VIET NAM

The Origins of Revolution

PUBLISHED FOR

the Center of International Studies, PRINCETON UNIVERSITY

John T. McAlister, Jr.

VIET NAM

The Origins of Revolution

Alfred A. Knopf · New York · 1969

THIS IS A BORZOI BOOK
PUBLISHED BY ALFRED A. KNOPF, INC.

TO

ÉMILE MUS

Sous-Lieutenant,
2ᵉ Régiment parachutiste d'Infanterie de Marine,
mort en Algérie, le 21 juillet 1960,
de blessures reçues au combat.

WITH THE HOPE THAT
THIS BOOK MAY SERVE
HIS MEMORY WELL

PREFACE ✪ ✪ ✪

The publication of this book marks the passage of a decade devoted to trying to understand the convulsive political life of Viet Nam. During my senior year in college in the autumn of 1957, after persuading the faculty at Yale to inaugurate the country's first university course in Vietnamese, I began studying the language with an able teacher, Huynh Sanh Thong, who had come to New Haven to teach three students. As I learned to speak and read Vietnamese, I also began work on the culture and history of Viet Nam under the direction of Professor Paul Mus, a French scholar of the prestigious faculty at the Collège de France in Paris who has regularly spent half the academic year at Yale for nearly two decades.

Paul Mus's unique background and his sensitivity made him an ideal teacher, mentor, and friend. As a small child he went to Viet Nam, where his father founded the colonial education system shortly before World War I. He stayed on to become a scholar of Vietnamese and Southeast Asian culture at the École Française d'Extrême-Orient in Hanoi before being mobilized into the French Marine Corps at the outbreak of World War II. As a representative of the Free French, he was parachuted into Japanese-occupied Viet Nam in early 1945 for a brief intelligence mission and returned later in the year as political adviser to General Philippe Leclerc, the French commander in the Far East. Through his public statements and behind-the-scenes negotiations, Paul Mus tried desperately to head off the clash between the French and the Vietnamese over independence and national unity. Since he had worked hard to prevent war, Mus's bitterest experience was probably his mission as France's final emissary to Ho Chi Minh in May 1947, just before the Indochina War began in earnest; because Mus had no latitude from his superiors to bargain with Ho, this last meeting with the Viet Minh leader was a somber, tragic, and fruitless confrontation—qualities that also characterized the bloody conflict which followed.

I was graduated from Yale in 1958, commissioned a reserve officer in the U.S. Navy, and assigned to a destroyer escort in the far Pacific. Through more persuasion, this time of the Navy, I was reassigned to the Navy section of the U.S. military mission in Viet Nam in the summer of 1959. Due to the prevailing contingency planning which regarded Viet Nam as another Korea, I got the job of adviser to the River Force of the Vietnamese navy, which operates on the waterways of the Mekong Delta south of Saigon. A young ensign could be sent alone on a mission into the Delta in 1959 because it was considered a minor task in a rear area. If an invasion were launched across the 17th parallel in Viet Nam, as one had been initiated across the 38th parallel in Korea in June 1950, then the fledgling Vietnamese navy would be of little use and a river-gunboat flotilla in a presumed rear area would be almost ludicrously irrelevant.

But Viet Nam was not another Korea. And so, at the end of the rainy season of 1959, in late September and early October, there was surprise and uncertainty when a series of guerrilla clashes suddenly erupted in the countryside of the Delta, where ripe stalks of rice awaited harvesting. These clashes were the first signs of the renewal of a war that has now grown to a scale so unprecedented for such a small country that it is not only destroying cities and ravaging the countryside, but also weakening the shaky foundations of Vietnamese society. No small part of the tragedy is that in 1959–61, when the U.S. military mission still numbered no more than 685 men, including support personnel, we had no clear idea as to how to respond to the conflict. Today many people would argue, with justification, that we had no right or responsibility to respond at all.

Yet such an argument overlooks the popular attitude at that time toward the "loss" of territory from the Western world to the Communist bloc and the pressures on elected officials resulting from these sentiments. A more realistic question, it seemed to me from my vantage point in the Mekong Delta, was whether we would act politically—in the character of our assistance to the Republic of Viet Nam and in our diplomatic bargaining—to resolve what was essentially a political problem, or whether, lacking the political sophistication, we would react by encouraging the Republic of Viet Nam to use primarily military force.

Because of my academic training and language ability, and my experience in the Mekong Delta, where the conflict had initially flared, I felt I had something to offer toward a political resolution of the problem; so I decided to stay on beyond the normal one-year tour in Viet Nam. At first, my recommendations focused on the gap in political communications and mutual respect between villagers and the provincial institutions of the Republic of Viet Nam. In my judgment this cleavage was the government's most serious political weakness, because within the gap an alternative governmental structure was being created that involved the villagers in politics in ways that won their loyalty and dedicated effort. However, since President Ngo Dinh Diem had been responsible for abolishing elected village councils and appointing instead village officials of his own choosing, and since almost all of Diem's province chiefs were military officers who were rotated so frequently that they rarely got to know their provinces very well, any suggestions for closing the political gap with the countryside became a criticism of President Diem himself.

In the autumn of 1960 I was given six weeks off from my duties in the Mekong Delta to prepare a staff study on the political dimension of the conflict. It was then I found how unproductive any analysis would be that reflected poorly on Diem. My recommendations for political action were ignored, and instead, my study was used as the basis for a steady move toward a primarily military response to the guerrilla challenge. I thought perhaps I was still too young for my views to have much influence, or perhaps I hadn't been able to present my ideas precisely or forcefully enough. Later I learned that my report had been blocked from wide dissemination within the U.S. government because its characterization of the Diem regime was regarded as too extreme, even though the study was considered substantive enough to be used in framing the first military counterinsurgency program in Viet Nam. Of course, I thought my assessment of the Diem regime was accurate and candid, and I wondered if the United States had become so wedded to Ngo Dinh Diem that we could not even afford candor in appraising his strengths and weaknesses. But Diem's shortcomings, even when they were rationalized away in public or when severe appraisals were blocked in private, were well known.

The real problem was that the United States did not know what to do about the political weaknesses of the Republic of Viet Nam, and rather than expose our perplexity, we preferred to minimize in public those of Diem's errors that might have called for a strong reproach. But despite Diem's intransigence, the United States never seriously considered dissociating itself from him until it was too late; any earlier disavowal would obviously have entailed a repudiation of long-standing American policies that Diem at least appeared to be fulfilling. At the heart of the American dilemma, therefore, was an uncertainty about the nature of our predicament and an unwillingness to examine the full range of options potentially open to us.

Not surprisingly, there was an almost total absence in Saigon of American specialists trained in Vietnamese culture and politics, people who could perform, in the political sphere, comparably to our military advisers who were building up the Vietnamese army. For nearly two years, I was the only officer in the U.S. military mission who knew Vietnamese, and while there were many able political analysts in our Saigon embassy, some of whom knew Vietnamese, there were virtually none trained in Vietnamese culture or prepared to participate in a program of political action. Because our available expertise and cadre of activists were military, our response was inevitably a military one, and because the Vietnamese were unprepared for the political demands of a militarization of the conflict, the United States progressively shouldered more of the cost and manpower required.

As the military trend accelerated, I concluded that my experience would have little relevance to the course the United States was choosing to follow. At the same time I realized that what I knew about the character of Viet Nam's politics and culture was very small in comparison to what there was to be known. In the summer of 1961, as Ngo Dinh Diem was launching his strategic hamlet program in a vain effort to bring the people in the countryside under his political control, I left Viet Nam to return to graduate school. I felt the strategic hamlet was a counterproductive approach to bridging the political gap between villagers and the government's provincial institutions; the program emphasized physical control over people as well as territory, so as to deny their commitment to the Communist-led guerrillas, but not the full involvement of villagers in the politics of the Diem government.

Because of previous failures, the strategic hamlets were superseding the abandoned agroville program, which had been an attempt to force villagers into stockaded areas where, instead of being safe, they became conspicuous targets for the guerrillas. Following the strategic hamlet program there was the "New Life" hamlet program, then the "pacification" program, and more recently the revolutionary-development program. Despite semantic shifts, all of these programs were designed to secure Saigon's political control—primarily by means of physical surveillance and force—over village Viet Nam, rather than to close the gap of political legitimacy through an identification with the villagers on their own terms.

Questions of political legitimacy in an unstable, slowly modernizing country like Viet Nam, the sharing of political power by modern, urban elites with peasant villagers in the countryside, and the political bases of guerrilla war all preoccupied me as I began my graduate studies. This book represents part of my effort to answer these questions, although in the

course of my studies many additional questions have arisen that
the book does not attempt to answer. The book was originally
written as a dissertation for the Ph.D. degree at Yale, but it has
been revised substantially out of a desire to reach the widest
possible audience. Initially I had planned to write a book on the
Indochina War of 1947–54, because I felt that an understanding
of the French–Viet Minh military experience would bring present problems more sharply into focus. But as my research progressed, I found that it was not possible to understand the full
meaning of France's war against the Viet Minh without a
detailed examination of the way the conflict began.

I have called this book *Viet Nam: The Origins of Revolution*
because I believe that the conflict in Viet Nam can best be
understood as a revolution, perhaps not in the classic sense of
revolution in France and Russia, but as a series of changes so
convulsive and pervasive as to call into question conventional
conceptions of revolution. The fact that Asian revolutions and,
in particular, revolution in Viet Nam do not conform to prevailing concepts of revolutionary politics is undoubtedly a part of
our problem of adapting our perceptions and policies to the situation as it exists. This book tries to relate the origins of the conflict in Viet Nam to an understanding of the nature of revolution
with the hope that this relationship will give the reader both
a historical and an analytical perspective on the continuing
crisis in Vietnamese politics. Now that the book is completed,
I intend to continue with my original plan and bring the perspective of revolution to bear on more recent phases of Viet
Nam's tortuous history.

Without my access to the still-secret archives of the French
army in the Service Historique de l'Armée at the Château de
Vincennes, just outside Paris, this book could not have been
written. In the bibliography I describe in detail how I drew upon
these classified documents. Here, I wish to express my deep
appreciation to the Ministry of Defense of the Republic of
France for permitting me to consult the documents in their
archives and to Captain John G. Noel, Jr., USN (ret.), former
U.S. Naval Attaché in Paris, for guiding me through the pro-

cedures required for admission to the archive. At the Service Historique, I was given a warm welcome and invaluable assistance by its director, General Cossé-Brissac, and the chief of the Overseas Section, Lieutenant Colonel Jouin. It was with the chief of the Indochina archive, Major Michel Désirée, a courageous survivor of Dien Bien Phu, that I worked most directly; despite the pain of his lingering wounds, Major Désirée performed innumerable kindnesses which ensured that I found the information I needed from the mass of 15,000 cartons of documents in his charge. According to the regulations governing my use of these archives, I am not permitted to make direct citation to the information collected there. Similar conditions have been observed in the publication of two other works: Bernard B. Fall, *Street Without Joy: Indochina at War, 1946–54* (Harrisburg, Pa.: The Stackpole Company; 1961) and George K. Tanham, *Communist Revolutionary Warfare* (New York: Frederick A. Praeger; 1961).

I also wish to acknowledge the financial support of the Foreign Area Fellowship Program, a joint committee of the Social Science Research Council and the American Council of Learned Societies, which made possible my research at the Service Historique de l'Armée in 1964 and also enabled me to return to Viet Nam for a research visit in 1965. I am most grateful for their support.

The preparation of this book has been sponsored by the Center of International Studies of Princeton University; I wish to express my gratefulness to the center's director, Professor Klaus Knorr, and to Professor Harry Eckstein for their willingness to support me in this undertaking. A portion of the funds for work on this book came to the Center of International Studies from the Special Operations Research Office, the American University, under Department of the Army Contract DA 49–092 ARO–7. Neither the Foreign Area Fellowship Program, the Special Operations Research Office, the Department of the Army, nor the Center of International Studies is responsible in any way for the contents of this book or the views it expresses.

For their guidance and concern, I wish to thank the faculty

committee at Yale that supervised the writing of my dissertation and helped me through my graduate studies: Professors Karl W. Deutsch, Harry J. Benda, David N. Rowe, W. Bradford Westerfield, and, of course, Paul Mus. I also wish to acknowledge my indebtedness to other scholars who have blazed the trail ahead of me in studying Viet Nam: Joseph Buttinger, Philippe Devillers, the late Bernard B. Fall, Ellen Hammer, Gerald C. Hickey, Paul Isoart, Roy Jumper, Jean Lacouture, Donald Lancaster, Le Thanh Khoi, and I. Milton Sacks. Their important works will be found in the bibliography.

I cannot begin to name all of the many friends who have been of such tremendous help to me in my decade of work, either in Viet Nam, in Paris, or in American universities; I think they know how much I appreciate their thoughtfulness and assistance. I must, however, mention my special thanks to Professor Richard L. Walker of the University of South Carolina, who, as my adviser at Yale, was instrumental in setting me on my decade of work on Viet Nam and in helping the Navy decide to send me to the Mekong Delta. Also not to be forgotten is Professor Frederick W. Mote of Princeton, who took a special interest in my research, read the manuscript of this book, and boosted my spirits when they were low. One of my closest Vietnamese friends, Truong Buu Lam, has read the manuscript and saved me from many pitfalls; most of all he contributed his friendship. While all of the scholars mentioned above have aided me in numerous ways to improve this book, the errors which may remain are my responsibility alone.

The task of transforming a bulky manuscript into a handsome book has been the special—and deeply appreciated—contribution of Ashbel Green, Managing Editor of Alfred A. Knopf, Inc. His careful, sympathetic attention to vocabulary, syntax, and style has made me more conscious of the duties of a writer and, in turn, made this book more readable. Not the least of his contributions has been to make this the first book—I believe—on Viet Nam in America to have the precise writing system for Vietnamese language words, complete with diacritical marks, in the printed text.

I regret that my father did not live to see the publication of this, my first book, but I know my mother realizes how deep is my sense of gratitude to them both. I also know that Mr. and Mrs. Henry T. Bourne of Woodstock, Vermont, understand how thankful I am for their love.

Finally, my gratitude to Paul Mus is so great and so hard to express that the most fitting gesture I can make is to dedicate this book to the memory of his son.

John T. McAlister, Jr.

Center of International Studies
Woodrow Wilson School of Public and International Affairs
Princeton University
Independence Day, 1968

CONTENTS ❈ ❈ ❈

PART ONE ❈ ❈ ❈

Introduction

❈
❈
❈

CHAPTER 1 ✠ ✠ ✠

REVOLUTION IN VIET NAM

IN PERSPECTIVE

✠

✠

✠

Understanding the politics of Viet Nam requires an understand-ing of revolution. For more than a generation Viet Nam has been convulsed by a protracted revolution which began in August 1945, amidst the chaotic collapse of Japan's wartime occupation of French Indochina, and is yet to be completed. Revolutionary strife in Viet Nam was at first focused on the elimination of colonial rule. However, even during the First Indochina War, 1947–54, the overriding goal was not merely driving the French from the country but deciding who would succeed to France's eighty years of political control. Tragically, the First Indochina War did not result in any decisive answer to this question of succession; instead it ended in a standoff between those with opposing concepts of political rule. At the heart of their con-tinuing controversy is a struggle for a political order which can unify the Vietnamese people—if they are to be unified at all. Here is a revolution which remains incomplete and which has consumed the vitality of the Vietnamese for more than two decades as they have tried to effect basic changes in the structure of their politics and achieve a unified political order.

By 1954, after seven years of revolutionary conflict, two competitor governments emerged: The Democratic Republic of Viet Nam in Hanoi and the Republic of Viet Nam in Saigon. Each claimed to be the sole legitimate government for all the Vietnamese people, yet each controlled only about half the territory of the country. When these two governments withdrew into separate territories divided at the 17th parallel by the Geneva Conference of 1954, the Western powers expected them to act like separate nation-states, instead of adversaries in a revolutionary war. But neither government did. Nor has either of them denied that "reunification" is its ultimate goal, and there has been little reason to expect that they would.[1]

The war now raging in Viet Nam is a continuation of the pattern of conflict launched during the First Indochina War; it is not a war being fought between two separate nations, but a revolutionary struggle within one nation. More conspicuously than in wars between nations, revolutionary war is, in the words of Clausewitz, a "continuation of politics by other means." It is a competition between two or more governments, each of which wants to become the sole legitimate government of a people. In wars between nations, political objectives are usually sought by destroying the military power of an adversary, but in revolutionary wars, political goals are sought more directly. The focus of conflict is to eliminate the political structure of an opponent and replace it with a political structure of one's own.

With a viable political structure a government can lose much of its regular military strength, and even much of its territory, yet still continue to be a serious competitor in a revolutionary war. But without a viable political structure linking it to the people a government may exist in name but not in fact. People

---

[1] In order to establish legitimacy over a portion of the Vietnamese population, it has seemed necessary to claim the right to rule over all Vietnamese. Since the Republic of Viet Nam in the south is in a poor position to emphasize such a claim, it has not done so. But it has not renounced legitimacy over all of Viet Nam. Needless to say, the United States has never supported the Repubic of Viet Nam as the sole government for the whole of Vietnamese territory.

cannot be rallied behind a political program of such a government because there will be no dependable means of sharing power and influence with those who participate in the government's behalf. Since it will be unable to win the political commitment of the people and deny their support to the adversary, a government without a viable political structure will have missed the essence of victory in revolutionary conflict.

Before 1954, the Democratic Republic of Viet Nam (Hanoi) had established a very extensive political organization in areas south of the 17th parallel, and this, the Hanoi leaders felt, entitled them to influence there despite the Geneva truce agreement to withdraw their regular troops from the region. Hanoi had expected to recoup this influence through the elections called for in the Final Declaration of the Geneva Conference, but when the elections failed to materialize in 1956, the northern regime demonstrated considerable strength in the south by guerrilla terrorism; through a concerted organizational effort, Hanoi also began to expand its political power there.[2] In response, the Republic of Viet Nam in the south has asserted, with accuracy, that its government is under attack and that its sovereignty is threatened by a Communist government in northern Viet Nam. Behind these assertions, however, is the implicit admission that the southern republic cannot command the loyalties or mobilize the energies of enough of the population south of the 17th parallel to rule even that portion of Vietnamese territory.

This impotence of the southern republic has been attributed to subversion from the north which over the years has grown into a large-scale military infiltration.[3] Yet, as has been made

2 For a discussion on the lack of agreement at the Geneva Conference see John T. McAlister, Jr: "The Possibilities for Diplomacy in Southeast Asia," *World Politics*, Vol. XIX, No. 2 (January 1967), pp. 258–305. See also Jean Lacouture and Philippe Devillers: *La fin d'une guerre* (Paris Éditions du Seuil; 1960), pp. 111–288. On election issue see Franklin B. Weinstein: *Vietnam's Unheld Election* (Ithaca: Southeast Asia Program, Cornell University, Data Paper Number 60; July 1966).

3 See U.S. Department of State: *A Threat to Peace: North Viet-Nam's Effort to Conquer South Viet-Nam*, Publication 7308, Far Eastern Series 110 (Washington: U.S. Government Printing Office; 1961); U.S. Department of State: *Aggression from the North: The Record of North Viet-Nam's Campaign to Conquer South Viet-Nam*, Publication 7839, Far Eastern Series 130 (Washington: U.S. Government Printing Office; 1965); for an interesting critique of the latter see *I. F. Stone's Weekly*, Vol. XII, March 8, 1965.

clear by United States efforts to eliminate northern units from
areas of the countryside, the Republic of Viet Nam has not had
any really effective political institutions for uniting the rural
population within a central government. Without such institutions it seems unlikely that purely military achievements can
be consolidated into any viable political order in southern Viet
Nam on other than Communist terms. Nor does it seem that
anything more than a stalemate between the military force of
the United States and the political-military potency of the Communists can be hoped for. Quite the contrary, a much less
favorable outcome remains a distinct possibility.[4]

Since the war now being waged in southern Viet Nam is a
continuation of the revolutionary war begun in 1945, the absence
of effective political institutions there has been a decisive consideration. Indeed, revolutionary wars occur because a substantial portion of a population is alienated from the prevailing
political structure and no longer accepts the legitimacy of an
incumbent government. In Viet Nam after World War II, such
a war broke out because a well-organized political movement, the
Viet Minh, led a determined effort to block the reimposition of
French colonial rule over the country. In launching the Democratic Republic of Viet Nam in 1945, the Viet Minh claimed
that it was the legitimate government of the Vietnamese people.
But not all Vietnamese accepted this claim. While those that
opposed the Viet Minh were, initially, few and ineffectual, the
majority of the Vietnamese were simply uncommitted to any
political movement. In the vast rural areas of the country where
more than 80 per cent of the people lived, there were no political
institutions through which they could participate in politics
beyond their village or develop a commitment to a national
government.

The French interpreted this lack of popular commitment to
mean that they could easily crush the Viet Minh by force without
having to accord it any long-term recognition as a legitimate

4 R. W. Apple, Jr.: "Vietnam: The Signs of Stalemate," *The New York Times*,
August 7, 1967, p. 1; Robert Shaplen: "Letter from South Vietnam," *The New
Yorker*, June 17, 1967, pp. 37–91.

political entity. Yet they did not calculate on the strength of the Viet Minh's political structure in the areas of the countryside under its control, nor did they try to eliminate this structure by replacing it with a more effective one of their own. As pressures of French and Viet Minh military operations mounted, it became increasingly necessary for the rural population to make political commitments in order to secure protection from one side or the other. Since the Viet Minh's political structure was more immediately accessible and offered more predictable political rewards than that of the French, it was the chief beneficiary of the intensification of the conflict.

Despite their lack of success the French were not unaware of the need to establish a political alternative to the Viet Minh. But since they had made no preparation before or during World War II for the eventual self-government of Viet Nam, the French had scant political resources to fall back on. They had to base their political alternative on the population in areas controlled by the French army, especially the cities and towns but also the rural pockets inhabited by religious groups (Catholics in the north and members of folk religions in the south) opposed to the Viet Minh. Known as the State of Viet Nam and led by the archaic emperor Bao Dai, this political alternative had as its bedrock a small Vietnamese upper class which had been formed through French colonial institutions. Most of the Viet Minh leadership was part of this upper class too, but unlike those who joined with the French, they had received fewer social and political rewards. Since these Viet Minh leaders saw French rule as a barrier to their aspirations, they were impatient for independence and sought it through revolution.

In building an alternative to the Viet Minh's revolutionary movement, the French found that the Vietnamese upper class was a shaky foundation. It did not have the coherence and strength of a well-established ruling class; internecine squabbles prevented it from providing effective political leadership, while its social and cultural status made it so distant from the mass of the people in the countryside that it could not communicate with them easily. But the greatest shortcoming of this French-oriented upper class lay in its restricted concept of politics. Its members seemed not fully to realize that they would have to forge new political links with the village population if the State of Viet Nam was to develop the power to become a serious contender in revolutionary war, instead of being just a dependency of France. They seemed to believe with the French that force alone was sufficient to destroy the Viet Minh. Some, however, were conscious of the political dimension of the conflict, but they concluded that needed actions could not be taken unless the French gave the State of Viet Nam its full independence. Because they did not recognize that independence from France or dominance over the Viet Minh required them to develop superior political strength, these protestors simply withdrew from politics altogether and became "attentists," or "those who waited," on the sidelines of the war.[5]

Though the State of Viet Nam was a government without a political structure to knit together the villages and towns and develop a widespread popular commitment in the countryside, it was not powerless. Its power lay in the superstructure of Vietnamese society, not in the village substructure. In the cities where the small modern enclave created by the French gave the appearance of a government in action, there was power to be had from industry, commerce, education, social services, and trained personnel. But this power could not be projected into the countryside except as military force. So at nights, the world outside of the towns and cities became the domain of the Viet Minh—except for these areas controlled by the French army and the slowly emerging army of the State of Viet Nam. These areas were not inconsiderable; they included the Mekong Delta in the south, the south-central plateau inhabited by the montagnards, and until 1952–3, the Red River Delta in the north. Within these areas, participation in the politics of the State of Viet Nam was significant. About a million people registered to vote in the elections of 1953, and by 1954 there were nearly 300,000

5 Probably the most prominent attentist was Ngo Dinh Diem, who left Viet Nam in 1950 not to return until 1954, when he was appointed Prime Minister of the State of Viet Nam.

Vietnamese fighting alongside 70,000 regular French troops and about 68,000 Legionnaires and Africans against approximately 400,000 in the Viet Minh ranks.[6]

Even with the aid of the United States, the power of the State of Viet Nam together with that of France was never sufficient to defeat the Viet Minh. Yet it was enough to prolong the war for seven years until 1954; and then there was adequate strength to get a favorable partition of the country, including a substantial evacuation of Viet Minh forces from the south.[7] After a successful struggle to eject the French in 1955–6, the south became the domain of the Republic of Viet Nam, the successor to the State of Viet Nam. Now, nearly a decade and a half later, the revolutionary conflict continues along much the same lines of earlier years. Like its predecessor, the Republic of Viet Nam is trying by force to stop the Communists' expansion of their revolutionary political structure. There is yet little recognition that this expansion of a new political structure throughout the countryside is effecting a revolution even as it lays the basis for a more sustained military effort against the Republic of Viet Nam.

The Communists are not simply trying to eliminate their adversary by force. They are attempting to win the political commitment of the mass of the people in the countryside and thereby deny legitimacy to the Republic of Viet Nam as a representative government of the Vietnamese people. To achieve this commitment the Communists are not primarily concerned with increasing the welfare of the peasant villagers, but with forging them into a political community—one which commands loyal-

6 Voting statistics are from Bernard B. Fall: "Political Development of Viet Nam: V-J Day to the Geneva Cease-Fire" (unpublished Ph.D. dissertation, Syracuse University, October 1954), p. 662. Military personnel figures are from Henri Navarre: *Agonie de l'Indochine (1953–1954)* (rev. edn., Paris: Plon; 1956), p. 46. One of the last useful prewar estimates of Viet Nam population put the total at 21.6 million. Gouvernement Général de l'Indochine, Direction des Services Économiques: *Annuaire statistique de l'Indochine*, douzième volume, 1947–1948 (Saigon, 1949), p. 19.

7 In the autumn of 1954 the Viet Minh indicated to the International Control Commission supervising the truce in Indochina that they had 130,000 persons to evacuate from four locations in the south. These included 87,000 combatants and 43,000 political cadres and families. B. S. N. Murti: *Vietnam Divided: The Unfinished Struggle* (New York: Asia Publishing House; 1964), p. 224. Before the evacuation had been completed, nearly 150,000 Viet Minh had been brought north, but the laxity of control procedures left authorities unsure of the exact number.

ties because it rewards performance by upward mobility in a hierarchical political structure. Through such mobility the villager can find a more predictable access to the attributes of modernity (i.e., literacy, technical skills, organizational ability, etc.) and to the rewards of political power than through any other governmental structure in Viet Nam. From this mobilization of the potential power of the peasants and a sharing of governmental authority with them, changes have been occurring in Vietnamese politics which are the very substance of revolution.

Revolution in essence is change, but there is very little agreement as to how much and what kind of change constitutes revolution. Despite, or perhaps because of, their profound character, social and political changes in Viet Nam have not usually been described as revolutionary. Unfortunately, the vocabulary with which an understanding of revolution is expressed has not been closely identified with the characteristics of a protracted revolution in a modernizing society. Yet, because of its protractedness, the events of two decades of upheaval in Viet Nam have cast in bold relief many aspects of revolution often obscured in the faster-moving revolutions of our time.

This conflict—first among the Viet Minh and the Frenchled State of Viet Nam and now between two Vietnamese republics—has shown once again that revolution is not merely the overthrowing of an old regime. It is a competition between opposing concepts of political community for a monopoly, or legitimacy, in holding power. And rarely can an alternative—revolutionary—government emerge as a competitor to the prevailing regime for poltical legitimacy unless it sets forth new ways of mobilizing and sharing power. In attempting to establish such a new legitimacy the revolutionaries are changing the structure of politics to conform to a new concept of political community—a change in the way who gets what, when, and how.[8]

The emphasis in this book is placed on revolution as being a permanent change in the structure of politics which results

8 Harold D. Lasswell: *Politics: Who Gets What, When, How* (Cleveland and New York: The World Publishing Company; 1958).

in new ways of mobilizing and sharing power. These two qualitative changes in managing political power are intimately related in the revolutionary process; if revolutionaries are to mobilize the popular strength to supersede an incumbent regime, it seems clear that they must develop new forms for participation in politics. In order for a potent following to be won to the revolutionary cause, new types of political status, institutions, and ideology will be a necessity. Through new institutions—such as revolutionary committees and assemblies, as well as military units and mobilization groups—individuals will have the chance to achieve a greater share of power as their participation contributes to revolutionary goals. Only when such institutional links reach out into the society and create political opportunities that are qualitatively different from those of the incumbent regime can revolutionaries mobilize increasing amounts of political power. Sustained by an effective ideology which rationalizes this mobilization of power and which dramatizes the presumed injustices of the incumbent regime, a revolutionary government can establish its legitimacy and gain increasing compliance with its will.

A crucial measure of the extent to which changes in the structure of politics are likely to occur during a revolution is the amount of popular strength required to overthrow an incumbent. If these changes—in political status, institutions, and ideology—are not far-reaching enough to accommodate those alienated from an incumbent regime, then the potential for revolution may still exist even though a new revolutionary government has displaced the incumbents and taken control of a country. From this perspective, *revolutionary potential* can be said to exist when there is a gap between the demands made on a government and its performance to meet them. A possible shortcoming of this definition is its implication that all societies have some potential for revolution—an implication which nevertheless seems useful for analytical purposes since it calls attention to the fact that incumbent governments usually try to establish political relationships which in some measure meet the demands placed on them. But when incumbents cannot respond with political changes that are extensive enough to satisfy popular demands, they will usually try to contain revolutionary potential by force and maintain themselves in power against the popular will.

Whatever its extent, revolutionary potential will not be translated into revolution unless it is specifically exploited by *revolutionaries*—those who are potential members of the prevailing political elite yet are denied or thwarted from participation in it and who excel in articulating demands left unfulfilled by the incumbents. In order for political protests to go beyond random events such as riots, strikes, demonstrations, or peasant revolts, the revolutionaries must establish an opposition political structure, a *revolutionary structure,* within the gap between demands and performance which will be called *revolutionary space.* In this book the term *revolutionary space* will be used as an approximate synonym for *revolutionary potential* except that it will indicate where the revolutionary potential lies in a society, i.e., in rural areas where demands for agrarian reform are going unheeded or among urban dwellers where protests for new policies have emerged, etc. Clearly, the goal of revolutionaries is to exploit the gaps of revolutionary space by advancing their revolutionary structure until it undercuts the existing regime and becomes the legitimate government of the people.

Some observers believe that there has been no revolution in Viet Nam at all, that the country has merely undergone an anticolonial revolt which has now been followed by an international war between two distinct Vietnamese states. The thesis of this book rejects this opinion and maintains that fundamental changes in the structure of politics, which are the essence of revolution, have occurred in Viet Nam over the past four decades. Moreover, the book has been written in the belief that Viet Nam's experience has much to contribute to an understanding of revolution, because events there have challenged many commonly held assumptions about the revolutionary process. By a detailed study of the new ways of mobilizing and sharing power that developed in Viet Nam during the 1930's and 1940's, this book will try to explain how and why revolution occurred and what the significance of this Vietnamese experience is for an understanding of the origins of revolution. While there will be no attempt to bring the story of revolution in Viet Nam beyond the year 1946, when large-scale revolutionary war broke out, a focus on the formative years should clarify the basic characteristics of revolutionary change in the country and provide a needed perspective on subsequent events.

Such a perspective seems necessary, since the problems that Vietnamese revolutionaries have had to cope with include the legacy of Viet Nam's historic inability to achieve durable unity as a nation. Central political institutions reached their apogee in precolonial Viet Nam during the four centuries between 1009 and 1400. Thereafter, the southward migration of the Vietnamese people from their homeland in the Red River Delta produced pressures which resulted in a tradition of political disunity. Rule over a unified nation was undercut by regionally based groups whose competition in the era prior to French intervention led to political turmoil rather than to the institutionalization of political power.

During eighty years of rule, France did little that contributed to developing institutions in which the politics of Viet Nam could be conducted. Instead, the modernizing influences brought on by French colonial policies served to reinforce old antipathies and to ensure that once France's hegemony was ended, traditional problems would be revived with an intensity never before known. As Vietnamese revolutionaries began to organize themselves in the 1930's and 1940's, they too found that regional pressures threatened to undercut their effectiveness in opposing French rule. In their attempts to unify a revolutionary movement, Vietnamese leaders had to do more than offer dependable political opportunities to those alienated from the colonial regime; they also had to overcome the antipathies which Vietnamese from various parts of the country and various social affiliations had—as a result of their historical experience—toward each other.

Even such a goal as independence from France could not by itself bring unity and discipline to Vietnamese political life. On the contrary, these qualities had to be sought through techniques of mobilizing and sharing power that would result in political commitments surmounting traditional and parochial antagonisms. In forging such commitments Vietnamese revolutionaries in the 1930's and 1940's were bringing about changes that would characterize revolution in Viet Nam for decades and would set examples challenging old assumptions about the nature of revolutionary politics. And for all its appearance as a mystifying web of contemporary politics interlaced with age-old conflict, there lies in Viet Nam a clear and unavoidable challenge to our understanding of revolution as well as a promise of wider knowledge if its complexities can be mastered.

PART TWO

The Historical Context of Revolution in Viet Nam

CHAPTER 2 ✿ ✿ ✿

REVOLUTION: A LANDMARK

IN VIETNAMESE HISTORY

✿

✿

✿

For a people with a two-thousand-year heritage of occupation, rebellion, and a troubled search for order, the revolution launched in August 1945 represented a major landmark. It not only inaugurated a new approach to politics in Viet Nam, but also marked a millennium of freedom from Chinese occupation. Before the year 939, when the Vietnamese threw off China's direct control over their affairs, they had been ruled as a Chinese province for a thousand years. Yet the tortuous history of the country even predates Chinese control. The record goes back to 208 B.C., when the Vietnamese first appeared in official annals as a minority people in the kingdom of Nam Viet, known in Chinese history as Nan-yüeh.[1]

Covering wide areas of present-day northern Viet Nam and southern China, the kingdom of Nam Viet was created by a

1 D. G. E. Hall: *A History of South-East Asia* (New York: St. Martin's Press; 1955), pp. 169-70. Also L. Aurousseau: "La première conquête chinoise des pays annamites," *Bulletin École Français d'Extrême-Orient,* Vol. XXIII (1923), pp. 137-264.

renegade Chinese warlord. He had taken advantage of the decay of China's first imperial dynasty to assert his marginal power based on regional military occupation. His political creation, Nam Viet, remained autonomous for nearly a century because the power of the emerging Han dynasty was restricted to north and central China, where it was struggling to consolidate dynastic control. In the pattern that was to become familiar on China's southern periphery when its imperial regimes were weak or preoccupied internally, Nam Viet was recognized as an autonomous kingdom over which the Han retained a nominal though unenforceable sovereignty. Within the loose structure of the kingdom, the forebears of the Vietnamese were permitted their own administration. This structure consisted of fiefs governed by hereditary chiefs in the sort of feudal system that still exists among the mountain peoples of northern Viet Nam. However, after 111 B.C., when the Han dynasty was strong enough to extend its power southward and absorb Nam Viet into the Chinese empire, the Vietnamese fiefs became provinces of China.[2]

Despite the deep imprint made on them by Chinese culture of the Han and T'ang dynasties, these early Vietnamese possessed a zeal for political autonomy. Among the numerous peoples on the southern periphery of China, only the Vietnamese adopted Chinese culture without becoming a part of the Chinese political system. Only in Viet Nam "did the [Chinese] culture outpace the [Chinese] political unit. The Vietnamese speak a Sinitic language related to Chinese; they derived their higher culture from China; and they were for a long period under Chinese rule." Yet eventually they managed to establish their identity as a separate country within East Asian civilization.[3] Indeed it may be that the adoption of Chinese culture made it

2 G. Coedès: *The Making of South-East Asia,* trans. by H. M. Wright (Berkeley and Los Angeles: University of California Press; 1966), p. 40.

3 Edwin O. Reischauer and John K. Fairbank: *East Asia: The Great Tradition* (Boston: Houghton Mifflin Company; 1958), p. 395. It is important to note that areas neighboring Viet Nam in what we now call China were not fully and permanently absorbed into the Chinese central administration (except for the delta province around the city of Canton) until the T'ang dynasty (A.D. 618–907) at the earliest, and some parts, like Yunnan province, not until the fourteenth century. This uneven pattern of integration emphasizes the changing nature of the Chinese interest in the southern frontier area of which Viet Nam was a distant part.

possible for the Vietnamese to free themselves from political control by China. In the view of the noted scholar Henri Maspero, Viet Nam was able to assert its autonomy because Chinese occupation, "by breaking the power of particularist institutions and local groups, and by introducing Chinese ideas and social organization, gave it a cohesion and formal structure which its neighbors lacked."[4] Whether or not the imposition of Chinese culture was instrumental in winning the Vietnamese their autonomy, it seems certain that the way the culture was imposed provided the motivation for them to seek an end to rule by China.

Efforts to absorb the Vietnamese into the Chinese empire were carried on sporadically and haphazardly throughout a millennium of occupation. In fact it seems that the Chinese overlords were more concerned with pacifying these peripheral minority peoples than in assimilating them. As the pressure of the Chinese occupation progressively curtailed the influence of Vietnamese feudal leaders, they were afforded virtually no compensating opportunities to join the broader political and cultural world of the Chinese empire. Because the local aristocracy saw that a continuation of Chinese policy threatened to wipe them out, their hostility toward the occupation rose sharply until it culminated in a rebellion in A.D. 40. Crushed by an expedition of Chinese reinforcements, this desperate revolt by a decaying feudal regime was followed by one of the most thorough attempts to implant Chinese culture among the Vietnamese ever undertaken. Perhaps the most important result of this program was to speed the intermarriage of Vietnamese with Chinese settlers and functionaries. A new elite emerged with a commitment to Chinese language and culture that would have been difficult to obtain by coercion alone. Although this new racially mixed local elite enjoyed none of the privileges or influence of their feudal predecessors, they too were a hereditary aristocracy, but with family ties now based on Chinese customs.[5]

4 Henri Maspéro: "L'expédition de Ma Yuan," *Bulletin École Française d'Extrême-Orient,* Vol. XVIII, No. 3 (1918), p. 27.

5 Henri Maspéro: "La dynastie des Li antérieurs," ibid., Vol. XVI, No. 1 (1916), pp. 25 ff. Also see Hisayuki Miyakawa: "The Confucianization of South China," in

The emphasis on cultural assimilation which had produced a Chinese-oriented aristocracy among the Vietnamese was not matched by efforts to absorb them into Chinese politics. Only gradually and hesitantly was this local elite allowed to participate in the Chinese provincial administration over the Vietnamese. They had to qualify for appointment by mastering the same examinations in Chinese literature and philosophy that were required of Chinese administrative officials. But, as the Han dynasty was in the decline, these administratively qualified Vietnamese demanded and were granted a status—equal to that of any qualified Chinese—which entitled them to be assigned anywhere in the empire. Mixed-blood Vietnamese were actually appointed as subprefects in two Chinese provinces. But these promising beginnings in cultural and political integration came abruptly to an end with the fall of the Han dynasty in A.D. 220.[6]

Thereafter, China suffered several centuries of internal political disintegration. Not only did Chinese preoccupation with domestic politics reduce pressures on the Vietnamese, but it also encouraged them to seek their own political identity separate from China. Significantly, the abortive attempts to establish an autonomous Vietnamese kingdom between 542 and 602 were led by the local racially mixed aristocracy. Their short-lived kingdom was an expression of the political consciousness and skills they had acquired through Chinese culture but had been able to use only slightly within the Chinese empire. Although their flimsy kingdom was easily destroyed by the Chinese, little was done to resolve the underlying causes of the uprising. When China was once again brought under centralized control, in 618 by the T'ang dynasty, little effort was made to integrate the Vietnamese into Chinese political life. The T'ang simply used

Arthur F. Wright, ed.: *The Confucian Persuasion* (Stanford: Stanford University Press; 1960), pp. 21–46, and Harold J. Wiens: *China's March Toward the Tropics* (Hamden, Conn.: Shoe String Press; 1954), Chap. vi.

6 Le Thanh Khoi: *Le Viet-Nam: Histoire et civilisation, le milieu et l'histoire* (Paris: Les Éditions de Minuit; 1955), p. 106. This book is the most comprehensive history of Viet Nam available; it is based on French and Vietnamese monographic sources.

their burgeoning power to impose the most severe occupation the Vietnamese had ever known. But the power of the T'ang, like that of previous dynasties, had its limits and when it had run its course the resultant weakness in China coincided with an increasing political strength among the Vietnamese. By 939 an autonomous Vietnamese kingdom was able to defend itself against direct Chinese control.[7]

This assertion of local strength did not mean complete independence for Viet Nam. Reimposition of Chinese rule—as was threatened during the Mongol invasion of 1285, and as occurred briefly, 1413–37, during the Ming dynasty—was always a factor in Vietnamese politics. Instead of asserting their independence of China, which would have run the risk of frequent struggles over the reintroduction of Chinese military occupation, the Vietnamese had earlier become one of China's tributary states.[8] Until France gained control in 1885, the Vietnamese ritually acknowledged the supremacy of China and periodically sent missions bearing tribute. Moreover, these ritual ties contained a fiber of strength in the recognized prerogative of the Chinese court to invest the Vietnamese emperors with their legitimacy to rule. Rather than stimulating Chinese interference in Vietnamese affairs, this symbolic investiture contributed to stability because of the careful scrutiny given to new claimants of political legitimacy.

Once the Vietnamese had freed themselves of a millennium of Chinese domination, they struggled for another millennium with the consequences of their own autonomy. The ending of Chinese control did not mean that the Vietnamese had achieved

7 Henri Maspéro: "Le protectorat général d'Annam sous les T'ang," *Bulletin École Française d'Extrême-Orient*, Vol. X (1910), pp. 539 ff. See also Josephs Buttinger: *The Smaller Dragon: A Political History of Vietnam* (New York: Frederick A. Praeger; 1958), Chap. iii, pp. 129–97.

8 A. B. Woodside has called this fifteenth-century attempt to make Viet Nam a province of China "the greatest policy disaster suffered by the early Ming empire." See his excellent study of the tribute system: "Early Ming Expansionism (1406–1427): China's Abortive Conquest of Vietnam," *Papers on China*, Vol XVII (Cambridge: East Asian Research Center, Harvard University; December 1963), pp. 1–37. For another important study of the tribute system see Truong Buu Lam: "Sino-Vietnamese Relations at the End of the Eighteenth Century: A Study of the Tribute System," Paper No. 3 prepared for the *Conference on the Chinese World Order*, September 1965 (Cambridge: East Asian Research Center, Harvard University).

political unity and stability. For nearly ten centuries they fought among themselves in attempting to institutionalize political power into a unified government having authority over all the Vietnamese. Significantly, the incipient dynasty that was instrumental in asserting Vietnamese autonomy from China was unable to consolidate its power in Viet Nam. Persisting feudal groups thwarted the ephemeral Ngo dynasty (A.D. 939–69) in its ambition to unify the Vietnamese. Even less durable regimes followed the Ngo as competing families sought to subdue their rivals by military force and impose their hereditary rule on the country. Not until 1009, nearly a century after Chinese rule ended, did one group prevail over its rivals and consolidate political power into a durable regime.[9]

The leaders of the resilient Ly dynasty (1009–1225) succeeded in institutionalizing their power by stages. First they established a military administration to translate their predominant strength into territorial control over the country. But the durability of the dynasty for over two centuries undoubtedly resulted from their capacity to transform coercive force into a governmental authority widely accepted as having the legitimate use of power. This institutionalized strength was achieved by sharing power more widely and making the access to power more orderly than under military control. Specifically, a civil administration was established with recruitment based on the Chinese examination system. From this procedure a bureaucracy was created that represented those most thoroughly knowledgeable in Chinese language and culture.[1]

Selection to the bureaucracy, or mandarinate, as the Europeans baptized this scholar-administration, was theoretically open without regard to social standing to all who could satisfy the qualifications. Since education in Chinese culture became the primary criterion for political mobility, some members of the mandarinate, called mandarins by the Europeans, did come from modest social origins. However, since only those with extensive resources could

---

9 Maspéro: "La dynastie des Li antérieurs," pp. 25 ff.
1 Le Thanh Khoi: Le Viet-Nam, pp. 145-9. The first examinations for selection of the scholar-bureaucrats were given in 1075.

afford the leisure of long years of preparation for these examinations, the bureaucracy in fact institutionalized the power of the families with the greatest wealth and cohesion. Instead of turning their resources into military power with which to fight for dynastic succession, the Vietnamese families gradually accepted competition for political power on a more orderly basis. But despite the rigor of the examinations, power in Viet Nam was still largely hereditary.[2]

For nearly four hundred years, between the eleventh and the fourteenth centuries, the mandarin system of bureaucracy provided relative internal order under conditions of almost constant threat of invasion by aggressive neighbors and dynastic usurpation at home. Domestic challenges to dynastic rule, often militant in character, were never sufficient to bring down the mandarin system, at least not until other factors weakened internal order. Even when the long rule of the Ly dynasty came to an end in 1225 for lack of a male heir, there was no outbreak of internal war. The Tran dynasty (1225–1400) succeeded to dynastic rule by arranging a marriage with the female heir of the Ly family, but it was by preserving the mandarinal system that they maintained the continuity of power. The Tran thus perpetuated a period of political coherence, nearly four centuries long, that was in sharp contrast to the turmoil of both earlier and later epochs.[3]

The institutionalization of power that the mandarinal system had helped to achieve was eventually undermined by critical requirements for external defense. While the threat of invasion was a perennial dilemma, it was not until the late fourteenth century that a sustained external challenge appeared. Until then China and the other bordering states periodically attacked the Vietnamese. But in the fourteenth century, as well as in earlier periods, the main threat came from Champa, a hostile kingdom

---

2 On hereditary character of scholar-bureaucrats, Roy Jumper: "Vietnam: The Historical Background," in George McTurnan Kahin, ed., *Governments and Politics of Southeast Asia* (2nd edn., Ithaca: Cornell University Press; 1964), pp. 377–8, cites Tran Van Giap: "La vie d'un mandarin annamite du XVe siècle," *Cahiers de l'École Française d'Extrême-Orient,* Vol. XXVI (1941), pp. 24–5.

3 Coedès: *The Making of South-East Asia,* pp. 86–7.

founded about A.D. 192 on Hindu cultural traditions. Champa was located just south of the Red River Delta in present-day central Viet Nam. The great Vietnamese vulnerability to spoiling attacks by Champa was reduced only after autonomy from China had been won in A.D. 939 and the forces necessary for external defense had been mobilized. By the middle of the eleventh century the Vietnamese were able to sack Champa's capital and kill its king in retaliation for a Cham invasion. As a result of such military strength the Vietnamese acquired in 1069 their first portion of Champa's territory in what was to become a steady southward expansion. Under relentless pressure the Chams were diminished by the twentieth century to a minority status in a greatly enlarged Viet Nam.[4]

Ultimately the Vietnamese had reacted to Cham invasions by a program of territorial expansion aimed at destroying the kingdom of Champa and absorbing its domain. Yet this action was not without its political costs. They emerged when a series of Cham campaigns over a thirty-year period (1360–90) brought an unexpected military challenge to institutionalized political power in Viet Nam. The threat came not from the invaders, who were effectively repulsed, but from a trusted military leader, Le Quy Ly. He had saved the Vietnamese kingdom from destruction and occupation, yet in the process his power had gone beyond the level that could be controlled by dynastic political authority; so had his ambitions. In 1400 he overthrew the Tran dynasty, proclaimed himself Emperor Ho Quy Ly and in effect returned the country to a competition for political power through control of military force. His actions set in motion a sequence of events that increased Viet Nam's reliance on military might and made a return to institutionalized political power increasingly difficult.[5]

After Ho Quy Ly's usurpation the resulting turmoil among the Vietnamese weakened them internally and invited the intervention of China. The former overlords came ostensibly to restore the Tran, but in fact they wished to annex the country. For two decades, 1408–28, a fierce resistance against Chinese occupation was carried on through guerrilla warfare until Le Loi—a great hero of Vietnamese history and the founder of the Le dynasty

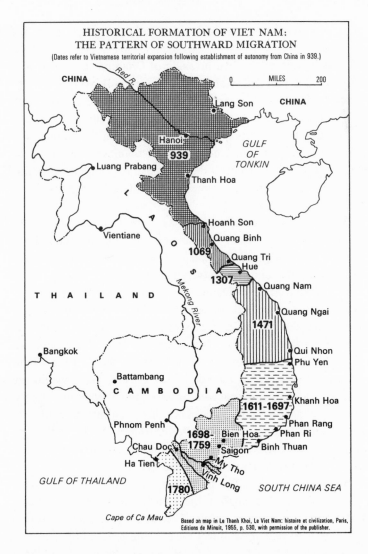

HISTORICAL FORMATION OF VIET NAM:
THE PATTERN OF SOUTHWARD MIGRATION
(Dates refer to Vietnamese territorial expansion following establishment of autonomy from China in 939.)

CHINA

Red R.

Lang Son

CHINA

GULF
OF
TONKIN

Hanoi

939

Luang Prabang

Thanh Hoa

Vientiane

L
A
O
S

Hoanh Son

Quang Binh

1069

Quang Tri
Hue

1307

Quang Nam

T H A I L A N D

Mekong River

Quang Ngai

1471

Qui Nhon
Phu Yen

Bangkok

Battambang

C A M B O D I A

Khanh Hoa

1611–1697

Phnom Penh

1698   Bien Hoa

Phan Rang
Phan Ri

1759   Saigon

Binh Thuan

Chau Doc

Ha Tien

My Tho

Vinh Long

GULF OF THAILAND

1780

SOUTH CHINA SEA

Cape of Ca Mau

Based on map in Le Thanh Khoi, Le Viet Nam: histoire et civilization, Paris,
Éditions de Minuit, 1955, p. 530, with permission of the publisher.

(1428–1527)—recaptured control over the country and obtained recognition of autonomy from China. Although his successors made great strides in restoring order to the war-ravaged
country, their most enduring achievements were also in the field

4 For a map showing the phases of southward expansion at the expense of the
Chams, see Pierre Huard and Maurice Durand: *Connaissance du Viet Nam* (Hanoi:
École Française d'Extrême-Orient; 1954), p. 33.

5 Coedès: *The Making of South-East Asia*, pp. 205–7; André Masson: *Histoire
du Viet Nam* (Paris: Presses Universitaires de France; 1960), pp. 21–2.

of military operations. An invasion of Champa succeeded in destroying the political viability of the rival kingdom in 1471. Severely diminished in territory, Champa lingered on for another two hundred years before the Vietnamese finally occupied and settled the whole of its territory.[6] However, in the course of this occupation the expansiveness of Vietnamese military power merely posed more sharply the challenge to Vietnamese political ingenuity. Could the Vietnamese consolidate their gains through resilient institutions?

Southward migration (known as *Nam Tiến* in Vietnamese), following in the wake of the conquest of Champa, altered Vietnamese life fundamentally. Vietnamese territory almost doubled its original size, and the country's population, formerly concentrated in the Red River Delta, became scattered throughout areas more than six hundred miles away. The problems of increased scale produced parochial pressures too great for traditional politics to manage, and Viet Nam's central institutions gave way. Though these institutions were modeled on those of the Chinese empire—within which the total area of Viet Nam would have been no more than a province or two—the Vietnamese, as their territory expanded, could not make these institutions work effectively. Even through military administration the Le, unlike previous dynasties, could no longer maintain territorial control over the whole country. Regionalism had become the stronger force.[7]

By 1516 three families had emerged with a disproportionate amount of armed strength in the society while the ruling dynasty had virtually no power at all. The country fell into a state of anarchy, with rich agricultural areas being pillaged by mercenary troops hired by rival families; farming was interrupted and famine spread over the land. It seemed impossible to repeat the previously successful strategy in which the Ly dynasty (1009–1225) had achieved control over the whole country by force and then transformed military power into political institutions. With the

6 Georges Maspéro: *Le royaume de Champa* (Paris: Van Oest; 1928), pp. 206–16.
7 On the problems of political unity see Paul Isoart: *Le phénomène national viêtnamien: De l'indépendance unitaire à l'indépendance fractionnée* (Paris: Librairie Générale de Droit et de Jurisprudence; 1961), pp. 33–80.

expansion of Vietnamese territory it had become easier for more numerous and formidable military groups to develop from fertile agricultural bases; regionalism was ascendant.[8]

In the midst of this breakdown of central authority, one of the three dominant families, the Mac, attempted in 1527 to unify the country under its dynastic control. Instead, their bid for power precipitated a fratricidal internal war that continued spasmodically until just before the French intervened in Viet Nam, almost three hundred years later. As the war became more protracted, the conflict was gradually stabilized by a partition of the country into defined territories controlled by the rival families. The beginning of this trend toward partition occurred in 1592 when the Mac were driven out of the Red River Delta by the force protecting the vestigial Le dynasty. Rather than restoring unity, the victory over the Mac merely aggravated an already strong spirit of enmity between the Trinh and the Nguyen, the two other dominant families. While they were united in opposing the Mac, these two families were divided by their desire to exercise unchallenged influence over the impotent Le rulers. They both regarded the Le as the only legitimate authority in the country, yet each accused the other of fomenting rebellion. On the outcome of this dynastic impasse rested the unity and stability of Viet Nam for more than two centuries.[9]

Lines between the two rival families hardened as the Nguyen steadily consolidated their strength south of the Red River Delta along the strategic coastal plain. Unable to reconcile their struggle for dynastic influence and regional power, in 1620 the two adversaries confronted each other with fierce combat. This conflict persisted tenaciously for fifty years until it subsided into an armed stalemate which divided the country, north and south, into distinct areas of political-military control. The disintegration of the country into two warring states was symbolized by a wall built across the narrow waist of Viet Nam at the 18th

8 Charles Maybon: *Histoire moderne du pays d'Annam, 1592–1820* (Paris: Plon; 1920). This work is the most thorough and well-researched study available in a Western language for any period of Vietnamese history.

9 Ibid., pp. 1–12.

parallel, near the town of Dong Hoi, just north of Hue. Erected by the Nguyen, the wall of Dong Hoi rose to a height of eighteen feet, extended a distance of eleven miles, and in 1672 proved strong enough to withstand a major military test from the Trinh in the north.[1] Thereafter the country remained divided for another century on almost the same territorial basis as it is today.

1 L. Cadière: "Le mur de Dong Hoi: étude sur l'établissement des Nguyen en Cochinchine," *Bulletin École Française d'Extrême-Orient*, Vol. VI (1906), pp. 87–254.

CHAPTER 3

VIET NAM'S TRADITION
OF POLITICAL DISUNITY

❁
❁
❁

Besides stimulating divisive political tendencies, territorial expansion also brought to Viet Nam an unusual geographic shape—one especially conducive to regionalism and rebellion. The striking dimensions of the territory that has resulted from relentless southward movement are its length of approximately one thousand miles and its width of only three hundred miles at its widest and about forty-five miles at its narrowest. Striking as they are, these dimensions do not reflect the fact that Viet Nam lacks geographic unity. Overall, it is an S-shaped country fragmented with mountain chains and held together by a thin coastal plain loosely connecting two deltas at extreme ends of the territory. Except for the generous extent of seacoast with frequent harbors, few natural avenues of communication span the length of the country. Isolated areas—especially those in the narrow central coastal plain, but also in the mountainous regions surrounding the deltas—have historically posed difficulties for central administration and given a haven to rebels.[1]

In creating problems of regionalism and rebellion, the character of the terrain has been emphasized by the pattern of population settlement. If military conquest alone had been the instrument of Viet Nam's expansion, it is doubtful the Vietnamese would occupy the territory they do today. Close behind the military forces were the settlers ready to bring the land under cultivation. Yet the terrain, in addition to limiting communications, also restricted the locations in which the Vietnamese population could settle. Only land permitting the cultivation of rice under irrigation, the very foundation of the country's agricultural society, was suitable for Vietnamese migration. Such areas were extensive in the deltas located at either end of the territory; but in the approximately six hundred miles in between there were only small and frequently isolated fragments of land, snatched from the encroachment of the mountains on one side and the sea on the other. Not only was it difficult to adapt the Vietnamese style of wet rice agriculture to the surrounding mountains, but these highlands were infested with the malaria-carrying anopheles mosquito.[2]

The overall limits these barriers imposed upon Vietnamese settlement are best seen in the curious pattern of population distribution that has emerged from southward migration. Today, roughly 30,000,000 Vietnamese are crowded into less than 20,000 of the country's approximately 128,000 square miles of territory. More than 90 per cent of the population is concentrated in less than 20 per cent of the land area, a fact which results in some of the densest population clusters anywhere in the world. Because of their rice agriculture and vulnerability to upland malaria, the Vietnamese live in the fertile lowlands. The remaining 100,000-plus square miles of plateau and mountains are sparsely

---

1 Great Britain, Admiralty, Naval Intelligence Division: Georgraphical Handbook Series, B.R. 510, *Indo-China* (Cambridge: Cambridge University Press; 1943). This is the best available geography of Viet Nam. Also see Canada, Department of Mines and Technical Surveys, Geographical Branch: *Indo-China: A Geographical Appreciation* (Ottawa, 1953).

2 For a map showing these rice-growing areas see Masson: *Histoire du Viet Nam*, p. 10.

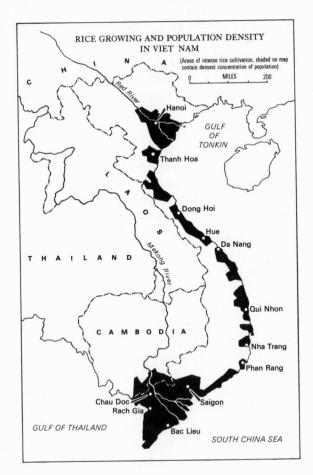

RICE GROWING AND POPULATION DENSITY
IN VIET NAM

(Areas of intense rice cultivation, shaded on map
contain densest concentration of population)

0   MILES   200

CHINA

Red River

Hanoi

GULF
OF
TONKIN

Thanh Hoa

LAOS

Dong Hoi

Hue

Da Nang

Mekong River

THAILAND

Qui Nhon

CAMBODIA

Nha Trang

Phan Rang

Chau Doc
Rach Gia

Saigon

GULF OF THAILAND

Bac Lieu

SOUTH CHINA SEA

populated by non-Vietnamese ethnic minorities, who are less
advanced culturally than the lowlanders. Thus a major dichotomy
between the upland and the lowland areas is reinforced by ethnic
as well as other cultural differences.[3]

A focus on this settlement pattern of the Vietnamese people—
their reliance on irrigated rice agriculture and their history of
territorial expansion—illuminates much that is complex and obscure in their past. Such a perspective sheds light on strengths
and weaknesses of Vietnamese politics and society. A hypothesis

3 These statistics are from Georges Condominas: "Aspects of a Minority Problem
in Indochina," *Pacific Affairs,* Vol. XXIV, March 1951, p. 77. See also John T.
McAlister, Jr.: "Mountain Minorities and the Viet Minh: A Key to the Indochina
War," in Peter Kunstadter, ed.: *Southeast Asian Tribes, Minorities and Nations*
(Princeton: Princeton University Press; 1967), pp. 771–844.

of the geographer Pierre Gourou is that in a tropical country the cultivation of rice in flooded fields is what alone gives rise to the development of an advanced civilization, while at the same time limiting it both culturally and geographically.[4] In Viet Nam these strengths and limits are best seen through the prime module of social development—the village. It was due primarily to the cohesion and flexibility of the Vietnamese village that popular migration followed upon military conquest. The village was the institution that translated the potential of the newly occupied land into the reality of productive habitation.

A system of sponsored settlement developed in which established villages sent out pioneers. They were usually young people or others without land who were eager to get new fields and create new villages. Support from the parent villages continued until the offspring were self-sufficient. Then official recognition was requested from the emperor, who bestowed a name, a communal seal, and a guardian spirit upon the new village. These imperial articles were traditionally kept in a communal house (known as the đinh) which was in effect the symbol of village unity: a place for religious ceremonies and public occasions and in a sense a ritual link with the rest of the country.[5]

Through this process the Vietnamese village facilitated the southward territorial advance that simply went beyond the country's capacity to consolidate its gains through political centralization. The experience after 1500, of nearly three centuries of regionalism and disunity—trends never fully resolved before France assumed control over the country—raises several fundamental questions about traditional politics in Viet Nam. Perhaps the key question is why the village was such an effective instrument of cultural expansion while central institutions were not.

4 Gourou is quoted by Paul Mus: *Viet Nam: Sociologie d'une guerre* (Paris: Éditions du Seuil; 1952), p. 18. Role of the village in Vietnamese expansion is discussed, pp. 13-22.

5 In Viet Nam's archaic ideographic writing, the character for village is composed of two roots which "together give the idea of a place where individuals sacrificing to the spirits come together," Paul Ory: *La commune annamite au Tonkin* (Paris: Augustin Challamel; 1894), p. 3. The manner in which a new village was created is described in Pierre Pasquier: *L'Annam d'autrefois* (Paris: Société d'Éditions Géographiques, Maritimes et Coloniales; 1929), p. 42.

The answer seems to lie in the deeply rooted autonomy of the village, which, though guaranteed by statute, had evolved through custom and practice. According to an old Vietnamese proverb, "the laws of the emperor yield to the customs of the village."[6]

The substance behind this proverb came from the restraint village institutions imposed on the power of the central authorities. The development of these local institutions, it seems, predated those of the central administration; their origins are often traced to the period before China's occupation was overthrown. The most important of these local institutions was a council of notables which, among other things, was responsible for the external obligations of the village; the central administration did not deal directly with individual villagers. Members of the council were chosen from the small village oligarchy, based on age, education, family standing, and, to a lesser extent, wealth. They represented the cohesive ties of the village—family, Confucian learning,[7] and property. Only the council of notables could inform the state on village resources when collective obligations were levied for taxes, *corvées,* and contingents of soldiers for the national army. And their information was purposely falsified in order to lessen the weight of collective exactions. Because there was no compulsory registration of births and deaths, the village rolls were an inaccurate and incomplete indication of village population. Yet the state refrained from enforcing a greater surveillance over village productivity and population because of its respect for village autonomy. If this autonomy were violated, as the French learned later to their misfortune, then the bedrock upon which political stability might be founded would be destroyed. Thus, Vietnamese regimes treated this autonomy with

6 Gerald Cannon Hickey: *Village in Vietnam* (New Haven: Yale University Press; 1964), p. 276. The most comprehensive work dealing with village government is Vu Quoc Thong: *La décentralisation administrative au Viet Nam* (Hanoi: Presses Universitaires du Viet Nam; 1952); also see Nguyen Xuan Dao: *Village Government in Viet Nam: A Survey of Historical Development* (Saigon: Michigan State University, Vietnam Advisory Group; September 1958).

7 Although the Vietnamese kept abreast of developments in Confucian thought in China, their concept of Confucianism followed a pattern that was uniquely Vietnamese. At the village level it mixed with Buddhist and Taoist beliefs. Huard and Durand: *Connaissance du Viet Nam,* pp. 48-9.

respect in order that they might perfect a stable political super-structure above the village.[8]

The limits on centralized authority arising from the official anonymity of individual villagers and the prestige of the council of notables caused the village and not the state to have the largest executive role in Vietnamese politics. A skillful division of labor evolved in which the state performed the military, judicial, and religious functions while all public works and services were in the hands of the village authorities. They had the resources, they built the roads, dikes, bridges—the state was essentially a co-ordinator. The state did all the countrywide planning and then issued directives for decentralized execution. In the face of frequent instability the effectiveness of such a division of labor rested on the Confucian political tradition as well as the common bond of self-interest. Villagers were brought up to believe that their survival and the success of their labors depended on ritualistic ob-servances which the emperor—as the mediator between heaven and earth—prescribed and in some cases performed. Through ritual observances complementary to those of the emperor, the villagers won the favor of heaven and assured their harmony with nature. Overall the dynastic authorities attempted to establish a balance between the strength of the village and the necessary requirements of power for political centralization.[9]

Although the division of responsibility between an administra-tive superstructure and autonomous villages was skillful when in operation, it created profound weaknesses in Vietnamese po-litical organization. With their autonomy and command over local resources, the villages could easily survive if cut off from the administrative superstructure. But a concern for peace and security caused the villages to seek the protection of the dynastic regime. Conflict or the threat of it would interfere with the steady routine required for rice farming; the very basis of village life would then be challenged. However, when the incumbents were unable to respond to village needs for security, it was usually

8 Mus: *Viet Nam: Sociologie d'une guerre*, pp. 23–5.
9 Paul Mus: "Viet Nam: A Nation Off Balance," *Yale Review*, Vol. XLI, Summer 1952, pp. 524–33.

both convenient and advantageous for villages to come under the protection of political movements opposing the prevailing dynasty.

While village resources made it relatively easy for rebels to develop support in localized areas, it was quite difficult for the rebels to achieve legitimacy throughout the country. Faced with the same type of problems as the incumbent dynasty, they had to institutionalize political power. If they failed to devise ways of assuring security, mobilizing a population for political and military action, regularizing the access to political power, and sharing power among those who had obtained it, then the rebels would have little likelihood of overthrowing the existing dynasty. Moreover, they might find themselves subject to rebellion in their own ranks, just as they had rebelled against the incumbent dynasty. The village character of Vietnamese society seemed to lend itself to rebellion while discouraging political consolidation. At least this was the nature of Vietnamese politics after the sixteenth century; neither the Trinh nor the Nguyen regime had been able to defeat the other or even consolidate in political institutions the military power they had in opposing regions of the country.[1]

By the end of the eighteenth century a stalemate had endured for a century between the northern (Trinh) and southern (Nguyen) regimes without there having been a major military engagement. But this lack of conflict did not indicate that the sources of rebellion had been resolved. During the seventeenth and eighteenth centuries the Nguyen had continued Vietnamese expansion southward until they had occupied the Mekong Delta over the opposition of its Cambodian inhabitants. Just as this expansion was reaching it apogee, a rebellion broke out in the Nguyen territory south of Hue, in central Viet Nam. Breaking a century of stalemate, this uprising gave the northerners, the Trinh, an unexpected opportunity to extend their control over the whole of Viet Nam. Through ineptness, however, the Trinh alienated the southern rebels, known as the Tay Son, who turned on the Trinh while also fighting the Nguyen. Except for the

1 Maybon: *Histoire moderne du pays d'Annam,* pp. 15–20.

male heir to their familial leadership, the Nguyen had been virtually eliminated by 1777, and less than a decade later, Trinh rule in the north had been defeated decisively by the Tay Son.[2]

Although rebellion had brought disunity in the sixteenth century, it was out of this Tay Son rebellion that Viet Nam found unity in the nineteenth. At the conclusion of the Tay Son rebellion in 1802, Vietnamese territory was united from the China border to the Gulf of Siam for the first time in history. But this historic achievement was not accomplished by the Tay Son. In an epic conflict the surviving heir to the Nguyen regime capitalized on the Tay Son's preoccupation in the north to return from exile, recapture the Mekong Delta, and in 1788, seize control over the strategic region around Saigon. The heir, who later proclaimed himself Emperor Gia Long, might have been unable to consolidate these territorial gains and unify the country had it not been for the arrival of substantial military and naval reinforcements from France. Arranged by the French missionary prelate, Bishop Pigneau de Behaine, this vital aid marked the revival of a dormant interest in Viet Nam by the French church.[3]

Opportunities for outside involvement in Viet Nam's internal conflict had existed since warfare divided the country in 1620. French interests in Viet Nam had stemmed from this earlier period in which the Nguyen regime had also been dependent on external aid. French priests had been in the country since the early seventeenth century, when the Nguyen's initial weakness against the Trinh had led them to seek sophisticated weaponry from the Portuguese. These French priests, part of a Portuguese Jesuit mission, were so successful in winning converts that they were expelled when the armed stalemate reduced the Nguyen's dependency on foreign aid. Not until the 1780's with the outbreak of the Tay Son rebellion, did France's freedom from worldwide commitments coincide with an opportunity for influence in

2 Ibid., pp. 290–331.
3 John F. Cady: *The Roots of French Imperialism in Eastern Asia* (Ithaca: Cornell University Press; 1954), pp. 11–12.

Viet Nam. But the French revolution cut short the participation of forces raised by the influence of the French clergy at Versailles. Once again France's interest in Viet Nam subsided.[4]

When Emperor Gia Long unified Viet Nam in 1802, the country's capacities for political centralization reached a high-water mark. Realizing that this unity had been essentially a military achievement, the new emperor tried to overcome the regionalism that had divided the country for centuries. Institutions were created to promote the political integration of the Vietnamese people, but regional and parochial identities continued to exert stronger pressures. Beneath the surface of apparent political unity the governors of the various regions held the real power while formally acknowledging the sovereignty of the emperor. Unfortunately for the future of Vietnamese politics, even this promising trend toward unification was ended with Gia Long's death, and in 1820 an authoritarian and xenophobic policy was inaugurated by his heirs.[5]

Once again internal tensions created opportunities for outside intervention. Through the xenophobic policies of Gia Long's successors, the French were denied the influence in Vietnamese affairs they had enjoyed during the fight for unification and had come to expect during the period of consolidation. Not surprisingly, it was the Catholic missionaries who were the hardest hit. Gia Long's successors saw Christianity as a threat to the Confucian traditions upon which Vietnamese politics were founded. They proscribed Christian missions and eventually put some of the French clergymen to death. Since protection by the Far Eastern fleet for French missionaries became a significant issue

---

4 With the signing of a treaty at Versailles on November 28, 1787, Louis XVI agreed to provide military assistance to Nguyen Anh, the future Emperor Gia Long. Among the 360 men in the French-led force that fought in Viet Nam, many were veterans of the American Revolution. Philippe Vannier, the captain of a ship in the French squadron, had been present for the surrender of Cornwallis at Yorktown. John F. Cady: *Southeast Asia: Its Historical Development* (New York: McGraw-Hill; 1964), pp. 281–4.

5 Jumper: "Vietnam: The Historical Background," pp. 380–3, A. B. Woodside: "Some Features of the Vietnamese Bureaucracy Under the Early Nguyễn Dynasty," *Papers on China*, Vol. XIX (Harvard University, East Asia Research Center; December 1965), pp. 1–29.

in France, the Vietnamese attacks on the church provided a convenient opportunity for Napoleon III to solidify the tenuous domestic position of the Second Empire.[6]

After initial setbacks, the intervention in Viet Nam launched by Napoleon III in response to domestic religious sentiment became the special interest of the French navy. More interested in acquiring territory than religious converts, the navy's enthusiasm resulted in the occupation of Viet Nam and the ethnic and culturally distinct areas of Cambodia and Laos. These disparate countries were formed, in 1897, into a territory known thereafter as Indochina—a name chosen as a semantic compensation for French colonial failures in India and China at the hands of the British.[7]

[6] Louis–Napoleon's "susceptibility to Catholic propagandist pressure developed largely from his determination to deny to his Legitimatist political enemies of the Right the backing of the French Church." Cady: *Southeast Asia*, p. 415.

[7] Cady: *The Roots of French Imperialism*, pp. 267, 296.

CHAPTER 4 🏵 🏵 🏵

FRENCH RULE IN VIET NAM

🏵

🏵

🏵

In administering their territorial acquisition, the French created a state in which colonial administration virtually supplanted indigenous politics. Obviously, the primary French concern was to prevent Vietnamese opposition from threatening their colonial rule. Although they could not stop rebellion entirely, the French did neutralize it through military and administrative control. Yet the effect of these preventives was to eliminate all but the most circumscribed and stylized political activity. In becoming the country's incumbent government, the French suppressed the energies that had gone into centuries of political conflict among the Vietnamese. Almost no legitimate channels for political expression existed; the politics of the Vietnamese became synonymous with sedition in French Indochina. Unintentionally, however, Vietnamese political energies were enlarged by the unexpected social consequences of colonial programs. Ultimately, when French strength wavered in the 1940's, pent-up political energies erupted in a revolution that no amount of French force could subdue.[1]

1 Virginia Thompson: *French Indochina* (London: George Allen and Unwin; 1937) is the standard work in English on the French colonial regime.

The suppression of Vietnamese political life was begun by the adminstrative partitioning of the country, which occurred initially through the uneven pattern of French military occupation. Viet Nam would have been occupied all at once except for the limits on French resources imposed by other foreign commitments; a combination of far-flung imperial ambitions and domestic counter-pressures made the French occupation a piecemeal affair. By the treaty of June 1862, the southernmost portion of Viet Nam, called Cochinchina by its French occupiers, came under French control. The central and northern parts of the country, known to the French as Annam and Tonkin, did not become parts of the French empire until more than twelve years after Cochinchina was occupied. Annam—the former Chinese name for all Viet Nam and a term considered derogatory by the Vietnamese—and Tonkin were acquired throught treaties of 1884–5 with the Vietnamese government at Hue and the Chinese at Peking.[2] The resulting fragmentation of the country was perpetuated by a colonial mythology which regarded Viet Nam not as one country but three: Annam, Tonkin, and Cochinchina. Even the name *Việt Nam*, with which the country had been baptized by Gia Long in 1802, was outlawed and uttered only as a rallying cry of revolutionaries.[3]

Partitioning Viet Nam into three parts aided the security of France's colonial state against countrywide uprisings. Administrative barriers were imposed to discourage the Vietnamese from unifying their potential resources against the French. Such obstacles helped to perpetuate the traditional pressures of regionalism and parochialism that had previously limited Vietnamese political unity. Prior to French intervention, administrative regions (known as *kỳ* in Vietnamese) had existed and the tripartite subdivision of the French roughly approximated the

2 In hopes of maintaining their autonomy, the Vietnamese tried to play off the Chinese against the French. See Hall: *A History of South East Asia*, pp. 569–71. Also see Cho Huan-Lai: *Les origines du conflict franco-chinois à propos du Tonkin jusqu'en 1883* (Paris: Jouve; 1935). A documentary history of the French conquest is Georges Taboulet: *La geste française en Indochine: Histoire par les textes de la France en Indochine des origines à 1914* (2 vols., Paris: Adrien Maisonneuve; 1955-6).

3 Jean Chesneaux: *Contribution à l'histoire de la nation viêtnamienne* (Paris: Éditions Sociales; 1955), p. 7.

territories of the three *kỳ*. But under the Vietnamese these regions were apparently intended, especially in Gia Long's regime, to promote the unity of a disparate and difficult-to-administer country. With the French, however, the three *pays* or "countries" appeared as manifestations of the well-worn technique "divide and rule."[4]

Of course, administrative subdivisions alone could not ensure political impotence among the Vietnamese. But new and more important bases for disunity were created through separate French policies and programs for each administrative region. Perhaps the sharpest of these regional differences was between Cochinchina and the other two *pays*. Partly because it was occupied more than two decades before the rest of Viet Nam and partly because it was ruled as a colony of France with fewer treaty or legal restraints, Cochinchina developed in a distinctive pattern.

A difference in public administration was one of the more significant aspects of this distinctiveness. In Viet Nam, as elsewhere, the selection and training of civil servants is a key political act indicating where power lies. Originally, the French navy expected to govern Cochinchina through the existing mandarinal administration. However, after the French occupation, local officials fled northward into central Viet Nam, leaving the French with the task of administering the territory directly. Because the number of French personnel was limited, it became necessary to recruit a wholly new cadre of Vietnamese to consolidate French colonial control. Chosen without regard to traditional criteria and trained in French language and procedures, a totally new kind of Vietnamese official appeared. Enjoying a status of authority and prestige by virtue of their loyalty to alien rule, these new Vietnamese officials were committed to France even before the whole of Viet Nam had come under French control.[5]

By contrast, the other areas of Viet Nam, when occupied two decades later, were administered indirectly through the traditional

4 Hoang Van Chi: *From Colonialism to Communism: A Case History of North Vietnam* (New York and London: Frederick A. Praeger; 1964), pp. 10-13.

5 Isoart: *Le phénomène national viêtnamien*, pp. 126-37.

bureaucracy, the mandarinate. Although some mandarins resisted the French, they had no sanctuary where the majority of
them could flee. Moreover, in Annam and Tonkin, France's
occupation was in theory a "protection" of Viet Nam's traditional
government. In principle, the continuation of the mandarinate
was sanctioned by treaty. But despite its treaty commitments,
France actively interfered with the administration of these "protectorates" in order to ensure the perpetuation of its colonial
rule. Instead of abolishing the mandarinate outright, the French
sought to decrease its continuity with traditional politics and to
increase its bureaucratic capacities to fulfill colonial programs.
Entrance examinations for the mandarinate which tested Confucian learning were discontinued in Tonkin in 1915 and in
Annam in 1918. Classical knowledge also lost more of its relevance for social mobility and political opportunity as the University of Hanoi was opened in 1918, to train limited numbers
of Vietnamese for technical specialities and administration. Over
the twenty-five years before revolution broke out, the distinction
between direct and indirect rule became virtually meaningless
except as a legal distinction.[6]

Even though administrative personnel throughout Vietnam
were eventually trained in essentially the same manner, definite
regional differences persisted. By the time direct rule was considered for the whole of the country, Cochinchina already had
had more than half a century of experience with its effects. The
French-oriented functionaries of Cochinchina contrasted with
the curious mixture of administrative personnel in Tonkin and
Annam. In these protectorates there were the older mandarins,
submissive to the French yet loyal to the monarchy, and alongside them the younger Western-trained administrators, whose
loyalties were uncertain. When the revolution occurred, these
administrative elites formed only a portion of the political leadership of the country, yet they had a substantial impact on the
course of events by attempting to lead the various regions in

6 Joanne Marie Coyle: "Indochinese Administration and Education: French Policy
and Practice, 1917–1945" (unpublished Ph.D. dissertation, Fletcher School of Law
and Diplomacy, Tufts University, 1963), pp. 54 ff.; see also Jumper: "Vietnam:
The Historical Background," pp. 383–4.

separate directions.[7] And until the revolution broke out their diversity was a helpful guarantee that they would not combine their energies against French rule.

Differences in administration, despite their significance in shaping a potential political leadership along regional lines, were overshadowed by social and economic changes in creating new bases for regionalism. Rather than being randomly distributed, these changes were clustered regionally. Industrial development in the north, and plantation agriculture along with a vast increase in cultivatable land in the Mekong Delta in the south produced conspicuous regional peculiarities in Vietnamese society. What industrial labor force there was in Viet Nam was concentrated in the north, while a previously nonexistent class of Vietnamese absentee landowners arose in Cochinchina as a result of land development.[8]

From these regionally clustered changes came regional identities which were often stronger, especially in Cochinchina, than any lingering feelings for a unified and independent Viet Nam. Of all the regions, the south was the most susceptible to such changes in attitude. It had been settled by the Vietnamese for less than a century before French occupation occurred. Vietnamese traditions and population had not yet been firmly implanted before they came under the forceful influence of France. Consequently, Cochinchina became known as the most Gallicized area of colonial Viet Nam while Annam, which on the whole had the least amount of social change, was known as the most traditional area of the country. Although Tonkin, the administrative and academic center of all Indochina, underwent substantial social change, it nonetheless retained a close identification with Vietnamese traditions.

Colonially induced regionalism tended to reinforce cultural differences that had arisen during the Vietnamese's southward

7 Harry J. Benda has discussed these regional distinctions among political elites in Viet Nam in his perceptive essay "Political Elites in Colonial Southeast Asia: An Historical Analysis," *Comparative Studies in Society and History*, Vol. VII, No. 3 (April 1965), pp. 233–51, especially pp. 248–9.

8 A sharp critique of French colonial policies in promoting social disequilibrium and regionalism is Chesneaux: *Contribution à l'histoire de la nation viêtnamienne*, pp. 158–82. See map on p. 169 for regional configuration of French enterprises.

migration. Parochial characteristics have become convenient symbols of regional identity, and between north and south, one of the most easily noticed has been the difference in dialect and pronunciation of the Vietnamese language. The southern tongue is less inflected, flatter, and softer,[9] but it is thought by northerners to be a less proper, provincial accent. In addition, village customs and family structure in the less densely populated Mekong Delta have been more informal and less rigid than traditional practices which originated in the thickly settled Red River Delta homeland of the Vietnamese.[1] These characteristics have made the southerners more amenable to change yet have given them less stability during the uncertainty of social change. Speaking a parochial tongue and showing less respect for traditions, southerners have been looked down upon by northerners as being less cultivated. In turn, northerners have been thought to be overly formal and haughty by their more gregarious southern brethren. Eventually such popular conceptions limited the possibilities for cooperation among the Vietnamese and affected their potential for common action.

The changes that gave regionalism a new emphasis in Viet Nam were symbolized by the superficial contrasts that developed between the regional centers of Hue, Hanoi, and Saigon. In Annam, in the center of the country, Hue remained virtually unchanged except for its increasing impotence and irrelevance to the changes occurring elsewhere. It continued to be a small sedate town where the obsolete imperial court of Viet Nam periodically performed Confucian rituals amidst the decaying monuments of the archaic Nguyen dynasty. Court mandarins presided over a government that had been the first to unite Viet Nam, yet by the beginning of the twentieth century lacked all but the anachronistic vestiges of power.

9 Laurence C. Thompson: *A Vietnamese Grammar* (Seattle: University of Washington Press; 1965) is a text which uses the northern pronunciation, which it describes as "the most widely accepted as a sort of standard." Robert B. Jones, Jr., and Huynh Sanh Thong: *Introduction to Spoken Vietnamese* (Washington: American Council of Learned Societies; 1957) uses the southern pronunciation and gives a comparison with the northern style.

1 Hickey: *Village in Vietnam*, pp. 280–2.

To the north, Hanoi became a mandarin-red brick administrative city built on the ruins of an ancient Vietnamese capital. Here, in the period after 1920, were found the new men of Vietnamese politics: the recently trained administrators who, despite uncertain political loyalties, helped carry the burden of administering Indochina. In the little more than two decades between the beginning of their recruitment in the 1920's and the outbreak of revolution in 1945, these administrators did not develop a close identification with French interests; their opportunities were too restricted for that, so when the revolution arrived, they went along, taking their administrative talents with them. At the other end of the country, in Cochinchina, were the Francophile Vietnamese who had found wider opportunities through French colonialism, and who supported France when the challenge came. Saigon—their "Paris of the Orient"—emerged from a marsh through an elaborate French construction program to become a gleaming commercial port-city which often reminded visitors of a provincial town in the south of France.

Besides reinforcing old—mainly regional—tensions, French colonial policies created new ones. Although colonially sponsored social change became clustered regionally, it was not planned that way. A reinforced regionalism was a by-product of changes that resulted from programs directed toward other, primarily economic, purposes. In broad outline these changes occurred from the creation of an export economy in primary products— mainly rice and rubber, but some minerals—with a protected market for French manufactured imports; from the introduction of taxation in money to finance expenditures of the colonial budget; and from the expansion of primary education. While these changes held out the promise of modernization, they were insufficient to achieve that goal; they left Viet Nam halfway between the traditional and modern worlds. Viet Nam's colonial economy was vunerable to fluctuations in international commodity and monetary markets and did not possess the institutional structure for sustained economic growth. Moreover, it lacked a self-generating industrial sector to absorb the people drawn into the towns in hopes of gaining access to the monetary economy.[2]

Under the impetus of colonial programs, wide segments of Vietnamese society were moving from traditional toward modern ways of life. Such a movement has been described as a process of social mobilization. As an analytic concept, social mobilization is defined by Karl Deutsch "as the process in which major clusters of old social, economic, and psychological commitments are eroded or broken and people become available for new patterns of socialization and behavior."[3] Two distinct stages are implied in this process. The first stage involves "the uprooting or breaking away from old settings, habits, and commitments," while the second stage is concerned with "the induction of the mobilized persons into some relatively stable new patterns of group membership, organization, and commitment."[4] During the colonial era in Viet Nam the first stage was fairly widespread, but the second touched the mobilized population only slightly. The Vietnamese were only partially mobilized. They had moved away from traditional lives, but they had not been reintegrated into a new pattern, nor had the institutions for this reintegration been established.

Viet Nam's halfway house on the road to modernization was neither stable nor tension-free. Many Vietnamese were caught between the deterioration of old commitments—to the village and the clan—and the lack or uncertainty of new commitments to factory, foreman, teachers, work group, classmates, and the like. Voluntary associations so closely identified with social integration in highly mobile modern societies did not come easily to Vietnamese. They fell back upon fictive or real kinship identities and secret societies. Moreover, there was little hope of reintegration through the institutions of the colonial state; it sought only to keep tensions arising out of the imbalances of Vietnamese society from erupting out of control.

2 Donald Lancaster: *The Emancipation of French Indochina* (London: Oxford University Press, under the auspices of the Royal Institute of International Affairs; 1961), pp. 65–8.
3 Karl W. Deutsch: "Social Mobilization and Political Development," *The American Political Science Review*, Vol. LV, No. 3 (September 1961), p. 493.
4 Ibid.

Potential reintegration through economic growth was restricted by the mercantilist system of colonial trade, in which the colonies were supposed to absorb the exports of French industry while supplying tropical products in return. Unfettered indigenous economic development would have reduced French imports into Viet Nam. Politics also could not play its potentially conciliatory role, much less act as a force for reintegration. The colonial bureaucracy absorbed most of the functions of Viet Nam's political life down to the village; the role that mandarinal recruitment had once played in institutionalizing political power, conciliating tensions, and integrating far-flung villages into a centralized political system was neglected. The colonial administration could fulfill none of these functions. Instead it became a training-ground for a new type of bureaucratically competent Vietnamese elite. In the uncertainty of the colonial world their understandable anxiety for prestige and occupational mobility, outweighing their concern for the problems of politics of the country, generated yet another set of tensions.

The existence of unreconciled tensions was nothing new to Viet Nam. Prior to the French intervention the Vietnamese political capacity for resolving conflict was conspicuously poor; violence and internal warfare were endemic. Yet on occasions when unity had been achieved, determined efforts were made to institutionalize political power. France was both eager to quell violence and capable of doing so, but it gave little attention to the long-range consequences of holding power by force rather than by institutionalized compliance. Political, as distinct from administrative, institutions were not a part of the French colonial state, except for high-level advisory councils composed of a small number of French and Vietnamese in each of the three *pays* of Viet Nam.[5] While the French administrative structure was suppressing a traditional system of politics that had its own unique criteria for mobility and power based on Confucian concepts, it was establishing a system with little mobility and almost no power for indigenous participants. At the same time, when

5 Isoart: *Le phénomène national viêtnamien*, pp. 191–219, presents a detailed account of the structure of the French colonial state.

social change was occurring more rapidly than ever, no legitimate channels for expressing or reconciling social tension were permitted to a people with a long tradition of lively political life. In destroying the old structures of politics and neglecting to create new ones, France was undermining its own interests in Viet Nam.

The destabilizing effects of French colonialism had several important consequences in developing the potential for revolution in Viet Nam. At the lowest level of the institutional hierarchy, the Vietnamese village was no longer the vital cohesive force it had once been. These qualities were lost to it largely because the French had violated the anonymity of the villagers and the autonomy of the village. This occurred through three major reforms:

> (1) the institution of regular registration of births and deaths, which permitted the composition of more accurate tax rolls; (2) the imposition of tighter French control over the Council of Notables, particularly in tax and bugetary matters; and (3) the substitution of election for co-optation of council members. The first two of these reforms undermined the patriarchal system by curtailing the considerable administrative—and consequently financial—latitude with which the councils of notables had been accustomed to function. The third reform encouraged the tax payers to look after their own affairs.[6]

By weakening traditional village leadership and promoting the legal autonomy of the individual villagers without establishing new forms of political organization to encompass these relationships, the French were inviting the disintegration of the Vietnamese social system.

Perhaps the most important change in creating the potential for revolution in Viet Nam was the formation of new sets of elites. These elites emerged from French colonial institutions which were bringing Viet Nam into closer contact with the modern world. Besides the administrative cadre, this included

---

6 Paul Mus: "The Role of the Village in Vietnamese Politics," *Pacific Affairs*, Vol. XXII, September 1949, p. 266.

people who were naturalized as French citizens, those who received French education, those who became commercial entrepreneurs and property owners, and finally those members of the traditional elite who adapted their talents to qualify for colonial elite status. Although by definition these elites had more opportunities than did the mass of the population, still their social and occupational mobility was limited. Restrictions arose because the institutions into which they were mobilized were circumscribed by the confines of the colonial society. Moreover, most of the important positions in these institutions were held by Frenchmen. Therefore, in seeing a new privileged class take form under its aegis, the French were unprepared to prevent its frustration by ensuring that these Vietnamese would have opportunities commensurate with their expectations, especially in access to positions of authority.[7] For the French to have shared such power would have required the creation of a mutually beneficial relationship with the Vietnamese to protect France's colonial interests. Such a political relationship or community of interest the French conspicuously failed to create.

Under the impact of French colonialism, Viet Nam became "a nation off balance."[8] Social changes had been induced by colonial programs, but there was hardly a harmonious relationship between the new society and the old Viet Nam. These changes had "dislocated the traditional mode of life and produced a poorly integrated society in which a small, urban-oriented Westernized elite was largely alienated from the bulk of the village based population."[9] Although harmony had been intermittent in traditional Viet Nam, it seems to have been a widely shared ideal, especially in the life of the villages. The basis for this harmony had been a structure of authority based on Confucian precepts and buttressed by strong patrilineal kinship ties. The social changes wrought during colonial rule were undoubtedly necessary if Viet Nam were to participate in the

7 In 1935 all the schools of the University of Hanoi, with the exception of law and medicine, were closed because of "intellectual unemployment." Coyle: "Indochinese Administration and Education," p. 82.

8 Mus: "Viet Nam: A Nation Off Balance," pp. 524–33.

9 Jumper: "Vietnam: The Historical Background," p. 383.

interdependent life of the modern world. However, too little attention was given to the effects of this process on the structure of authority or popular compliance. Since the village has been and continues to be the foundation of Vietnamese society, the deterioration of its resiliency was certain to have a strong impact on the stability of the society as a whole. Because the villages lay outside the modern sector that France was creating in the urban centers, this social instability was not apparent. French administration, commerce, and military force provided a veneer of stability on a society halfway between the traditional and the modern world.

Despite the instability emergent in Vietnamese society during colonial rule, revolution might never have occurred. Although rebellions broke out periodically, they were usually localized affairs and rarely threatened to overwhelm the colonial regime. Before 1940, a force of only 10,776 regular French troops, 16,218 men of the indigenous militia, and 507 French police agents was sufficient to keep order among 19,000,000 Vietnamese.[1] In 1954, 140,000 French and African troops and 280,000 indigenous troops were forced to withdraw from the field of battle after seven years of revolutionary war.[2] Initially, rebellions against French rule were led by men loyal to the imperial government at Hue, but then rural uprisings became virtually leaderless protests of discontented peasants. However, in the early 1930's a new type of leadership appeared to take advantage of incipient rebellion. Paradoxically, the rural areas did not produce these leaders; they came from the French schools and bureaucracy in the urban centers. They were part of the modern elite that France had created to facilitate the development of a colonial economy and administration. Yet this new class had not been assimilated into the world they were being asked to create. Their lack of a stake in the colonially created world induced many French-trained Vietnamese to seek through rebellion against France the fulfillment they had come to expect.

1 *Annuaire statistique de l'Indochine, 1936–1937*, pp. 25, 241.
2 Navarre: *Agonie de l'Indochine (1953–1954)*, p. 46.

Not surprisingly, the rebellions led by these Vietnamese were no more successful than previous traditionalist uprisings. Gradually, it became clear that the old-style Vietnamese rebellion could not affect French power, that a more comprehensive, structured, and enduring movement was required. When the Japanese wartime occupation broke the French hold on Viet Nam, a small but strategic portion of this frustrated upper class went into action. They had learned that only a broad-scale revolution could achieve the objectives they sought.

PART THREE ✖ ✖ ✖

The Colonial Background to the Vietnamese Revolution, 1885-1940

✖
✖
✖

CHAPTER 5 ✪ ✪ ✪

THE TRANSFORMATION

OF VIETNAMESE POLITICS

✪

✪

✪

The treaties of protection of 1883–4, imposed upon Viet Nam by the military force of France, did not mean the end of opposition to French rule; this opposition continued intermittently until France was finally forced to retreat from Viet Nam in 1954. In opposing France, the greatest lack of Viet Nam in the mid-nineteenth century was her greatest asset in the mid-twentieth: a political organization capable of mobilizing and directing a large body of men in military and political action; and a political appeal to sustain the functioning of this organization and to maintain the loyalty of the populace toward it. Throughout the seventy years between 1884 and 1954 the Vietnamese opposition to France underwent a substantial transformation to achieve this position of strength. In order to understand more fully how the French were overthrown, it is necessary to trace the lines of Viet Nam's internal political transformation back to the imposition of alien control over the country.

The development of revolutionary sentiment in Viet Nam passed through several distinct phases. The first of these was transitional. It ranged from the militant yet uncoordinated and largely ineffectual protests of those identified with the traditional political structure to the formation of the new political parties based on the ideologies of nationalism and Communism in the year 1925. The second phase, covering a sixteen-year period, was characterized by the frustrated attempts of nationalist and Communist parties to overthrow French rule. This era of unresolved political conflict was superseded in 1941 when both Communists and nationalists organized political fronts against the Japanese and French occupation of Viet Nam. This third broad phase, leading to the August Revolution of 1945, saw the emergence of a well-organized, Communist-led revolutionary movement. The movement succeeded in capturing the aspirations and many of the adherents of Vietnamese nationalism and in forging the nucleus of an armed force.

These phases can be distinguished by particular changes in the structure of Vietnamese political life brought on by the impact of French colonialism. The first of the phases is distinctive for the destruction of the countrywide effectiveness of the traditional political system and the persistence of its uncoordinated fragments in militant protest against French occupation. It also reflects the attempt by leaders identified with traditional concepts of politics to find new bases of power with which to sustain their protest against France. It saw the end of the imperial restoration movement as a meaningful political appeal, and at the same time it witnessed the laying of the foundation for later political movements. What is perhaps most significant about this period is that it occurred before the major transformation in Vietnamese society—before the creation of a French-educated elite, an industrial labor force, or a landless peasantry with monetary debts.

These effects of colonialism were absorbed during the second phase of Vietnamese political development under French dominance. In this second period, broadly based political organizations were formed, although the limitations of regional political identities were not surmounted to a significant degree. Such parochial affinities were equally as important an obstacle to countrywide political movements as were the surveillance and the repression of French authorities. And after the Japanese *coup de force* of March 1945, which effectively ended French colonial sovereignty in Viet Nam, these centripetal forces in Vietnamese politics reappeared with vigor. But as the postwar experience showed, it had been the Communists who used the Japanese interregnum to build a cohesive political organization capable of overcoming at least some of the persisting parochial tendencies among the politically conscious Vietnamese.

The initial transition from traditional politics to movements based on imported ideologies is best personified by Phan Boi Chau, a well-known political leader born in the central Viet Nam province of Nghe An. Prepared for the mandarinal exams by a classical education, Chau, upon scoring first place in the tests, refused to accept an appointment in the French-dominated mandarinate.[1] Instead, he went into exile in Japan, taking with him the last representatives of the *Cán Vương*, the loyalists to the old regime. The most outstanding of these faithful was the twenty-four-year-old Prince Cuong De, a direct descendant of Emperor Gia Long, who had in 1802 reunified Viet Nam.[2] While in exile, Chau founded the *Việt Nam Duy Tân Hội* (The Association for the Modernization of Viet Nam), whose energies were directed toward three main goals: national liberation, restoration of the monarchy, and the promulgation of a constitution on the Japanese model.[3]

In addition to the obvious influence of his Japanese political supporters, Chau's efforts to give greater structure to the Vietnamese resistance was also affected by his early political experiences. It is reputed that Chau took part in the militant uprising in Nghe An and adjoining Ha Tinh province, which was led by one of Viet Nam's most outstanding scholars, Phan Dinh Phung.[4] Whether or not Chau was an active participant in this revolt

1 Le Thanh Khoi: *Le Viet-Nam*, pp. 386–7.
2 A Vietnamese source on the relationship of Chau and Cuong De is Trang Liet: *Cuộc Đời Cách Mạng: Cường Để* ("Life of a Revolutionary") (Saigon: Tôn Thất Lễ ; 1957), pp. 12–18.
3 Isoart: *Le phénomène national viêtnamien*, p. 229.
4 Ibid., p. 228.

from 1893–5, which breached French lines of communication across central Viet Nam and into Laos, there is little doubt that he was impressed by its consequences.[5]

This Nghe-Tinh revolt was only one of the localized protests led by the scholar bureaucrats of Viet Nam against French occupation from 1885–97; they broke out all the way from the mountainous Chinese border area to the Tonkin Delta to the lowlands of central Viet Nam. Although there was virtually no coordination between these rebellions, they were fought for ostensibly the same purposes and led by men of similar backgrounds and probably of close personal familiarity. The shortcomings of these leaders lay not only in failing to establish lines of communications and trust between each other, but also in placing more emphasis on military action than political preparation. Consequently, there was no symbol of this protest although it was directed toward monarchical restoration and expulsion of the French. On the local level there was also a neglect of political organization to replenish the ranks of the traditionalist rebels, to provide supplies and information, or to ensure loyalty in the face of French occupation.

While modern weapons were available to them, the tactics and techniques employed by the Vietnamese neither included the innovations which these new circumstances required nor were they effective. It remained for the French—through two of their most celebrated officers, Galliéni and Lyautey—to develop a doctrine of pacification adapted to the exigencies of this political warfare in Viet Nam. The pacification doctrine became a standard for French colonial warfare from Madagascar to Morocco, but it was one which ultimately found its impoverishment in 1954 in the hills of Tonkin, where it was first forged.[6] In the face of

5 Tran Trong Kim: *Việt Nam Sử Lược* ("History of Viet Nam") (6th edn., Saigon: Tân Việt; 1958); p. 567, contains a summary of the revolt.

6 The conduct of French "pacification" in Viet Nam during this period is best covered by Jean M. A. de Lanessan: *Le colonisation française en Indochine* (Paris: Félix Alcan; 1895), pp. 1–113. Comments on the limitations of the Vietnamese scholar-bureaucrats are found in Le Thanh Khoi: *Le Viet Nam*, pp. 382–5. The French doctrine of colonial warfare is treated in Jean Gottman: "Bugeaud, Galliéni, Lyautey," in E. M. Earle, ed.: *Makers of Modern Strategy* (Princeton: Princeton University Press; 1943), pp. 236–49. Also Lt. Col. Lyautey: "Du rôle colonial de l'Armée," *Revue des Deux Mondes*, Vol. CLVII, février 15, 1900, pp. 308–28.

superior French forces and techniques, the regionally based scholar-bureaucrats did not have the chance to become warlords, as occurred with the end of central traditional authority in China. Rather, the feeble protests of the traditional political leaders were as doomed as the Vendée Militaire in late eighteenth-century France, whose Vietnamese counterpart it is often said to be.[7]

While it had fairly extensive cultural activities, the Duy Tan Hoi never developed an active program of political operations to challenge French authority in Viet Nam. Brought into existence largely by overseas support, the Duy Tan Hoi was dissolved by the same influences. For in July 1910 the Japanese, having agreed to respect the integrity of French colonies as one of the terms of a much needed loan from France, expelled both Phan Boi Chau and Cuong De and closed the special schools where Vietnamese students had come to be educated in modern techniques.[8] The two exiles sought temporary refuge in Thailand, but upon receiving the news of the Chinese revolution of 1911 they proceeded to Canton, a city which became the most important center of Vietnamese exile politics over the following two decades.

There Phan Boi Chau received his most substantial support for political efforts in Viet Nam when he made contact with Hu Han-min, one of the leaders of the nationalist Kuomintang Party. With this backing, Chau reorganized his political forces in May 1912, when he launched the Việt Nam Quang Phục Hội (The Association for the Restoration of Viet Nam). Perhaps induced by the financial assistance of the Kuomintang, the program of the Quang Phuc Hoi no longer spoke of an imperial restoration but claimed the formation of a Vietnamese republican government. Prince Cuong De was no longer supported as a claimant to the throne of Viet Nam, but in the new government he would become the Tổng Đại Biểu, or the General Representa-

7 A comparison can be made by seeing Peter Paret: *Internal War and Pacification: The Vendée. 1789–1796* (Princeton: Center of International Studies; 1961). A more thorough study is Charles Tilly: *The Vendée* (Cambridge: Harvard University Press; 1964).

8 Le Thanh Khoi: *Le Viet-Nam,* p. 229.

tive of the Vietnamese people, a position similar to chief of state in a parliamentary form of government.[9]

But the importance of this tie with the Kuomintang was not merely reflected in a programmatic change since the relationship set a precedent for the conduct of Vietnamese anticolonial politics over the decades ahead. It was from among Vietnamese exiles attracted to Canton by Chau's political movement that Nguyen Ai Quoc (the early pseudonym of Ho Chi Minh, who was also a native of Nghe An province) founded in 1925 the antecedent to the Indochinese Communist Party. Moreover, Vietnamese cadres were trained at the Whampoa Military Academy, the Chinese Nationalists provided assistance for the formation of the first Vietnamese Nationalist party, and eventually China played a crucial role in the organization of wartime resistance groups against Japanese occupation (1940–5). Clearly the fortunes of Vietnamese political groups were now linked with their counterparts in China.

Although foreign support was the major strength of Phan Boi Chau's political movements, he did have an extensive organization functioning inside Viet Nam. One measure of its strength under the Duy Tan Hoi was its ability to send more than a hundred students to Japan for education in modern disciplines between 1906 and 1909.[1] But the character of this organization was more important than its strength, for it too set a precedent in the methods of organization in Vietnamese politics. Both the Duy Tan Hoi and the Quang Phuc Hoi depended on a network of secret societies for their internal strength in Viet Nam.[2] The use of this time-honored social institution for political purposes by the Quang Phuc Hoi was both an indication of its ties with traditional techniques and traditional leadership as well as its lack of intellectual and material resources to recruit and train a political cadre indoctrinated in new organizational methods.

Secret societies have always played an important role in Viet

9 Georges Coulet: *Les sociétés secrètes en terre d'Annam* (Saigon: Imprimerie Commerciale, C. Ardin; 1926), p. 6.
1 Ibid., p. 9.
2 Ibid., p. 8.

Nam because of the lack of culturally integrative institutions and the absence of a coherent "great tradition" of commonly accepted beliefs.[3] As a result there has been a strong persistence of magic and superstition as widely accepted beliefs in the Vietnamese countryside. Taking advantage of this cultural residue, men who trained themselves as geomancers and magicians would organize secret societies and from them derive a comfortable income and a circle of influence. The adherents to a secret society would gain magic intercession with the implacable forces of nature and a group of friends for potential mutual assistance as well as personal identity and social status.[4]

Prior to the French intervention one of the principal means of discouraging secret societies was through the examinations for the mandarinate. This culturally integrative institution provided an avenue for the social mobility of the villager; it also provided him with tangible incentives—by exemption from the corvée, military service, and the head tax—after he passed the first of three qualifying examinations for an appointment to the mandarinate.[5] Until the French began to tamper with Vietnamese cultural institutions, there was a greater incentive to study the Chinese classics in hopes of passing an examination rather than to practice sorcery in a secret society.

But upon the French occupation of southern Viet Nam (Cochinchina), the bureaucracy fled and the colonial masters, after discontinuing the traditional examinations, were unable to establish any culturally integrative institutions, except for a small school for interpreters. In 1903 a knowledge of French was made a prerequisite for admission to the mandarinate in Annam and

---

3 In the sense used by Robert Redfield: *The Little Community and Peasant Society and Culture* (Chicago: University of Chicago Press, Phoenix Books; 1953), p. 48. By contrast, there has been more cultural integration of the Thai village into a larger framework largely because of the role of the Buddhist bonze and the temple, or Wat. There is no counterpart to the Thai bonze in a Vietnamese village—a person representing a countrywide cultural hierarchy and a structured set of beliefs. A discussion of the Wat and the village bonzes can be found in H. K. Kaufman: *Bangkhuad: A Community Study in Thailand* (Locust Valley, N.Y.: Association for Asian Studies; 1960).

4 Coulet: *Les sociétés secrètes en terre d'Annam*, pp. 26–142.

5 Pasquier: *L'Annam d'autrefois*, p. 248.

Tonkin while there were only the most-limited opportunities to gain Western education.[6] With the end of the tax exemption and the corresponding deterioration of established patterns of authority in the rural areas of Viet Nam, the environment was created for a leadership thwarted from traditional recognition to aspire to influence and income through secret societies.

An exile political organization with countrywide aspirations, like the Quang Phuc Hoi, could make contact with existing secret societies or help to start new ones by issuing honorary charters, commissions of rank in the new republican government to society members, paper money with emblems of the new government, and other means of creating a symbolic tie between the central organization and the local units.[7] In the absence of means to recruit and train political cadres, the Quang Phuc Hoi was using the best available resources for political organization, and though no estimate has been made of how extensive an organization was assembled, some indication can be gained through an analysis of its militant demonstrations against French rule.

On the night of March 23–4, 1913, the city of Saigon was the target of a bomb attack with eight public buildings being the specific objectives. The attack was discovered before the bombs exploded, but it was followed four days later by a nonviolent demonstration by six hundred unarmed peasants who had come from the countryside in hopes of seeing Emperor Phan Xich Long descend from heaven and begin a war against the French.[8] On April 12 a provincial mandarin in the Tonkin province of Thai Binh was assassinated, and on the 26th a bomb was thrown on the terrace of a hotel in Hanoi, killing two French officers and a Vietnamese bystander. The repression for these acts was swift and forceful: 254 persons were arrested, 64 were brought before a court, and 7 were executed and both Phan Boi Chau and Cuong De were condemned to death in absentia.[9]

Facing the loss of the goodwill of their adherents, the Quang

6 Roy Jumper and Nguyen Thi Hue: *Notes on the Political and Administrative History of Viet Nam 1802–1962*, (Saigon: Michigan State University, Vietnam Advisory Group; 1962), p. 101.

7 Coulet: *Les sociétés secrètes en terre d'Annam*, p. 16.

8 Ibid., p. 17.

9 Isoart: *Le phénomène national viênamien*, p. 231.

Phuc Hoi launched no violent incidents until 1916, when the city of Saigon was once again the target. During the night of February 14–15, a group of three hundred armed men entered the city unnoticed in sampans. Their objective was the central jail, where they hoped to free some of their compatriots and then attack key administrative offices. However, before reaching the jail they were discovered and routed, sustaining numerous casualties in their flight.[1]

On the surface, these attacks were unimpressive by almost any criteria of political warfare. They dramatically pointed to the classic requirement for any realistic seizure of power: a specially trained and equipped armed force. In their amateurishness, however, these attacks did not obscure a solid accomplishment; coordination of operational effort was demonstrated in the planned simultaneous uprising in thirteen of the twenty provinces in Cochinchina in the spring of 1916 by the Quang Phuc Hoi.[2] These simultaneous attacks did not mean that a general plan was drawn up by the central organization of the Quang Phuc Hoi in its Canton exile and passed down to its local units for execution, but it does show that the local leadership had the capability to launch a concerted program. These then were the first steps away from the fragmented revolts of the scholar-bureaucrats.

More important for future operations was the internal strength of the Quang Phuc Hoi, which showed that a local-level leadership could make substantial progress in rural political organization even under French surveillance. This came not as a result of giving voice to social or economic discontent, but through organizational efforts in areas where a traditional structure had been dissolved and no alternative for political expression had been provided by the conquering power. Moreover, the fact that revolutionaries operating from exile could form a continuing political link with a local leadership was significant evidence that the first steps in building a new Vietnamese political system had also begun. These political energies had not been motivated by

1 Ibid., p. 236.
2 Coulet: *Les sociétés secrètes en terre d'Annam*, pp. 20–1.

new ideologies or revolutionary theories or from some economic calamity. They had originated from a colonial occupation which discouraged political participation and thwarted the mobility of those with traditional social and political skills. Limited though their accomplishments were, these traditionalists had adapted their skills to the exigencies of French dominance and thus had begun the transformation of Vietnamese politics.

The failure of a more potent opposition to France to appear was due in part to the fact that the Quang Phuc Hoi and its leader, Phan Boi Chau, were in a real sense neither nationalist nor revolutionary. If we accept Hans Kohn's dictum that nationalism "recognizes the nation-state as the ideal form of political organization and nationality as the source of all creative cultural energy and economic well being,"[3] then we cannot find extensive evidence that Chau was the first important articulator of Vietnamese nationalism. Moreover, there is some evidence to suggest that Chau was more opportunistically motivated. For in addition to altering his political program to fit the ideals of first his Japanese and then his Chinese supporters, Chau finally became a partisan of Franco-Vietnamese collaboration.[4]

Perhaps a partial explanation for the lack of vigor in Chau's leadership and the absence of a more dynamic development in Vietnamese politics at this period can be found by referring to Rupert Emerson's observation that

> the greater the disruption of the old society under the intruding impact of Western force—assuming that disruption takes the form of a development of modern enterprise and administration and not merely the suppression of the native population—the speedier and more complete the assertion of nationalism is likely to be.

Emerson's analysis continues that those "most drastically divorced from the close knit pattern of their traditional society are the most susceptible to the appeal of nationalism," but this ap-

---

3 Hans Kohn: *The Idea of Nationalism* (New York: The Macmillan Co.; 1961), p. 16.

4 I. Milton Sacks: "Marxism in Viet Nam," in Frank N. Trager, ed.: *Marxism in Southeast Asia* (Stanford: Stanford University Press; 1960), p. 114.

peal awaits "the appearance of a Westernized elite . . . the new intelligentsia and the professional men—which translates to the local scene the nationalist experience and the ideology of the West and serves as the crystallizing center for the inchoate disaffections of the mass."[5]

Prior to the mid-1920's, Vietnamese politics did not have such an intelligentsia, nor had traditional patterns of life been so completely disrupted. What had been disrupted was the old, tenuous political system, and in its absence a clandestine structure of politics had developed to oppose French rule. It was only after France had begun a program of colonial development, including education and industrialization, that a more fundamental change in the structure of Vietnamese society occurred. When political groups reflecting these changes in Viet Nam began to form, they found in the vague beginnings of the transition from traditional politics valuable forms of experience which they were to use in new ways and with new justification to oppose French domination.

5 Rupert Emerson: *From Empire to Nation* (Boston: Beacon Press; 1960), p. 44.

CHAPTER 6 ✺ ✺ ✺

THE TRANSFORMATION

OF VIETNAMESE SOCIETY

✺
✺
✺

The structural transformation of Vietnamese society resulted from the impact of World War I and the enthusiasm for colonial development which followed in its aftermath. The period between the two world wars saw changes from four principal sources: 1) the formation of an industrial labor force; 2) the emergence of an indigenous wealthy class whose holdings were in newly developed agricultural lands; 3) the creation of an educated elite whose instruction had been exclusively in the French language and had included the assimilation of French cultural values as well as training in technical specialities, with the promise of employment in the French sector of the colonial society; and 4) the deterioration of cohesive social institutions in the rural areas.

The first three of these changes attracted Vietnamese away from traditional pursuits to positions of greater physical and social mobility. However, the latter accelerated the decline in vitality of suprafamilial institutions which had given coherence to traditional society. A gap was thus established between what had become the modernized sector and the remaining peasant sector. Unlike their urban brethren, however, the peasants were left without vital institutions and traditions to sustain them. The French did not attempt to bridge the gap by building institutions for the eventual self-generating development of Vietnamese society; instead, they stabilized this gap and thereby created a potential for social and political instability. Having decided on this course, France could have avoided the political consequences of this social change only by absorbing the energies or gaining the loyalties of the modern classes it had created.

During World War I, France's demands upon her colonies fell most heavily upon Indochina, which had to provide "more than half of the wartime loans and gifts made to France by her colonies, more raw materials than any other part of her empire except West Africa; and more than 43,000 Indochinese soldiers and almost 49,000 workers were sent to Europe."[1] The magnitude of this levy upon Viet Nam can be measured by the fact that the total industrial labor force before World War I was only approximately 62,000 workers.[2] In addition to exporting manpower, it was necessary to recruit increased numbers of workers for local production of raw-material exports as well as to step up the output of manufactured goods which France could not supply. Therefore, a 33 per cent wartime increase in the work force in the mining industry—from 12,000 in 1913 to 16,000 in 1918—was representative of the growth in other fields.[3]

At the end of the war, the industrial labor force continued to expand because of the economic growth which resulted primarily from the monetary stability in Viet Nam, contrasting with inflation in France, and from the initial success in growing rubber in the red lands of southern Viet Nam. From 1913 the labor force expansion was almost fourfold when it reached its pre-World

1 Albert Sarraut: *La mise en valeur des colonies françaises* (Paris: Payot; 1932), pp. 44, 47, 50, as cited by Ellen Hammer: *The Struggle for Indochina* (Stanford: Stanford University Press; 1954), p. 60.

2 André Dumarest: *La formation des classes sociales en pays annamite*, thèse, Université de Lyon, Faculté de Droit (Lyon: Imprimerie P. Ferrol; 1935), p. 59.

3 Ibid., p. 62.

War II maximum in 1929, estimated at more than 221,000 workers in all of Indochina. The distribution of these laborers was over three major fields of economic activity: commercial and industrial undertakings, plantation agriculture, and mining. The largest of these fields was the first with 39.2 per cent of the total (86,000 workers), while the other two comprised 36.8 per cent (81,000 workers) and 24.0 per cent (53,000 workers) respectively.[4]

Although these figures indicate that the labor force of Viet Nam did not represent more than 1 per cent of the population, they do not reflect the overall social mobility which resulted from industrialization.[5] Because of the high turnover in the labor force, there were more persons mobilized to the modern industrial sector of the economy than was indicated by the figures for the work force at any one time. For example, in order to maintain the work force on the rubber plantations in southern Viet Nam at a constant 22,000, it was necessary to recruit more than 75,000 laborers between 1925 and 1930.[6] Moreover, in this example, substantial geographic mobility was involved because the rubber plantation workers were recruited in the north, since suitable workers could not be found in the less populous southern region. The mining companies in northern Viet Nam did not, however, face the problem of recruiting at a distance because they were located adjacent to the densely populated Tonkin Delta. Yet this proximity to the workers' homeland meant that mining companies would usually have to recruit new workers each year because the miners would often not return from their lunar New Year vacation. The importance of this rapid turnover was not only that it added to the numerical percentage of the work force

4 League of Nations, International Labour Office: *Labour Conditions in Indo-China* (Geneva, 1938), pp. 294–5. Ethnic Vietnamese and other peoples residing in Viet Nam made up all but a small portion of the whole, with Cambodians compromising only 2.4 per cent and Laotians 2.0 per cent of the total work force. However, with Vietnamese labor being used in each of the other two countries of Indochina, it is difficult to be more specific about the size of the labor force in Viet Nam by using existing statistics.

5 In 1931 Viet Nam had a population of 17.7 million. *Annuaire statistique de l'Indochine, 1936–37*, pp. 19–20.

6 Charles Robequain: *The Economic Development of French Indo-China* (London and New York: Oxford University Press; 1941), p. 82.

of Viet Nam, but also that it "delayed the formation of a distinct, self conscious working class and it postponed the establishment of a strict line of demarcation between the wage earner and the peasant. On the other hand, it extended the effects of the new way of life to a rather large portion of the population."[7]

Even though this labor force was loosely structured, it did not lack the cohesiveness to stage labor protests and strikes; between 1922 and 1934, there were more than a hundred strikes, the majority of which occurred in northern Viet Nam (Tonkin), where the industrial labor force was concentrated.[8] Disputes grew out of grievances over wages and working conditions, and one demonstration resulted in the assassination of M. Bazin, the French director of a firm engaged in recruiting agricultural labor for the plantations in the south. Problems of repatriating rubber workers were eventually overcome by establishing a savings plan which left them with a sum to cushion their readjustments to life in their home areas.[9] But the most pervasive problem of labor readjustment occurred during the depression, when the total industrial labor force declined by nearly 33 per cent when it fell from its 1929 high to an estimated 150,000.[1] With few other alternatives the unemployed either sought to be reabsorbed into their peasant villages, burdening already overtaxed institutions, or chose to remain idle in the cities. In both cases their presence contributed greatly to social instability.

The opening up of new land and the credit requirements to bring it under productive cultivation are always crucial forces for change in agrarian societies. In Viet Nam these factors brought fundamental changes in the characteristics of landholding and production; between 1880 and 1937 a French public works program in southern Viet Nam (Cochinchina) constructed drainage and irrigation canals which made 4½ million acres of new land available for cultivation.[2] France was more interested

7 Ibid.
8 League of Nations, International Labour Office: *Labour Conditions in Indo-China*, p. 168.
9 Ibid., p. 75.
1 Robequain: *The Economic Development of French Indo-China*, p. 81.
2 Lancaster: *The Emancipation of French Indo-China*, p. 61.

in recouping the capital investment which this public works program had required than in the social consequences of the ownership of this newly developed land. Moreover, a program designed to establish smallholders as owners of their land would have had an administrative overhead and required an extension of credit to moneyless peasants, which the French did not wish to undertake. Instead, the land was sold in virtually unlimited amounts to an emerging group of Vietnamese who had already learned the requirements for participating in a commercial environment.

The pattern of landholding which resulted in southern Viet Nam was therefore conspicuously different from that in other parts of the country. In the center and the north (Annam and Tonkin), smallholders continued to predominate; in the center those who owned less than 1½ acres constituted 68.5 per cent of the area's landholders in 1930, while in the north this portion of the landholders was 61.6 per cent of the total for the region. By contrast, in the south those with less than 2½ acres composed only 33.6 per cent of the total number of landholders. However, the most startling development is that out of 6,530 landowners in all of Indochina to have more than 125 acres of land by 1930, 6,300 were located in southern Viet Nam.[3] An even more dramatic statement of the landholding pattern is that 45 per cent of the cultivatable area of the Mekong Delta was by 1930 in the hands of 2 per cent of all the landholders. Moreover, of the 244 landowners having more than 1,500 acres of land in Viet Nam, all were located in the Mekong Delta.[4]

Along with the emergence of this landed upper class there was also the formation of a tenant class who, not having access to easy purchase of property, actually worked these domains and provided the landlords with their income. No accurate figures are readily available on landlessness and tenancy, but an estimate can be derived from existing statistics. In the south in 1930 there

3 Yves Henri: *Économie agricole de l'Indochine* (Hanoi: Gouvernement Général de l'Indochine, Inspection Générale de l'Élevage et des Forêts; 1932), pp. 108–9, 144–5, 182–3, 212.
4 Ibid, p. 191.

were some 255,000 persons owning agricultural land; of this number, only 165,000 cultivated their land directly while the rest, or 25 per cent, were absentee landlords.[5] By allowing these farmer-owners a family of 10 persons for purposes of estimation, there is the indication that out of a rural population of 4,000,000 in southern Viet Nam in 1930, more than half, or 2,400,000, were tenants or landless agricultural laborers. This would mean that the tenant class in the Mekong Delta alone was nearly 14 per cent of the total population of Viet Nam in 1930. By comparison, in the Tonkin Delta in the north, there were 964,000 individual property owners in 1930 and only 12,000, or slightly more than 1 per cent, were absentee landlords.[6]

The emergence of this landowning upper class in southern Viet Nam as a distinct social grouping can be given another dimension by analyzing the naturalization of Vietnamese as French citizens.[7] In 1937 there were 2,555 Vietnamese who had received French citizenship, and more than half, or 1,474, were from southern Viet Nam. The north had the next largest number, a third of the total, and the center, a continuing stronghold of traditional values, had less than 10 per cent of the naturalized Vietnamese.[8] Some allowance must be made for the fact that there were more naturalized Vietnamese women than men, which leads to the assumption that many had become the wives of Frenchmen. Since there was a certain uniformity in this pattern throughout Viet Nam, it does not detract from another assumption. Based on the fact that southern Viet Nam had only 20 per cent of the population of the whole country but more than half the naturalized French citizens, it appears that the landowning class, which had already been favored by French policies in land development, was becoming more closely identified with French rule by adopting the citizenship of France.

5 Ibid., pp. 182–3.
6 Ibid., pp. 108–9.
7 The legal and administrative problems involved in citizenship are discussed in J. Mérimée: *De l'accession des indochinois à la qualité de citoyen français*, thèse, Université de Toulouse, Faculté de Droit (Toulouse: Imprimerie Andrau et LaPorte; 1931), especially pp. 110–57.
8 *Annuaire statistique de l'Indochine, 1936–1937*, p. 23.

These statistics lend substance to the rather arbitrary analysis of the effects of colonialism on Vietnamese social structure made by the French economist Paul Bernard, who in 1934 divided Vietnamese society into three general categories based on income.[9] The wealthy were those who received an average annual income of 6,000 piasters or more in 1931 (about U.S. $5,500 in 1957 prices); the middle-income group received an average of from 160 piasters in the north and center to 180 in the south (about U.S. $145–65 in 1957 prices); and the lowest income group received the remainder of the money income of the country, which averaged 49 piasters (about U.S. $44 in 1957 prices). Numerically, these categories indicated sharp divisions in Vietnamese society, with the wealthy consisting of 8,600 persons, the middle-income group of 1,600,000, and the low-income group of 14,900,000.[1]

Of greater interest than these aggregates are the regional variations which Bernard's figures reflect. Among the top income group, 8,000 out of the total 8,600 were residents of southern Viet Nam, and based on our statistics of 6,300 wealthy landowners there appears to be some justification for this number. Of equal interest is that central Viet Nam, traditionalist in outlook, had just slightly more than 1 per cent (100 persons) in this upper-income category while the north had about 6 per cent, or 500 persons. In the middle-income group the regional positions were reversed; it was the north where almost 45 per cent of the middle-income receivers lived, while the center actually had a larger portion, some 500,000 to 400,000, than did the south's middle-income group, which made up only 25 per cent of the countrywide total.

Even though these estimates are not based on thorough documentation, it appears that when compared with information on the labor force and landownership they present certain possibilities for generalizations. In the south an extremely small and

9 Paul Bernard: *Le problème économique indochinois* (Paris: Nouvelles Éditions Latines; 1934), pp. 19–21.

1 According to population statistics this leaves 1,100,000 people unaccounted for. This and lack of documentation are the limitations of Bernard's analysis.

wealthy (both in comparison with other Vietnamese and with the incomes of French administrators) upper class was emerging under French aegis, identified with France and adopting French citizenship. At the same time a small middle class of about 10 per cent of the regional population was taking form, consisting of the population of the one metropolitan center, Saigon-Cholon, and about a dozen provincial centers. While at the bottom of this southern hierarchy was a tenant class of recent origin representing about half of the regional population and approximately 14 per cent of the countryside population.

In the north the upper income group was of lesser importance both regionally and countrywide, but a relatively large middle-income group reflected an industrial work force devoted to mining, cement manufacture, and textiles; an indigenous administrative cadre at the seat of the colonial government in Hanoi; and a group of commercial assistants handling foreign and domestic trade. At the foundation of the society in the north, and indeed the country as a whole, were approximately 7.5 million peasant proprietors—representing 45 per cent of the population of Viet Nam—living in the densely populated Tonkin Delta.

The foundation of society in central Viet Nam was peasant farmers largely tilling their own land, who composed 25 per cent of the population of the entire country. An almost minutely small upper class in the center reflected the lack of involvement in commerce or in vast landholdings and a persistence of a traditional outlook. The one hundred persons whom Bernard indicates formed this upper class in the center were probably affiliated with the monarchical adminstration at the court of Hue. Rounding out the social categories in central Viet Nam there was a middle-income group with almost 10 per cent of the regional population, which lived in the provincial towns—working in a few industrial plants such as the match factory at Vinh—and in the only major port-city in the center, Da Nang.

Taken as a whole there emerges from these estimates the following social profile of the transformation of Vietnamese society up to 1931 by the effects of colonialism:

SOCIAL PROFILE OF VIET NAM IN 1931

APPROX. NUMERICAL PORTION OF POPULATION IN MILLIONS	APPROX. PERCENTAGE OF POPULATION	DESCRIPTION OF SOCIAL CATEGORY
1.6	9%	Mobilized into participation in the monetary sector of the colonial economy; living in towns with some degree of access to urban facilities for health, education, and information.
2.4	14%	Tenant-farmer class located on newly developed land in Mekong Delta, producing about half of all the rice exported from Indochina, which at its prewar, 1929 high was 1.5 million metric tons (other source of exportable rice was Cambodia since north and center of Viet Nam did not have surplus and often had to import to meet needs); tenants exceedingly vulnerable to 70 per cent drop in price of rice between 1929–34.[2]
1.5	7%	Peasant proprietors in southern Viet Nam also having advantage of new land, which resulted in their average holdings being almost nine times larger than average in Tonkin Delta.[3]
4.6	25%	Peasant farmers in central Viet Nam, most tilling their own land, but with local concentrations of tenancy and a regional absentee landlord group of about 10 per cent of the total number of property owners.

[2] Davy Henderson McCall: "The Effects of Independence on the Economy of Viet Nam" (unpublished Ph.D. dissertation, Department of Economics, Harvard University, 1961), pp. 4–5, 29.

[3] Great Britain, Admiralty, Naval Intelligence Division: *Indo-China*, p. 292.

7.5	45%	Peasant farmers in northern Viet Nam located in densely populated Tonkin Delta, with an average holding of roughly two tenths of an acre. Some localized tenancy but a minute part of total producers.[4]
17.6	100%	

From this social profile it would appear that the impact of colonialism had little effect on the 70 per cent of the population who were peasant villagers in northern and central Viet Nam, but clearly this was not the case. The colonial impact on the peasantry was undoubtedly as pervasive an influence for the future of Viet Nam as was the mobilization of a small upper class. For when France established—under the regime of Governor-General Paul Doumer (1897–1902)—the principle that taxes gathered in Indochina not only had to support the superstructure of French administration, but also had to supply funds to the metropolitan budget for France's military forces in the colony, the localized subsistence economy of the peasant villager was rendered obsolete.

Formerly the peasant had produced, or attempted to produce, enough food for his family's consumption plus a surplus to barter for staples and to provide for taxes in kind, but under the colonial regime both taxes and staples required cash. However, the monetary sector of the economy was neither large enough nor efficient enough to permit extensive peasant employment for wages or a market for an agricultural surplus at stable prices. This new situation produced two important results: a decline in peasant welfare and, because communal institutions had been superseded in administration and tax collection, the absence of meaningful mutual assistance beyond the extended family. Both results led to a deterioration in social cohesion and offered potential for political instability.

The sharpness of the dichotomy between the peasant sector and the modern sector is demonstrated by the extent of the inequality in income distribution. In 1931 the peasantry, which made up 90

4 Henri: *Économie agricole de l'Indochine*, p. 110.

per cent of the population, was receiving only 63 per cent of the money income of the colony, while the French administrative class and the Vietnamese wealthy class, which together represented less than 1 per cent of the population, were receiving almost 17 per cent of the income.[5] Although the income distribution was not a fair measure of peasant welfare because of their nonmonetary income from subsistence agriculture, it did indicate tax-paying capacity. The portion of total income devoted to governmental expenditures during the 1930's was about 15 per cent,[6] but there are no readily available statistics of the burden borne by either sector of the economy. Assuming that there was an equality of tax burden based on the share of income received, this would suggest that the peasantry paid 9 per cent of its total annual income in taxes, thereby reducing its net income to 54 per cent of the total income for a year comparable to 1931.

It is highly unlikely that the tax burden was either equal or progressive because, in addition to capitation and land taxes, a substantial portion of colonial revenue came from French monopolies on salt, tobacco, rice alcohol, and opium. However, another perspective, a microcosmic one, of the demands of peasant taxation can be derived from a survey of 1939 in which

the annual budget of a peasant family with eleven members was found to be 32 piasters—a sum indicative of a static economy. Of this total, direct taxes took 6 piastres, or 19%. Yet in certain areas it was customary to pay but one cent for a whole day's work. For a workman to receive one cent for a day's work and to have to pay six piasters as an annual personal tax makes no sense whatsoever. The first figure reflects the monetary value of labor in the traditional society; the second expresses its value in the modern economy. Such a state of affairs, in which the people's livelihood is calculated in terms of one world and their taxes in another, cannot endure.[7]

5 McCall: "The Effects of Independence on the Economy of Viet Nam," p. 20.
6 Robequain: *The Economic Development of French Indo-China*, p. 152.
7 Mus: "The Role of the Village in Vietnamese Politics," p. 269.

As this observation emphasizes, it was not the harshness of the taxes themselves which posed the burden for the peasant, but the duality of the economy which had developed under colonialism. The real impact in transforming Viet Nam into a society with a double standard of economic and social values was that the French

> introduced an economy based on exchange without being sufficiently aware of the need to adjust it to the whole country. It was necessary to bear with the economy already in operation (an economy based on autonomous villages) for a time, but the object should have been to eliminate it by gradually educating the people for something else. . . . Instead of that progressive policy, the French chose to maintain an old order, with the laudable motive of avoiding any shock to the local social structure, but with the practical result that in the country the economy continued to be based on little trade and local consumption while the cities developed a modern commercial economy based on worldwide exchange. Those who organized trade maintained the worker on the level of the traditional economy but sold the product of that work on the level of the city economy. The difference between the two went into their own pockets.[8]

The economy remained divided because there were no institutions for integration. The end to the duality could have been approached by bringing peasants into commercial occupations at a rate greater than the increase in population and by transforming agriculture from subsistence into market-oriented production. This would have required institutions to mobilize indigenous capital; to convert peasants, by technical training, into a commercial work force; and to increase the capital equipment in agriculture by a generous program of agrarian credit. None of these institutions was established, and thus the dichotomization of Vietnamese society persisted.

This dual character of Viet Nam's society was accentuated by a comprehensive education program, launched by the French administration at the close of World War I, which trained a few

8 Mus: "Viet Nam: A Nation Off Balance," *The Yale Review,* p. 535.

Vietnamese to a level of sophistication far beyond their peers. The purpose of this program, as set forth in the *Règlement général de l'enseignement supérieur* of December 25, 1918, was to train an indigenous cadre for both governmental and commercial administration.[9] Significantly, the inauguration of this French-language education program for Viet Nam coincided with the exhaustion of the traditional education system. The last purely indigenous schools were theoretically abolished by an imperial decree of July 14, 1919, and the last classical mandarin examinations were given, in central Viet Nam, in 1918 and, in the north, in 1915. Preceding the end of education in the Confucian classics was another radical change: the official adoption of *Quốc Ngữ,* the romanized script which displaced the ideographic characters based on the Chinese writing system for primary instruction and public notices.[1]

The system of instruction established for the Vietnamese by the colonial administration was never intended to offer wide educational opportunities. However, during its existence it did experience a significant expansion. The number of students receiving primary instruction in all of Indochina increased from approximately 164,000 in 1921–2 to 373,000 in 1930 and to 731,000 in 1942. But the 1930 level of primary school attendance represented only 1.7 per cent of the total population of Indochina, and at the high point of the primary education expansion, in 1942, the school population was only 3 per cent of the entire population of the three countries. The ratio for Viet Nam was somewhat higher than for all of Indochina, but it never exceeded 4 per cent.[2]

The results of the French policy in creating a Westernized upper class through education can be seen more clearly in the number of persons to pass the degree examinations which were set up at the various levels of the academic hierarchy. The lowest

9 J. de Galembert: *Les administrations et les services publics indochinois,* deuxième édition, revue et augmentée par É. Érard (Hanoi: Gouvernement Général de l'Indochine; 1931), pp. 704–5.
1 Coyle: "Indochinese Administration and Education," p. 54.
2 Ibid., pp. 177–8.

degree given by the French colonial educational system was the *Certificat d'études primaires élémentaires,* which was awarded after three to five years of instruction. Because this degree was a prerequisite for all subsequent education, the number receiving it, a total of 149,452 between 1919 and 1944, was a reliable indication of the size of this new elite.[3]

However, the holders of this degree could expect to get employment only in clerical or other minor administrative positions, while advancement to the next academic degree marked a difficult obstacle to educational opportunity. Only 14,393 persons were able to complete primary education and receive the Diplome d'études primaires supérieures in all of Indochina before the end of World War II. From this group came persons qualified for primary-school teaching as well as more responsible nonclerical jobs in commerce and public administration. Finally, to round out the preuniversity educational opportunities there was the handful of students who got to one of the four *lycées* in Indochina (three in Viet Nam) and were among the 827 persons who qualified for the *baccalauréat* in the interwar period.[4]

The University of Hanoi did not become an institutional reality until 1918. Before 1931 it consisted of a group of higher-level technical schools which met the personnel needs of the French administration and the professional requirements of the newly urbanized Vietnamese. Undergoing a major change in character during the worldwide depression, the university in 1931 eliminated its technical schools and instead emphasized law and medicine, bringing the quality of these schools up to the standards of instruction in France. There were always at least 400 students at the university from its opening, and its maximum enrollment came in 1943–4 when it had 1,222 students. In over two and a half decades the university enrolled an estimated 3,000 students and trained 408 lawyers, 229 doctors, and before discontinuing

3 This figure and all subsequent figures on number of degree holders is for all of Indochina. Total figures for Viet Nam are not readily available. However, Viet Nam represented 85 per cent of the population of Indochina in 1931. These figures are based on unaggregated statistics presented in the Appendix, pp. 179–85, of ibid.
4 Ibid.

the programs in 1930, 337 public works engineers and 160 teach-ers for secondary schools.[5]

Thus the impact of the newly educated elite on Vietnamese politics can best be assessed on the basis of its numerical profile in 1931. By that year the depression had made its full imprint on Viet Nam and the discontent of segments of the population from this and other causes had been felt widely, yet the upper class was still a very tiny fraction of the population. Avoiding

EDUCATED ELITE IN 1931[6]

1,200 (APPROX.)   Opportunity for some form of technical or profes-sional training at University of Hanoi.

305   Received *baccalauréat* from one of the four *lycées* (three in Viet Nam, one in Cambodia).

4,146   Received diploma after successfully completing approximately nine years of primary education.

39,223   Received certificate after successfully completing approximately five years of primary education.

double counting of those with higher degrees, it can be concluded that a little more than 39,000 persons had received some form of higher instruction in the French educational system in Indo-china. Not only was this elite characterized by the minuteness of its size, but the sharp divisions within this educated class were equally as striking as its distinctiveness from the population as a whole.

The consequences of this sophisticated upper class for political leadership in the Vietnamese independence movement can be viewed from several perspectives. But the origin of political dis-content from lack of status and intellectual unemployment is the most important one for a study of revolution in Viet Nam. On a

5 Ibid. The number of university students is based on an average of 120 graduates over the twenty-five years from 1918–19 to 1943–4. This is admittedly a very rough estimate, but it does indicate an order of magnitude.

6 Ibid. This is the educated elite for all of Indochina. The estimate for the college educated is again based on the average of 120 a year for the twelve years from 1918–1919 to 1930–1. This is a rough estimate.

quantitative basis it seems that there was enough employment for those Vietnamese being trained in the new educational system. The number of indigenous persons serving in the French administration in Indochina rose from 12,249 in 1914 to 16,915 in 1922 to 22,570 in 1937.[7] This did not include those persons serving permanently with the Garde Indigène, a militia force which was an auxiliary to the French military establishment in Indochina that consisted of 11,536 men in 1914 and had grown to 16,218 by 1937.[8] On the basis of these statistics the estimate that there were 40,000 indigenous employees of the French administration by 1929 seems reasonable,[9] and also appears adequate enough to have absorbed the approximately 39,000 persons who had received some Western education. While one could not expect an educated militia, the government also could not be expected to be the only employer of the educated.

A more understandable source of personal dissatisfaction and latent political discontent within this newly educated class was the lack of advancement to positions of authority. But even among the French administrators, power was held in a very few hands. Those with authority were about 10 per cent of all French personnel, a number varying from 309 in 1914 to 292 in 1937.[1] This did not compare unfavorably with the 286 Vietnamese who had reached responsible positions in colonial administration by 1934, the majority of whom were located in southern Viet Nam, where they were provincial chiefs of administration.[2] However, this favored group represented only slightly over 1 per cent of all the indigenous personnel working in the French civil administration in Indochina.

Although it would appear that the professionally trained university graduates enjoyed good prospects for advancement, the fortunes of the primary-school graduates seem to have been less bright. The principal source of employment for this middle level

---

7 *Annuaire statistique de l'Indochine, 1913–1922,* p. 247. *Annuaire statistique de l'Indochine, 1936–1937,* p. 241.

8 Ibid.

9 Coyle: "Indochinese Administration and Education," p. 122.

1 Ibid., p. 126.

2 Jumper and Nguyen Thi Hue: *Notes on the Political and Administrative History of Viet Nam, 1802–1962,* p. 96.

of educated Vietnamese was as teachers in the lower section of
the primary-education system. But in 1937 there were only
1,559 men and 217 women who held these teaching positions in
Viet Nam, while the total number of primary-school degree
holders in Indochina had risen to 7,122.[3] While figures on employment or the lack of it cannot be conclusive, it appears that if a
case is to be made for political leadership in the independence
movement resulting from the thwarted mobility of the new educated elite, it is best founded on the situation of those in the
middle level. Here were those who had not only absorbed a
substantial knowledge of French culture, but were oftentimes
passing on this learning by teaching in the French language to
other Vietnamese. Blocked from higher teaching positions because of the higher-degree requirement and prevented from getting the degree because of the lack of educational facilities, this
group was caught between the decay of traditional avenues of
mobility and the insufficiency of those created by the French.

The structural transformation of Vietnamese society brought
on by the French in the years following World War I produced a
potential for political instability. The potential resulted from the
creation of a small modern social sector without the establishment of institutions for the eventual mobilization of the whole
society into a modern framework. The exploitation of this potential awaited a political leadership which the French had in
large measure helped to create.

3 *Annuaire statistique de l'Indochine, 1936–1937*, p. 241.

CHAPTER 7 ✿ ✿ ✿

THE GENESIS OF

VIETNAMESE NATIONALISM

✿

✿

✿

When Ho Chi Minh arrived in Canton in June 1925 as an agent for the Comintern—disguised as an interpreter in the mission of Mikail Borodin—his first task was to cause the arrest of Phan Boi Chau, the living symbol of the traditionalist protest against French rule.[1] The irony of this act was that Ho Chi Minh, the future leader of Communist Viet Nam, was causing the political death of a man from his own native province of Nghe An who for twenty years had led the movement for Vietnamese independence. In a development that contained strong elements of both continuity and change, this Moscow-trained Communist, absent from his country's politics for almost fifteen years, was asserting his control over the small Vietnamese exile group that had congre-

---

1 Gouvernement Général de l'Indochine, Direction des Affaires Politiques et de la Sûreté Générale: *Contribution à l'histoire des mouvements politiques de l'Indochine française* (Hanoi, 1933). Vol. III, *Les Émigrés du VNQDD*, p. 6. This is part of a massive six-volume documentary of the initial formation of the modern political parties in Viet Nam. It is an indispensable source on the subject.

gated in this south-China city. Within days, Ho Chi Minh had gathered about him six political exiles he had found in Canton—all from his native province—and with them he organized the *Việt Nam Cách Mệnh Thanh Niên Chi Hội* (the Viet Nam Revolutionary Youth League), popularly known as the Thanh Nien.[2]

These events were to mark the beginning of a second phase in the transformation of Vietnamese politics. Over the following six years—from 1925 to 1931—parties based partially on ideological programs but more on local and particularistic loyalties would be formed. Their formation was the result of new leadership from Vietnamese who had received training abroad or who had found new opportunity in some segment of the French educational or administrative systems. In their attempts to establish a framework of support for their political ambitions, these Vietnamese were, out of convenience and necessity, to utilize the persisting fragments of the traditionalist structure of politics. Thus there developed a struggle for control over existing political organizations because of the strength they would contribute to the revolutionary cause. While the shift in control over existing groups provided some benefits to the modern revolutionaries, the degree of success these new leaders achieved depended on their ability to transform Vietnamese politics by creating mass-based political organizations having an ideology that would attract the widest possible support.

Obviously, such efforts required, as an immediate priority, the organization of the small, but most politically conscious, portion of the population that had moved away from traditional social patterns as a result of the modernizing influences of colonial rule. But the transformation of Vietnamese revolutionary politics, so that it involved the recently modernized portion of the population in the opposition to French rule, was not a smooth one. A conflict soon developed—masked by an almost continuing controversy over ideology—between those whose power stemmed

2 Ibid., Vol. IV, *Le Đông Dương Công Sản Đảng (Parti Communiste Indochinois)*, p. 16.

from traditional loyalties and those who represented new social and political identities designed to appeal to the mobile population. The dilemma of Vietnamese revolutionary politics lay in creating an organizational structure that would link together parochial political loyalties with modern ones and thereby develop the strength to drive the French from the country. Such a basis for Vietnamese politics was not developed in this second phase, but the new revolutionary groups did gain enough strength by 1931 to pose several militant challenges to colonial rule before they were eclipsed for more than a decade by the counterthrusts of the French.

The arrest of Phan Boi Chau produced political changes inside Viet Nam that were a corollary to those which the Canton exile group had undergone. In Viet Nam a new generation of political activists had emerged which recognized Chau's leadership only in the organizational sense. With his arrest and the end of the moribund phase of the exile movement, a different category of political leadership began to come forward in Viet Nam. For example, as a result of the action by minor officials in the colonial administration and urban groups in provincial towns, a party later known as the Tan Viet (a short form for *Tân Việt Cách Mệnh Đảng*, or New Viet Nam Revolutionary Party) was formed in 1926 in north-central Viet Nam from among secret societies formerly allied with Phan Boi Chau.[3]

For the little more than four years of its existence, 1926–30, this party underwent rapid modifications and internal strains in an attempt to preserve its autonomy; yet all the while it was hoping to negotiate an alliance with the Comintern-backed exile group, the Thanh Nien. The party's leadership became fragmented because some of its members were attracted to the more appealing ideology of Marxism and wanted to lead the Tan Viet in its direction. This position was refuted by Dao Duy Anh in one of the first important theoretical works of modern Vietnamese politics, entitled *Study of the Vietnamese Revolution.*

3 Ibid., Vol. I, *Le Tân Việt Cách Mệnh Đảng (Parti Révolutionnaire du Nouvel Annam)*, p. 4.

He argued that the party's program ought to be nationalist in emphasis in order to avoid antagonizing diverse social groups.[4] But Anh's effort did not overcome the divisiveness of the leaders, and as a consequence the Tan Viet succumbed to the influence of the Thanh Nien, though its local-level structure, which had been the object of the exiles' envy, maintained its integrity as a separate organization.

In searching for an indigenous organizational foundation, the Thanh Nien had hoped to capitalize on the provincial support of this loosely knit party made up of minor administrative personnel and the *fonctionnaires de l'enseignement,* or primary teachers. However, the Tan Viet organizational structure was not widespread but was concentrated in the contiguous north-central Viet Nam provinces of Nghe An, Ha Tinh, and Thanh Hoa, where by 1928, 24 of its 42 cells were located.[5] Its strength tapered off rapidly in other areas for there were only 7 cells in all of southern Viet Nam and 5 in the north. Yet, until 1927 the Tan Viet was the only significant indigenous political organization in Viet Nam, even though the weakness of the Tan Viet in the north and the south reflected the identity of the party's founders with their native province of Nghe An and the sedentary nature of their occupations. Being teachers and functionaries, these part-time political activists in the Tan Viet could not easily move from their jobs in a campaign of political organization in the countryside.[6] But enjoying the traditional respect toward their occupations, the local Tan Viet leaders developed strength in depth in provincial areas,[7] which gave their party its unique basis of popular support in Vietnamese politics. Significantly, the Tan Viet contained no workers or big city middle-class func-

4 Ibid., Vol. I, pp. 51–5.

5 Ibid., Vol. I, pp. 34–5. The party organization consisted of 42 cells in 1928 located as follows:

central Viet Nam:	Nghe An —	9
	Ha Tinh —	8
	Thanh Hoa —	7
	Hue —	3
	Quang Ngai —	3
southern Viet Nam:		— 7
northern Viet Nam:		— 5

6 Ibid., Vol. I, p. 25.

7 Ibid., Vol. I, pp. 20–1.

tionaries in its membership, and although it had an elaborately written nationalist program, the parochial mold of the party and its organizational limitations prevented it from winning more than several hundred adherents.[8]

In the face of overtures by the Thanh Nien to take over the Tan Viet organization, the only way the party could maintain itself as a non-Communist national force was to join forces with the Việt Nam Quốc Dân Đảng, or VNQDD (the Viet Nam Nationalist Party). Organized in Hanoi in November 1927, the VNQDD, like the Tan Viet, was a regionally based political party concentrated in the north.[9] For these two parties, founded primarily on regional loyalties, to have united into a countrywide, instead of a regional, nationalist movement would have required the formation of commitments and the sharing of organizational responsibilities on a broader basis of political identification than then existed. Although nationalism was beginning to emerge as an ideal in Viet Nam, practically it was able to give coherence and structure only to parochial and not to countrywide political organizations. In their incapacity or unwillingness to seek a wider basis for political activity, the leaders of the Tan Viet showed a preference to rely on provincial loyalties even when this meant the loss of their personal political power. For in 1930, the Thanh Nien exile group—principally from Nghe An province and now relocated in Hong Kong—founded the Indochinese Communist Party, which succeeded in having the Tan Viet leaders arrested and in assuming control over their provincial organization.

In contrast to the Tan Viet experience the expansion of the VNQDD in northern Viet Nam, between 1927 and 1930, was undoubtedly due to the concentration of the labor force there, the presence of the University of Hanoi, and its location as the center of the colonial administration. With nearly half the population of Viet Nam in and around Hanoi,[1] the organizational

8 Ibid., Vol. I, p. 46; also Sacks, p. 120.

9 Ibid., Vol. II, Le Việt Nam Quốc Dân Đảng (Parti National Annamite du Tonkin), p. 4.

1 Annuaire statistique de l'Indochine, 1936–1937, p. 19. Of the 17 million people in Viet Nam in 1931, 8 million were in north Viet Nam, and the majority of them were concentrated within 60 miles of Hanoi.

efforts of this nationalist party were also facilitated, permitting those with sedentary occupations to overcome the obstacle of geographic immobility in contacting potential adherents. In addition the greater differentiation of the northern population favored the development of a political party with a broader social foundation. But while these factors, combined with the relatively sophisticated organizational techniques of the VNQDD, resulted in the strongest Vietnamese political group of the moment, with approximately 1,500 persons affiliated with 120 cells by 1929, it still remained a force localized in northern Viet Nam.[2] Primarily because of its limited strength, the VNQDD decided on a program of overt militancy to demonstrate what power it had, with the vain hope of winning wider support by proving itself to be the vanguard party in overthrowing the French.[3]

The VNQDD launched its first attack against the French administration on the night of February 9, 1929, when M. Bazin —the director of an enterprise which recruited laborers for employment in the rubber plantations in the south and in New Caledonia—was assassinated in a public place in Hanoi.[4] By this dramatic event the VNQDD hoped to provide a symbol of the readjustment problems and discontent of the workers returning from the south and to win their support, but the quick response of the French authorities led to the capture of party documents and then to the arrest of 229 members of the VNQDD.[5] From the arrests, detailed information emerged on the strengths and weaknesses of the party, which makes more understandable some of the reasons prompting its choice of overt political action.

In the table below it can be seen that although there was a broad occupational distribution among the arrested party members, more than 50 per cent of them were in the service of the French administration and almost all of them were of an educated or intellectual background. Moreover, all but about 15 per cent

---

2 Gouvernement Général de l'Indochine: *Contribution à l'histoire des mouvements politiques de l'Indochine française,* Vol. II, p. 12.
3 Ibid., p. 51.
4 Ibid., p. 13.
5 Ibid.

of those arrested were in urban occupations and were therefore best prepared to participate in such urban forms of violence as the assassination of a prominent French official. As subsequent events were to show, the VNQDD did not lack strength in the rural areas of northern Viet Nam, but this support was obviously subordinate and was there as a refuge when bolder moves in the city failed. Clearly, the VNQDD leadership saw that its best opportunity in seizing power lay in organizing the urban educated classes, especially those in the French administration.[6]

While these arrests led to several convictions, the majority of those arrested were released and rejoined the party, which during the crisis of French repression, had come under the leadership of Nguyen Thai Hoc. A founding member of the VNQDD, Hoc was a graduate of the École Normale of the University of Hanoi with a degree entitling him to be one of the few Vietnamese high-school teachers.[7] Undeterred by the French reprisals for the Bazin assassination, Hoc now spurred the VNQDD

OCCUPATIONS OF VNQDD MEMBERS ARRESTED
FEBRUARY 1929

Secretaries to the French administration	36
Agents of indigenous administration	13
Primary public-school teachers	36
Teachers of Chinese characters	4
Students	6
Primary private-school teachers	4
Publicists	4
Employees of commerce and industry	10
Shopkeepers and artisans	39
Property owners, cultivators, and traditional medicine men	37
Militiamen	40
	229

6 Ibid.
7 Ibid., p. 6.

on to a more ambitious plan, which called for a general uprising at key points throughout northern Viet Nam during the lunar New Year holiday, in the first week of February 1930. Taking advantage of the more than 120 VNQDD members in the French colonial army or the indigenous French-led militia, Hoc planned a mutiny in remote outposts to occur simultaneously with demonstrations in Hanoi.[8]

Reacting to a last-minute compromise of his communications network, Hoc ordered the uprising delayed for five days, but at this point the discipline of the VNQDD command structure—a loosely united group of geographically dispersed lieutenants—broke down. The followers of Nguyen Khac Nhu, located at military outposts and in administrative positions in the mountains and foothills northwest of Hanoi, were ordered by their chief to proceed with their original plans.[9] Thus, on the night of the first anniversary of the Bazin assassination, February 9, 1930, two companies of Vietnamese troops garrisoned at the hill town of Yen Bay revolted, killing three French officers, two NCO's, and five loyal Vietnamese before they were overwhelmed by loyal troops aided by French reinforcements.[1] Of course, this precipitous move prejudiced the general uprising, which Hoc then canceled.

Sensing the immediate danger of capture but still hoping to provoke an uprising, Nguyen Thai Hoc and his principal lieutenants in Hanoi fled the city and relocated in the Delta village of Co Am, in Hai Duong province east of Hanoi. From this rural base they hoped for a peasant uprising. However, after staging demonstrations in two provincial towns the VNQDD followers were dispersed by loyal militia, and in the first air raid in Viet Nam, the village of Co Am was bombed by French aircraft.[2] Finally, on February 18, 1930, while the party leaders

8 Ibid., p. 12.
9 Ibid., pp. 18–19.
1 The New York Times, February 13, 1930, p. 6. Also Bốn Mắt (pseud., in Vietnamese means "Four Eyes"): La nuit rouge de Yen Bay (Hanioi: Imprimerie Le Van Tau; n.d.), pp. 9–28. There is a discrepancy in the number of persons killed and wounded in these accounts.
2 To Nguyet Dinh: Tân Phá Cô Am (Destruction of Co Am) (Saigon: Tân Phát Xuât Bán; 1958), pp. 71–89. This is a short popular history of the VNQDD.

were launching an attack on the Tonkin Delta town of Sept Pagodes, they were captured, and the top thirteen men of the VNQDD were executed. The party was left moribund, with the remnants falling into the hands of Le Huu Canh, who had opposed the tactics of Nguyen Thai Hoc and had wanted a longer period of revolutionary preparation.[3]

The final blow was administered to the party in October 1932, when seventy-four members were arrested in Hai Duong province; thereafter, the influence of the VNQDD ceased to exist inside Viet Nam. The remaining members escaped to Yunnan, where they joined other party exiles. A gradual impoverishment caused this Yunnan exile group to join with a hollow vestige of Phan Boi Chau's old forces in Canton, which also called themselves the VNQDD,[4] under the aegis of the Kuomintang. After a decade of inaction, the VNQDD came to life again during the wartime 1940's as a part of a Kuomintang-sponsored liberation front for Viet Nam, but it never again recaptured its former strength inside the country. It remains one of the ironies of the Vietnamese Revolution that, in the late 1940's, when the French were attempting to block the Communists, they vainly sought for a nationalist alternative, the roots of which they had already destroyed almost two decades before.

With the demise of the VNQDD, the center stage of Vietnamese politics became occupied by the Communist movement which Ho Chi Minh had set in motion before he was forced to flee Canton for Russia in April 1927, following the Kuomintang crackdown on the Chinese Communists. Launched as a nationalist revolutionary force with the formation of the Thanh Nien in June 1925, the Communist effort made rapid strides, and by May 1929 some 250 persons had been given revolutionary training outside Viet Nam and at least 200 of them had been returned to the country. Moreover, the Thanh Nien's membership had risen to approximately 1,000; while this was less than the VNQDD in 1927, it was probably a more disciplined and

---

3 Gouvernement Général de l'Indochine: *Contribution à l'histoire des mouvements politiques de l'Indochine française,* Vol. II, p. 20.

4 Ibid., Vol. III, p. 17.

widespread group, with regional committees in every area of Viet Nam.[5] However, after Ho Chi Minh's retreat to Russia, schisms began to develop in the absence of a strong party leader to enforce a working consensus. Before January 1930, when Ho reappeared to reunite the party, the principal issues dividing its members were those of nationalism versus Communism or proletarian internationalism.[6]

A major confrontation of the contending forces within the Thanh Nien came at the first party congress in May 1929, when the conflict between Communism and nationalism took form in the appeal of members from northern Viet Nam to change the party name to the Indochinese Communist Party.[7] Although the motion was voted down, it did lead to a schism within the party which followed regional lines. In northern Viet Nam the party affiliates adopted the title Indochinese Communist Party, and those in the south chose Viet Nam Communist Party, while dissidents from the Tan Viet opted for Indochinese Communist Federation.[8] To compound the dilemma the exile group in China, now driven from Canton to Hong Kong by the wrath of the Kuomintang, retained the title of Thanh Nien in an effort to preserve unity. But behind the apparently superficial controversy over the party's title in the various regions of the country, there was a struggle for control over the Vietnamese revolutionary movement by a multiplicity of factions. In the move to redesignate the party with the title "Indochinese Communist" lay the claim for a Communist successor state for the whole French colony, rather than an emphasis on independence for the three nations founded on the historic cultural identities of the peoples of Viet Nam, Cambodia, and Laos.

While a nationalist program seemed to offer the greatest long-range potential for overcoming the divisive parochial tendencies in Vietnamese politics, the immediate support of the urban, educated population appeared best obtained by Communist appeals directed toward their frustration over the limited oppor-

5 Ibid., Vol. IV, p. 19.
6 Ibid., p. 23.
7 Ibid., p. 20.
8 Ibid., pp. 22–3.

tunities for a modern elite under French rule. The controversy between long-range goals and short-term needs was resolved not by a careful assessment of the potential of the political alternatives, but through a test of political influence among party leaders. For after three years without contact with the Vietnamese revolutionary movement, Ho Chi Minh returned to Hong Kong in 1930 in order to restore unity among the quarreling factions. Acting in the name of the Comintern, Ho imposed unity on the fragmented movement, proclaimed its name to be the Indochina Communist Party, and set forth a program for a "bourgeois democratic revolution led by the Vietnamese working class, aimed at overthrowing imperialism and feudalism and securing national independence and freedom."[9] Probably the Comintern was hoping to avoid the complications it had encountered with nationalism in China, and undoubtedly Ho saw that without the allegiance of the modernized population, his goals for Viet Nam would be unfulfilled.

The urgency for the reunification of the Communist-sponsored revolutionary movement in late 1929 was underscored by both the numerical strength of the VNQDD and the audacity of their political demonstrations. Realizing that these northern Viet Nam nationalists were making an attempt to establish themselves as the leaders of the anti-French independence movement inside the country, the Communists decided to act. But with the sudden elimination of the VNQDD by the reprisals of the colonial authorities, serious competition to the Communists ceased to exist, though the force of French surveillance remained constantly alert against revolutionary activity. Aware that the potential for attracting widespread support depended on a successful demonstration of strength, the Communists sought to launch an operation in areas where the forces of the French were weakest and their own resources most potent.

A combined peasants' and workers' uprising in the provinces of Nghe An and Ha Tinh in north-central Viet Nam seemed

9 Democratic Republic of Viet Nam, Central Committee of Propaganda of the Viet Nam Lao Dong Party and the Committee for the Study of the Party's History: *Thirty Years of Struggle of the Party,* Book One (Hanoi: Foreign Languages Publishing House; 1960), p. 24.

to provide the best opportunity for the embarrassment of the French administration and the demonstration of Communist strength. Such an operation would draw upon the Communists' local political resources, especially those of the now-absorbed Tan Viet Party which were concentrated in these provinces; the predominance of men from this area on the Central Committee of the party; the close ties between workers in the provincial towns and their relatives in the peasant villages; and the deterioration of the welfare of the rural population because of the failure of several harvests.[1] Yet this provincial movement merely emphasized the reliance of the Communists on the vestiges of traditionalist political organization and their lack of strength in other areas, especially the north, where a larger-scale revolt might be ignited from an uprising in Nghe-Tinh. However, for reasons that are still not clear it appears that Ho Chi Minh, as a confirmed Communist and a tough-minded politician, was against the Nghe-Tinh uprising, but he lacked the control over the party to prevent it.[2]

The Communists commenced their organizational effort in late February 1930, when, coinciding with the capture of Nguyen Thai Hoc of the VNQDD in northern Viet Nam, a member of the Central Committee, Nguyen Phong Sac, was sent to Nghe An to begin organizing workers in the match factory and railway repair shop in the provincial center of Vinh and the adjoining port town of Ben Thuy.[3] Overt demonstrations were launched in the form of protest marches on May Day, 1930, and political manifestations continued throughout the two-province Nghe-Tinh area for over a year until they subsided in August 1931 and

1 Tran Huy Lieu: *Les Soviets du Nghe-Tinh (de 1930–1931) au Viet Nam* (Hanoi: Éditions en Langues Étrangères; 1960), p. 11.

2 "During the period when the Nghe-An Soviets were being organized, Ho's attitude was somewhat ambiguous. While he most certainly did not approve of the action taken (a repetition of Mao's Hunan campaign which Stalin held to be anathema) he took no steps to stop it. During a Thought Reform course in 1953, it was disclosed that Ho had voted against the resolution calling for a peasant uprising, but he was in a minority of one and submitted to the will of the majority. . . . Whatever the truth there is no doubt that this was the first occasion on which Ho lost control of the movement under his charge." Hoang Van Chi: *From Colonialism to Communism: A Case History of North Viet Nam* (New York and London: Frederick A. Praeger; 1964), p. 52.

3 Tran Huy Lieu: *Les Soviets du Nghe-Tinh*, p. 19.

ceased in October. During this period the French administration recorded 231 separate incidents occurring throughout all Viet Nam which it attributed to the Indochinese Communist Party. The distribution of these acts of political violence provides an important index in the regional variation in strength of the party, for only 7 of these incidents occurred in the north and 58 in the south; of the 166 manifestations in central Viet Nam all but 17 took place in the Nghe-Tinh provincial area.[4]

Within these provinces a distinct pattern consisting of two separate phases can be seen in the acts of political protest and violence that erupted during this period. The turning point in the two distinguishable phases that together endured for a year and a half, came on September 12, 1930, when bands of peasants gathered at scattered points to mass gradually in a march on district administrative centers, passing from them to the ultimate goal of the provincial center of Vinh. When they reached the town, the crowd numbered about 6,000 persons,[5] and according to Communist sources the protestors were spread out over 4 kilometers of the main road as they entered Vinh. There the column was attacked by French aircraft, which killed 216 persons and wounded 126.[6]

The march on the province capital marked the climax of four and a half months of mass public demonstrations, which had included demands for an augmentation in the price paid for locally made salt by the government monopoly, the destruction of district tax rolls, and workers' demands for increases in wages. Undoubtedly reflecting fear at the vulnerability of large, essentially unarmed public groups, the Communist-sponsored political uprising next entered a phase where clandestine political organization and terrorism were the hallmarks. In this second phase, the incidents were smaller in scale but they occurred more frequently and in the more remote rural areas, where they usually took the form of assassinations of persons who informed on or

4 Gouvernement Général de l'Indochine: *Contribution à l'histoire des mouvements politiques de l'Indochine française,* Vol. IV, pp. 124–39. This data is unaggregated in the document.

5 Ibid., p. 31.

6 Tran Huy Lieu: *Les Soviets du Nghe-Tinh,* pp. 25–6.

refused to join the Communist Party or one of its adjunct political organizations. Therefore, it is not surprising that of the 149 incidents which the French recorded during the period of the Nghe-Tinh soviets, 126 took place after September 1930 and consisted almost entirely of murders by beating or stabbing, but rarely by shooting.[7]

The change in the form of political manifestations in Nghe-Tinh is indicative of a more fundamental transition in the Communist revolutionary operations; until the September 12 march on Vinh the party tactics had emphasized giving momentum and form to an apparent popular responsiveness for mass public demonstrations. A tightly organized and widespread revolutionary structure was not even begun until after the spectacular march on the provincial capital, but thereafter the village soviets were formed in Vo Liet and other locations in the Song Ca river valley of Nghe An.[8] These revolutionary village governments which attempted to supplant traditional forms of authority gradually spread to Ha Tinh province and before the suppression of the Communist influence in Nghe-Tinh, there were sixteen village soviets in operation.[9] The purpose of these village organizations was not just to lay the groundwork of a clandestine party structure, but, more ambitiously, it was to assume wide governmental and social functions and thereby become the sole institution of authority in rural areas. Of course, the ultimate goal of this system of village soviets was the mobilization of the Vietnamese to overthrow French rule and establish an independent government for the country. The Nghe-Tinh soviet was obviously too weak a framework for such a task, but its leaders hoped it would generate a widespread revolutionary movement. Though their schemes were smashed, the experience of the Nghe-Tinh soviets went beyond the previous forms of rural political organization in the secret societies and the Tan Viet party cells

---

[7] Gouvernement Général de l'Indochine: *Contribution à l'histoire des mouvements politiques de l'Indochine française*, Vol. IV, pp. 124–39. From unaggregated data in the document.

[8] Tran Huy Lieu: *Les Soviets du Nghe-Tinh*, p. 26.

[9] Ibid., map at end of book. This compares favorably with the seventeen cells of the Tân Việt which were formerly existing in these two provinces.

to develop techniques of popular participation in politics. These techniques were direct antecedents of the "parallel hierarchies" of complementary political and military organizations that were so successfully used in the period after 1945.[1]

Where the Communist Party succeeded in establishing soviets in Nghe-Tinh, it was largely because of the deterioration of village institutions and the unresponsiveness of both the French administration and the mandarinate. With the soviets they attempted to gain political power by meeting village needs through an administrative committee formed by the party cell and its adjunct popular associations: the Peasants Association, the Youth Organization, and the Women's Association. These committees superseded the traditional Council of Notables and took into their hands all of the affairs of the village. The popular associations provided roots into the village population through which the party cadre could ensure their control and from which they could receive recruits for political action; both this popular control and support were strengthened by nightly propaganda sessions held in the village hall, where party newspapers were read aloud. More direct action occurred through the organization in each hamlet of the village soviet of self-defense units armed with sticks, knives, and other primitive weapons. Rounding out the schemes to capture village political power, the Communists sought the adherence of the heads of extended family groups through whom there was a more natural structure of communications and control.[2]

The village soviets were more tightly structured institutions for holding political power than their predecessors, and they gave more potential mobility for participation in politics outside the village. But for this potential to have been realized, a more extensive regional organization was required, and this second stage in creating a revolutionary political system was not achieved

1 "Parallel hierarchies" is a phrase indicating the vertical integration of geographically dispersed Communist organizations for popular participation. This technique allows the centralization of power with a flexibility in executing commands through dispersed units. See Col. Charles Lacheroy: *Une arme du Viet Minh: Les hiérarchies parallèles* (Paris; 1953), p. 21.

2 Tran Huy Lieu: *Les Soviets du Nghe-Tinh*, pp. 33–4, 26–8.

in the days of the Nghe-Tinh soviet. The Communists' attempt
to establish a revolutionary base in north-central Viet Nam in
1930–1 was ultimately thwarted by the intensive and eventually
successful French efforts to capture party leaders and to eliminate their rural organizational foundation. The first important
results of the drive against the party by the French Sûreté came
with the arrest of the top-level leaders outside the Nghe-Tinh
operating area in December 1930 and in April 1931.[3] But this
led almost immediately to the capture of the directors of the
Nghe-Tinh movement, such as Nguyen Phong Sac, a special
envoy of the Central Committee, and Nguyen Duc Canh, a member of the regional committee for central Viet Nam. With the
arrest of Ho Chi Minh in Hong Kong in June 1931, followed
by the apprehension of the southern Viet Nam regional committee, the Communist movement became a body without a
head.[4]

In Nghe-Tinh the French accelerated their "pacification" program aimed at restoring their administrative control. They established a network of security posts—sixty-eight in Nghe An,
fifty-four in Ha Tinh—manned by loyal militia; brought in
officials of the mandarinate who were natives of Nghe-Tinh in
order to establish firmer contact with those potentially loyal to
the colonial regime; formed paramilitary groups; and even tried to
create a local political party called the Lý Nhân, or Party of the
People with Good Hearts.[5] This combination of counterrevolu-
tionary measures brought an end to the Nghe-Tinh soviets by
late September and early October 1931, and with it a cessation
in overt revolutionary activity for almost ten years.

Despite their defeat, the Communists had given the French
their most serious challenge to continued sovereignty in Viet
Nam; at its apogee in January 1931, the Communist Party had
a strength estimated by the Sûreté at 1,500 members, with
about 100,000 affiliated peasants.[6] The Communists claimed to

3 Gouvernement Général de l'Indochine: *Contribution à l'histoire des mouvements
politiques de l'Indochine française*, Vol. IV, p. 35.
4 Ibid.
5 Tran Huy Lieu: *Les Soviets du Nghe-Tinh*, pp. 33–4.
6 Gouvernement Général de l'Indochine: *Contribution à l'histoire des mouvements
politiques de l'Indochine française*, Vol. IV, pp. 4–5.

have had 1,300 members in Nghe-Tinh alone, with about 10,000 affiliated followers.[7] While these figures do not correspond, they emphasize the success of Communist efforts in proportion to their real strength. Even with their organizational limitations these successes could have been greater had the Communists not committed several crucial tactical errors in the turbulence of their operation in Nghe-Tinh.

Perhaps the most fundamental mistake was that the Communist terrorism was almost exclusively directed at lower-echelon Vietnamese officials who were exercising authority for the French administration, rather than at the French themselves. As one observer has noted, "Even at the height of the disturbances, Europeans could circulate freely and unarmed in these provinces."[8] The Communists attributed this misstep to the shortcomings of the Thèses on the Bourgeois Democratic Revolution in Viet Nam, adopted by the Indochinese Communist Party in October 1930 and written by its secretary-general, Tran Phu.[9] As one Vietnamese Communist critic has seen it, this program "committed the error of advocating the overthrow of the national bourgeoisie at the same time as the French colonialists and the indigenous feudalists . . . [for] this bourgeoisie had interests which were in conflict with the imperialists . . . [and] they ought to have been drawn into the ranks of the bourgeois democratic republic and not systematically separated."[1]

The meaning of these criticisms seems clear. The Communists found in the central Viet Nam provinces of Nghe An and Ha Tinh a smoldering antagonism born of a rapid decline in welfare in a rural area—an antagonism focused not on the colonial power, but on the most immediate object of discontent: the low-level indigenous officials and local social leaders. Because of its ties with Nghe-Tinh through the Tan Viet and the native origins of its top leaders, the Communists were in a good position to

7 Tran Huy Lieu: Les Soviets du Nghe-Tinh, p. 44.

8 Roger Levy: "Indo China in 1931–1932," Pacific Affairs, Vol. V, No. 3 (March 1932), p. 210.

9 Nguyen Kien Giang: Les grandes, dates du parti de la classe ouvrière du Viet Nam (Hanoi: Éditions en Langues Étrangères; 1960), pp. 20–2, contains a resume of the Theses.

1 Tran Huy Lieu: Les Soviets du Nghe-Tinh, p. 51.

give form and encouragement to this discontent. But their inability to make this protest something more than a workers' and peasants' rebellion was largely due to limitations of organization and political ideology. Moreover, the Nghe-Tinh soviets demonstrated that local issues were still the lifeblood of Vietnamese politics and that neither Communism nor any other political movement had come to grips with a program broad enough to incorporate the variety of these interests into a larger political whole. However, the Communists had succeeded in giving more structure and momentum to one set of particular interests than had any previous political movement. They had also developed organizational techniques in rural areas that went beyond secret societies in their political effectiveness, and furthermore, they had united village soviets into a viable, if only temporary, system of revolutionary politics.

Curiously, the extensiveness of the Communists' success was attributed by a French journalist to their cleverness in using the "nationalist movement to their advantage. We therefore see this paradoxical situation: in Indo-China, Communism, the primary principle of which is internationalism, is based on nationalism."[2] The paradox here is far more subtle. The Communists had not been able to create a national myth which would be meaningful to both modernized Vietnamese and the peasantry in areas like Nghe-Tinh who they were attempting to recruit to a revolutionary cause.[3] The Communists were trying to establish new forms of political communications in a country where even lines of cultural communications no longer existed. The framework of traditional society had been disrupted, but a new society binding together the modern and mobile classes with the traditional and stagnant ones had not occurred.[4] In short, Viet

2 Jean Dorsenne, *Faudra-t-il évacuer l'Indochine* (Paris: La Nouvelle Société d'Édition; 1932), as quoted in Roger Levy: "Indo China in 1931–1932," p. 209.

3 Chalmers Johnson has described the national myth as a doctrine which "will provide an ideological framework within which the mobilized people may understand and express their behavior as a nation," and he sees this myth drawn "from doctrines that are independently respected in society and reinterpret[ed] . . . so that they will tend to mobilize popular imagination in support of a national government." In *Peasant Nationalism and Communist Power* (Stanford: Stanford University Press; 1962), p. 27.

4 In broad form this is the "plural society" expressed by J. S. Furnivall in his *Colonial Policy and Practice* (New York: New York University Press; 1956), pp. 303–

Nam was not, in the terminology of Karl W. Deutsch, a nationality, and the fragmentation of its politics reflected the divisiveness and parochialism of the Vietnamese people.[5] More than any other cultural force, politics brought greater unification to Vietnamese society because, in the eventual struggle against France the modern revolutionary leadership of the country had to create a common bond with the peasants in order to wage war successfully. Clearly, the Communists did not have the capacity to unify Vietnamese society and achieve national independence at the beginning of the 1930's, but the contours of their failure provide important criteria for measuring the scope of the revolutionary problem and the efforts which would be required for success.

---

12. A more recent critique of the concept of pluralism is contained in Manning Nash: "Southeast Asian Society: Dual or Multiple," *The Journal of Asian Studies*, Vol. XXIII, No. 3 (May 1964), pp. 417–24, and also Benjamin Higgins: "Southeast Asian Society: Dual or Multiple," ibid., pp. 425–8, and Lucian W. Pye: "Perspective Requires Two Points of Vision," ibid., pp. 429–32.

5 ". . . *nationality*, then, means an alignment of large numbers of individuals from the middle and lower classes linked to regional centers and leading social groups by channels of social communication and economic intercourse, both indirectly from link to link and directly with the center." Karl W. Deutsch: *Nationalism and Social Communication* (Cambridge: The M.I.T. Press; 1953), p. 75. Also, "The Growth of Nations," *World Politics*, Vol. V, January 1953, pp. 182–3.

CHAPTER 8 ✿ ✿ ✿

THE COLONIAL BACKGROUND TO
THE VIETNAMESE REVOLUTION

✿
✿
✿

For any Vietnamese revolutionary movement to have been successful prior to the military intervention of Japan in Indochina in 1940, it would have been necessary, theoretically at least, for it to overcome the opposition of only 10,779 regular French troops, 16,218 men of the indigenous militia, and 507 French police agents.[1] In the era before World War II, the whole of Indochina was controlled for France by a commercial and official population of 42,000, of which a little more than half were wives and children.[2] To the potential advantage of the revolutionaries was the dispersement of French forces throughout the states of Indochina, with the greatest concentration of military strength being in the mountains of northern Viet Nam along the China border. Moreover, the Communists and the

[1] *Annuaire statistique de l'Indochine, 1936–1937*, pp. 25, 241.
[2] Ibid., p. 25.

nationalists of northern and central Viet Nam were not the only revolutionaries leading movements to overthrow the French regime. Besides other exile and northern splinter groups there were in southern Viet Nam several significant political associations.

The most important of these was the group known by the name of its newspaper, *La Lutte* ("The Struggle"). Perhaps reacting to the forceful repression of the VNQDD and the Nghe-Tinh soviets, it became after 1932 a legal political movement in the narrowly circumscribed colonial politics of Saigon. Led by the Trotskyite Ta Thu Thau, The Struggle entered candidates for the Saigon city council and the Cochinchina colonial council in 1933, 1935, 1937, and 1939.[3] During the course of the 1930's The Struggle was joined in an electoral coalition by both a moderate evolutionary political group, the Constitutionalists—which had been formed in Saigon in 1925—and the Communists, led by Moscow-trained Duong Bach Mai.[4] Success at the polls held this diverse group together, but internal frictions developed before both the Communists and Trotskyite organizations were decimated in late 1939 by the French police, in the wake of the collapse of the French Popular Front and the outlawing of the Communist Party in France.[5]

With the exception of the Communists, none of these groups staged any overt political demonstrations, nor did they have any organizational links with the countryside. And while the Communists had organizational resources sufficient to launch fifty-eight demonstrations in southern Viet Nam between May 1, 1930, and December 31, 1931, they did not succeed in establishing a system of village soviets in rural areas. Nor did any of their manifestations approach the proportions of the Nghe-Tinh soviet until their protest against the Japanese occupation, which lasted for only a few days in November 1940 and resulted

3 Anh Van and Jacqueline Roussel: *Mouvements nationaux et lutte de classes au Viet Nam* (Paris: Publications de la IVe Internationale; 1947), pp. 54–8.

4 U.S. Department of State, Office of Intelligence and Research: *Political Alignments of Vietnamese Nationalists*, by Milton Sacks, OIR Report #3708 (Washington, 1949), pp. 39–40.

5 Ibid., p. 41.

in the elimination of the party structure in the south.[6] By contrast, the most successful of the rural movements in Viet Nam had almost no numerical strength in urban areas except for its leadership, who were former officials of the French administration. This movement was the occult syncretic religion known as Cao Đài, which started in southern Viet Nam in 1926 and had won at least 100,000 adherents by 1930—although its leaders claimed five times that many.[7] Even though it attempted no overt political strategy, this religion—created on the traditional techniques of the secret societies—was consciously building a structure of influence, as was to be shown with the appearance of its own armed force after 1945.

Until the coming of World War II, the political experience of Vietnamese revolutionaries in widespread portions of the country had displayed a marked similarity. Although clandestine systems of politics had been launched, they had not developed to a point where opposition to French sovereignty could be sustained. The limitations to revolutionary activity did not all lie in the strength of the French colonial regime in arresting party leaders and smashing peasant demonstrations, but, as was obvious when the French regime was displaced, the revolutionaries themselves had obstacles of organization and ideology to overcome. However, the revolutionaries had demonstrated the existence of a potential for political protest and violence which sprang from the unresponsiveness of the colonial administration to the disruption in peasant society and the absence of a satisfying personal identity for those torn away from traditional modes of life. Attempts to translate this potential into revolution had been unsuccessful because various political groups had done little more than give expression to parochial interests. Without the creation of an effective countrywide revolutionary structure and the formation of military units, there could be little hope of exploiting the vulnerabilities of the relatively small and dispersed French forces.

6 Ibid., p. 45. Gouvernement Général de l'Indochine: *Contribution à l'histoire des mouvements politiques de l'Indochine française*, Vol. IV, pp. 124–39.

7 Ibid., Vol. VI, *Le Cao Đài*, p. 83. Gabriel Gobron: *Histoire et philosophie du Caodaïsme* (Paris: Derby; 1949).

The five wartime years, 1940–5, of Japanese occupation in Viet Nam, brought several major developments creating the potential for revolution. As a result of the isolation from France and the sharp curtailment of external trade, the colonial society in Viet Nam became totally dependent on internal resources, and this in turn resulted in the involvement of greater numbers of Vietnamese, especially young people, in the educational, administrative, and economic systems of the colony.[8] Since the French were concerned that the Japanese overlords would capture the sympathies of these active young Vietnamese, they established an extensive sports and youth program to try to hold the loyalties of the young people of the country.[9] But the program merely heightened the consciousness of those who were to become the political activists in the postwar period and gave them experience in organization and self-discipline.[1]

The motivation for France to maintain its sovereignty during the Japanese occupation was the determination that it alone would make whatever postwar settlement might occur involving the future of Indochina. However, there took place on March 9, 1945, the event which the French had labored to avoid: the suspension of French sovereignty by the Japanese and the encouragement of Vietnamese independence movements. Into this gap came the group best prepared to take advantage of it: the Communist-led Viet Minh (short for the *Việt Nam Độc Lập Đồng Minh Hội* or Viet Nam Independence League) which had been formed in May 1941 by Ho Chi Minh.[2] During the war the Viet Minh had developed a broad, nationalist liberation program with an extensive political organization, but it had functioned primarily as an intelligence network for Chiang Kai-shek's government, which had been responsible for providing the Viet Minh and other Vietnamese exile groups with the financial support to sustain themselves. The Viet Minh had preserved its

8 Adm. Jean Decoux: *À la barre de l'Indochine* (Paris: Plon; 1949), pp. 353–464.

9 Maurice Ducoroy: *Ma trahison en Indochine* (Paris: Les Éditions Internationales; 1949), p. 103. About 86,000 persons were regular participants in the sports program.

1 Ibid., in preface by Decoux.

2 Nguyen Kieng Giang: *Les grandes dates du parti de la classe ouvrière du Viet Nam*, pp. 42–3.

autonomy and strength over its rivals, principally the Kuomin-
tang-backed Dong Minh Hoi, by establishing more-effective
intelligence-gathering units, and in December 1944 it began to
create guerrilla teams; starting with 34 men and growing to 1,000
by the time of the Japanese *coup de force* the following March,
the Viet Minh units had reached approximately 5,000 men when
Hanoi was occupied in August 1945.[3]

Without the interaction of the two major wartime events—
the weakness of France both in Europe and in Indochina and
the growing strength of the Viet Minh—revolution in Viet Nam
might have been delayed but certainly not avoided. The extensive
political discontent stemming from the social problems of the
colonial period when combined with the catalytic effects of the
Japanese occupation created an opportunity to develop revolutionary power and sustain a seven-year war which humbled
French military might. What the colonial background to the
Vietnamese revolutionary war has to show is the origins of that
political discontent and some of the techniques which had been
used to exploit it and arouse the populace in the revolutionary
cause. Here was a harbinger of the revolutionary tumult to
come.

3 Democratic Republic of Viet Nam, Viet Nam News Agency: *Ten Years of Fighting and Building of the Vietnamese People's Army* (Hanoi: The Foreign Languages
Publishing House; 1955), pp. 11–15.

PART FOUR ❂ ❂ ❂

The Wartime Impact on Revolutionary Politics: The Japanese Occupation of Indochina, 1940-1945

❂
❂
❂

CHAPTER 9 ✿ ✿ ✿

THE STRATEGIC ASPECTS

OF THE JAPANESE OCCUPATION

✿

✿

✿

The occupation of Indochina by Japan came not as a sudden sneak attack as did the capture of the Philippines or Malaya; it was a gradual process achieved largely without violence but through blunt diplomatic measures in response to specific strategic needs. The slow paralysis of French sovereignty came in a series of Japanese ultimatums demanding the right to station increasingly large numbers of troops and to build air and naval bases. After June 1940 the fall of metropolitan France had left Indochina isolated and vulnerable to such external pressure; the French felt that the lack of firm material and diplomatic support from the United States in the summer of 1940, and the absence of any anti-Japanese East Asian power, left them with only two alternatives: either fight the obviously futile battle to maintain their colonial sovereignty against overwhelming Japanese military power or meet Japanese demands and thereby preserve what autonomy they could.[1]

---

1 The lack of American support is discussed in Gen. Catroux: *Deux actes du drame indochinois* (Paris: Plon; 1959), pp. 54–8.

Out of a strict regard for self-interest an anomalous situation arose: The Japanese, despite their commitment to the independence of the peoples of Asia, confirmed French colonialism in Indochina, the only place that a European regime remained standing in East Asia during World War II. Conversely, France, now under the control of the puppet administration at Vichy, was giving support and advantage to the enemy of the Allied powers in Asia. Japanese bases in Indochina were especially useful for attacks on European possessions in Burma, Malaya, and Indonesia, a condition which had to incur the wrath of the Allies and suggest potential postwar consequences.

Initially, the French colonial administration and military establishment were left intact side by side with the Japanese occupation forces. The Japanese did not have the administrative personnel to supplant the French and were apprehensive over the possibility of internal disorder resulting from such a change. Since the principal wartime utility of Indochina to the Japanese was as a base for their operations in other areas of Southeast Asia, their military forces varied greatly in size from month to month and a good portion of them remained in a transient status. No effort was made to match the French forces in strength, for the sanction on their obedience was not only the proven docile attitude of the colonial administration, but the certainty of substantial Japanese forces available in neighboring areas.

A total of 99,000 armed men were under French command during the occupation; more than 74,000 of them were regulars, including 19,371 Europeans in three services together with 54,649 indigenous troops. The remaining French forces consisted of a local militia of 24,680 men with a cadre of 362 Europeans. By contrast, the largest contingent of Japanese troops in Indochina during the occupation came only toward the end of the war in February 1945, when 61,775 men were stationed there; the lowest number was around 25,000—about a third the size of the French regulars—in August 1943. The average Japanese troop strength appears to have been about 35,000 men.

If means of force were only incidental to the maintenance of this unusual relationship, the heart of the guarantee was the attitude of the French governor general in Indochina, Admiral Jean Decoux. He was firmly committed to the Vichy government as long as it lasted and was under no illusions about the interests of the Japanese, who he knew would keep their part of the bargain only as long as it was convenient for them. As Admiral Decoux was believed to have seen it, his duty was

> to resist the Japanese as far as he dared and yield to their demands where he must, playing the one good card he held—the desire of the Japanese to avoid destroying his administration— to the utmost of its value. Thereby he hoped to maintain the Government-General until such time as the Japanese should meet with defeat in the war, when it might be possible to arrange for a peaceful evacuation of their forces and in this way preserve the colony for France. He knew that if the Japanese were provoked into sweeping away his administration and setting up Annamite [Vietnamese] and Cambodian regimes there would be a small chance of the peaceful restoration of French authority, and in this judgement events were to prove him correct.[2]

Since the circumstances which had sustained this wartime situation in Indochina were of an international character, it was to be expected that the establishment of the de Gaulle government in metropolitan France and the American landings in the Philippines would bring fundamental changes. With these two developments the ability of Admiral Decoux to maintain even nominal French sovereignty was severely reduced. The Japanese were understandably apprehensive over a possible Allied landing in Indochina, while at the same time the de Gaulle government, and especially its military and intelligence representatives in south China, was suspicious and publicly noncommittal in its relations with the Vichy holdovers inside the colony. Moreover, de

2 Royal Institute of International Affairs: *Survey of International Affairs, 1939– 1946, the Far East, 1942–1946*, by F. C. Jones, Hugh Borton, B. R. Pearn (London: Oxford University Press; 1955), p. 26.

Gaulle's hypersensitivity was heightened even further by his awareness that President Roosevelt was prepared to make an effort after the war to place Indochina under an international trusteeship.[3] This feeling took form in a memorandum of January 14, 1944, to Secretary of State Cordell Hull, in which Roosevelt made his now famous assessment of Indochina: "France has had the country—thirty million inhabitants—for nearly one hundred years and the people are worse off than they were in the beginning."[4]

While Roosevelt considered the support of Chiang Kai-shek and Marshal Stalin for the trusteeship as certain, the British were incredulous and probably would have blocked it. However, de Gaulle understood clearly that unless France took some active part in the liberation of Indochina, French reoccupation of the territory might be prevented. As events developed, the Gallic fear proved unnecessary for the end of the international-trusteeship plan came with the death of Roosevelt in April 1945. But in the interim the French, lacking any available troops to dispatch to East Asia, decided to encourage resistance movements for undermining the Japanese position despite Admiral Decoux's warnings against such steps. Paradoxically, the implementation of this decision gave benefit to those Vietnamese who were not only resisting the Japanese, but were also seeking the independence of Viet Nam. The resulting guerrilla sabotage gave substance to Japanese apprehensions and strengthened their determination to eliminate the Vichy colonial administration.

In his memoirs Admiral Decoux charges that the essential cause of the Japanese *coup de force* of March 9, 1945, which eliminated the French civil administration and military presence, was the imprudence of the "resistance" launched by de Gaulle in Indochina during the summer of 1944.[5] According to the governor general a lack of discretion arose from the rivalry of interests and political divergences within the French colonial army

3 Allan B. Cole: *Conflict in Indo-China and International Repercussions, a Documentary History, 1945–1955* (Ithaca: Cornell University Press; 1956), p. 48.
4 Cordell Hull: *The Memoirs of Cordell Hull* (New York: The Macmillan Company; 1948), Vol. II, p. 1597.
5 Decoux: *À la barre de l'Indochine*, p. 315.

and administration, which were, initially, supposed to be the principal resistance force in Indochina. Certain colonial officials developed an autonomy of their own by authority of secret instructions from the de Gaulle government which undercut Decoux's discipline over them almost completely. Repeatedly, Decoux asked to be relieved of his position but was told by Paris to remain at his post and exercise his "nominal power." De Gaulle obviously felt that the departure of Decoux, more than any indiscretion of his "resistance" subordinates, would alarm the Japanese.[6]

While General Sabattier, the French military commander in northern Viet Nam during the occupation, tends to support Admiral Decoux's charges that the Japanese were alarmed by the indiscretion of the resistance and especially by the Free French radio broadcasts asserting that an Allied landing was to be made in Indochina, he believes that the *coup de force* was in response to broader considerations. In his view the decision to eliminate the French presence in Indochina was made in Tokyo in the autumn of 1944, out of a recognition of the inevitability of the Japanese defeat and the desire to have as strong a position as possible either for negotiation or fanatic resistance.[7] Sabattier's analysis is in general accord with the revelations of postwar investigations; by Supreme War Council Decision #6 of February 1, 1945, the Japanese determined to extract greater assistance from the French, and in the event of a noncooperative response their forces in Indochina were authorized to "elevate and support the independent position of Annam."[8]

In tactical terms the *coup de force* of March 9, 1945, meant that approximately 60,000 Japanese troops in Indochina had the task of eliminating a more numerous French civil and military establishment. The French presence consisted of around 50,000 French men, women, and children in addition to approximately 80,000 local personnel in the military and administra-

6 Ibid., pp. 316–18.

7 Gen. G. Sabattier: *Le destin de l'Indochine* (Paris: Plon; 1952), pp. 138–9.

8 Williard H. Elsbree: *Japan's Role in Southeast Asian Nationalist Movements, 1940 to 1945* (Cambridge: Harvard University Press; 1953), pp. 25–6. Decision #6 is Exhibit #661 of the International Military Tribunal for the Far East.

tion.[9] Despite the intensive intelligence gathering and preparation of the French-led "resistance," as is carefully documented by General Sabattier, it seems that the French forces were caught off their guard and were unable to react against the Japanese in time to preserve themselves. Of the 74,000 regulars of the Colonial Army, only about 6,000 were able to escape to south China, and of these only 2,150 were French.[1] Although the fate of the Vietnamese serving with the Colonial Army who did not escape is unclear, their French superiors along with their civilian counterparts were placed under confinement in the major cities of the country.

Upon this colonial cadre of businessmen, administrators, and soldiers plus their indigenous subordinates had rested French sovereignty in Indochina. With the elimination of the cadre that had put down the peasant revolts, kept a constant surveillance over the local political movements, filled the jails with the recent graduates of the freshly constructed French schools, broken the strikes at the new French factories, arrested the assassins of the indentured-labor contractors, in short, with the demise of both those who had created the tensions in the colonial society and those who had prevented their violent expression, a new environment for the politics of Viet Nam had been created. Unquestionably the disappearance of its colonial authority in Indochina, in the space of a few short days in early March 1945, was for France the gravest consequence of the Japanese intervention. Once broken, its administrative control was never reestablished over all of Indochina. But this was more than just a problem of discontinuity in administration. In the absence of colonial restraint the latent political forces in Viet Nam, which had been blocked or provided only narrow channels of expression before the war, now received new opportunities for protest.

The sovereignty of France in Indochina had not been founded on 50,000 French men and women plus their local auxiliaries, but on the compliance or passivity of the people who inhabited the territory. Before the Japanese war, French sovereignty

9 Sabattier: *Le destin de l'Indochine*, p. 80.
1 Ibid., p. 455.

over 24,000,000 Vietnamese could be maintained by approximately 11,000 French soldiers plus half again as many native troops, assisted by a very efficient security police. This was all the force needed to contain those who didn't comply. In the postwar reoccupation, compliance progressively decreased and the need for armed forces to maintain colonial sovereignty increased until an extensive military establishment was insufficient.

It was this consequence of the *coup de force* which Paul Mus, a clandestine envoy of the de Gaulle government and a scholar who already had twenty years' experience in Indochina, was able to observe. Amidst the popular reactions of the Vietnamese peasants who concealed him from capture by the Japanese, there was a definite change of attitude; Mus felt that the events of March 9, 1945, liberated feelings which had remained masked by the Vietnamese personality. Since in Vietnamese society, misfortune does not evoke sympathy, but rather a denunciation of the hidden faults for which the misfortune is a punishment, opportunities were present for a reorientation of attitudes toward compliance. As Professor Mus has related it, "The continuance of French sovereignty had been in France's favor, but the sudden eviction of France had incited the Vietnamese to play another card. They thought it a punishment of heaven and justified in their eyes a re-examination of the situation. Moreover, they were ready to believe anything bad about the French."[2] While the urban population was probably more sophisticated than M. Mus's peasant protectors, the city people were the ones who had felt the French impact the most and had the most to gain in preventing the reimposition of colonialism.

Given the policies that the Japanese were pursuing elsewhere in Southeast Asia in encouraging nationalist independence movements, a simliar pattern of supporting an independent Vietnamese government might logically have been expected to follow the *coup de force* in Indochina. But once again larger strategic considerations were guiding the policies of Japan in

2 Paul Mus: *Problèmes de l'Indochine contemporaine: La formation des partis annamites* (Paris: Collège Libre des Sciences Sociales et Économiques; n.d.), P.M. 5, p. 3.

Indochina. Paradoxically, such reins of government as were then handed over to Vietnamese immediately after March 9, 1945, went to a Francophile group of scholars and bureaucrats identified with the monarchy and with their home area of central Viet Nam. They did not enjoy a wide popular appeal, had not articulated goals of nationalist independence, had played no significant political role prior to the occupation other than as members of the colonial administration, and had not been allied with the Japanese until the late summer of 1944.

The paradox was not only that the "independent" government the Japanese were sponsoring had greater continuity with the French than with the prewar nationalist parties, but also that it was theoretically sovereign only in central and northern Viet Nam. It also excluded the Vietnamese political groups which the Japanese had given more long-standing assistance and encouragement; these groups were concentrated in the south, where the occupation continued to rule in name as well as fact until the capitulation six months later, in August 1945. This curious and discontinuous pattern of Japanese political action in Viet Nam suggests that assistance to local political groups resulted not so much from a coherent plan as from particular interests and unsanctioned maneuvers of bureaucratic cliques within the occupation forces. When it was established in March 1945, the "independent" government was formed more in response to Japanese strategic needs for continuity and stability in Viet Nam than to considerations of internal political influence.

The random and largely uncoordinated political action of the occupation only served to strengthen already existent regional and parochial tendencies in Vietnamese politics. Japanese initiatives intensified the limitations to Vietnamese nationalism rather than encouraging efforts to overcome barriers to a countrywide political identity, as was being done under Japanese auspices elsewhere. While this ill-defined Japanese dabbling in the politics of Viet Nam can explain much about the internecine conflict that erupted with the August Revolution of 1945, the overall impact of the occupation was to set loose a chain reaction which affected the whole fragmented mosaic of Vietnamese political life. These reactions had occurred almost simultaneously with the arrival of Japanese troops in Indochina in the autumn of 1940, and quickly reflected both the indecisiveness of the political programs of the occupation and their potential consequences for the development of revolutionary movements in Viet Nam.

CHAPTER 10 ✖ ✖ ✖

UPRISINGS TOUCHED OFF BY

THE JAPANESE OCCUPATION

✖

✖

✖

After the signing of a general military accord between Vichy and Tokyo in August 1940, an agreement was reached for the entry of Japanese troops into Indochina. Ostensibly for the purpose of facilitating Japanese operations against China, this arrangement was concluded on September 22, 1940, by Governor General Decoux and the Japanese military representative, General Nishihara.[1] By the terms of the agreement the Japanese forces were supposed to cross into northern Viet Nam from south China at the frontier town of Lang Son. Because of the specific terms regulating this maneuver, the French were unprepared for the attack on their border positions which the Japanese forces launched as they penetrated the frontier of Viet Nam. Although this border assault might have been a deliberate attack to underscore Japanese determination to dominate the French, the units involved were later punished by the Japanese High Command

1 Decoux: *À la barre de l'Indochine*, pp. 103–12.

for what were termed arbitrary actions.[2] It seems rather that this was the first instance of a local Japanese military clique's using its occupation advantage, unsanctioned by higher authority, to assist a Vietnamese political group in obtaining a foothold inside the country.

The Japanese attack on Lang Son was carefully coordinated with a revolt staged in the surrounding mountainous frontier region adjacent to China by cadres of the Phuc Quoc movement, who had come in the vanguard of the occupying force. The Phuc Quoc was a vestige of the *Việt Nam Quang Phục Hội*, or Restoration Association, which Phan Boi Chau had organized in China before World War I. Its adherents were traditionalist in political orientation and still held hopes of restoring Prince Cuong De to the leadership of a new Viet Nam. Through the generosity of the Japanese, the Phuc Quoc cadres had equipment estimated at 5,000 rifles and 20 automatic weapons along with 25,000 rounds of ammunition and 3,000 grenades available to them. Backed by this firepower, these cadres were able to recruit around 3,000 men from the Vietnamese troops who had served with the French and been captured by the Japanese at Lang Son. In addition to these trained men they also got the services of exiles, border pirates, and members of several mountain ethnic minorities inhabiting the border area.[3] It seems clear the Japanese role in this revolt was to divert the attention of the French frontier forces and weaken their capacity to crush the insurgent challenge. But after several days of rampage the Japanese may have found the disruption of communications no longer in their interest or higher echelons of command may have reacted swiftly to what they considered insubordination. In any event, through negotiation with the local French commander, the Japanese ceased their armed opposition to the Colonial Army and withdrew their support from the revolt.[4]

The momentum created by this pocket-uprising in the hills of north Viet Nam did not come to an end with the fleeing of

2 Ibid.
3 Pierre Dabezies: "Forces politiques au Viet Nam" (thèse pour le Doctorat présentéet soutenue le 31 mai 1955; Université de Bordeaux, Faculté de Droit), p. 135.
4 Ibid.

the Phuc Quoc cadres to the safety of Japanese protection in China's neighboring Kwangtung province. The revolt continued against isolated militia posts and elements of the French army retreating from Lang Son through the mountain passes and defiles of the border territory inhabited by the Tho minority peoples. Because of their antipathies toward the French, these highland tribesmen had sought avenues of protest which had prompted them to act as guides for the invading Japanese, to follow the Phuc Quoc cadres in purposeless revolt, and beginning around September 27, 1940, to accept the leadership of Communist cadres in ambushes against fragments of the French frontier forces. Springing from the mountain-enclosed upland valley known as Bac Son, the uprising of the Tho people was given needed coherence by Communist cadres led by a principal member of the party, Tran Dang Ninh, who organized guerrilla units among them.[5] Lacking any more-fundamental military preparation, the Thổ insurgents were dispersed by hastily dispatched French reinforcements. Even though the French regained their defensive posture, the spasmodic outbursts of Tho insurgency were to continue; with 5,000 weapons scattered throughout the mountains along the northeastern frontier of Viet Nam, it was impossible to restore to what it had been before the occupation.

From the perspective of the Japanese impact on Vietnamese politics, the Lang Son attack and resulting Bắc Sơn uprising were significant initial examples of the random character of the political activities which the occupation was to bring. Since the Phuc Quoc movement was the principal Vietnamese political group with which the Japanese had had extensive relations before the Pacific war, it is not surprising that their first foray into politics in Viet Nam would be through their best-known local contact. These ties had developed from the exile of Prince Cuong De, who shortly after the turn of the century, with his political tutor Phan Boi Chau, had sought refuge in Japan, where they attempted to establish a reform movement in the style of the Chinese exiles Liang Ch'i-ch'ao and K'ang Yu-wei.

5 Democratic Republic of Viet Nam: *Thirty Years of Struggle of the Party*, p. 66.

Despite the convulsive changes in the structure of Vietnamese society over the ensuing four decades and their growing irrelevancy to them, the Phuc Quoc movement still nourished hopes from their exile that their opportunity for political power might arrive. While they received more tangible assistance from the Japanese during the occupation than at any other period in their political life, the Phuc Quoc, just as their expectations had reason to rise, had to content themselves with limited and short-term aid. The support they received, which seems to have been opportunistically acquired from subordinate Japanese military men, fell far short of fulfilling their grandiose scheme to place Prince Cuong De on the throne of Viet Nam as a constitutional monarch with Japanese support. Such a broad design clashed with the overriding concern of the Japanese occupation authorities for stability and order. Indochina was important to Japan as a base and support point against the complexities of colonial resistance elsewhere in Southeast Asia. They had no intention, at least not initially, of making Viet Nam a laboratory for political experimentation and reform.[6] But the assistance that was extracted by the Phuc Quoc from local Japanese commanders in the Lang Son encounter was not unique; it was only the opening note of an important theme of Japanese political operations during the occupation. Ironically, the results of the Phuc Quoc's uprising were extremely advantageous for the adversaries of the restoration movement.

To the Vietnamese Communists these events in the autumn of 1940 had a seminal character. As their party's official history chronicles, "The Bac Son insurrection opened a new historical page of armed struggle for the Vietnamese people. It broke out while the people throughout the country were not yet prepared. But the lesson drawn from the Bac Son insurrection was very useful and served as a basis for preparation for the August general insurrection later."[7] Of more tangible importance than the lessons drawn from the insurrectionary experience of Bac Son was the opportunity it afforded the Communists in establish-

---

6 Elsbree: *Japan's Role in Southeast Asian Nationalist Movements*, pp. 23–4.
7 Democratic Republic of Viet Nam: *Thirty Years of Struggle of the Party*, pp. 66–7.

ing the first "people's armed force" under party control, and to extend their organizational network into a strategic area of Viet Nam. In sharp contrast to the Phuc Quoc cadres, who lacked any indigenous political organization of substance, the Communists launched a systematic consolidation of the guerrilla bases which had been hastily formed in the intensity of the Bac Son fighting.

Decisions concerning the creation of a guerrilla zone were reached at the pivotal Eighth Session of the Central Committee of the Indochinese Communist Party, which was convened by Ho Chi Minh on May 10, 1941, after his return from a decade of foreign activity. Although this historic meeting had far-reaching consequences in refashioning the fundamental approach of Communist revolutionary strategy in Viet Nam, one of its most quickly implemented results was the appointment of a command committee for the guerrilla units in the Bac Son area. This included Phung Chi Kien, Le Van Chi, and Chu Van Tan. The latter was a Tho leader who had organized the "first platoon of national salvation" in January 1941, and whose subsequent vital contributions to the revolution were to make him the minister of defense in the first government formed by Ho Chi Minh, in August 1945.[8]

By the autumn of 1941, the Viet Nam National Salvation Army, as the guerrilla force became known, was large enough to be organized into two sections. Chu Van Tan led the one located in Thai Nguyen province, the nearest to the heartland of the Vietnamese population in the Red River Delta. The other section, operating further to the north under the command of Phung Chi Kien, fell into an ambush in the vicinity of Bac Kan sometime in late 1942 and suffered such heavy losses that it ceased to exist as an organized formation. Meantime, Chu Van Tan's southern force continued to wage guerrilla warfare by succeeding in maintaining its own force while wearing down the French-led Vietnamese militia. However, in February 1942, after eight months of campaigning, difficulties in obtaining arms and am-

8 Ibid., p. 70.

munition forced the unit to scatter into lightly armed groups devoted to political organization among the Tho.[9]

From this effort, revolutionary political-military bases were created in wide areas over four mountainous provinces adjacent to the China border. And after less than a year's operation, at the beginning of 1943, Chu Van Tan had been able to establish more than nineteen assault sections comprising more than one hundred armed propaganda cadres, which permitted the work of organizing a revolutionary structure to be intensified. By the time the Japanese eliminated French control in Indochina in 1945, the Communists had succeeded in perfecting a network of mountain bases where, with the aid of airdrops of weapons and ammunition in the spring of 1945, they developed a revolutionary armed force which was to play a key role in the August Revolution.

The insurgency growing out of the Bac Son uprising was virtually the first genuine experience of the Vietnamese Communists with systematic guerrilla warfare, even in its most rudimentary form. It taught the party that protracted guerrilla warfare could wear down a stronger adversary if secure bases were created for the support and development of guerrilla units. In this form of armed struggle the Communists were learning the hard way that the absence of extensive political organization was one of the sharpest limitations to widespread guerrilla operations. They also saw the need for continual growth, extreme mobility, and constant adaptation for guerrilla forces, as well as the precaution against precipitous action because "If guerrilla units stand on the defensive and coil themselves up, divorcing themselves from the masses they will be crushed. When the situation requires it, they must disperse, be able to stick to the masses, and build bases, and when the situation is favourable, gather again and wage the struggle."[1]

Despite this more systematic approach of the Communists to the task of revolutionary war, their advantage resulted from

9 Ibid., pp. 72–3.
1 Democratic Republic of Viet Nam: *Thirty Years of Struggle of the Party*, p. 73.

a chance combination of factors producing the Bac Son insurrection; it gave them the opportunity to assume the leadership of a parochial protest among a highland ethnic minority and through it to gain a strategic foothold in Viet Nam. The scattering of Japanese weapons by the Phuc Quoc cadres fed like inflammable drops upon smoldering Tho antipathies, whose origin lay in the antagonism which a mountain people might be expected to feel against the lowland representatives of central authority who had tried to force cultural conformity on them. Moreover, because of their strategic location across the major routes of communication between south China and the Red River Delta, the Tho had played an unenviable role during the twenty centuries in which Viet Nam fought to maintain its autonomy from the court at Peking. Like other areas of the Sino-Vietnamese border region, the Tho homeland had served as both a battleground and buffer, with the Tho, as did other people, shifting their loyalties to their own advantage. However, it was also because of their location that the Tho became more Vietnamized than any other highland group despite the fact that they shared the same fierce desire of other mountain peoples to maintain their autonomy.

Besides its frontier aspect, the northern highlands area has also been used historically as a base for fractional groups in internal fights for political power in Viet Nam. One of the major antagonists to central authority during the seventeenth century was the Mac family, who lodged themselves in the border area of Cao Bang province, from where, with Chinese aid, they harassed the mountain region.[2] Out of the military campaigns to eliminate the Mac and pacify the mountains, the Vietnamese developed a more long-range program for Vietnamizing the Tho, who had served the insurgent family. One of the important aspects of this program was the sending of Vietnamese mandarins to the Tho country, where they intermarried locally. The mixed-blood descendants of these mandarins came to be known as Tho-Ti and were recognized as a local aristocracy, which the rest of the Tho tended to imitate in their social style of speaking

2 Le Thanh Khoi: *Le Viet-Nam*, p. 250.

Vietnamese and wearing Vietnamese dress.[3] As new Tho leaders emerged, they too would adopt the Tho-Ti style of life so that a continuing mechanism of social regulation came to be accepted which fulfilled the Vietnamese objective of bringing stability and control by lowlanders over the Tho country.

The pressures that helped to spark the Bac Son insurrection had their source in the fact that, in addition to their positions of social prestige, the Tho-Ti had been the leaders of the loose and decentralized political system among the Tho. Their mode of politics was a curious mixture of the Vietnamese mandarinal administrative system, with the bureaucratic positions filled not by rigorous examinations, but by the hereditary prerogatives of the Tho-Ti. Besides heredity these prerogatives also stemmed from the ritualistic role which the Tho-Ti performed in the official cults to Confucius that had been introduced by the Vietnamization and mixed over the years with the local cult of the god of the soil.[4] Tensions were created in this synthesized social system in the late nineteenth century by the French when they decided to suppress the Tho leaders. This resulted through colonial regulations making political offices randomly appointive or elective so that many non-Tho-Ti were placed in positions of authority.[5] While this French policy successfully destroyed the political prerogatives of the Tho-Ti, they were still able to maintain their positions of social leadership and prestige among the Tho. Despite the opposition of the French, the Tho-Ti's influence persisted because of their ritualistic role and distinctive cultural traditions.[6]

Although extensive and detailed information on the political reaction of the Tho-Ti is lacking, especially in the events of the Bac Son uprising, it is significant that the Communist effort in organizing a revolutionary base among the Tho found its success concentrated in areas where the Tho-Ti were influential. Since the position of the Tho-Ti was such a vital characteristic of the Tho

3 Gerald C. Hickey: "Social Systems of Northern Viet Nam" (unpublished Ph.D. dissertation, Department of Anthropology, University of Chicago, 1958), p. 33.
4 Ibid., p. 198.
5 Ibid., p. 169.
6 Ibid., p. 106.

society and because their status had been the special object of
French opposition, it seems reasonable to suppose that it was
the Tho-Ti who led the Tho in insurrection against the colonial
administration and then into the mutually advantageous union
with the Communist Party. But whatever specific pressures may
ultimately be verified as having caused the Bac Son revolt, it
appears clear that the Tho were actively seeking some outlet of
expression against the French. In providing the means for such
a manifestation of pent-up feelings, the Japanese impact on
Vietnamese politics was twofold. It not only contributed to a
heightened political consciousness within the country, but also
to the weakening of the capacity of the colonial administration
to control these developments. By decreasing the capacity of
the established authority and increasing that of its antagonists, the
momentum of the occupation was advancing the time when
the accumulation of relative changes in political power would
tip the balance toward the violent outburst of the revolution.

It is of importance for an understanding of revolution in Viet
Nam to note that this initial occasion for the establishment of
a Communist revolutionary base occurred not in the lowland
deltas densely populated with Vietnamese. The ensuing revolutionary war for Vietnamese independence was largely fought
and won in the thinly inhabited northern mountain areas pre-
dominantly settled by a people known generically as Tai. Sharing many cultural qualities with the people who settled the lowlands of the Menam River and created the foundation for the
modern state of Thailand, these minority people of northern
Viet Nam are part of a larger group of Tai-speaking people who
live in mountain areas scattered throughout mainland southeast
Asia.[7] Unlike their lowland relatives, the highland Tai settled in
upland valleys where they too became wet-rice cultivators. Because of their mountainous habitat and the difficulty of communications, separate cultural groupings developed although certain
basic characteristics remained. Thus the upland Tai of Viet Nam
are part of a mosaic of Tai peoples stretching across Laos, northern Thailand, and into the Shan states of upper Burma as well

7 Hall: *A History of Southeast Asia*, pp. 144–58.

as extending into the southern border regions in China. Their social communications, such as they are, have been more within the loose cultural unity across international boundaries than with the lowland Vietnamese. Through the necessity of economic and administrative relations, frictions developed between the uplanders and lowlanders in the latter's attempts to "pacify" the peoples of the mountainous areas.

A microcosm of this broad mosaic is formed in northern Viet Nam by three distinct groupings of Tai peoples: the Tho, the Black Tai, and the White Tai. The White Tai and the Black Tai are concentrated to the northwest of the Red River Delta in the area of the Black River Valley. Their numbers spill over into Laos, where they have close contacts with similarly labeled Tai groups.[8] To the northeast of the Red River is the homeland of the Tho, the largest of the Tai groups in Viet Nam, with a population of approximately 400,000[9] Interspersed among these groups are the Man, Meo, Muong, and Nung, who have widely dissimilar characteristics from the Tai as well as among themselves. These other groups provide a tension and dimensionality to the settlement pattern of the mountainous ethnic groups whose major theme is the scattered communities of the Tai.

The Communists' success in establishing a base area among the Tho enabled them to prepare and sustain their bold occupation of Hanoi and the Red River Delta when the Japanese surrender created the opportunity for the August Revolution of 1945. Moreover, it assured them of a refuge when the French

8 These contacts are discussed on the basis of field research by K. G. Izikowitz: "Notes About the Tai," *Bulletin of the Museum of Far Eastern Antiquities*, No. XXXIV (Stockholm, 1962), pp. 79–91.

9 The Tai population of northern Viet Nam in 1936 was listed officially at 686,000 persons. No estimate for the specific population of the Tho, Black, or White Tai was given. See Georges Condominas: "L'Indochine," in André Leroi-Gourhan and Jean Poirer: *Ethnologie de l'Union Française, tome second: Asie, Océanie, Amérique* (Paris: Presses Universitaires de France; 1953), p. 543. In 1952 the northern Viet Nam Tai population was estimated at 830,000, with no details as to the size of the three major groups. See G. Morchand: "Notes démographiques sur un canton Meo blanc du pays Tai," *Bulletin de la société des études indochinoises*, XXVII (1952), pp. 354–61. It appears that the accepted population figure for the Tho in the mid-1950's was 400,000; see Hickey: "Social Systems of Northern Viet Nam," p. 93. Some estimates for the 1940's have been as low as 200,000, for the Tho population. For the period under discussion it appears reasonable to assume that the Tho were about 400,000 in number.

pushed them out of the cities of northern Viet Nam in early 1947. It was not only the Tho's history of long-sought autonomy and the fortuitous incorporation of the Tho uprising into the Communist revolutionary movement that led eventually to the formation of the base area. It was also the geographic character- istics of the region itself. The advantage from these characteris- tics is best demonstrated in the sharp population differential between the mountains and the lowlands.

Out of an estimated population in 1943 of 9,800,000 in northern Viet Nam (Tonkin), two thirds were concentrated on the 10 per cent of the land area of the region in the fertile Red River Delta.[1] There, population density was an average of 430 persons per square kilometer, making it one of the most thickly inhabited areas of the world.[2] This meant, of course, that ap- proximately 90 per cent of the land area of northern Viet Nam contained only 10 per cent of the population of the region. While a portion of this sparse population was Vietnamese, the bulk of the inhabitants outside of the Delta consisted of moun- tain ethnic minorities. The Vietnamese portion of this population was located in the midlands which bordered the triangular- shaped Delta on its two inland sides and formed the geographic transition to the mountainous arc which separated the lowland Vietnamese from the Mekong Valley to the west and the Chinese to the north. Perhaps a single example of the disparity in pop- ulation distribution can serve to underscore the suitability of the terrain for guerrilla bases. Lai Chau province in the north- west, homeland of both the Black and White Tai, had a 30-per- cent greater surface than the entire Red River Delta. Yet it contained only an estimated 67,000 persons, as contrasted with the 7,500,000 peasant farmers of the Delta.[3] The sparsity of population was an indication that Vietnamese settlement patterns depended on easily irrigated lowlands for wet-rice agriculture.

---

[1] *Annuaire statistique de l'Indochine, 1943–1946*, p. 28.

[2] Pierre Gourou: *The Peasants of the Tonkin Delta: A Study of Human Geography*, trans. by Richard R. Miller (New Haven: Human Relations File; 1955), Vol. I, p. 2. The French edition is *Les paysans du delta Tonkinois: étude geographique humaine* (Paris: Éditions d'Art et d'histoire; 1936).

[3] *Annuaire statistique de l'Indochine, 1943–1946*, p. 28.

The Tai peoples were also wet-rice cultivators, and thus could live only in the small number of upland valleys. This factor limited the growth of their population while the mountain barriers circumscribed their communications. These mountain ranges in the northwest rise from plateaus of from 1,800 to 3,000 feet to peaks of 10,000 feet. By comparison those in the northeast are less rugged and rarely extend beyond 6,000 feet.[4] Since these mountain pockets of ethnic minorities were in close proximity to the Red River Delta, the protection their areas afforded for guerrilla bases did not result in a remoteness from potential targets.

Partly because of its extreme geographic characteristics, which other areas of Indochina shared only as an approximate pattern, northern Viet Nam became the major area of conflict in the seven years of the Indochina War. Of course, there were other more profound factors in making the north the central theater of combat, but the geographical context did the most to set the pattern and pace of the combat once it was begun. Although the Tho provided the Vietnamese Communists with their initial opportunity to establish bases in the highlands, this did not give them control over all the minority peoples. The same cooperative attitude was absent from the other less Vietnamized groups of the mountains, especially the White and Black Tai of the northwest region, who were antipathetic to all Vietnamese, Communist or not. Because of their strong feelings against the Vietnamese, the Black and White Tai sought protection from the French, but far from assuring their safety the French presence made the Tai Highlands a major target for the Viet Minh.[5]

That the French conducted their last stand of the Indochina War in the Tai country at Dien Bien Phu is not without its larger significance. For with the exception of a series of battles in the winter and spring of 1951, in which the Communists hurled themselves at the formidable French fortifications in the

---

4 Great Britain, Naval Intelligence Division: *Indo-China,* pp. 14–16.
5 This attitude is discussed in R. Bauchar: "Fleuve Rouge–Rivière Noire," *Revue des Troupes Coloniales* (juin 1947, numéro 289), pp. 17–31, and Lt. Col. Lhermite: "Les opérations 'Bénédictine' et 'Geneviève,' " *Tropiques: Revue des Troupes Coloniales* (juin 1948, numéro 300), pp. 27–31.

Red River Delta, all of the major battles of the Indochina War were fought in the highlands of northern Viet Nam and adjacent areas of Laos.[6] It was eventually the tension created by the Communists' increasingly successful guerrilla infiltration and base-area organization within the Red River Delta and their simultaneous wide-ranging war of movement in the mountains that brought the French military effort to its end. Paradoxically, it had been in these mountains of Tonkin that the French had perfected their concepts of colonial warfare in their campaigns from 1884 to 1896 to pacify the area. Battles that marshals Lyautey and Galliéni had fought when they were colonels at Thai Nguyen and Cao Bang were to be repeated sixty years later, but with less favorable results.[7]

If the events of the Bac Son insurrection in the mountains of Tonkin were to have an effect on the August Revolution and the course of the Indochina War, there occurred almost simultaneously in southern Viet Nam (Cochinchina) in late 1940 an uprising which had a quite different impact. By its complete contrast with the Communist reaction to the revolt among the Tho, this revolt in the Mekong Delta illustrates the sharp regional differences then present in the party and gives some explanation for the striking dissimilarities which emerged in the character of the August Revolution. While this southern uprising was sparked by the Japanese occupation of Indochina, it was not, unlike the Lang Son attack, sponsored by them. As Japanese troops entered Tonkin from China, Thailand (or Siam, as the country was then called) took the occasion, when the French were faced with a challenge in the north, to threaten to attack the western border of the Indochina state of Cambodia, an act which they carried out in January 1941.[8] Anticipating this second-front threat, the French began to mobilize civilian Vietnamese in Cochinchina and Cambodians for military action, and in this atmosphere of crisis the Communists in southern Viet Nam felt

6 The assault on the delta is discussed in Gen. Jean Marchand: *Le drame indochinois* (Paris: J. Peyronnet; 1953), pp. 143–71.

7 See L. H. G. Lyautey: *Lettres du Tonkin et du Madagascar, 1893–1899* (Paris: Librairie Armand Colin; 1920), deux tomes.

8 Decoux: *À la barre de l'Indochine*, pp. 123–47.

that these circumstances would permit them to capitalize upon popular discontent to launch a revolutionary uprising. But at that moment, several key Central Committee members, including Le Duan and Le Hong Phong, were arrested, an event which denied to the party in the south leadership vitally needed for a successful armed venture.[9]

Before any action was taken, a party representative from the south, Phan Dang Luu, was sent in early October 1940 to seek directives on the projected revolt from the Central Committee, which was then meeting at Bac Ninh, a provincial town to the northeast of Hanoi. Because of the failure of the Bac Son insurrection and because the preconditions for an effective insurrection throughout the country had not been met, it was concluded that a revolutionary uprising should not be launched in the south. As the party's leaders assessed the situation, "It was necessary to prepare the conditions, and wait for a favorable opportunity when conditions were ripe throughout the country, to launch an armed insurrection to defeat the French and the Japanese. If the insurrection were launched it would be isolated and annihilated by the joint French-Japanese Army."[1]

According to the party's official history, upon the return of Phan Dang Luu to the south with the assessment of the Central Committee members, he found that the order for the insurrection had already been issued. Supposedly it could not be withdrawn.[2] There is some discrepancy as to what day in November 1940 the uprising actually broke out, but there has been no disagreement on its consequences. By the middle of December 1940, three Frenchmen and thirty Vietnamese soldiers serving with the French army or local Vietnamese notables had been killed and six Frenchmen and thirty Vietnamese had been wounded.[3] At the price of rendering their party in the south almost nonexistent by the resulting repression, the Communists were able to block the highways leading from Saigon into the Mekong Delta and to attack and hold public facilities in provincial areas. The re-

9 Democratic Republic of Viet Nam: *Thirty Years of Struggle of the Party*, p. 67.
1 Ibid., p. 68.
2 Ibid.
3 Mus: *Problèmes de l'Indochine contemporaine*, P.M. I, p. 12.

pression that followed included more than 6,000 arrests and several dozen executions in addition to those lost in combat.[4]

This precipitous action was almost exclusively the responsibility of Tran Van Giau, who, reportedly, was condemned by the Central Party organs.[5] This reprimand seems to have had little effect, for much of the same sort of compulsiveness was demonstrated later on by the party in the south during the tense days of the August Revolution. Since it was the Communists who were to benefit most from the Japanese occupation and to benefit most in northern Viet Nam, it is ironic that at the outset of the occupation the party organization was strongest in the south, primarily due to the work of Tran Van Giau. The southern Communists had taken advantage of the Popular Front era in France, which had allowed them to consolidate their urban political organization. Then in 1939, when upon the outbreak of the European war the Communist Party was outlawed, they responded by moving their cadres and many followers to the countryside, where they extended their organization, established popular participation groups tied to the party, and formed paramilitary units located in the strategically positioned swamp area southwest of Saigon, the Plaine des Joncs.

Before the beginning of the Japanese occupation, the strength of the Communist Party in the south was estimated at 800 effective cadres, 700 well-indoctrinated members, and about 1,000 persons in associated groups. After four years of rebuilding following the repression in the autumn of 1940, the party was believed to have had less than 200 members and only about 600 participants in associations tied to the party.[6] Yet this heavy toll did not seem to dissuade the leadership group around Tran Van Giau from taking further uncalculated, compulsive steps during the August Revolution. Indeed these self-defeating acts following the capitulation of Japan were undoubtedly attributable to the narrowed range of alternatives which the unpreparedness of the southern Communists for the seizure of power made

4 Ibid.
5 Ibid.
6 Ibid.

VIET-BAC GUERRILLA ZONE
1940-1945

Red River

CHINA

Pac Bo 1941
HA GIANG   CAO BANG
Tran Hung Dao Forest
BAC KAN
Tan Trao 1945   Binh Gia
Bac Son   **BAC SON UPRISING**
LANG SON   **1940**
TUYEN QUANG   Trang Xa
Yen Bay   Vu Nhai   THAI NGUYEN
1930   1940, 1945
Son La   Cam Pha
Hanoi   Hong Gai
Haiphong
THAI BINH
Nam Dinh

CHINA

GULF
OF
TONKIN

Luang Prabang

THANH HOA

NGHE AN   **NGHE-TINH SOVIET**
Do Luong   **1930-1931**
Vo Liet   Vinh
Ben Thuy
HA TINH

Vientiane

Udorn

L   A   O   S

Savannakhet

Mekong River

Hue

Da Nang

QUANG NAM

QUANG NGAI
QUANG NGAI   **GUERRILLA ZONE**
Ba To   **1945**

KONTUM

THAILAND

Ubon

Pakse

Korat

Qui Nhon

kok

Battambang

CAMBODIA

Ban Me Thuot

Kratie

Nha Trang

Kampong Cham

Loc Ninh
Ba Ra
Quan Loi   Da Lat

Phnom Penh

Dau Tieng

Hoc Mon-Ba Diem 1937
Saigon 1931

SOUTH CHINA SEA

MY THO
SADEC
VINH
LONG
SOC
TRANG
BAC LIEU

MEKONG DELTA UPRISING
OF 1940

RISINGS AGAINST FRENCH
ULE BEFORE THE AUGUST
REVOLUTION OF 1945

Limits between the three regions of Viet Nam.

Scene of particularly fierce French response
to anti-colonial uprising.

Place and date of an important meeting of the
Indochinese Communist Party.

Strikes in factories, mines or rubber plantations.

Peasant uprisings.

Guerrilla bases.

Areas where uprisings occurred.

French detention camps for political prisoners.

Zones controlled by the Viet Minh on the eve
of the August Revolution of 1945.

Province names

Cities and towns

0   MILES   150

almost inevitable. Thus the severe penalties of the Mekong Delta uprising of 1940 appeared to betray in the Nam Bo (southern region) leadership of the Communist Party a fetish for momentary advantage and a corresponding inability to cope with the fundamentals of revolutionary political organization in the more diffuse social context of southern Viet Nam.

The experience of the Bac Son and Nam Bo uprisings had, in addition to the organizational consequences it held for the course of the Communist revolution, an impact on the party's approach to the task of obtaining political power. The lessons which the party drew from the two spasmodic challenges to continued French dominance were, as set forth in its official history, structured around three general categories of guidelines. In abbreviated form these may be stated: (1) the importance of appropriate timing for success in seizing power, (2) that in an agricultural colony the most exposed places to be seized and occupied as bases are in the countryside and from there the towns can be seized when conditions have matured, and (3) that a successful insurrection must rely on the force of the masses of the population as well as on propaganda among the ranks of the enemy to win them to the revolutionary side.[7] While these principles may not appear startling or even novel from the perspective of subsequent Communist operational doctrine, they chronicled the initial steps in an eventual comprehensive definition of revolutionary strategy.

They also marked a distinguishable departure from the random acts of political protest before the Japanese occupation. Then, in response to specific opportunities present in the erratic course of colonial politics, the revolutionary structure of the Vietnamese Communists had been variously centered among students and exiles in south China in the 1920's, among the peasants in north-central Viet Nam in the early 1930's, and in Saigon and the southern provincial towns during the Popular Front period of 1936–9. Now that more fundamental changes were taking place to reduce French power, the party was empha-

7 Democratic Republic of Viet Nam: *Thirty Years of Struggle of the Party*, pp. 69–70.

sizing that it was the countryside "where the enemy's machinery of rule was relatively weak. The party had more opportunity to come into close contact with the peasant masses to make propaganda, organize them, and transform the countryside into a revolutionary base."[8]

The significance of this assessment was not its discovery of a recent radical change in French power. French rule had always been *relatively* weaker in the countryside than in the more easily controlled towns. The Communist recognition of this fact was an important revolutionary milestone. While the impact of the occupation was overburdening the capacity of the French to control developments in Indochina, an already existing gap between the colonial administration and the countryside was only being reinforced. Most of the French administrators and their military colleagues had always been concentrated into the cities and provincial towns.[9] In the absence of a political structure to secure indigenous political loyalty, the French had been able to put down any threats of noncompliance with their efficient security police and military forces. But with the Japanese intervention diverting the attention of the French forces from their colonial mission and sponsoring indigenous threats to French control, the gap—the revolutionary space—was increasing. Yet this accentuation was less significant than the fact that some Vietnamese, led by the Indochinese Communist Party, were making more deliberate and comprehensive plans for exploiting this gap than they had ever before considered.

8 Ibid., p. 64.
9 *Annuaire statistique de l'Indochine, 1936–1937*, p. 25.

CHAPTER 11 ✿ ✿ ✿

THE CREATION OF VIETNAMESE

INDEPENDENCE MOVEMENTS

✿

✿

✿

The Communists' realization that the Japanese occupation had created a new potential for revolution in Viet Nam was demonstrated by the organizational strategy conceived at the Eighth Session of the Central Committee of the Indochina Communist Party, held from May 10 to 19, 1941. This meeting brought Ho Chi Minh together with the party leaders for the first time that is recorded in the party's official history since the founding meeting in January 1930. It seems reasonable to assume that the pivotal doctrinal results of this session were due in large measure to the impact of the returned leader's personality.[1] The keystone of these strategic decisions grew out of the belief that the occupation had profoundly changed political conditions in Viet Nam and consequently the nature of the party's task. As the Central Committee's resolution analyzed it, the situation required that "For the moment the partial and class interests must be sub-

1 Democratic Republic of Viet Nam: *Thirty Years of Struggle of the Party*, p. 70.

ordinated to the national problem. If the independence and freedom of the whole nation could not be recovered, not only the
whole nation would be further condemned to slavery but the
partial and class interests would be lost forever."[2]

Through its intervention, Japan had further complicated the
colonial character of Vietnamese politics; another layer of foreign control had been introduced and another actor had entered
the Vietnamese political scene. This increased external pressure
seems to have stimulated a greater sense of national identity
among Vietnamese and heightened nationalist expectations that
independence might be secured through Japanese support. Yet
what appears of greatest significance is not these factors of the
occupation in themselves, but the Vietnamese Communists' response to them. For if the analysis of the Central Committee
resolution was valid at all, it should have been equally true before the occupation. In that prewar period how could the independence of the nation have been recovered by emphasizing class
interests over broader nationalist ones? This question seems
especially pertinent when the lack of widespread political consciousness is taken into account. But during the 1920's and
1930's the Communists had neglected wider nationalist appeals
to take advantage of random and particular political opportunities. They had evoked the parochial interests of peasant discontent, exile anxiety, and elite alienation without attempting to
integrate them into a larger ideological whole. In this period the
opportunities for political action had outdistanced the Vietnamese Communists' doctrinal capacity and organizational ability
to translate these events into challenges with broader revolutionary impact. Significantly, the wider political focus being
adopted by the Vietnamese Communists in May 1941 was not
merely a change in idiom and perspective; a fundamental change
in strategy was occurring through new organizational forms and
operational doctrine.

The shift of the Communists' attention away from a class
revolution against indigenous feudalism to a national revolution
against imperialism was symbolized in the decision of the Eighth

2 Ibid.

Session of the party's Central Committee to found the *Việt Nam Độc Lập Đồng Minh Hội,* the Viet Nam Independence League, known as the Viet Minh. The purpose of this new organization was to facilitate "the mobilization of the masses' national spirit."[3] In theory the Indochinese Communist Party became a member of the Viet Minh front, but in practice the two were indistinguishable. The term "Viet Minh" became a virtual synonym for the Communist Party, the government it was to found in August 1945, and thanks to the Communists' successes, the whole anti-colonial nationalist movement. Although the Indochinese Communist Party was publicly dissolved in a shrewd tactical move in October 1945, and the Viet Minh was formally dispensed with in May 1951, with the founding of the *Việt Nam Lao Động Đảng,* Viet Nam Labor Party, there has been no misunderstanding by the Communists themselves that there has been a firm line of organizational continuity since the founding of the party in 1930. Thus the title of their party's history published in 1960: *Thirty Years of Struggle of the Party.*[4]

(The launching of the Viet Minh was not simply a change in façade; it brought deep-seated organizational changes including the formation of mass associations for "national salvation," *Việt Nam Cứu Quốc Hội,* known as the Cuu Quoc associations, whose purpose was to extend throughout the country a network complementary to the Communist Party for popular participation in politics.)The new emphasis on popular associations in Communist tactics committed the party in principle to establishing widely diffused organizations for political mobilization, a significant contrast to their pre-occupation policy in which virtually all recruiting resulted in party membership. These subsidiary Cuu Quoc associations in theory gave the party a flexibility it could not previously have had by maintaining its requirements for discipline and ideological control within the heart of the party ranks.

3 Ibid.

4 The editor's note on the inside cover of this publication states: " 'Thirty Years of Struggle of the Party' was written in commemoration of the thirtieth anniversary of the founding of the Indochinese Communist Party, now the Viet Nam Lao Dong Party."

While the results of organizing Cuu Quoc associations during the Japanese occupation are almost impossible to assess, their immediate importance to revolution in Viet Nam was more qualitative than quantitative. The quantity of participants in the August Revolution was significant only because of the smallness of their number. It was the effectiveness with which a few well-trained activists were able to establish themselves in authority that was of underlying importance in the Communist success of 1945. Besides these qualities of flexibility and decisiveness in action, the organization which the Viet Minh evolved during the Japanese occupation was distinguished by its capacity to mobilize large numbers of Vietnamese for political participation. This was a long-term development closely related to the intensity of the ensuing seven years of revolutionary war with France, the requirements for military personnel, and the extent to which combat operations affected the civilian population. Yet the reasons for the eventual effectiveness of this structure of political mobilization can be traced back to its initial framework which took form as a result of the Eighth Session of the Central Committee of the party in May 1941.

The basis for this whole structure of revolutionary organization was the *Chi Bộ*, or cell, made up of a relatively few persons whose leader was the only one to have contact with superiors. These groups shared many of the characteristics of secret societies and thus the Communists capitalized on the appeal of such organizations to the Vietnamese as well as their experience in utilizing its institutional form. The Communists were making use of native organizational capacity just as had the earlier Tan Viet Party; cells were to be established on the basis of the limited categories of social differentiation that existed in colonial Viet Nam, such as women, youth, laborers, military men, and whatever homogeneous groups might be found.[5] Cells based on these functional distinctions in Vietnamese society had already been attempted as part of the Communists' operational proce-

---

5 Philippe Devillers: *Histoire du Viet Nam, 1940 à 1952* (Paris: Éditions du Seuil; 1952), pp. 100–1. Because of Devillers's great fund of first-hand information, this is an indispensable book.

dure during the Nghe-Tinh soviet, but they had only meager success due to poor upper-echelon coordination. Through learning by past mistakes the Viet Minh displayed its organizational ingenuity during the Japanese occupation by linking the Chi Bo to a larger revolutionary framework.

The superstructure of the communist revolutionary organization was formed by functionally distinctive horizontal and vertical dimensions. The vertical dimension was the countrywide structures for each Cuu Quoc association, the Communist Party, and the future military command. Through this vertical structure there was to be a unity of effort in long-range policies for organizational growth determined by the top-level leadership of each of these groups. The horizontal dimension was to be a territorial unification of all the vertical structures: the popular participation associations, the party, and the military into an operational chain of command beginning at the level immediately above the village and continuing through the district and province level in a pyramidal form until the ultimate level of revolutionary decision-making was reached. At each territorial echelon —village, district, province, region, etc.—there was operational control over each of the vertical structures—party, Cuu Quoc, military, etc.—in the revolutionary organization. The functioning of these two organizational hierarchies permitted a maximum flexibility in action by concentrating operational decisions in each level of the territorial hierarchy while at the same time maintaining centralized control through the party, Cuu Quoc, and military hierarchies. The matrix thus formed was manipulated by the party through territorial representatives at each echelon; they monitored the activities of the militia and the Cuu Quoc at their level and controlled the selection of the leaders of each militia unit and Cuu Quoc association. In its later refinements this framework came to be known as the "parallel hierarchies," which is meant to describe the parallel horizontal lines tying together the territorial organizations of party, popular association, and militia into a pyramidal apex of centralized control.[6]

6 Lacheroy: *Une arme du Viet Minh: Les hiérarchies parallèles*, pp. 11–12.

It was through this matrix that the party expected to mobilize a people who had not had any dependable opportunity for political participation beyond their village since the discontinuation of the mandarinal examinations in 1917. Yet this mobilization could not follow immediately from the Eighth Session of the Central Committee, but developed gradually as the Communists were able to train more cadres and to expand their foothold from the mountainous area of northern Viet Nam. The most significant conclusion reached at this party meeting was that nationalism offered the best formula for a Communist revolution in Viet Nam and that this nationalist identity was not widespread in the country, but had to be "mobilized" through organization and propaganda.

Another area of great doctrinal importance to Communist revolutionary strategy which was given a significant reorientation at this session of the Central Committee in the spring of 1941 was the question of land policy. Attitudes toward land reform have always been a key indicator of the general Communist policy line as well as of party strength; they indicate how pressing its need is for compromise with and support of landed interests. Therefore, it was of strategic significance that the Central Committee decided to put aside their "land to the tillers" program and replace it with an emphasis on confiscating the land of "traitors" and "imperialists," which seems to have meant absentee landlords who could not control their holdings under wartime conditions.[7]

A more pervasive and "revolutionary" land policy initiated in principle at this time was the decision to divide communal lands. This struck at the very heart of Vietnamese rural social structure and cohesion, for communal lands were maintained by villages, family groups, and a multitude of private associations, such as former students of the same teacher. Communal lands are a Vietnamese rural equivalent to the modern-day trust funds, and their rents supported the welfare and philanthropic purposes of the sponsoring groups. By 1938 communal land represented

7 Democratic Republic of Viet Nam: *Thirty Years of Struggle of the Party*, p. 71.

as much as 20 per cent of all cultivated land in northern Viet Nam (Tonkin) and 25 per cent in the center (Annam).

In areas of heavy population concentration, where intense bidding on rent prices for communal land might have made these lands the domain of the rich, they were made available according to age-old customs only to those who owned no land or had amounts too small to support their families.[8] Thus the Communists' policy decision to divide communal lands was not so much a means to win the support of landless elements of Vietnamese society, but to break down existing structural relationships at the village level so as to facilitate new forms of organization. But because of the solid implantation of the French and the Japanese at the time these land policy decisions were made, they did not have an immediate impact. Since the few Communist cadres available were at work in the Tho country, where communal land was not a social characteristic, the effects of that policy were delayed.

The various themes running through the meeting of the Eighth Session of the Central Committee of the party and reorienting its revolutionary doctrine were perhaps best reflected in the election of Truong Chinh as the party's secretary-general at the age of about thirty-two. The significance of this development lay in the fact that through his subsequent writings, Truong Chinh was to become the chief political theoretician of the party—a role Ho Chi Minh in his pedestrian publications never attempted—and, because of the content of his work, the presumed leader of the pro-Chinese sentiment within Vietnamese Communism.[9] The Chinese affinity is in part substantiated by the name Trường Chinh—an alias for its bearer, whose real name is Dang Xuan Khu—which means "Long March" in the Vietnamese language. The name was an obvious identification with the most celebrated chapter in Chinese revolutionary history until that time. (This was the 6,000-mile march of the Chinese Communists from

8 Hoang Van Chi: *From Colonialism to Communism*, p. 202. J. Price Gittinger: *Studies on Land Tenure in Viet Nam* (Saigon: United States Operations Mission to Viet Nam; December, 1959), pp. 16–29.

9 P. J. Honey: "The Position of the DRV Leadership and the Succession to Ho Chi Minh," *The China Quarterly*, No. 9 (January-March 1962), p. 27.

Kiangsi in south China to the northwest in Shensi province, covering more than a year between late 1934 and late 1935 and depleting their forces from over 100,000, to less than 20,000.[1] Although attempts have been made to identify Truong Chinh as trained by the Chinese Communists, there is no positive documentation for it. There is only the information that in December 1939, following the crackdown on the Vietnamese Communists by the colonial administration, he escaped into Yunnan province, where he joined other members of the Central Committee of the party. While in the ensuing year and a half it would have been possible for Truong Chinh to have been a student at Yenan or a comparable training center, the available data suggests that he led missions for the party back into northern Viet Nam.

Whatever the ultimate explanation of Truong Chinh's actual experience with the Chinese Communists, it seems unmistakable that the decisions of the Eighth Session of the Central Committee bore an identifiable relationship to the thrust of Mao Tse-tung's wartime reorientation of revolutionary strategy known as "New Democracy," and defined in a pamphlet of the same name published in January 1940.[2] The Vietnamese obviously

---

1 John King Fairbank: *The United States and China* (new edn., New York: The Viking Press; 1958), p. 234.

2 Mao Tse-tung: *On New Democracy* (English language edn., Peking: Foreign Languages Press; 1954). The essence of this theoretical reorientation has been summarized by John King Fairbank as follows: "The Chinese Revolution, Mao says, must be divided into two stages: first, a 'democratic revolution' (the New Democracy), and then a 'socialist revolution.' The two are quite different. The New Democracy must take its first steps by changing the old 'semi-feudal' society into an independent 'democratic' society. . . . The New Democracy in China must have bourgeois help, says Mao, for this new government cannot be a Soviet-style socialist republic ruled by the proletariat . . . even though that will become in time the ruling form of government in all advanced countries. Since that newest style is not suited to a semi-colonial country, China's New Democracy must be a third type, ruled neither by bourgeoisie alone nor by the proletariat alone, a transitional form for a certain historical period. . . . In form the New Democracy should have a government of 'democratic centrism' based on elections in which all participate, but graded through a hierarchy of people's assemblies from the village on up to a national congress. . . . In actual fact Mao's 'innovations' had been in the realm of practice, not theory. . . . His real 'contribution' had been the creation of a state within a state—a party, an army, and mass support in a territorial base. . . . Thus as Benjamin Schwartz puts it, 'the *New Democracy* is a Marxist-Leninist scaffolding which conceals as much as it reveals.' Its appeal to liberal-minded individuals was very great. The ambiguity of its terminology catered to their hopes while actually building a framework in which to control them." *The United States and China*, pp. 241–3. The Vietnamese were adopting the state-within-a-state concept without being specific at this point in dividing their revolution into "democratic" and "socialist" phases.

shared the goal Mao stated in this publication of wanting a broader base for the Chinese revolutionary movement. Yet it is impossible to relate the sources of the Viet Minh's operational and organizational decisions of 1941 directly to these doctrinal developments in China. It is true that by 1943 the Vietnamese party had committed itself "to develop the culture of new democracy in Indochina," and had incorporated much of the idiom of Mao's program into their public statements.[3] However, it seems that the Vietnamese Communists were elaborating their own distinctive strategy, which involved a deep commitment to nationalism. As they saw it, the main purpose of their Viet Minh front was "to rally the different strata of the people and the national revolutionary forces in the struggle against the main enemy of the nation, that is the French and Japanese fascist imperialists."[4] This emphasis on nationalism in Viet Nam was probably a reflection of the wide difference in level of revolutionary development compared with China, where the recent history of internecine warfare dated back at least eighty years to the T'ai-p'ing rebellion. Although internal conflict among Vietnamese had not been lacking, it remained more an elite affair without the mass involvement that had resulted from the revolutionary warfare in China. Moreover, opposition to continued French dominance was a unifying theme which tended to overcome many, if not all, of the regional and parochial tendencies in Vietnamese politics. Clearly, there seemed more potential power to be derived from a nationalist program in Viet Nam than one which championed any more particular interest.

Despite these features distinguishing the revolutionary situation in China from that in Viet Nam, Truong Chinh's election was an indication of a more pronounced Chinese Communist influence than the Vietnamese party had until then experienced. From the founding of the Thanh Nien in 1925, to the establishment of the Indochinese Communist Party in 1930, until the Eighth Session of the Central Committee, Vietnamese Communism had been the reflection of the Russian training of its

3 Democratic Republic of Viet Nam: *Thirty Years of Struggle of the Party*, p. 76.
4 Ibid., p. 71.

founder-leader, Ho Chi Minh. Unquestionably, the Chinese experience during the 1930's had great relevance for Vietnamese Communism from the perspective of operational effectiveness. For reasons of their own autonomy and flexibility, the Vietnamese probably wished to adopt the relevant and immediately useful substance of the Maoist innovations without a close public and ideological identification with Chinese Communism. It was such a role that Truong Chinh was able to fulfill with unusual effectiveness. Chosen in 1941 to be the party's secretary-general, he was to become the virtual embodiment of the principles and techniques of political mobilization upon which subsequent Communist success in Viet Nam has been based.

Some of the reasons why the Vietnamese party did not wish to identify itself closely with the Chinese Communists became clear after the Central Committee session of May 1941. Its relations with politics in China were much more subtle and complex than might be suggested by the incorporation into Viet Minh operational doctrine of many recent innovations from their Chinese counterparts. The principal reason for this subtle relationship was the fact that the Chinese Communists were in no position to give any direct assistance, material or otherwise, to the Viet Minh. Their bases of strength lay outside the south China border area, which was still the domain of warlords despite the proximity of Chiang Kai-shek in Chungking and the deep inroads of the Japanese occupation. These Chinese warlords were in a position to exert some influence in Viet Nam because of the significant number of Vietnamese political exiles who had sought refuge from the French in south China during the 1930's. As a result of their presence, there was established in Kwangsi province in October 1942 the *Việt Nam Cách Mệnh Đồng Minh Hội,* the Viet Nam Revolutionary League, known as the Dong Minh Hoi. This group, which was subsequently to play a significant role in the August Revolution, was formed under the sponsorship of the south China warlord and commander of the Fourth War Zone, Chang Fa-k'wei.[5]

This association brought together five groups of Vietnamese

5 Dabezies: "Forces politiques au Viet Nam," p. 144.

exiles, two of which were based in Yunnan province and the others in Kwangsi. Included were remnants of the Phuc Quoc group, still faithful to Cuong De, which had sought political sanctuary in Kwangsi province after the failure of their attack on Lang Son. Also located there was a group centering around Nguyen Tuong Tam, who had had a long career as an exile politician and had organized a student political group in Hanoi in 1940, only to flee the city the following year. Contrasted with these Kwangsi groups the exiles in Yunnan had been based in south China a longer time and had firmer contacts among the Vietnamese community there, as well as with the local authorities. Of greatest prominence was Vu Hong Khanh, who was the titular leader of the VNQDD and who since 1933 had attempted to revitalize the nationalist party, which had been driven into exile by the French.[6]

In order to eliminate opportunities for external exploitation which competition between these political exiles presented, Chang Fa-k'wei had enforced unity upon them by establishing the Dong Minh Hoi. This tenuous unification was achieved by utilizing an older group of exiles who had no continuing party affiliations and were in reality political anachronisms. Principally this involved Nguyen Hai Thanh, who became head of the Dong Minh Hoi in 1942, and Trung Boi Cong, who became president of the provisional Vietnamese government which Chang Fa-k'wei sponsored in 1944. Nguyen Hai Thanh, who was born in 1878 in northern Viet Nam, had participated in the original Phuc Quoc renovation movement of Phan Boi Chau. With the nationalist leader he had gone into exile in China in 1912, where in Canton he had tried to regroup young Vietnamese, but without any significant success. Growing old, long out of touch with Vietnamese politics, and even rumored to have forgotten his native language, Nguyen Hai Thanh seemed an improbable figure to give purpose or coherence to political exiles in China. But Thanh had come into close contact with Chang Fa-k'wei, who had convinced himself that this was the personality who might bring unity to the squabbling factions. Aided by the weight

6 Ibid., pp. 142–3.

of Chang's personal influence and a monthly stipend of 100,000 Chinese dollars, the Dong Minh Hoi became a reality. However, the qualities that commended Nguyen Hai Thanh for this figure-head role among Vietnamese exiles was in turn his greatest weakness in fulfilling a more fundamental purpose the Chinese had in creating the Dong Minh Hoi.[7]

Because of the relatively small numbers of Japanese troops in Indochina, there was the potential that developments there could affect the pressures on the China front through shifts in military contingents. Such a shift did in fact occur but not until the last year of the war when in January 1945, the Japanese 37th Infantry Division was relocated from Kwangsi to northern Viet Nam.[8] In anticipation of events of this kind, information on trends in Viet Nam was obviously of great concern not only to the border warlords and Chungking but to the Allies as well. Therefore, the effort to create the Dong Minh Hoi was not merely to get control over Vietnamese exiles in China, or to establish lines of political hegemony in Viet Nam—although some Chinese were anxious for such advantage—but to fill the pressing needs for wartime intelligence from that region. Such a function the aging exile Nguyen Hai Thanh could not command the Dong Minh Hoi to perform, for none of its member groups had any organizational ties in Viet Nam capable of such activity. Chang Fa-k'wei was aware that the only organizational network of any effectiveness throughout Viet Nam was that of the Communists, which extended from the strategic mountain base in the Tho country to include informational contacts with the party in the south.[9]

According to the party's official history, however, a major obstacle to utilizing the Communist organization lay in the fact that its leader, Ho Chi Minh, had been arrested on orders from the Chungking government and was not released until September 16, 1943, presumably to enable him to be used for Chinese intelligence purposes.[1] This extended detention and the change

---

7 Ibid., p. 144.
8 André Gaudel: *L'Indochine en face du Japon* (Paris: J. Susse; 1947), p. 143.
9 Mus: *Problèmes de l'Indochine contemporaine*, P.M. 1, p. 15.
1 Democratic Republic of Viet Nam: *Thirty Years of Struggle of the Party*, p. 75.

of the future Vietnamese president's name to Ho Chi Minh (from Nguyen Ai Quoc) appear symptomatic of the suspicions which Chungking had about his Communist affiliation and his activities in the 1920's with the Borodin mission. However, contrary to the generally accepted view, Chang Fa-k'wei has maintained that the man known as Ho Chi Minh did not have to change his name to get out of jail or that he was ever imprisoned in China in the 1940's.[2] Chang Fa-k'wei states that when he first met the Vietnamese Communist leader in Liuchow in 1941, he was bearing the name "Ho Chi Minh" and shortly thereafter was sent to Kunming for training at the request of American military men there. Whatever may eventually be the truth in the matter, it appears that, despite the Chinese antipathy to Ho Chi Minh's ideological identity, they now regarded him as indispensable in fulfilling their intelligence requirements. The contradiction in the stories relating to the wartime experiences of Ho Chi Minh may reflect a conflict in Chinese operational priorities. This conflict manifested itself following Ho's appointment to replace Nguyen Hai Thanh as head of the Dong Minh Hoi.

Strengthened by a monthly stipend increased to 200,000 Chinese dollars, Ho Chi Minh began to consolidate his hold over the Dong Minh Hoi by accusing certain elements antagonistic to him of being sympathetic to the Japanese.[3] Faced with pressures of this sort the leading nationalist exile, Vu Hong Khanh, returned to Yunnan with his lieutenant, Nghiem Ke To. There he tried in vain to set up serious contact with northern Viet Nam through agents along the border and also through employees of the Yunnan Railway. Although the effort did not meet with any immediate success inside Viet Nam, it did bring advantage to the nationalists. By raising once again the problem of the tenaciousness of exile political competition, the frustrated antagonism of the VNQDD and the obvious success of the Communists aroused once more the suspicions of the Chinese. Now the question of the priority of their intelligence requirements in Viet Nam as com-

2 An interview with Chang is reported in King Chen: "China and the Democratic Republic of Viet Nam, 1945–1954" (unpublished Ph.D. dissertation, The Pennsylvania State University, September 1962), pp. 40–1.
3 Dabezies: "Forces politiques au Viet Nam," p. 144.

pared with their desire to exert a controlling influence over Vietnamese exile political elements was more sharply posed for
Chang Fa-k'wei.

At this point the assessment of the Chinese was subject to
pressures brought to bear by French intelligence operatives, who
were alarmed by the opportunities the Communists were receiving
to build up their strength.[4] Whatever results in intelligence-gathering the Communists had been able to produce, it appears that
they were insufficient to counterbalance the Chinese determination to manage Vietnamese exile politics and to thwart any
autonomous consolidation of power within their circles. This
attitude was demonstrated by Chang Fa-k'wei through a reor-
ganization of the exiles into a provisional government of Viet
Nam, which again brought a tentative unity by using the archaic
older exiles for their symbolic value and their innocuousness. At
a meeting held in March 1944, at Liuchow, a provincial town in
Kwangsi, close to the Vietnamese frontier, the Viet Minh leadership after less than a year in favor was replaced by Trung Boi
Cong, an old and weak personality who received the vague puppet
authority of president of the provisional government.[5]

But if this ease in manipulating Vietnamese exiles facilitated
the immediate purposes of the Chinese, it also demonstrated with
perhaps unintended conspicuousness the rootlessness of these
exiles. Since they did not represent structures of political interest
wider than a handful of the educated and alienated elite, the
exile parties were more concerned with personal prestige and
position than more long-range goals. While this meant that their
objectives were easier to satisfy, it also indicated that their range
of political impact within Viet Nam was limited to an urban
competition among a small upper class rather than being able
to widen the context of politics to include the peasant and upland
minority population. In choosing their political allies among the
Vietnamese, the Chinese settled for those who were easier to
control rather than those who had wider influence and political
capability within their home country. The consequences of this

4 Sacks: "Marxism in Viet Nam," p. 149.
5 Mus: *Problèmes de l'Indochine contemporaine*, P.M. I, p. 15.

choice were to provide an important dimension to the August Revolution and to illustrate again the incapacity of the nationalists as a coherent effective force in the politics of Viet Nam.

Following the organization of the provisional government, in which Ho Chi Minh had only a minor role, the Communist Viet Minh developed its activities autonomously inside Viet Nam, paying particular attention to strengthening its mountain base area. The relationship with the Chinese had been a most useful one while it had lasted. If it did not result in getting Ho Chi Minh out of jail, as Chang Fa-k'wei maintains, it at least gave him a freedom of action advantageous to the Viet Minh. The financial support had not been unimportant, and it had undoubtedly allowed the Viet Minh to extend its intelligence-gathering and political organization. Moreover, some of the cadres were a part of the approximately five hundred Vietnamese who received guerrilla training at the hamlet of Ta Ch'iao, fifteen miles from the frontier town of Liuchow. This camp seems to have given more emphasis to political reorientation than the fundamentals of military tactics, but the politics of the camp were diffuse rather than doctrinaire. Chang Fa-k'wei says that both Vu Hong Khanh and Ho Chi Minh were lecturers at the training center and that such diverse guests as Archbishop Paul Yu and Chou En-lai came to give talks.[6]

This training center and its program, along with the financial support and advantages available to Ho Chi Minh, serve to underscore the heterogeneous character of the relationship of the Viet Minh to the politics of China and the absence of a close wartime tie between it and the Chinese Communists. Indeed the relationship was an expression of warlord politics in south China, and its character was to set a pattern for relations between China and Viet Nam that was to endure until centralized power became more pronounced in both countries. Perhaps the best example of this trend was that the subordinates of Chang Fa-k'wei with whom the Vietnamese dealt during the Japanese occupation and in the Chinese occupation of northern Viet Nam after the capitulation, were the same personalities to represent the Chinese

6 King Chen: "China and the Democratic Republic of Viet Nam," pp. 39-40.

Communists in their early relations with the Viet Minh, following the extension of their control over south China in the late 1940's. Most notable among these personalities was Hsiao Wen. Appointed in 1942 by Chang Fa-k'wei to handle Vietnamese exile affairs, he was also political adviser to the occupation command in Hanoi in 1945–6, and after joining the Chinese Communists he conducted negotiations regarding aid to the Viet Minh.[7] Seen from a historical perspective, it was obviously not a new phenomenon that the Chinese were willing to intervene in Vietnamese politics. However, the fact that its intervention was more an extension of the warlord politics of south China rather than a tie with any central political group in China— Communist or Nationalist—was to have important consequences for revolution in Viet Nam.

7 Ibid., p. 39.

CHAPTER 12

THE FORMATION OF VIET MINH GUERRILLA BASES

For the Communist Viet Minh these consequences of warlord politics were to mean, until the confused events of the Chinese occupation in the autumn of 1945, an end to the cooperation and support from the Kwangsi war zone. Following this break in 1944 with Chang Fa-k'wei, the Viet Minh turned to the consolidation of fragmented guerrilla units and the extension of its base area among the Tho people. The Viet Minh entrusted these tasks of military and organizational preparation for the anticipated Japanese collapse to Vo Nguyen Giap. If Truong Chinh, the party's secretary-general, was the embodiment of the Communists' strategy of political mobilization, then Vo Nguyen Giap was the personification of the evolving doctrine of revolutionary warfare and the man who forged an army of six divisions from a guerrilla band of thirty-four men.[1]

[1] Democratic Republic of Viet Nam: *Ten Years of Fighting and Building of the Vietnamese People's Army*, p. 12.

Giap had been a member of one of the pre-Communist revolutionary parties, the Tan Viet, and had been arrested by the colonial authorities for his activities. Despite this background Giap, upon his release from prison, was permitted to continue his education in French schools and in 1938 was awarded the highest French degree given in Indochina, the Doctorat en Droit, or Doctor of Laws. The future commander of the Viet Minh army then became a history professor at a private school in Hanoi, the Lycée Thanh Long, where he succeeded in winning many of his colleagues to his revolutionary perspective; from the faculty of Thanh Long were to come many of the nonparty leaders in the August Revolution. When France declared war in Europe in 1939, the Indochinese Communist Party was outlawed and its key members arrested, but Giap escaped capture and departed for China, leaving his wife and family in the town of Vinh. His wife, known as Minh Thai among revolutionaries, was arrested in 1941 by the French Sûreté for her liaison activities and condemned to fifteen years of forced labor. She died in detention sometime during the years 1942–3, from what Giap considered mistreatment and the lack of proper facilities. This personal blow heightened his revolutionary zeal and his hatred for the French, propelling him onward in his guerrilla activities in the mountains of northern Viet Nam. Out of this wartime experience he developed a close alliance with the Tho guerrilla leader Chu Van Tan, and through his increasingly strong ties with the Tho people, Giap prepared himself for the effort—undertaken with greater earnestness after March 9, 1945—to develop a "liberation armed force" for the August Revolution. Here was the nucleus of the "People's Army" which was to win spectacular victories in seven years of war against the French.

While there had been much Viet Minh political activity in the mountains of northern Viet Nam throughout the occupation, it was only 2½ months before the Japanese *coup de force* that Vo Nguyen Giap launched the first platoon of the "People's Liberation Troops," consisting of 34 men equipped with 2 revolvers, 17 rifles, 14 flintlock rifles and 1 light machine gun.[2] Formed on December 22, 1944, in a Tho settlement in Cao Bang province, on the border of China, this platoon was separated by several mountain ranges from the main Japanese military concentrations in the Red River Delta as well as from the more seasoned Tho units further to the south. The unit got its first taste of battle by attacking the small French-led militia outposts scattered throughout Cao Bang province, which were manned by only 450 troops.

The weapons captured in these attacks permitted the small guerrilla platoon to expand its strength through a tactic which set a pattern that was to be repeated on a vaster scale during the Indochina War. The Viet Minh attacks in this early period succeeded because the adversary was tied down in numerous static defense posts, which enabled the guerrillas to concentrate a relatively superior force in order to overwhelm the posts one at a time. Theoretically the militia could have adopted a mobile defense, but this would have inevitably left some of its territory unprotected, and the mountainous terrain, a natural habitat for guerrillas, would have circumscribed its mobility. Because the militia lacked extensive political ties to the Tho and was burdened with the legacy of Tho antagonism and revolt, its response was limited to ineffective static defense. From these isolated and modest victories the Viet Minh obtained the weapons to increase its Cao Bang contingent.

Despite their preparations the Communist-led guerrillas in the mountains of northern Viet Nam were still a relatively insignificant force when the Japanese *coup de force* occurred. In early March 1945 the whole "liberation force" numbered no more than a thousand men.[3] Moreover, the Viet Minh could not derive the maximum strength from its forces because there was no unified command to coordinate its operations. The Cao Bang forces under Giap's direct control were still not in operational

2 Democratic Republic of Viet Nam: *Ten Years of Fighting and Building of the Vietnamese People's Army*, p. 12.
3 Ibid., p. 14.

coordination with the more seasoned guerrillas in the heart of the Tho country to the south. But by taking advantage of the *coup de force,* the Viet Minh was able to disarm some French who were off their guard in attempting to escape the Japanese. This increased its fund of weapons and also reduced the obstacles to its movement, since the Japanese made no attempt to replace the French in their mountain defense positions. With greater freedom to maneuver, the Viet Minh, by the middle of April, succeeded in uniting its guerrilla troops around the mountain town of Cho Chu in Thai Nguyen province. Unaware that it had only four months to prepare its revolutionary bid for power to take advantage of the Japanese capitulation in August, the Viet Minh nevertheless launched the task with a determination and comprehensiveness unmatched by other Vietnamese groups.

Immediately upon learning of the Japanese *coup de force,* the Standing Bureau of the Central Committee of the Indochinese Communist Party met to consider the new situation. After their deliberation they issued an instruction which would guide their party and its Viet Minh front in the preparation for an insurrection against an occupation enemy that would, surprisingly, offer them no opposition. On the contrary their ostensible Japanese adversary would aid them passively at first, then actively. The results of the party meeting formally confirmed what all of its members must have known: ". . . conditions are not yet ripe for an uprising because" indecision did not yet prevail among the Japanese, the country as a whole was not yet ready to fight, and because "the 'neutral' strata of the population must necessarily go through a period of disillusionment with the disastrous results of the coup d'état before they give way to revolutionary forces. . . ."[4] Although the moment for a bid for power had not arrived, the *coup de force* had increased the potential for revolution by destroying existing authority, and the exploitation of this potential through political and military organization was the

<hr />

4 Democratic Republic of Viet Nam: *Breaking Our Chains: Documents of the Vietnamese Revolution of August 1945* (Hanoi: Foreign Languages Publishing House; 1960), pp. 8–9.

chief concern of the party. As the party assessed the situation, "French administration has completely disintegrated and the Japanese have not yet had time to set up as effective an apparatus of repression as that of the French."[5]

Two important events helping to increase revolutionary potential were the absence of Japanese troops in the highlands of northern Viet Nam—now held only by colonial militia remnants following the retreat of the French army into China—and the famine which ravaged the Red River Delta from March through May 1945, taking between 500,000 and 600,000 lives and sending urban rice prices soaring.[6] But if opportunities for revolutionary organization were available in the countryside, it was beyond the capacity of the modest Viet Minh cadre to take advantage of them. Yet the cities where the few determined cadres could be, and eventually did become, extremely effective were still tightly held by the Japanese, who, in the face of a potential Allied landing, were preoccupied with local continuity and stability.

Because of this dichotomy between revolutionary opportunity and capacity, the Standing Bureau instruction attempted to define a program which made best use of existing capacity while preparing for the exploitation of available and future opportunities. Due to the convulsiveness of events as well as the modesty of military organization and cadres, emphasis was placed on the psychological preparation of the population. In addition to slogans and printed matter this required the party to switch over to so-called "higher forms" of propaganda, including "parades, demonstrations, political strikes, public meetings, strikes in schools and markets, non-co-operation with the Japanese in all fields, opposition to the requisition of paddy [rice] and refusal to pay taxes."[7] Shock teams were to be formed to create new political-military bases, liberation committees were to be set up in factories, mines, villages, and public and private

5 Ibid., p. 28.

6 André Volait: *La vie économique et sociale du Viet Nam du 9 mars 1945 au 19 décembre 1946* (Paris: École Nationale de la France d'Outre-Mer, Section Afrique-Noire; 1948), p. 7.

7 Democratic Republic of Viet Nam: *Breaking Our Chains*, p. 13.

offices, while "People's Revolutionary Committees" were to be established in areas under Viet Minh control.[8]

Although the organization of this revolutionary structure was to lead to a provisional government, it was through guerrilla warfare that the party saw it could best "keep the initiative in the struggle to drive Japanese aggressors out of the country . . ."[9] But this analysis of the efficacy of guerrilla tactics in extending the party's revolutionary organization and gaining power from the Japanese was tempered with the warning that only where natural features of the country, such as mountain areas, were favorable was guerrilla warfare to be launched. However, within this framework, quickly laid down after the *coup de force,* a more specific program of guerrilla politics for exploiting revolutionary space was hammered out.

Following the arrival of Vo Nguyen Giap and his "liberation army" in the forward base area in Thai Nguyen province, the North Viet Nam Revolutionary Conference was convened by the Standing Bureau of the Central Committee of the party. As its first steps the conference unified the disparate guerrilla units which had been created under the auspices of the Viet Nam Liberation Army and placed it under the command of a Revolutionary Military Committee of North Viet Nam consisting of Vo Nguyen Giap, Chu Van Tan, and Van Tieng Dung. Moreover, the Military Committee was made the focal point of revolutionary activity by its responsibility for both "the political and military command of the resistance bases in north Viet Nam."[1] As a further advance toward a more coherent military command structure, four "resistance zones" were established in northern Viet Nam along with two in central and one in southern Viet Nam. Within these zones additional bases were to be created where conditions were auspicious, "as to natural features, mass organizations, food supplies, and a favourable balance of forces between ourselves and the enemy . . ." In northern Viet Nam these conditions were best met in the arc of mountains that

8 Ibid., p. 15.
9 Ibid., p. 16.
1 Democratic Republic of Viet Nam: *Thirty Years of Struggle of the Party,* p. 88.

surrounded the Red River Delta, where bases could "serve as spring boards for the general insurrection and constitute the nucleus of a future independent and free Viet Nam."[2]

Within the base area, guerrilla warfare became the principal form of struggle for both the consolidation of control over the territory and the expansion of the Viet Minh forces. In this initial phase of guerrilla warfare the Viet Minh placed a premium on the maintenance of its force and on the rule of attacking only when that would increase its strength. Thus, its operational watchword was "to ambush and attack the enemy by surprise in small engagements when we are quite certain of success."[3] These guerrilla tactics were closely coordinated with those of armed propaganda units, whose task included "repression of traitors, puppet notables, and ruffians, warnings to mandarins and puppet officials of villages, and cantons, opposition to requisitions of rice and refusal to pay taxes to the Japanese," which were to be linked with public speeches by shock teams in markets, transportation centers, schools, enterprises, and theaters.[4] Through techniques of this kind the modest Viet Minh resources were made to serve the purpose of extending the revolutionary organization by taking advantage of the mountain area, where the population was sparse and mobility difficult. By eliminating the existing remnants of the colonial administration or persuading its officials to become part of the People's Committees, the Communists were consolidating their hold. At the same time they were establishing a new organization to mobilize the mountain population for participation in revolution.

In early June 1945, six mountain provinces which had come under more than partial Viet Minh control—Cao Bang, Lang Son, Ha Gaing, Tuyen Quang. Thai Nguyen, and Bac Kan—were united into a single administrative entity known as the "Free Zone." A Provisional Committee was placed in charge of the Free Zone, assuming control from the Military Committee, which continued to exercise authority in the military sphere.

2 Ibid., p. 34.
3 Democratic Republic of Viet Nam: *Breaking Our Chains*, p. 36.
4 Democratic Republic of Viet Nam: *Thirty Years of Struggle of the Party*, p. 91.

These two committees were charged with executing a program broadened to include economic, cultural, and social affairs as well as political operations. Particular emphasis was given to a three-month program of heightened preparedness which indicated the specifics of the political mobilization the Viet Minh desired. Of primary importance there was to be a "mobilization of the minds of the masses," which was to be achieved by requiring each administrative district to have a propaganda committee. Its members were required to go into every village with theatricals, displays of force, and to hold meetings at which newspapers would be read and commented upon. The next step involved the organization and the development of the youth movement. This was followed by a program to unify all Viet Minh organizations up to the provincial level within three months, and from this framework there were expected to be significant results to give needed support to the military effort. Each village was expected to organize at least one self-defense group of twelve men in addition to a guerrilla group of five who were to be trained for operations outside the village. But the population of the base area was also to yield recruits for the Viet Nam liberation army, which was to create its first battalion-size unit during June 1945.[5]

Thus after two months of intensive effort, following years of experimentation and preparation, the Communists through their Viet Minh Front succeeded in establishing their hegemony over a territory with an estimated population of 856,000 persons. Of these only 12 to 15 per cent were Vietnamese, with many of them living in the foothills or adjoining lowlands beyond immediate control. But the Communists could claim to control a third of the territory of northern Viet Nam by virtue of the absence of political opposition in the 37,000 square kilometers of the six-province Free Zone. However, this made them masters of only 10 per cent of the population of Tonkin, a fact which emphasized the Communist isolation from the mass of the Vietnamese population.[6] Moreover, this underscored not only the features making

5 Democratic Republic of Viet Nam: *Breaking Our Chains*, pp. 52–7.
6 *Annuaire statistique de l'Indochine, 1934–1946*, p. 28.

the mountains a convenient base, but also the limitations on the Viet Minh expansion so long as it did not have ties to the delta heartland of northern Viet Nam.

While the Japanese *coup de force* had given the Viet Minh the chance to establish itself in the highlands, it had also created other opportunities which the consolidation of the base area helped to strengthen. The Viet Minh believed that the elimination of the French served to improve its "diplomatic" relations with the Allies, "because the Japanese aggressors have become our only enemy and because the revolutionary people have become the only forces fighting against the Japanese . . ."[7] Although the military occupation of the Japanese prevented the immediate seizure of power by the Viet Minh, it offered advantages which might not have occurred had Japanese authority collapsed simultaneously with that of the French and been followed by a quick Allied intervention. Based on the experience of New Guinea and other Pacific islands, the Allies had good reason to suspect that the Japanese resistance would be protracted and tenacious. The swiftness of the Japanese surrender was not anticipated in the late spring and early summer of 1945, since the bomb that was to bring that quick collapse only received its final tests in Alamogordo on July 16, 1945. For the Viet Minh, being recognized as the only effective anti-Japanese group inside Viet Nam brought opportunities from both the United States and France. The overriding concern of the French was the reestablishment of their colonial sovereignty in Indochina, while the interests of the Americans were on immobilizing the Japanese troops from participating in other war theaters or opposing an Allied landing in Viet Nam. For both allies there was a convergence of purpose in seeking to work with the Viet Minh.

After numerous tentative communications with the Viet Minh through intermediaries, a French reconnaissance detachment was ordered by Jean Sainteny, the chief of the French military mission in Kunming, to move south from Tsin Tsi in Kwangsi province into northern Viet Nam's adjoining province of Cao Bang. On July 2, 1945, it made contact with the local Viet Minh author-

7 Democratic Republic of Viet Nam: *Breaking Our Chains*, p. 28.

ities, who, significantly, were Tho. Through them a request was made for Viet Minh assistance in infiltrating French troops into the Red River Delta. Under the pretext that they would have to refer this proposal to higher authorities for decision, the local Viet Minh indicated that it would take about two months to get an answer. In turn the Viet Minh representatives in Cao Bang asked that they be given arms and instructors in order to continue their activity against the Japanese. Whether or not in response to this specific plea, a mixed Franco-American mission of six men was parachuted into Viet Minh headquarters on July 16, 1945.[8] Their liaison prepared the way for airdrops of arms, ammunition, and other supplies, which did much to transform the Viet Minh from a ragged bunch of irregulars into units that had standardized weapons if not an extensive degree of military training.[9]

Even though it appears widely accepted that the Viet Minh received external material aid during its preinsurrectionary preparation, the size of this assistance and its impact on the August Revolution have been less well known.[1] Without being able to determine the precise circumstances, it seems certain that approximately 5,000 weapons were air-dropped to the Viet Minh during the summer of 1945.[2] Certainly it is not coincidental that the number of Viet Minh regular troops at the moment of the Japanese capitulation, both claimed by the Communists and estimated by the French, was 5,000 men.[3] Although the weapons

8 Jean Sainteny: *Histoire d'une paix manquée: Indochine 1945–1947* (Paris: Amiot-Dumont; 1953), pp. 57–8.

9 A comparable experience of arming a psychologically indoctrinated but militarily untutored guerrilla force for anti-Japanese purposes occurred in Malaya. See Lucian Pye: *Guerrilla Communism in Malaya* (Princeton: Princeton University Press; 1956), pp. 68–9.

1 "In 1944 he [Ho Chi Minh] created an Army of Liberation and our OSS dropped supplies and ammunition to help it carry on guerrilla activities against the Japanese." William O. Douglas: *North From Malaya, Adventure on Five Fronts* (Garden City, N.Y.: Doubleday and Company; 1953), p. 165. Also Thomas E. Dewey: *Journey to the Far Pacific* (Garden City, N.Y.: Doubleday and Company; 1952), p. 215. Bernard B. Fall: *The Two Viet Nams: A Political and Military Analysis* (New York and London: Frederick A. Praeger; 1963), p. 100.

2 These arms included 3,000 rifles and carbines, 1,000 Colt 45-caliber pistols, 600 Thompson submachine guns, and an undetermined number of 50-mm. mortars and bazookas.

3 Democratic Republic of Viet Nam: *Ten Years of Fighting and Building of the Vietnamese People's Army*, p. 15.

supplied the Viet Minh were of American manufacture and the Americans were virtually the only Allied force having the air capability in the area for such an undertaking, the material support of the Viet Minh was not a unilateral policy of the United States. The French were also interested in the Viet Minh as a client force, beyond their request for assistance in infiltrating their men into the Red River Delta and in the parachuting of their teams into the mountain base area. In an interview in early 1947 with the East Asian correspondent of *The New York Times*, Robert Trumbull, there is significant information in this regard. It comes from an anonymous French official in Hanoi who is described as a member of the highest echelon of the French administration in northern Viet Nam and a former French resistance figure. This personality seems to be Jean Sainteny, a celebrated resistance hero in France who at the time of this interview was French commissioner for northern Viet Nam. Commenting on the character and the consequences of French policy toward the Viet Minh, the official said:

> Ironically, the Viet Minh received aid from us because the Allies thought they were fighting the Japanese. The first French agents dropped into Tonkin made contact with the Viet Minh and supplied them with arms, including the Sten guns that are now being used against the French . . . so the mass of the population said "These Viet Minh have the aid of the Allies; they are strong, they are the champions of the nationalists, they have destroyed the mandarinal system" . . . which was unpopular with the masses because all authority is unpopular. The Viet Minh told them, "Now you are a free people."[4]

Since the weapons air-dropped to the Viet Minh in northern Viet Nam before the Japanese capitulation were a small part of the more than 80,000 weapons it was estimated to possess when open warfare broke out in December 1946, the observation of the French official suggests that the greater long-range impact of the aid was psychological rather than material. While these

4 *The New York Times*, interview on January 21, 1947, printed January 23, 1947, p. 16. Copyright 1947 by The New York Times Company, Reprinted by permission.

weapons permitted the Viet Minh to enter Hanoi in force on August 19, 1945, it was the acquiescence of the Japanese rather than Viet Minh strength which ensured Communist predominance over the disoriented Vietnamese caretaker government. Moreover, the view that the deterioration in the respect for or compliance with the established pattern of authority was one of the principal effects of the aid to the Viet Minh tends to reinforce the earlier observation of Paul Mus. It was not so much the elimination of colonial administrative and military personnel, as its consequences for the Vietnamese attitude toward the French hegemony that was the real significance of the Japanese intervention.

In the gap between the loss of French authority and the absence of any other authority, the Viet Minh came forward to fulfill routine tasks such as settling everyday disputes and disagreements, registering transactions, and maintaining order against the insecurities of the period.[5] Complemented by its propaganda but limited by its meager cadres, these measures served to win acceptance for the Viet Minh. The Communists, becoming ever immaculate in their nationalist garb, were also able to extend their influence beyond the reach of their cadres; shrewdly they endowed with a new legitimacy those locally influential groups which lacked any larger identity. They merely called upon them to form liberation committees in order to participate in the fight for independence. These committees served to structure the gaps of revolutionary space and to provide a justification and direction for what might otherwise have been random and halfhearted protest.[6] Success in actions of this kind was in no small part due to the feeble efforts of the Japanese and their Vietnamese associates to create an acceptable alternative authority. Because of the lack of real competition in filling this gap, the Communists were able to galvanize many of the politically influential behind them.

While the preparations of the preinsurrectionary period had demonstrated its growing capacity to carry out guerrilla politics

5 Democratic Republic of Viet Nam: *Thirty Years of Struggle of the Party*, p. 91.
6 Ibid.

in the countryside, the Viet Minh was aware that "it was in the three big cities: Hanoi, Hue, and Saigon, that the August general insurrection . . . [would win] victories of a main and decisive meaning."[7] Even though these guerrilla bases and forces would be vital to the Viet Minh after the August Revolution had run its course, they were a complementary rather than a decisive factor in winning control over Hanoi and Hue, and the lack of such bases in the south was not the key determinant in the loss of Saigon. These guerrilla forces were another psychological tool in the arsenal of a political movement which, during the Japanese occupation, had shrewdly adapted itself to the goals of a broader segment of Vietnamese society and developed more flexible revolutionary techniques than they had displayed during the 1920's and 1930's.

This acceleration of Viet Minh influence resulted from a subtle though fundamental transformation within the Vietnamese Communist movement. In personalities it reflected the return of Ho Chi Minh from almost a decade of aloofness from Vietnamese politics as well as the rise of two indigenously cultivated party activists, Truong Chinh and Vo Nguyen Giap. Contrasted with their impetuous Moscow-trained southern Viet Nam counterparts, these men devised techniques of political mobilization and guerrilla warfare which by their sophistication and appropriateness created new dimensions of power for Communism in Viet Nam.

The guiding spirit of these innovations was a new-found meaning for and identity with nationalism, which led to the formation of organizations for popular participation in politics. As this goal had become more attainable through the Japanese occupation, culminating in the capitulation, the Viet Minh was virtually the only Vietnamese group to exploit these fluid circumstances by a broad appeal based on nationalism. Within this context the Viet Minh's nationalism did not include any more specific definition than the goal of independence, and probably did not require it until the question of parochial autonomy among local groups clashed with central party control.

7 Ibid. p. 94.

Feeding upon the relief felt at the demise of the colonial administration and upon the anxiety over the uncertain consequences of a French return, the Viet Minh won wide support for their advocacy of independence.

Complementing their capacity for decisive if not widespread action, this psychological conditioning of an anxious population through a nationalist idiom prepared the Viet Minh for its bid for power. In this task the one thousand armed troops that entered Hanoi on August 19, 1945, while a tangible manifestation of the advantages to the Communists from the occupation interlude, were not the decisive element in the successful seizure of power. Their source of strength had come from a fundamental change in political strategy that resulted in the party's adapting itself effectively to the requirements for mobilizing political power and articulating the nationalist aspirations of those Vietnamese who were determined to end French rule.

CHAPTER 13 ✿ ✿ ✿

POLITICAL MOBILIZATION

DURING THE OCCUPATION

✿

✿

✿

It was through the elimination of the French administration and the acquiescence to the Viet Minh take-over that the Japanese contributed most conspicuously to revolution in Viet Nam. However, their direct aid to diverse Vietnamese political groups and their sponsorship of the trappings of independence did much, in an often contradictory manner, to develop the nationalist sentiment which the Communists capitalized upon. On March 11, 1945, only two days after the *coup de force,* the Japanese prompted Emperor Bao Dai to issue a declaration from his royal capital at Hue in which he abrogated the French Treaty of Protection of 1884 and proclaimed the independence of Annam.[1] Such an act could serve only to tantalize Vietnamese nationalists, for the declaration failed to use the name Viet Nam and it significantly left the area of southern Viet Nam (Cochin-

1 Text of remarks in Devillers: *Histoire du Viet Nam,* p. 125.

china)—legally still a French colony—in the hands of the Japanese.

This continued separate status for the south reflected a special Japanese interest in the area. Their purpose was to use the south as a guerrilla base where they felt they could more easily tie down an Allied invasion force, immobilizing it from activity against Japanese positions in China or the home islands.[2] If the south were left under Japanese control without an intervening layer of indigenous government, it would permit the necessary political base for guerrilla warfare to be developed more conveniently. Although this special interest in the south was to cause substantial political tension during the August Revolution, it had originated in Japanese desires for preparedness and stability. Again for strategic reasons, stability was the over-riding concern, and this fact led to another anomalous situation; the French administration, though disarmed, had not been totally eliminated. Therefore,

> When the Japanese replaced the French administration on 9 March 1945, they were anxious to avoid any economic or administrative dislocation which might interfere with military security for they believed an invasion of the country was possible at any moment. They were willing, therefore, to maintain the French in the lower brackets of administration. . . .[3]

However, after a month the French began to disappear rapidly from the scene and the Japanese were pressed to set up a more substantial Vietnamese regime. While their diffuse programs in the south appeared to serve short-run Japanese purposes, they decided it was necessary to replace the monarchical government at Hue, headed by Pham Quynh.

The selection of a new administration was not as simple as it might have seemed. The Japanese found themselves faced with a disputatiousness and unconciliatory attitude among the nationalists, which was later to frustrate the French in their attempts to

2 Mus: *Problèmes de l'Indochine contemporaine*, P.M. V, pp. 5–6.
3 Elsbree: *Japan's Role in Southeast Asian Nationalist Movements*, p. 97.

"choose and form" a nationalist alternative. Ngo Dinh Diem, who had proven a stubborn bargainer for political advantage with the Japanese in preceding years, was the almost unanimous choice of the Vietnamese non-Communist political elite. But maintaining a political hostility against Bao Dai which dated from 1933 and which continued until his assassination in 1963, Ngo Dinh Diem refused to form a government under the Emperor of Annam.[4] Perhaps it was wisest for Diem not to accept the auspices of the Japanese when their defeat seemed so near and their benediction so unpromising for future prestige.

Yet the importance of his unconciliatory behavior for nationalist politics was that Diem's alternative was to retire to the inactivity of his study, leaving the field of political conflict to others. Consequently, it was out of a desire to take what opportunity there was to get a nationalist political force in motion that Tran Trong Kim agreed on April 17, 1945, to form a Vietnamese government. Unhappily for the development of an effective and coherent nationalism, the contributions of this government were minimal. However, these initial efforts of non-Communist politicians, circumscribed as they were by the control of the Japanese, were illustrative of characteristics which limited their success in the August Revolution as well as their nationalist successors throughout the years up until the present.

The majority of the officials and supporters of the Tran Trong Kim government were members or sympathizers of the *Đại Việt Quốc Dân Đảng,* or Great Viet Nam Nationalist Party, known as the Dai Viet. The Dai Viet had been formed among university students in Hanoi in the autumn of 1940, in the hope that the Japanese occupation would help their nationalist cause.[5] The party had immediately suffered a setback at the hands of the Sûreté, although it remained clandestinely alive among the Hanoi students and was reconstituted with Japanese encouragement in 1945, when it underwent a major transformation. While the student origin of the Dai Viet remained significant, the party

4 Devillers: *Histoire du Viet Nam,* p. 126.
5 Dabezies: "Forces politiques au Viet Nam," p. 140.

now became the focus of what has been called the "bourgeois nationalists."[6] These men had advanced through the French education system to receive the very highest degrees and subsequently to enjoy positions of importance in the colonial life and administration of Indochina. The background of Tran Trong Kim, who has written the most comprehensive popular history of the country in the Vietnamese language and who was an education inspector in the colonial administration, is a good example of those of his political associates.

In the Tran Trong Kim cabinet there were four medical doctors, a professor, and a distinguished jurist, Tran Van Chuong, who was considered the mainspring of the government, which comprised individuals who had received many privileges in a land where there were few available.[7] Their political experience had been intense, but it had also been limited to what might be called "elite politics." Their activities prior to March 1945 had not included years of frustrated attempts to establish a popular political organization, but had centered on the infighting for educational opportunity, official position, and that elusive quality known best to colonial upper classes, "prestige." The anti-French spirit they manifested was emphatically not a rejection of French culture, but a result of their impatience at being blocked in their occupational mobility within a French-made framework just short of managing the affairs of their country. And while this characterization obviously cannot cover all of the diverse personalities and groups attracted to the Tran Trong Kim government, it does typify its decision-making core and can begin to explain why the August Revolution was a Communist and not a nationalist affair.

The popular reaction to the Japanese *coup de force* which Paul Mus observed in the Vietnamese countryside was also present in the cities and provincial towns. Here it was expressed by the expansion of the Vietnamese-language press and the

6 Ibid.
7 The composition of the cabinet is in Devillers: *Histoire du Viet Nam,* p. 128. Tran Van Chuong, a close confident of Ngo Dinh Diem, was the Ambassador to the United States from 1954-63 and is the father of Diem's sister-in-law, the widely known Mme Ngo Dinh Nhu.

organization of public demonstrations, all of which reflected a spontaneity far short of mass uprising. Conscious of the importance of these sentiments, the Tran Trong Kim government attempted to respond, but on the whole its actions, reflecting its training, were bureaucratic and legalistic. Through the pronouncements of Emperor Bao Dai there was a commitment to the preparation of a written constitution which was to be based on principles of religious and political liberty. The constitution never appeared, but there was an administrative reform unifying the old monarchical bureaucratic structure with the parallel French-created one, although this did not notably increase efficiency.[8] At the beginning of July 1945 in some of its most popular measures the Tran Trong Kim government proclaimed the name of the country as "Viet Nam," adopted a national anthem, and unfurled a national flag of three horizontal crimson stripes on a yellow background which is still in use today. Finally and grudgingly on August 8, after the bomb on Hiroshima had sounded the knell for the Japanese, the occupation authorities turned back sovereignty over the southern area, Cochinchina, to the imperial government at Hue. Thus for the first time since 1864, the country was united under its historic name of Viet Nam, but this unity, the object of subsequent unending fratricidal conflict, was resilient enough to last only a little less than two weeks.[9]

In sharp contrast to these formal and bureaucratic measures which might have been expected from the personalities directing the Tran Trong Kim government, there was also action which reflected another important facet of its political resources. Organizational activity and the stimulation of political participation among the youth of Viet Nam had more long-range consequences than almost any other effort initiated by the Dai Viet-backed government. The impact of these efforts was in large measure due to the social changes occurring during the war which had affected the attitudes and expectations of Vietnamese

8 Ibid., p. 129.
9 Ibid.

youth. Paradoxically, these changes resulted from a range of activities included in the educational and sports programs inaugurated by the administration of Admiral Decoux. Fearing that the Japanese would capture the sympathies of Vietnamese youth through their propaganda and desiring to win to the allegiance of France the future leaders of Indochina, Decoux had expanded social and educational opportunities as a pragmatic alternative. In four years 4,800 additional rural schools were created, and the total students at all schools increased by a half from 450,000 in 1939 to 700,000 in 1944. Particular emphasis was given to the University of Hanoi, where a school of science and a school of architecture were created and a *cité universitaire* constructed as a center for student activities.[1]

Parallel to this expansion of educational opportunities was the formation of a youth and sports corps structured around a selected cadre. These young people were brought to the southern coastal town of Phan Thiet for training as group leaders and then returned to their localities to organize teams for gymnastics, soccer, and other mass-participation sports. At the height of the development of this corps there were about 86,000 young people all over Indochina regularly participating in the programs, led by an additional 1,016 cadre members.[2] One of the major purposes of these educational and sports programs was to "safeguard French grandeur," to use the words of Admiral Decoux, but the practical effect was to heighten the social consciousness of the participants and give them experience in organization and group discipline.[3] While pledging an athlete's oath to the French flag and pronouncing the Vichy slogan of "Family, Work, Country," the young Vietnamese were being initiated into social patterns that would later be transferred to other loyalties. Although available statistics are conflicting, it would seem probable that the organized sporting youth combined with their less disciplined student colleagues must have

1 *Annuaire statistique de l'Indochine, 1943–1946*, pp. 273–4, and Decoux: *À la barre de l'Indochine*, p. 403.
2 Ducoroy: *Ma trahison en Indochine*, p. 103.
3 Decoux: *À la barre de l'Indochine*, p. 401.

added approximately 500,000 young persons to the mobilized population.[4]

While the French were responsible for the social mobilization of this wide segment of the youth of Viet Nam, it was left to the Japanese and to the enterprising members of the Tran Trong Kim government to make political capital of this reservoir of talent. In the spring of 1945 they launched programs giving the youth a political organization and, under Japanese sponsorship in southern Viet Nam, a partial militarization. It was a thirty-three-year-old lawyer, Phan Anh, minister of youth in the Dai Viet government; his talented assistant, Ta Quang Buu; and in southern Viet Nam, under Japanese auspices, Dr. Pham Ngoc Thach who were responsible for giving political direction to Vietnamese youth.[5] The distinctiveness of the program in the south was due to the particular political interests the Japanese had in connection with their preparations to resist a potential Allied invasion. The swampy and mountainous Cambodian–southern Viet Nam border region seems to have been chosen by the Japanese as the center of a resistance area from which guerrilla war would be launched at the rear of the Allies as they pushed northward through Viet Nam.[6]

The effectiveness of this guerrilla scheme required that the Japanese have a close accord with indigenous groups for assistance and flexibility. Since the activities and membership of the Sports and Youth movement had been concentrated in the south, it lent itself to a transformation, on July 2, 1945, into the *Thanh Niên Tiên Phong,* or Advanced Guard Youth, which formed the nucleus of an indigenous army. This paramilitary unit became the special preserve of its organizer, Pham Ngoc Thach, who led the Advanced Guard Youth to a decisive role in the August Revolution in the south, where they fought tena-

4 United States Department of State, Office of Intelligence and Research, and Analysis Branch, OIR Report #3369, 10 August 1945, *Programs of Japan in Indochina.* This contains monitored broadcasts of Radio Saigon which on November 8, 1943, said the total membership of the Movement of Sports and Youth was 800,000 (p. 331), on December 7, 1943, the figure of 690,000 was used (p. 356), and on August 8, 1944, the figure of 240,000 (p. 339).

5 Devillers: *Histoire du Viet Nam,* pp. 127–8.

6 Mus: *Problèmes de l'Indochine contemporaine,* P.M. V, p. 6.

ciously against the reoccupying French. To the charge that in the Advanced Guard Youth the Vichy colonial regime had merely trained the forces to expel France from Indochina, Admiral Decoux retorted:

> The truth is that the youth of Indochina have not been more traitorous to the French cause than have been the soldiers formed under our discipline, or than the students or intellectuals of this messy country have been to French culture. . . . The crime is not that. It is imputable to Frenchmen who, by their foolishness or ambition, made inevitable the *coup de force* of the Japanese of 9 March 1945, creating an extremely dangerous hiatus in the exercise of our sovereignty in Indochina.[7]

Following a pattern similar to that of the Advanced Guard Youth, both Phan Anh and Ta Quang Buu joined their Dai Viet youth with the Viet Minh upon the outbreak of the August Revolution.[8] They took with them their youthful followers, drawn largely from the students at the University of Hanoi, who had been given their opportunity for higher education through the program of Admiral Decoux. The wartime governor-general's action expanding higher education had been based on the belief that those Vietnamese educated in France had, upon their return, only infrequently found positions commensurate with their preparation and expectations. This he attributed to the fact that no requirements were placed on their curriculum, with the consequence that their preparation usually bore little relationship to needs and opportunities in Viet Nam. The admiral's remedy was to expand the University of Hanoi by emphasizing schools for professional training in order to tie a university education more closely to existing and anticipated occupational requirements.[9]

Had this trend been understood and acted upon during the 1930's, it might have served to establish more of an identity with France among the emerging Vietnamese elite. As it turned out, Decoux's *cité universitaire* provided the revolutionary set-

7 In preface to Ducoroy: *Ma trahison en Indochine*, p. 16.
8 Dabezies: "Forces politiques au Viet Nam," p. 141.
9 Decoux: *À la barre de l'Indochine*, pp. 397–8.

ting, on August 21, 1945, for a meeting of the General Association of Students, which demanded the abdication of Emperor Bao Dai and called for the formation of a government of national union under the Viet Minh.[1] In this crippling move the Tran Trong Kim government was to a significant extent undermined by the efforts of its defecting youth leaders, who had gained their strength from the student origins of the Dai Viet Party. The irony of these wartime developments was thus compounded: Decoux, with hopes of winning the allegiance of Vietnamese youth through expanding their opportunities for education, had facilitated the organization of an anti-French student movement; Tran Trong Kim's interim Dai Viet government, in hopes of broadening its base of popular strength, had encouraged the political organization of university students who were to be the very ones to demand its overthrow.

Of far greater impact than these defections upon the Tran Trong Kim government's capacity to establish a countrywide nationalist movement was the intense emphasis of Japanese political and military programs in southern Viet Nam after the *coup de force*. This was a separate and almost contradictory activity from their support of the Dai Viet government at Hue. There were historical reasons for this divisive effort, since Japanese political programs in southern Viet Nam, having begun at the outset of 1942, had antedated similar activity in other parts of Indochina. Their decision to focus operations in the south was due in part to the fact that the non-Communist Vietnamese opposition to the French had been more conspicuous there and that Japanese officials had interests which had been cultivated before the start of the war. One of the key Japanese figures in this operation was a businessman named Matsushita who had opened an export-import firm in Indochina in 1925, known as the Dai Nan Koosi. This firm had a rather lusterless career and in 1938, after committing "indiscretions," Matsushita was asked to leave the country. Following the Japanese occupation Matsushita returned to use his Dai Nan Koosi as a cover for espionage and clandestine political activity in southern

1 Devillers: *Histoire du Viet Nam*, p. 137.

Viet Nam. At the same time the prewar Japanese consul general in Saigon, Yoshio Minoda, was placed in charge of similar activities in the north. While overt support for Vietnamese political groups did not result from this network until 1943, clandestine activity, frequently in lively competition with the French Sûreté, did take place.

The vigorous opposition of the religious-political sects to the French in southern Viet Nam and the concern over reprisals against them caused the Japanese to become involved in the early part of the occupation in specific issues of Vietnamese politics. By 1938 the Cao Dai were the largest folk religious sect in southern Viet Nam, with approximately 300,000 followers. In the first blush of enthusiasm over the French defeat in Europe and the Japanese occupation in Indochina, they attempted to extend their religious organization overtly into politics. But their initiative provoked a stern reaction from the French authorities who deported their pope, Pham Cong Tac, to Madagascar and occupied the papal see in Tay Ninh, west of Saigon, on December 27, 1941. In his prewar activities Matsushita had been in touch with the Cao Dai, for they had expressed interest in the establishment of Prince Cuong De on the throne of Viet Nam as part of a neotraditionalist reform movement which would bring wider status and prestige to the sect. Being a close friend of the exiled prince—who remained the symbol of the monarchical restoration movement, the Phuc Quoc—Matsushita capitalized upon this tie to gain a position of influence with the Cao Dai. He was, however, unable to prevent the deportation of their pope in 1942, an event which complicated his goal of gaining local political influence. Matsushita then had to find a leader who could bring some coherence to the now faction-ridden and disorganized Cao Dai sect; ultimately he decided on Tran Quang Vinh, whose activities after 1943 greatly stimulated the political consciousness of the sect. Although the Cao Dai were increasingly prepared for action, it was not until the imminence of an Allied landing that the Japanese made use of the political capacities that Vinh had developed.[2]

2 Ibid., p. 91.

A similar sort of Japanese relationship developed with the Hoa Hao. The founder and spiritual chief of this folk religion, Huynh Phu So, was felt by the French to be exercising too great an opposition to them even though they kept him under careful surveillance, in house arrest. Unlike their acquiescence to the deportation of the Cao Dai pope, the Japanese intervened to prevent Huynh Phu So from being sent out of the country and thereby won the confidence of the Hoa Hao sect. With these loyalties from the Hoa Hao and the Cao Dai giving the Japanese political roots in the Vietnamese countryside, they hoped to create a structured force in southern Viet Nam's politics. It was for this reason that they sponsored the formation of the *Việt Nam Phục Quốc Đồng Minh,* or Viet Nam Restoration League, under the leadership of Tran Van An.[3]

The Japanese seemed to desire a political movement which would encompass both the rural folk religions and the parties which had developed among the more sophisticated urban population. Because of its continuity with the monarchy and its traditionalist orientation, the national renovation movement appeared to the occupation authorities to offer the best means for bridging the wide political spectrum which the Japanese wished to cultivate. If this coalition had become a reality, it would have given its creators a flexibility and a depth of influence in Vietnamese politics that would have been unmatched by subsequent non-Communist movements. But the Japanese and their protégés were unable to escape the pitfalls which also were to ensnare their successors. The political distance between the rural sects and the urban-based parties was too great for them to be joined together by the Phuc Quoc Dong Minh. It was not an impossible task, although it has yet to be achieved by any non-Communist Vietnamese political movement. Certainly, the Japanese approach to the problem maximized their chances for failure.

Tran Van An, a Trotskyite lacking strong legitimate ties to the monarchical restoration movement in Vietnamese politics,

3 Ibid.

was a poor choice to lead a broad political coalition.[4] The Japanese had tried to get Ngo Dinh Diem to head such a campaign when the plans for its formation were taking shape. Diem was the most prominent and authentic link to the monarchical restoration element in Vietnamese politics. His father, Ngo Dinh Kha, had been responsible for preserving what prerogatives the monarchy continued to enjoy under the French, and Diem himself maintained a close friendship with Prince Cuong De until the latter's death in 1950. However, Diem refused these, as well as later, Japanese overtures and probably ended any real chance that Cuong De ever had of returning to prominence from exile.[5]

In addition to problems of leadership the Japanese never really attempted to make their Phuc Quoc Dong Minh a countrywide movement. It seems clear that their purpose was to provide the political base for guerrilla resistance in the south rather than to create a successor government to the French colonial regime. This could explain why they made no effort to bring the genuine Phuc Quoc leadership from exile in south China or Japan into the center of their occupation plans for Vietnamese politics, and why no relationship was established between the Phuc Quoc Dong Minh and the monarchy under Bao Dai. Because they were unwilling to take the steps necessary to make their Phuc Quoc a credible countrywide movement, it proved incapable of serving even the regional purposes of the Japanese.

Since they could not develop an effective political coalition in southern Viet Nam, the Japanese adopted a policy of militarizing certain Vietnamese groups to involve them in the anticipated resistance to Allied amphibious landings in the country. As a result, some parochial elements acquired the armed means of asserting their autonomous purposes. Their new strength intensified the political friction among the Vietnamese factions and made the problem of the creation of central institutions and political integration more difficult.

It is not surprising that the Cao Dai were the first to undergo

4 Ibid.
5 Ibid., pp. 93–4.

this militarization, since they had the strongest relationship with the Japanese. Under the cover of a Japanese naval construction project, Cao Dai followers were assembled on the edge of Saigon, where they were given military training and equipment, and with a strength of 3,000 men, units were formed which became known as the Bạch Mũ Đoàn (the White Berets) and the Nội Ứng Nghĩa Binh (the Volunteers of the Interior).[6] By contrast the arming of the Hoa Hao is obscure and was probably done, if at all, on a most rudimentary scale, which suggests that it occurred not so much by the design of the Japanese as by consequence of the availability of weapons in the occupation environment. The culmination of the Japanese military transformation of southern Vietnamese politics was the creation of the Advanced Guard Youth in the summer of 1945. That group became the core of a much touted volunteer army which—so Radio Tokyo announced on June 29, 1945—was being created in Indochina.

Since these forces were never utilized directly by the Japanese, the most significant feature of this militarization was its impact on the August Revolution and therefore on the course of Vietnamese politics. It was not just that the capacity and expectations of divergent Vietnamese interests were increased, but that these militarized groups were exclusively concentrated in the south, that gave a special character to the revolution. In the north the militarization of Vietnamese politics was the exclusive affair of the Viet Minh, aided initially by Allied airdrops and later by Japanese aquiescence to confiscation of former French armament. Meanwhile, the Tran Trong Kim government was allowed to develop no military establishment at all and had theoretically available to it as an instrument of authority only the truncated remnant of the colonial militia, which had consisted of only 18,000 men in all Viet Nam before the *coup de force* (of course, the Dai Viet regime could not have expected to control the 3,500 of these militiamen in Cochinchina). With its political deficiencies, it is doubtful that the government at Hue could have employed an armed force

6 Dabezies: "Forces politiques au Viet Nam," p. 139.

decisively, but the lack of a forceful extension of its authority merely condemned it further to the periphery of Vietnamese politics.

With the Communists forming the largest military force in the north and the various Japanese-supported groups increasing their armed strength in the south, it seems that the Tran Trong Kim government could have overcome its potent opposition only by a penetrating psychological program. This might have developed as a complement to armed force as was successfully done by its competitors, but such a psychological appeal, necessarily nationalist in content, was beyond the talent of Dai Viet politicians. Moreover, the fact that the Japanese did not incorporate those groups affected by occupation political activities into the structure of one central government, even formally or superficially, until their surrender was near caused further difficulties for the Hue government in mounting a nationalist campaign. By their encouragement of so many conflicting interests and their generally inept efforts to coordinate indigenous political groups, the Japanese set the stage for fractricidal clashes which were to sap potentially nationalist energies and give the tightly structured Communists one of their major advantages. Of course, the parochial and unconciliatory forces within Vietnamese society were certainly not of Japanese creation, but their encouragement made these interests more difficult to resolve.

Obviously, out of their concern for expediency in the wartime situation, the Japanese never considered their task from the point of view of building institutions for a stable nation-state in Viet Nam. Yet it is significant that the consequences of their occupation undercut whatever potential effectiveness a country-wide successor government might have had. Sharp antagonisms resulted from Japan's conflicting political operations in the various regions of Viet Nam. Paradoxically, it was the French who profited initially from this intensification of parochialism and regionalism. After their reoccupation they were able to detach the parochial groups, especially the folk religions, from the Viet Minh nationalist coalition. However, the French found, as the Japanese had, in their attempts at developing political coherence that the religious-political sects among the rural people were difficult to combine with the political parties among the urban population. The common experience of both the French and the Japanese was that the political parties, with the notable exception of the Communists, were fractious and ineffective in mass political techniques.

As a general rule Vietnamese parties have not had the capacity to expand their organizations into mass-based totalitarian monoliths, as have the Communists. Yet each of them has acted as though it were already the predominant force in a single-party state. Either as a cause or effect of this attitude, the parties have not possessed the abilities of compromise and bargaining necessary to maintain stable political coalitions. Thus they have been caught in a dilemma of being unable to grow autonomously and unwilling to expand through alliances. And since no one group, the Communists included, has yet to become totally predominant, it seems that the parochial tendencies of Vietnamese society have been an effective barrier to countrywide political organization and integration. But these objective limits have been less of an obstacle to non-Communist political movements than other considerations.

Although this is primarily a study of Communist revolutionary strategy, it has become so because of the absence of a revolutionary doctrine on the part of the Vietnamese nationalists. They had, it seems, anticipated no possibility of seizing power upon the expected downfall of the Japanese. Apparently they had no contingency planning and they had within the Tran Trong Kim government no motivation to form a military organization even in skeletal form. Yet the lack of tactics related to the competition for power was only one aspect of the absence of a specific concept of revolutionary politics. Unlike the Communists, they seemed not to appreciate the political consequences of the structure of Viet Nam's colonial society, nor of the need for symbols and effective phrases to interpret the turbulent events of the Japanese occupation and capitulation to at least the urban population of Viet Nam. Because of these shortcomings they were unable to win wide support in opposing the return of the French. Also beyond their understanding in the August Revolution was the relationship of political organization to forms of armed struggle and seizure of power.

This sharp contrast in outlook, expectations, and capacities was a not-unexpected consequence of the difference in political background among Vietnamese political activists. The Communist leadership consisted of a Moscow-trained as well as a Chinese-influenced cadre who had carefully absorbed the theory and tactics of Marxism-Leninism and had applied them to their own environment in analyses of Vietnamese society. By comparison the nationalists had received little overseas political training and their preparation had been almost exclusively in technical and functional areas. In their political activities at home they had been devastated by the efficiency of the Sûreté and by their own organizational incompetence. Consequently, this gap in political experience and ability between the Communists and their disoriented nationalist adversaries was to be manifested clearly during the August Revolution and through the seven years of revolutionary war as a decisive characteristic of Vietnamese politics.

If it was this disparity in political ability that was ultimately the crucial determinant between the political factions in the August Revolution, rather than any tangible advantage or military capacity, then the Japanese occupation did not so much contribute to the development of this talent as give it the opportunity to be demonstrated. This is not to minimize the effect of the occupation in accentuating most of the existing trends in Vietnamese politics. Moreover, the Vietnamese had the occupation as a foil against which to sharpen their abilities. On numerous occasions, from the Lang Son revolt through the *coup de force* to the capitulation, their political sensitivity was obviously heightened and their practical experience deepened. Also, there can be no minimizing the specific advantages of the *coup de force* and of the capitulation, for even though the indigenous political groups had increased their capacity during the occupation, they were still very far from being able to eliminate by themselves the colonial apparatus of authority and compliance.

However, from the perspective of the occupation of 1940–5, the aspect of the August Revolution which seems most in need of emphasis is not the Japanese destruction of colonial authority. Rather it is the Vietnamese ability to exploit this opportunity to seize such instruments of authority as were available and to develop new structures for holding power. No uniform country-wide response to this opportunity occurred, and by its regional variation the revolution reflected the diversity and complexity of Vietnamese politics. But without this response attempting to fill the void left by the Japanese, there would have been no revolution. There would undoubtedly have been bids for territorial hegemony such as the Hoa Hao were to make in the Mekong Delta, and appeals for international recognition as voiced by the sinecure government at Hue. In themselves these were, strictly speaking, revolutionary acts, but they were paltry when compared with the comprehensive assertions of sovereignty which the Viet Minh articulated. These were based on claims of nationalist legitimacy and sustained by structures of political strength.

While comparable opportunities for revolutionary expression were unavailable prior to the Japanese occupation, the revolutionary capacity to exploit what occasions arose was also absent. Not only did the Japanese occupation and capitulation lay open Vietnamese society to virtually any form of social protest, especially by the removal of almost all formal restraints in August 1945, they also witnessed a maturation among the revolutionaries. It was this change—most pronounced among the Vietnamese Communists, who responded to the Japanese intervention by forming the Viet Minh Front and establishing guerrilla bases in the mountainous Tho country—that had fundamental consequences for the August Revolution. Although the Japanese had contributed both directly and indirectly to increasing the capacity of Vietnamese political factions, it was more the political flux and experimentation they created rather than any specific form of assistance that made the occupation the catalytic force in the Vietnamese revolution.

PART FIVE

The Bid
for Revolutionary Power:
The August Revolution
of 1945

❁
❁
❁

CHAPTER 14

THE REVOLUTION

IN HANOI AND HUE

✺
✺
✺

If the Japanese occupation of Indochina from 1940 to 1945 had not occurred, revolution in Viet Nam would certainly have been delayed, but it is hard to believe that a revolution would not have broken out at a later date. The potential for widespread opposition to French rule could have remained unexploited or been resolved by French programs to integrate Vietnamese elites into an autonomous political system. Yet it is difficult to imagine that the limitations of domestic politics in France would have allowed for such a development in French policy or that politically talented Vietnamese would have remained ineffective indefinitely. In the absence of more decisive political action by either the French or the revolutionaries, it was primarily the police power of the colonial state that prevented revolution in Viet Nam. Prior to 1940 the French police surveillance and military force had been able to thwart all attempts to challenge colonial rule. However, with the German invasion of France the maintenance of the political control of the colonial regime would have been difficult if not impossible, even if the Japanese had not occupied Indochina.

The effect of the Japanese presence went beyond its weakening of French control to encourage the consciousness and ambitions of Vietnamese political groups. Like the conditions the French themselves had created before 1940, these ambitions might still have been kept under control except for the hiatus in established authority in Indochina. In the absence of any stronger power the Communists were able to take advantage of the Japanese capitulation; within this gap in authority they staged a revolutionary scenario which reflected in a dramatic way much about the character of Vietnamese society and the politics of revolution.

• On the morning of August 19, 1945, about 1,000 armed troops of the Viet Minh entered Hanoi and assumed control over the city. They did not meet any resistance from approximately 30,000 Japanese troops stationed in the vicinity of Hanoi. The local administration of the "independent" government of Viet Nam, which had been launched under the auspices of Emperor Bao Dai four months previously by Japan's occupation authorities in Indochina, was caught off guard. Seeing the discipline and determination of these forces, the Hanoi police and the territorial militia wavered and were then caught up in the popular tide of the day. As a gesture symbolic of its popular strength, the Viet Minh led a crowd to storm the official residence of the imperial delegate, Phan Ke Toai, only to find that the Bao Dai representative had fled the city.[1] After the neutralization of armed units of the existing government and the occupation of key administrative offices and public utilities, the Viet Minh furthered its hold over the population of Hanoi by a propaganda meeting

1 Truong Chinh: *The August Revolution* (Hanoi: Foreign Languages Publishing House: 1958), p. 14.

reportedly held before 200,000 persons. There the Viet Minh publicly laid claim to political legitimacy when it was asserted that "Only the revolutionary people's government has prestige and strength enough to realize the common earnest aspirations of the whole people: independence, freedom and happiness."[2]

Two days before this successful armed coup, the Viet Minh had met its first and only real test in the propaganda conflict over the legitimacy of seizing power in northern Viet Nam. Sensing its vulnerability and feeling the need for a popular source of strength when its Japanese supporters surrendered, the local Bao Dai administration in Hanoi called a meeting of the General Association of Functionaries on August 17, 1945.[3] Since this government was headed by a French-trained scholar and colonial functionary, Tran Trong Kim, and had a distinct bureaucratic character, it might have been expected that it would seek to maintain its power through control over the existing administrative cadre. Although the meeting—held in Hanoi before a reported 150,000 persons—sought the support and the loyalty of this important element of the tenuous political fabric of Viet Nam, the gathering was wrested away from its organizers by the Viet Minh. As its press communiqué described it, the Viet Minh went into action:

> A functionary had hardly finished reading the agenda of the demonstration when suddenly Viet Minh flags appeared everywhere. One was seen waving immediately over the rostrum. A storm of applause and cheers greeted its appearance. Five minutes later, a Viet Minh militant took the floor. At the microphone he called on the people to join the general insurrection that was on the point of breaking out in order to win back the Fatherland and found the Democratic Republic of Viet Nam.[4]

Manipulated in this manner by Viet Minh propagandists, the functionaries' meeting was highlighted by an appeal of the Shock Group of the Democratic Party which asserted that "only

2 Democratic Republic of Viet Nam: *Breaking Our Chains*, p. 86.
3 Democratic Republic of Viet Nam: *Thirty Years of Struggle of the Party*, p. 95.
4 Democratic Republic of Viet Nam: *Breaking Our Chains*, p. 82.

a revolution of the entire nation will be powerful enough to
secure the withdrawal of the Japanese . . . and to cut short their
[the French] mad ambition to come back to this country."[5]
Combining its call for unity with an attack on the Tran Trong
Kim government, which it termed "completely powerless" and
headed by "wavering and weak minded leaders," the Democratic Party appeal urged the crowd to join with the Viet Minh
in the general insurrection: "Let us unite together into a single
bloc. The independence of the Fatherland can be won only by
blood. . . . We must take arms and rise up."[6] The rally then gave
way to a parade through the streets of Hanoi, with the gold-
starred red flag symbolic of the revolution and propaganda
banners supplied by the Viet Minh being carried by the throng.
Before the end of the demonstration, which lasted long into the
night, about one hundred *Bảo An* troops, or militiamen, of the
Tran Trong Kim government joined in the procession, bringing
their rifles with them.[7] By effective propaganda techniques the
Viet Minh was able to prepare the way for the *coup d'état* which
occurred two days later, and succeeded because there was no
force to oppose a revolutionary seizure of power.

Since mastery of Hanoi meant legitimacy at least over the
northern portion of the country, it is important that this task did
not require any absolute power but only a greater strength than
the existing government. Even had the 1,000 troops which entered the capital on the 19th met armed opposition, it is doubtful that they would have faced more than 750 militiamen, the
strength this unit was known to have had in Hanoi as late as
October 1944. But in addition to the weakness of its control
over the paramilitary and administrative bureaucracy, the Tran
Trong Kim government lacked any real political base, especially
among the literate and socially conscious population. Moreover, during the course of the Japanese occupation, Hanoi had
been the scene of two aspects of a general pattern of social
mobilization sponsored by the Vichy-French administration. One

5 Ibid., p. 83.
6 Ibid., p. 84.
7 Ibid., p. 83.

was the expansion of the student body of the University of
Hanoi, and the other was the increase in the numbers of Vietnamese in colonial administration, especially in the central
bureaus in Hanoi.[8]

It was among these bureaucratic and student elements of the
Vietnamese population that the *Việt Nam Dân Chủ Đảng,* or
Democratic Party, was founded in June 1944 by Duong Duc
Hien, who was then president of the Association of Students.
The creation of the Democratic Party fulfilled a double purpose:
It grouped in a popular party the students, intellectuals, and
urban upper classes of Hanoi having democratic ideals but
hostile to Communist ideology; and it allowed the Viet Minh to
benefit from the political enthusiasm of these groups without
having to bring them into the Communist Party, where their
nationalism might have conflicted with the requirements of
discipline.[9] Without this organization the more politically conscious people in Hanoi would not have participated in the August
Revolution, and without their participation the *coup d'état* in
Hanoi would probably have been primarily a test of armed force,
an eventuality which the Communists always sought to avoid.

In themselves the Communists' tactics suggested the elite character of the August Revolution, since there is no indication that
there was a mass uprising in Viet Nam. Even among the urban
population of Hanoi, one of the three cities where the principal
events of the revolution were acted out, the demonstrations were
carefully organized, not spontaneous. Such instruments of power
as existed in Viet Nam and could be considered objects of revolutionary seizures consisted of the small Vietnamese administrative
cadre, the remnants of the militia and Japanese-sponsored paramilitary groups, and key public facilities. They came under Viet
Minh control not so much by a contest of strength, but by

8 *Annuaire statistique de l'Indochine, 1943–1946,* pp. 45, 303; also Decoux: *À la
barre de l'Indochine,* pp. 395–403.

9 The Communist version of the founding of the Democratic Party is, "Our Party
deemed it opportune and necessary to help the Vietnamese national bourgeoisie
intellectuals found a revolutionary party. . . . Therefore, our Party helped Duong
Duc Hien's group of students and the *Thanh Nghi* group found the Viet Nam
Democratic Party which joined the Viet Minh Front." Democratic Republic of
Viet Nam: *Thirty Years of Struggle of the Party,* p. 75.

superior political organization and psychological preparation. It was this elusive but vital aspect of revolutionary competition that caused a French commentator to question whether "the phenomenon which took place in Hanoi around August 16 was a revolution, for the enthusiasm seemed artificial and forced. Can it be called a revolution when there was no one to thwart it. . . . In truth the place was free for Ho Chi Minh, there was nothing to oppose him. . . ."[1]

If this criticism missed the point, it was because it neglected to recognize the structured political coalescence of important elements of a Vietnamese elite which had been made aware of their potential social opportunities by French education and administration. For this colonially created upper-class independence and national unity presented opportunities for prestige and power that they knew would be threatened by the return of the French. Thus they seized what instruments of power were present in the cities, while in most of the countryside the politically unorganized but discontented peasantry continued its agricultural routine.

The Viet Minh as well as their adversaries were aware that the Japanese, despite their capitulation, could still play a decisive role in the August Revolution. The crowd that gathered in the streets of Hanoi on August 19 was told that the tactical requirements of the August Revolution meant that toward the Japanese "we must be very moderate and avoid all unnecessary clashes, disadvantageous to both sides. We can also use our diplomacy to make them understand the situation, approve our revolution, and hand over their arms to us."[2] This change from outspoken opposition to the Japanese was due to the overtures of the Japanese themselves. Their consuls general in Hanoi and Saigon gave, it has been asserted, carte blanche to their intelligence units to negotiate with the Viet Minh for the creation of a new provisional government. However, this Japanese acquiescence or support did not block the Viet Minh's understanding of the broader international aspect of the August Revolution. It knew

1 Volait: *La vie économique et sociale du Viet Nam*, p. 10.
2 Democratic Republic of Viet Nam: *Breaking Our Chains*, p. 86.

how much it needed the diplomatic recognition of its regime in order to have the freedom to consolidate its power, and it realized the necessity to avoid being "alone in our resistance to the Allied forces . . . which would invade our country and force on us a French or puppet government going counter to the aspirations of our people."[3] Whether or not it would be able to win one of the Allies to its side, the Viet Minh was under no misapprehension that "In this one and only opportunity, our people as a whole must bring into play all their resources and courage. . . ." and that "It is now or never for our people and army to rise up and win back national independence."[4] While diplomatic recognition was the guarantee of continuing.the hiatus of international force or of mitigating its reimposition, internal strength and legitimacy were thought to be the best paths to this guarantee.

By contrast the government of the Vietnamese monarchy felt that international recognition could compensate for the internal deficiencies which had led to its being physically and politically eliminated in Tonkin. On August 18, 1945, in the central Viet Nam capital city of Hue there was formed a National Salvation Committee under Tran Trong Kim, and an important statement was issued by Emperor Bao Dai, in which he sought in vain the formal recognition of the independence of Viet Nam under his rule. Messages were sent to President Truman, King George VI, and Chiang Kai-shek, but it was in his letter to General de Gaulle that his comments were most immediately meaningful: "You have suffered too much during four deadly years," it said, "not to understand that the Vietnamese people, who have a history of twenty centuries and an often glorious past, no longer wish, no longer can support any foreign domination or foreign administration." Then turning to a prophecy that even its author seemed to forget in future years, the Vietnamese emperor said:

> You could understand even better if you were able to see what is happening here, if you were able to sense the desire for in-

3 Ibid., pp. 66–7.
4 Ibid., pp. 74–5.

dependence that has been smoldering in the bottom of all hearts and which no human force can any longer hold back. Even if you were to arrive to re-establish a French administration here, it would no longer be obeyed; each village would be a nest of resistance, every former friend an enemy, and your officials and colonials themselves would ask to depart from this unbreathable atmosphere.[5]

Shifting their tactics in yet another attempt to compensate for their lack of internal political strength, Bao Dai and his advisers decided on August 22 to ask the Viet Minh to form a new government to take the place of the one led by Tran Trong Kim. But before initiatives could be undertaken, a message arrived from Hanoi in which the Viet Minh demanded that the Vietnamese emperor abdicate and recognize the Democratic Republic of Viet Nam.[6] Although it never received any public response, the Viet Minh was obviously concerned by Bao Dai's international appeal. However, it seems that the initiative to demand Bao Dai's withdrawal sprang not so much from a fear of the remote possibility that the emperor's government might be given diplomatic recognition as from a desire to score a psychological victory within Viet Nam. The demand for the abdiction had come in a resolution "adopted" by the General Association of Students held at the *cité universitaire* in Hanoi, which had also included a call for the formation of a provisional government by the Viet Minh.[7] Through this tactic the Viet Minh was greatly strengthening its formal claim to legitimacy by having itself acknowledged as the successor government to the monarchy. Moreover, it was increasing its popularity, especially in the north, among those who regarded the imperial government as a rallying point for a Francophile elite and who therefore sought its overthrow.

To capitalize on the propaganda value of the event, a delegation was sent by the National Liberation Committee from Hanoi to receive the abdication and to make contact with the People's

5 Printed in the newspaper *Việt Nam Tân Báo*, Hue, August 20, 1945, as cited in Devillers: *Histoire du Viet Nam,* p. 138.

6 Ibid., p. 137.

7 Ibid. See for text of resolution.

Committee in Hue, which had assumed control over the town without opposition on August 23.[8] The delegation was headed by Tran Huy Lieu, who was to become minister of propaganda in the first cabinet of Ho Chi Minh. It was Lieu who accepted on August 25, amid pomp and ceremony, the abdication of Bao Dai, in which the emperor "handed over the rule of the country to the Democratic Republic of Viet Nam" and declared he would "never allow anybody to utilize my name or the name of the Royal Family to deceive our countrymen."[9] Furthermore Bao Dai added additional weight to the claims of the Viet Minh to political legitimacy by accepting, under the name of citizen Vinh Thuy, the sinecure post of "supreme political adviser" to the new government.[1] Obviously the Viet Minh was striving for the broadest possible base of political support.

It was not until August 30, more than a week after the initial bid for power, that Ho Chi Minh arrived in Hanoi from the Viet Minh guerrilla base area in the mountains of northern Viet Nam. Two days later he addressed a crowd, reportedly numbering 500,000, gathered in Ba Dinh square, delivering the Declaration of Independence of the Republic of Viet Nam. In beginning his declaration, Ho reinforced the Viet Minh's efforts to gain international prestige and recognition by stating, "All men are created equal. They are endowed by their Creator with certain inalienable rights, among these are Life, Liberty and the pursuit of Happiness."[2] In addition to quoting from the American Declaration of Independence, Ho further identified himself with the mainstream of Western democratic liberalism by referring to the French Declaration of the Rights of Man and then went on to assert, "Nevertheless for more than eighty years the French imperialists, abusing the standard of Liberty, Equality and Fraternity, have violated our Fatherland and oppressed our fellowcitizens. They have acted contrary to the ideals of humanity and justice." The Vietnamese Communist leader then launched into a catalogue of political and economic transgressions which had

8 Democratic Republic of Viet Nam: *Thirty Years of Struggle of the Party*, p. 95.

9 Democratic Republic of Viet Nam: *Documents*, n.d., n.p.

1 Hammer: *The Struggle for Indochina*, p. 104.

2 Democratic Republic of Viet Nam: *Documents*.

been committed against the Vietnamese. This accounting concluded with an indictment that the French had not been able to
provide the "protection" on which their nineteenth-century
treaties of colonial dominance were based, for they had been
unable to prevent the Japanese occupation of Indochina.

With this preparation Ho then attacked the potential claims by
the French to continued political hegemony in Viet Nam while
justifying his own assertions of sovereignty by saying

> . . . since the autumn of 1940 our country has ceased to be a
> colony and had become a Japanese outpost . . . we have wrested
> our independence from the Japanese and not from the French.
> The French have fled, the Japanese have capitulated, Emperor
> Bao Dai has abdicated, our people have broken the fetters which
> for over a century have tied us down; our people have at the
> same time overthrown the monarchic constitution that had reigned
> supreme for so many centuries and instead have established the
> present Republican government.[3]

By its emotional vocabulary the Vietnamese Declaration of
Independence evoked ideals and symbols which were an intimate
part of the intellectual experience of the French-educated elite
of Viet Nam. Through this extremely effective propaganda, Ho
was articulating the feeling, especially widespread in northern
Viet Nam, that the expectations aroused by Western education
and culture had remained dramatically unfulfilled by French
colonialism. There were colonially created elites loyal to France,
particularly in the south, among landowners, professionals, party
politicians who had participated in prewar elections, and those
granted French citizenship. Yet even within those circles the
feeling of thwarted ambition under French dominance was widely
shared. Moreover, France had done little to win the support of
the upper classes they would confront upon their return; none
of their wartime propaganda statements had much of an impact
on these aspirations because French proposals were phrased in
bureaucratic language which talked of administrative reform.[4]

3 Ibid.
4 Primarily the French statement of March 24, 1945. For text see Cole: *Conflict
in Indo-China,* pp. 5–7.

Meanwhile, much of the Vietnamese upper class that had not already been organized by the Viet Minh was being steadily won over to the independence movement. The appeal of independence was meaningful, because it offered a path toward fulfillment or release for those not committed to some avenue of opportunity of French origin. For example, the breadth of the Viet Minh appeal and an indication of its effectiveness as a national independence movement was perhaps best demonstrated by its ability to win support from Vietnamese Catholics. Significantly, this affirmation came from three Vietnamese bishops in northern Viet Nam, where 1,100,000 Catholics made up almost 10 per cent of the population; while a bishop in the south (Ngo Dinh Thuc, a brother of the then-dormant political figure Ngo Dinh Diem), where Catholics were less numerous, did not give any backing to the independence movement.[5] Shrewdly, Ho declared Viet Nam Independence Day to be the first Sunday in September (September 2, 1945), which was the Feast of Vietnamese Martyrs, and appointed a prominent Catholic layman, Nguyen Manh Ha, as minister of economy in his provisional government on August 29, 1945.[6]

However, as events subsequent to the August Revolution were to show, the Catholics, like most other widely organized social groups, were more interested in sectarian autonomy than independence for the whole country.[7] Their enthusiasm for regional autonomy was a reflection of the character of Vietnamese society, which lacked a countrywide institutional framework for cultural or political integration above the level of the peasant village. In the absence of nationwide cultural institutions pen-

5 For statement of Catholic bishops see *Commonweal*, January 17, 1947, p. 15; for statistics on Catholics and indigenous priests see "L'église catholique en Indochine," *Revue des Troupes Coloniales* (février 1947, numéro 285), pp. 39–46. For further verification of the initial enthusiasm of the Catholics for the Viet Minh see Fall: "Political Development of Viet Nam," pp. 136–7.

6 Devillers: *Histoire du Viet Nam*, p. 186.

7 Nguyen Manh Ha in particular and Catholics in northern Viet Nam in general broke with the Viet Minh after December 1946, when the fighting against the French began. In their domain in the extreme south of the Red River Delta, the Catholics fiercely guarded their autonomy until circumstances made it necessary for them to rally to the side of France and the Bao Dai government in the autumn of 1949. Ibid., p. 447. Two of the top negotiators for the Bao Dai government at Geneva were Nguyen Quoc Dinh and Nguyen Dac Khe, who had been political advisers to Ho Chi Minh in 1945-6. Fall: "The Political Development of Viet Nam," p. 250.

etrating into Viet Nam's rural areas, parochial social and religious groups emerged as small, territorially defined organizations enjoying quasi-governmental authority as well as moral prerogatives over peasant villagers. Thus there was an area in the lower Red River Delta of northern Viet Nam which was virtually a Catholic fief. Corresponding to this in the Mekong Delta of southern Viet Nam were the domains of the Cao Dai, Hoa Hao, and Binh Xuyen, as well as a small Catholic group. Because these groups were minorities with little capacity of becoming a majority except in their own territories, they were more concerned with particular and relative rather than general and absolute problems of political influence. Due to their parochial interests, these groups eventually had an unsettling effect on revolutionary politics because their goals for territorial autonomy could be satisfied with less than full national independence.

Part of the success of the Viet Minh as an independence movement was achieved by outperforming any competitors in meeting the demands for autonomy of these groups. At the same time the Communist-led movement also had the capacity to incorporate the recently mobilized but still unorganized elements of the urban population of Viet Nam into their political structure. As will be seen presently, however, the Viet Minh in the south was substantially less successful in performing these two diverse political tasks. Its failure was due to a complex set of factors related to the more complicated political environment in southern Viet Nam. Chief among them were the more effective organization of urban political groups and the existence of more widely organized sects in rural areas. Strong regional variations of this kind have almost always affected Vietnamese politics, and the period of the August Revolution was no exception.

What these differences indicated was not only a contrast in political landscape between the regions of Viet Nam, but also fundamental limitations to the development of a nationalist identity. The Communists were virtually the only nationwide political group, but they too had regional stresses to contend with. Moreover, they were small. As Ho Chi Minh boasted, "When the August Revolution took place, there were about 5,000

Party members, including those in jail. Less than 5,000 Party members have thus organized and led the uprising of 24 million fellow-countrymen over the country to victory."[8] In leading its essentially urban uprising, an undertaking restricted to less than 20 per cent of the population of the country, the Viet Minh hoped that its nationalist appeal would win followers and it did. But it also faced a regional parochialism which saw in the Viet Minh a monolithic movement threatening the existence of sectarian identities.

In all regions of Viet Nam the impending intervention of international armed forces to receive the Japanese surrender, which would end the hiatus in which the August Revolution had been made possible, loomed larger than any internal obstacle to the consolidation of the independence movement under Viet Minh leadership. It was a recognition of this international power factor defining the limits of Vietnamese independence which also caused Ho Chi Minh to punctuate his Declaration of Independence with provocative images of the great disparity between Western democratic ideals and the French colonial record in Viet Nam. If the virtually unconditional commitment of the French to reintervention could have been blocked or somehow mitigated, it would have allowed the Viet Minh to avoid the anguishing discipline of mobilizing the human resources of a largely amorphous society for political and military action. At the same time the risk of losing the rural sects in a competition with the French over sect autonomy would not have been an issue confronting the Viet Minh. Therefore, as he concluded his Declaration on that day in Hanoi, Ho Chi Minh drove home the issue for the handful of Allied representatives among his Vietnamese audience by asserting that "We are convinced that the Allied Nations which have acknowledged at Teheran and San Francisco the principles of self-determination and equality of status will not refuse to acknowledge the independence of Viet Nam."[9]

The Viet Minh was to receive in the absence of Allied diplo-

8 Ho Chi Minh: "Our Party Has Struggled Very Heroically and Won Glorious Victories," in *A Heroic People: Memoirs From the Revolution* (Hanoi: Foreign Languages Publishing House; 1960), p. 12.
9 Democratic Republic of Viet Nam: *Documents*.

matic recognition another, perhaps unexpected, form of restraint upon French reintervention. This was the Chinese occupation of Viet Nam north of the 16th parallel, which occurred under the terms of arrangements made for accepting the Japanese surrender at the Potsdam Conference. The Viet Minh in the north was thus able to avoid a direct challenge by the French to its claims of sovereign independence for another seven months. However, the occupation brought with it limitations to the freedom of political action enjoyed immediately after the Japanese capitulation. The imposition of Chinese-sponsored Vietnamese exiles onto the body of the independence movement created new difficulties for the Viet Minh. The diversity, complexity, and often contradictory nature of Chinese political purposes in postwar Viet Nam was to be a major restriction to the Viet Minh. This was in part suggested by the size of the Chinese military contingent. Advance elements of a force that was to swell to an average of 125,000 troops during the seven-month occupation began to arrive in Hanoi on September 9, 1945. They came ostensibly for the disarmament of about 48,000 Japanese, a task that they never fulfilled.

CHAPTER 15 ✺ ✺ ✺

THE CONTRASTING PATTERN

OF REVOLUTION IN SAIGON

✺
✺
✺

The Chinese presence in the initial stages of the August Revolution was in sharp contrast with the pattern of international occupation in southern Viet Nam. When British troops entered Saigon on September 13, 1945, they caused French military units held under arrest by the Japanese since March 9, 1945, to be released and eventually rearmed.[1] When combined with a detachment of French commandos and troops of the 20th Indian Division under the command of Major General Douglas D. Gracey, these former prisoners comprised part of a 4,000-man force which was slowly augmented by reinforcements from France during the autumn and winter of 1945.

It had been determined in London that French administration would be restored by British occupation forces as soon as possible. Thus General Gracey announced upon his arrival that the responsibility for the maintenance of order would be trans-

[1] *Survey of International Affairs, 1939–1946: The Far East, 1942–1946*, p. 260.

ferred to the French as soon as they were in a position to take charge.[2] Although General Gracey attempted to avoid involvement in Vietnamese politics, this proved to be impossible; the violence that erupted between the French and the Viet Minh in Saigon in late September caught his troops in a cross fire which they could not have escaped without some positive action. Therefore, after his mediation efforts broke down, Gracey's troops were thrown into the fight to restore French rule in the south.

Although the strikingly dissimilar actions of the Chinese and British highlighted important differences in regional conditions, the political contrasts between northern and southern Viet Nam during the August Revolution were more profound than just the differing pattern of international occupation. Of fundamental significance was the distinctive character of the Communist Party in the south and its rather tenuous relationship with the Viet Minh. Unlike the party leadership in the north, which had developed out of the Thanh Nien exile youth movement in Canton in the late 1920's, with strong indigenous roots to the clandestine Tan Viet movement, the party in the south was headed by men with more cosmopolitan experience. They had become Communists as a result of education in France and had held elective office in southern Viet Nam during the Popular Front period of the late 1930's.[3] In Ho Chi Minh's absence from Vietnamese politics in the latter 1930's, there was no attempt to enforce countrywide discipline on the party. Therefore the organization in the south developed an autonomy which resisted efforts by the reinvigorated Central Committee to bring it under unified control during the Japanese occupation. Only after the southern party leaders had ruined their limited chances to exploit the opportunities presented by the Japanese capitulation and antagonized the regional political groups were the "bour-

2 Ibid.

3 Nguyen Van Tao and Duong Bach Mai, both of whom were educated in France and elected to the Saigon municipal council in 1937, were the best examples of this pattern. Tran Van Giau, although French-educated, spent more time in jail than in public politics. Ha Huy Giap was the major exception to the pattern, and unlike the others he was born in the north where he had a local education and a political experience more typical of northern party leaders.

geois" Communist chiefs replaced by trusted lieutenants sent from the north.[4]

The party's blunders in the south did not result so much from a jealously guarded autonomy as from the limiting conditions of the region's politics. The population was much more extensively organized for political action in the south, while more-numerous politically conscious and effective rural sects were also present. The actions of the French security police during the 1930's in smashing nationalist political groups in the north while such groups in the south were encouraged by electoral opportunities was fundamental to the many factors creating these conditions. In the north, where the Communists had mastered the techniques of candestine activity, the party reemerged to a fairly clear field among the urban population upon the Japanese capitulation, whereas in the south it faced efficient opposition. Moreover, one of the consequences of the Japanese interregnum was not only to heighten the already existent political consciousness of groups in the south, but to contribute to their militarization.

In contrast to the circumstances facing the Communist Party in the North, the situation in the south was more diffuse. In Tonkin the party was almost unchallenged in its organization of the population through the effective medium of the subsidiary Democratic Party. Moreover, as a result of covert Allied material aid the Viet Minh was virtually the only armed political group. Among all the groups affected by Japanese maneuvers in Vietnamese politics there resulted in the south at least two well-armed groups, neither of which was Communist in origin.[5] Furthermore, the southern party had not benefited from Allied aid (or from Japanese collaboration either, a fact that they used to their propaganda advantage) to build up an armed force of their own,

---

4 Duong Bach Mai and Tran Van Giau were sent on overseas missions, while Nguyen Binh, the new chief sent to the south in early 1946, had, as will be seen, relatively little success in the southern political environment. In 1951, after five years of effort, he was eliminated by being allowed to fall into a French ambush.

5 These were the Cao Dai and the Advanced Guard Youth, which had been militarized out of the French sports program. Less well-armed were the Hoa Hao and the Binh Xuyen. Although the strength of the latter groups was not decisive, it did add to the complexity of the situation.

nor were they able to get any such military means by guerrilla ambushes or other seizures. Therefore, they not only faced more autonomous and capable political groups than existed in the north, but they also had no instruments of power of their own to bring them under their control. However, the majority of these groups had no well-conceived program for taking the lead in an independence movement even limited to the south.

In joining with the French by 1948, all of the rural sects were to demonstrate, just as the Catholics did in the north, that autonomy for their territorial social organizations was more fundamental to them than independence for the whole country. Thus, for a coherent independence movement to have developed in the south, it would have required meeting the demands of sect autonomy and the aspirations of the urban parties while enforcing enough discipline upon both groups to achieve tactical effectiveness. This was the strategy of success of the Viet Minh in the less complex situation in the north, but the party in the south failed to repeat it because it emphasized discipline to the extent of causing the sects to fear for their autonomy. The party also neglected to articulate sufficiently broad goals of independence to win the unorganized but dissatisfied in both urban and rural areas. The lack of a common front led to internecine squabbles among the Vietnamese in the south, giving the French opportunities to bargain politically for what they could not obtain by superior force over the disorganized resistance.

The first indication that no single group in the south would be able to approximate the role the Viet Minh played in the north came with the announcement of the formation of the United National Front on August 14, 1945. This body was sponsored by the Japanese and consisted of political groups which they had aided to varying degrees during their occupation.[6] In addition, they superimposed on this political coalition lines of authority ostensibly emanating from the rapidly deteriorating imperial government at Hue. The treaties of 1864 with France, which had

6 This included the Cao Dai, Hoa Hao, Trotskyites, Phuc Quoc, Thanh Nien Tien Phong, and the Independence Party of Ho Van Nga. Devillers: *Histoire du Viet Nam*, p. 140.

made the south a legally separate French colony, were denounced, reunification was proclaimed, and a Khâm Sai , or imperial delegate, was appointed. The Japanese were waiting until the last moment before their capitulation to integrate into a governmental structure in the south groups to which they had given political encouragement, often along divergent and contradictory lines. The reasons for this delay are not altogether clear, but it suggests an unresolved competition between Japanese military cliques. Despite the apparent vagueness of their purposes the Japanese were to assume an active role in the tactical events of the August Revolution in the south that was crucial. Their first steps in this direction occurred when the imperial delegate, Nguyen Van Sam, arrived in Saigon on August 19 and began negotiations with the Japanese to obtain arms for the creation of militia forces under his control.

It was apparent to the Communists that once these arms were distributed, their already difficult task of gaining a controlling hand over political forces in the south might be made impossible. Therefore, under the leadership of Tran Van Giau the Communists were successful in securing a meeting of the United National Front on August 22, at which they argued that an identification with the Japanese would be disastrous. Their reasoning was that the Allies would consider the front a puppet movement. As an alternative, Giau held out the reputation of the Viet Minh as a countrywide anti-Japanese independence movement to which the political groups in the south could adhere.[7] Whatever merits the logic of Giau's argument might have had for the United National Front, it seems that the decision to acquiesce to the leadership of the Viet Minh was influenced to perhaps an overwhelming extent by the leverage of the Advanced Guard Youth. The leader of this youth group, Dr. Pham Ngoc Thach, had become a friend of Giau's during the occupation. The influence of the Advance Guard Youth, one of the two most significant groups composing the front, sprang from its having the most numerous armed force in the south, while the chief potential adversary of the developing Advanced Guard Youth–Communist

7 Dabezies: "Forces politiques au Viet Nam," p. 150.

coalition, the Trotskyites, derived their strength from having the largest popular following in Saigon.[8] Thach was undoubtedly fully conscious of his pivotal strength, and if he was not, as has been suggested, a secret member of the Indochinese Communist Party, then he had apparently assessed the opportunities of advancing his purposes as being better with the Viet Minh than alone or with the Japanese-sponsored United Front.[9] Whatever the basis of Thach's decision, it is unlikely that the Viet Minh would have been able to emerge on August 25 as the controlling political force in the south—supplanting the Japanese-backed Nguyen Van Sam regime—without the support of the Advanced Guard Youth and its armed units. Once predominant, the Viet Minh then made an arrangement to receive weapons from the Japanese, an act which they had so recently denounced.[1]

The consolidation of the Viet Minh in the south was publicly dramatized during an enormous day-long demonstration on August 25. Groups representing the United National Front and the Viet Minh paraded through the streets of Saigon. As a symbol of the Viet Minh's new armed potency the flag identified with the imperial government gave way to the red banner with yellow star.[2] The Nam Bo (southern region) Committee, which assumed governmental authority on that day, was tightly controlled by the Viet Minh, since six of its nine members were Communists.[3] The antagonism which the party's predominance

[8] The Trotskyites swept the Saigon municipal council elections in 1939, driving the Communists Nguyen Van Tao and Duong Bach Mai out of office. Devillers: *Histoire du Viet Nam,* pp. 68–9.

[9] Ibid., p. 140. Thach eventually held the post of Minister of Health in the first Ho Chi Minh cabinet and became a ranking official dealing with health problems in the Communist government. Whether this is the maximum he could have expected or wanted from his important position in 1945 is open to discussion.

[1] Lt. Gen. Numata Takazo, chief of staff to Count Terauchi, the Japanese commander, conceded that arms had been supplied to the Vietnamese after the capitulation, without specifying which group. It seems clear from subsequent events that it was not the Trotskyites or imperial government. *The New York Times,* September 29, 1945, p. 5.

[2] Truong Chinh: *The August Revolution,* p. 15, says that there were a million people on parade in Saigon-Cholon, but this is not substantiated elsewhere. This source says the manifestation took place on the 23rd, but the 25th seems more likely. Hammer: *The Struggle for Indochina,* p. 107.

[3] The six were Tran Van Giau, who was president and chief of military affairs; Dr. Pham Ngoc Thach; Nguyen Van Tao, who had been beaten by the Trotskyites in the Saigon elections of 1939; Huynh Van Tieng; Duong Bach Mai; and Nguyen Van Tay. Devillers: *Histoire du Viet Nam,* p. 142.

created was manifested on September 2, 1945, when a peaceful demonstration staged by the Communists was manipulated out of control into an anti-French riot, whose destructive force continued into the following day. Before it could be stopped, 4 Frenchmen, a woman, and 2 children were dead, 100 other persons were injured, and at least 500 homes were pillaged.[4] Realizing slowly that this was a serious psychological and political challenge to his power which could prejudice attempts to win the confidence of the Allies and generate anarchic conditions beyond his control, Tran Van Giau responded, but only after a week's delay. In hopes of neutralizing his political adversaries he reorganized the Nam Bo Committee on September 10 as a more broadly representative body, with only four of its thirteen members being Communists.[5]

The situation in the south contrasted with the pattern in the north, where a widely based provisional government under Communist control combined with enthusiastic national independence appeals from Ho Chi Minh had been sought from the start. The party in the south lacked a charismatic figure with whom popular aspirations could be identified, and it only adopted a coalition government under the pressure of violent provocation. Moreover, Pham Van Bach, whom Giau chose for the position of titular leader of the Nam Bo Committee, was an unknown lawyer who had been practicing in Cambodia. Neither he nor Giau displayed an ability to meet the fundamental demands of the groups active in the south. Because there was no resolution of their political expectations into a coherent independence movement, the strength of these groups was directed against each other rather than toward preparations to oppose the return of the French. While no one group can be documented as responsible for the excesses of September 2, these events formed part of a trend in the August Revolution in the south; as a consequence of widely differentiated social identity

---

4 *The New York Times,* September 9, 1945, p. 10. For the aspects of the manipulation see Hammer: *The Struggle for Indochina,* p. 109.

5 Although this included the spiritual leader of the Hoa Hao, a Cao Dai, and a Trotskyite, it was not a distinguished coalition. Devillers: *Histoire du Viet Nam,* p. 156.

and political power, sectarian predominance became a more urgent goal than national independence.

One important example of this internecine struggle was the drive of the Hoa Hao to establish its territorial hegemony in the Transbassac section of the Mekong River Delta, southwest of Saigon. Although this sect might have been successfully brought into a Communist-sponsored nationalist coalition, its basic territorial goals came sharply into conflict with the position of the Viet Minh. These differences were brought to a violent clash in the Mekong River port of Can Tho, which the Hoa Hao considered the rightful capital of their domain. Here on September 8, 1945, some 15,000 Hoa Hao followers, armed mostly with knives and other crude weapons, were bloodily put down by the Viet Minh-controlled Advanced Guard Youth, reportedly supported by the local Japanese garrison.[6] By its savagery the Can Tho massacre provoked reprisals against the Communists from Hoa Hao delta bases, and, the Hoa Hao momentarily looked to the French for a political alternative to the Viet Minh. However, the manner of France's colonial reoccupation of the Mekong Delta towns in the autumn of 1945 antagonized the Hoa Hao, so it sought an accommodation with Viet Minh—only to rejoin the French side in April 1947, when the founder and spiritual chief of the folk religion, Huynh Phu So, was arrested and subsequently executed by the Communists.[7] The death of Huynh Phu So, who had ironically been appointed by Tran Van Giau to the reorganized Nam Bo Committee on September 10, 1945, in an effort to placate the aroused feelings of the Hoa Hao, presented the French with a new political opportunity. They capitalized upon it by recognizing the territorial hegemony of the

6 It is Lancaster: *The Emancipation of French Indochina*, p. 137, who suggests that Japanese troops assisted the Advanced Guard Youth, and this is no doubt accurate although he gives no documentation.

7 "On 16 April 1947, Huynh Phu So was invited to a conciliation meeting with the Viet Minh leaders, Tran Van Giau and Nguyen Binh. He was arrested by the commander of the 22nd Vietnamese Regiment, Buu Vinh, on his way to the meeting, and tried by a Viet Minh court on charges of 'treason and rebellion.' A terse communique by the Central Executive Committee for Nam Bo dated 20 March 1947 announced Huynh Phu So's execution." Fall: "The Political Development of Viet Nam," p. 415.

sect and eventually arming 20,000 of its adherents in the fight against the Viet Minh in the Mekong River Delta. Although the Hoa Hao appeared on the surface to be politically unstable, because of wide pendulum-like swings in ideological affiliation, there was a fundamental consistency of purpose in its actions. The sect's chief goal, as the French found out, was territorial political hegemony.

The heavy-handed approach of the Communists to the political groups in the south did not confine itself to territorially defined social and political organizations such as the Hoa Hao; it was much more intense against the political parties among the urban population. These groups sought not geographic hegemony, but control over the instruments of power, such as they were, in the single metropolitan center, Saigon. The most avowedly determined enemies of the Communists in the south were the adherents to the Fourth International, the Trotskyites, whose antagonism had its origins in deep-seated ideological differences as well as enduring scars from political infighting in the late 1930's. The Communist dominance of the Nam Bo Committee had obviously done nothing to mitigate these antagonisms. There is almost no evidence available to suggest that the Tran Van Giau group wanted accommodation; instead they sought the elimination of the Trotskyites. Despite a moderate amount of assistance from the Japanese during the occupation, the Trotskyites found themselves unprepared for the situation that followed the capitulation. They had neither an armed force nor a well-developed party organization.[8] In early September 1945 the Communists moved swiftly against their enemy. The man who had guided the development of the Trotskyite movement, Ta Thu Thao, was arrested in Quang Ngai province in central Viet Nam on orders of Tran Van Giau and executed some time before the end of the year. By the end of October, five more Trotskyite leaders were known to have been assassinated by the Communists, and thereafter the party ceased to play a role in Vietnamese politics. While other less noteworthy mem-

8 Mus: *Problèmes de l'Indochine contemporaine*, P.M. I, p. 12.

bers of the party may also have been the object of violence or its threat, it appears that this was a case of eliminating a political movement by decapitation.

But the Trotskyites were not the only party to suffer such a fate, and the impressive results of its policy of assassination indicated the shrewdness and calculation with which the Communists conceived and executed it. In the year and a half following the Japanese capitulation to the outbreak of general hostilities in December 1946, approximately forty significant Vietnamese political figures were assassinated, not including, of course, large numbers of village and lower-ranking provincial officials. Among them were the leaders of seven different political groups in central and southern Viet Nam, including in addition to the Trotskyite and Hoa Hao chiefs already mentioned, the Constitutionalist Party; the Independence Party; Nguyen Van Sam of the National Union Front; Pham Quynh, the Prime Minister of Viet Nam before March 1945 and an influential nationalist in favor of the monarchy; and Ngo Dinh Khoi, chief of Quang Nam province, who was a leader of Vietnamese Catholics and a brother of Ngo Dinh Diem.

Whatever influence these violent deaths had on the remaining members of the various political groups in dissuading them from any anti-Communist activity or whatever impact these leaders might have had on Vietnamese politics if they had lived can only be speculated upon. What appears of greater significance from the successful results of these assassinations in quelling opposition, especially from urban-oriented parties, is the indication of the general lack of tight and resilient party structures and the small number of party adherents. This absence of widespread political participation and coherent party organization emphasizes a specific characteristic of revolution in Viet Nam. Despite the more broadly differentiated social and political structure in the south, the events in the August Revolution throughout Viet Nam were the sphere of a small portion of the total population. Except for the Communists and the religious-political sects, the effectiveness and endurance of parties was slight. Therefore, one of the major characteristics of the August Revolution was elite politics; mass participation could not be a meaningful alternative because organizations to mobilize large numbers of people for political action were lacking. With the exception of public demonstrations in the urban centers of Hanoi and Saigon, resulting from propaganda exhortations, the politics of the August Revolution was a tight competition between a handful of Vietnamese political figures.

Because of this preoccupation with competition among indigenous political groups the Communists were caught unprepared for a major turning point in the August Revolution in the south. This occurred on September 22, ten days after the first elements of General Gracey's British force had begun to arrive in Saigon. During this period Gracey had tried to get the Japanese to maintain order and prevent further clashes between the Vietnamese and the French, but the Japanese were far from resolute in this task, and finally, on September 20, Gracey had himself assumed the responsibility for the maintenance of order. On the 22nd the British general was persuaded by the French representative, Jean Cédile, to rearm approximately 1,400 men of the 9th and 11th Colonial Infantry Regiments, who had been imprisoned by the Japanese on March 9, 1945.[9]

Although these men were ostensibly to help General Gracey maintain order, once armed they followed an autonomous and provocative course. On the night of 22–23 under Cédile's orders, these troops moved to reoccupy all public buildings, and when morning came, the Vietnamese found that they had been the victims of a bloodless *coup d'état*. So tenuous were the instruments and institutions of power in the colonial capital of Saigon that, by evicting the unsuspecting Viet Minh from a handful of key public buildings, the French made themselves titular masters of the city. Because timing and coordination, rather than superior forces, made this French success possible, the Vietnamese were able to launch on the following day a large-scale counterattack on all the points they had lost. By this time, however, their potential superiority had vanished, for "The immediate collapse of all administration and the prospect

9 Devillers: *Histoire du Viet Nam*, p. 159.

of the outbreak of civil war caused General Gracey to intervene, and his forces evicted the Annamites [Vietnamese] from key points and restored these to the French."[1]

The potential effects of this action in support of the French might have been mitigated or entirely avoided had the preoccupation of the Communists with local aspects of the August Revolution not caused them to neglect their contacts with the British. For although the British came to Viet Nam committed to the restoration of the French, they were not necessarily committed to the expulsion of the Viet Minh from power. This distinction seems clear from the moves of General Gracey when faced with the excesses from the French side. With the power advantage now in their favor the French, who (with the exception of Cédile and about 500 commandos) were holdovers from the colonial administration, began to seek their revenge on the Vietnamese for the indignities of August and September. As one press report described it,

> Competent observers believe that ex-Vichyites ruined immediate hopes of a compromise settlement when last 23 September, they started their reign of terror by mass arrests.[2] The arrests touched off a wave of outrages by local French civilians against Annamese natives. While Vichyite patrols looked on civilians insulted and attacked unarmed Annamese on the street . . .[3]

Under the pressure of this type of criticism coming especially from foreign correspondents, General Gracey decided to neutralize the French Colonial Army units by having them confined to their barracks. Once again he charged the Japanese with the task of maintaining order. But the French reaction merely touched off a more intense reaction on the part of the Vietnamese. On the night of September 24, they broke into a French housing area known as the Cité Hérault, massacred 216 persons, mostly women and children, and wounded another 150.[4]

1 *Survey of International Affairs, 1939–1946: The Far East, 1942–1946*, p. 261.

2 Some 300 Vietnamese political activists were arrested on September 25 by the French, with Gracey's approval. *The New York Times*, September 26, 1945, p. 15.

3 Ivan Kingsley in *The New York Times*, January 4, 1946, p. 8.

4 Devillers: *Histoire du Viet Nam*, p. 160, says that 150 were killed and 150 injured.

There was no definite evidence to assign the responsibility for this outrage to any one Vietnamese group. It has been suggested that the massacre was the work of the Binh Xuyen, a small but effective neotraditionalist political sect which was organized largely for purposes of personal aggrandizement, during the Japanese occupation.[5] What is clear, however, is that like the events of September 2, the Cité Hérault incident was an obvious challenge to embarrass the position of Tran Van Giau and demonstrate the administrative incompetency of the Nam Bo Committee. The objective was to cause additional reprisals and sanctions against them by the French and British, but extra and probably unexpected force was to be added to these reprisals. To a much greater extent than on September 2, when they chose not to intervene, the Japanese were directly implicated, since they had been responsible for protecting the Cité Hérault. Moreover, they still had the most powerful force in the city, with 5,000 men under arms.[6] Perhaps embarrassed at their ineffectiveness in protecting French civilians and also because of Allied warnings that their irresponsibility might be grounds for war-crimes proceedings, the Japanese gave closer cooperation to the 2,500 Anglo-Indians under General Gracey's direct command in the face of Viet Minh attacks on September 25 and 26. With the coordinated efforts of French, Japanese, and British troops the armed units of the Viet Minh and other Vietnamese groups were driven from the center of Saigon to the northern and western suburbs, thus thwarting their attempts at a counter *coup de force*.

Although on September 30, Tran Van Giau spread a pamphlet through the city calling for a general strike and total evacuation of Saigon by the Vietnamese and exhorting, ". . . blockade the city . . . The Europeans will only occupy the town when it has been reduced to ashes,"[7] General Gracey was still in hopes of a negotiated settlement to avoid a more general conflict. The British commander arranged for a meeting between Cédile, the

---

5 Hammer: *The Struggle for Indochina*, p. 118.

6 *The New York Times*, September 29, 1945, p. 5.

7 Jean-Michel Hertrich: *Doc-Lap, L'indépendence ou la mort* (Paris: Jean Vigneau; 1946), p. 112.

French representative, and the Nam Bo Committee on October 2, but several days of negotiations indicated that the minimum conditions which the Communists would accept was a return to the *status quo ante* September 23. On the French side, Cédile had no desire or authority to meet the demands of a recognition of the legitimacy which the Nam Bo Committee had lost by being evicted from key public facilities and buildings in Saigon. Because of the imminent arrival of General Philippe Leclerc, who was to be the Commander of French Forces in Indochina, along with fresh reinforcements, there was no incentive for Cédile to treat the Viet Minh demands seriously.

By October 3 the French ship *Triomphant* began to debark the 5th Colonial Infantry Regiment, which gave at least another 1,000 men to strengthen the hand of the French. General Leclerc arrived by air on October 5, and a week later he began the push out of Saigon with the help of the British. Occupying the suburbs of Go Vap and Gia Dinh, the French then moved on northwestward to Bien Hoa on the 23rd and to Thu Dau Mot on the 25th of October. On the latter day the French were able to take My Tho in the south, the gateway to the Mekong River Delta, by a naval assault from the river estuary combined with a land force moving by road from Saigon. The two important Mekong Delta trading and communications centers of Vinh Long and Can Tho fell on October 29 and November 1, respectively.[8] Before the end of December 1945 most of the towns in Viet Nam south of the 16th parallel had been occupied, including extreme southern areas of the plateau country inhabited by a diffuse group of ethnic minorities faithful to the French. But this reoccupation did not include a strategic strip of territory running south from the key port city of Da Nang to just north of Nha Trang, in the central coastal area—a situation with much significance for future events.

8 Lancaster: *The Emancipation of Indochina*, p. 134.

CHAPTER 16 ✿ ✿ ✿

THE SHIFTING BALANCE OF

MILITARY FORCES IN THE SOUTH

✿

✿

✿

A complete shift in the balance of armed forces in the French favor had occurred on October 25, 1945, when the arrival of the 2nd Armored Division increased their forces in southern Indochina to 25,000 men.[1] This meant that the French could carry out their reoccupation policy south of the 16th parallel —at least in the towns and the rural areas of major economic importance—without the necessity of making political commitments or establishing negotiations with any local groups. During October the strength of the Viet Minh had consisted of approximately 20,000 men in the vicinity of Saigon, of whom about 15,000 were armed in one form or another.[2] Almost all of these were members of the Advanced Guard Youth except for about 3,000 under the command of the Cao Dai and about 1,300 in the Binh Xuyen.

---

1 *Survey of International Affairs, 1939–1946: The Far East, 1942–1946*, p. 261.
2 *The New York Times*, October 1, 1945, p. 4.

Besides having these forces in the Saigon area, local Viet Minh committees had organized armed units from among the leaderless remnants of the Vietnamese who had served with the French army and the militia known as the Garde Civile. It appears, however, that it was not until September 23, when they were being evicted from key points in Saigon, that the Nam Bo Committee ordered a general mobilization and in particular called on those with previous military experience. In addition to the late start the results of the mobilization were poor. In Vinh Long province in the Mekong Delta, for example, where there had been 135 Vietnamese stationed in the Garde Civile before the Japanese *coup de force* of March 9, only 20 responded to the mobilization call along with 100 inexperienced volunteers. The majority of these former militiamen who responded did so out of a fear of some vague consequences from the local revolutionary authorities. Although the respondents were confirmed in the ranks they had held in the Garde Civile, they were virtually the only persons with weapons, so that their command over unarmed volunteers was largely meaningless in terms of the immediate problem of holding provincial cities against French reoccupation.

How representative the situation in Vinh Long was for Viet Nam, even the south, cannot easily be determined. Whatever success the Nam Bo Committee might have had in its mobilization of provincial forces was surely limited, in quality at least, to the 6,000 Vietnamese who had been a part of the militia and the 17,000 who had served with the French Colonial Army in areas south of the 16th parallel.[3] While an additional 23,000 men could have made an important contribution to the Nam Bo resistance, after March 9 these troops—which had been stationed in small scattered groups all over southern Indochina—had either been interned with their French units, had escaped into China under French leadership, or had dropped out of sight. Had these men been brought under the Viet Minh's control, they might have played a decisive role in the August Revolution. But if the

3 A total of 54,649 indigenous personnel had served with the French army in all of Indochina.

attack on the Saigon suburb of Phu Lam on the night of October 13 is an example of a general condition, then the units hastily raised in the provinces from volunteers and ex-militiamen and soldiers were ludicrously ineffective.

The attack was led by a 24-year-old Vietnamese of French citizenship who had been an aspirant de réserve of the 11th Colonial Infantry Regiment stationed in Saigon. In a pathetic and almost comical assault on Phu Lam, his unit of 200 men— armed with only 70 muskets and 3 submachine guns—hoped to capture weapons from the Japanese. The abortive attack did more than point up the woeful lack in arms of these units. The subsequent interrogation of its chief and other men captured in the Phu Lam engagement indicated that at this stage of the August Revolution those who had received military experience exclusively under the French were men caught between two pressures: the dissolution of organizational structures to which they had previously been committed, and the uncertainty of participation with units that did not yet have stability of purpose or coherence in action. Hastily recruited to service, in many instances after months of inactivity, these exmilitiamen and colonial soldiers were illustrative of the military limitations of the revolutionaries. They could not rapidly forge new structures of deep commitment among those who had no identification with the revolutionary cause before the capitulation.

Organizational loyalty and operational coherence, and even tenacity, were more conspicuous among the Vietnamese military groups which had been formed with Japanese equipment and sponsorship. In addition to material aid, these diverse Vietnamese groups also received technical and operational assistance from Japanese officers and men who were present in the ranks of the Viet Minh and the sects during the resistance to French reoccupation. Of the 65,000 Japanese soldiers and 3,000 civilians in Indochina south of the 16th parallel at the time of the capitulation, approximately 1,000 joined actively with the various Vietnamese groups they had encouraged during their occupation. Before the end of 1946 nearly half of them had either been killed or captured or had given themselves up, which left a hard core of some 560 in the south, of whom the largest number, 220, were concentrated around Tay Ninh, the ecclesiastical center of the folk religion, the Cao Dai.[4] Because of the small percentage of Japanese activists with the Vietnamese and their concentration in homogeneous groups at key locations, the press and intelligence reports that they were almost exclusively agents of the Kempeitai (Japanese secret services) seem to be substantiated.[5] These military men provided the staff and training talent that gave coherence to what otherwise might have been fragmented armed bands; Japanese combat specialists in heavy and automatic weapons lent a potency to the units, and repair technicians gave them a logistical endurance.

Although this direct military assistance to the Vietnamese seems to have been carefully structured around the Kempeitai, the relationship of the Japanese High Command in Indochina to the events of the August Revolution was imprecise. There was clearly no evidence of massive support for local political groups by regular army units; yet a coordination, loose though it might have been, between the Kempeitai assistance and the action, or rather inaction, of the High Command—especially on September 2 and during the Cité Hérault incident of September 25—seems apparent. The repeated unwillingness of the Japanese to intervene in the violent clashes of September 1945, despite British demands that they be responsible for maintaining order, is a more straightforward indication that the High Command of Field Marshal Count Terauchi Isaichi was not interested in creating greater obstacles for the Vietnamese. It was only after the massacre at the Cité Hérault that the regular Japanese units were committed to assisting the French and British units. Thus, ironically, Japanese combatants became active on opposite sides.[6]

So long as the Japanese High Command was not willing to restrict their actions, the Vietnamese with Kempeitai assistance had a freedom of maneuver which could potentially have resulted

---

4 *The New York Times,* October 2, 1945, p. 4.
5 Ibid.
6 *The New York Times,* September 26, 1945, p. 15.

in the consolidation of the independence movement. But the Viet Minh was spectacularly unsuccessful in exploiting this latitude of action before the Allies and the High Command closed it, and the delicate balance of forces shifted decisively against the revolutionaries. Numerical inferiority was, however, only a part of the reason for the Viet Minh's being driven from Saigon and the provincial towns of southern Viet Nam. The divisiveness of indigenous political forces, in part a consequence of colonial development, in part the result of divergent Kempeitai encouragement, was the root of the problem. Exacerbated by the antagonizing moves of the Viet Minh, this divisiveness meant that the resistance could not compensate politically for its military limitations. Moreover, the Viet Minh suffered militarily by antagonizing its potential allies. It was the divisiveness, resulting in the excesses of September 1945 in Saigon, that caused the Japanese regulars, on orders of General Gracey, to be forced into the effort against the Viet Minh. It was concern with the effects of this divisiveness that resulted in the Nam Bo Committee's neglecting to exploit potential differences among the Allies or to win popularity locally among the uncommitted Vietnamese. Finally, it was the French who took successful advantage of this divisiveness by detaching nearly all of the sects and parties from the Communist–Advanced Guard Youth coalition.

In marked contrast to its urban performance the Nam Bo Committee when shifted to a rural environment and to a weaker position in the balance of forces shrewdly adopted forms of action—guerrilla warfare, sabotage, and terrorism—which maximized its modest strength and exposed the power limitations of the enemy. While the balance of forces had been unfavorable for maintaining a hold on the capital city and rural towns, it was sufficient for the Communists to prevent the consolidation of French control and to immobilize substantial portions of their army. Once the French forces were dispersed over the expanse of southern Viet Nam, they found themselves vulnerable to guerrilla attack as their troops spread over an ever larger area.

Thus the French came quickly to confront what was to be the main problem of the guerrilla phase of the Indochina War: how to divide their forces between those assigned to static defense elements and those given mobile intervention duty. This is perhaps the classic guerrilla war problem for the forces attempting to establish or maintain governmental authority. If forces are concentrated in order to wipe out an inferior guerrilla band, the adversary merely refuses combat and takes the occasion to hit emplacements left unprotected by the concentration of government forces. If government forces are dispersed to provide static security for routes of communication, military depots, economic installations, and a scattered rural population, then guerrilla forces concentrate to a strength sufficient to overpower the defenders and disrupt communications or capture supplies. Throughout 1946 the guerrilla activity in southern Viet Nam posed a challenge which the French were unable to surmount despite their estimates that at least 10,000 Vietnamese had been put out of action in the first half of that year. Yet, by June 1946 the French had about 33,000 officers and men in southern Indochina from their European army—a contingent 50 per cent greater than the highest force level for French troops during the Japanese occupation—plus more than 6,000 Vietnamese under their command. This great increase contrasted with the prewar situation when 10,779 regular French troops maintained all of Indochina for France with the assistance of 16,218 men of the local militia.[7] Why 39,000 men could not do the job that 27,000 had done with ease in twice the area before the war is explained only by the transformation that Vietnamese politics underwent during the Japanese occupation.

From this perspective on their guerrilla capacity the Viet Minh's task in obtaining political power during the August Revolution becomes more precise. Seizing revolutionary power, insofar as it meant getting administrative control over the key towns of Hanoi and Saigon, had merely facilitated the larger revolutionary task of establishing new structures of political organization. The public facilities and buildings gave no intrinsic power to the revolutionaries in order to help them stave off the return of the French; their usefulness was only as a bargaining

7 *Annuaire statistique de l'Indochine, 1936–1937*, pp. 25, 241.

tool and a hoped-for sanction in preventing the French from using force. But once the Nam Bo Committee was evicted from these locations in Saigon, what had changed was not the essential task of creating a structure of political power within the amorphous society of Viet Nam, where political participation was low, but only the environment in which this task would be accomplished. Thus in a real sense revolutionary power could not be seized, at least under conditions present in Viet Nam in 1945, it had to be developed.

Developing revolutionary power in northern Viet Nam was a less complex task than in the south, since in the north there was no meaningful autonomous opposition to the Communists. Those elements of the intellectual and administrative elite that had not been subdued by the superior arms and organization of the Viet Minh were mobilized behind the independence movement through ideological appeals. In the initial stages of the August Revolution around Hanoi there was no pressing need to bargain with an established opposition or to organize rapidly in the face of a hostile reoccupation. Later, however, the northern leadership was to demonstrate that when needed, it had impressive organizational qualities. The capacities of the southern leadership, on the other hand, were tested from the very beginning of the August Revolution. Its limitations lay in an inability to combine the very specific interests of the politically significant population into a broad independence movement. As the then secretary-general of the Communist Party analyzed it, the results in the south were due to

> the weakness of the Viet Minh organization in Nam Bo before the zero hour of the insurrection and to the lack of homogeneity in the ranks of the United National Front,

as well as

> . . . the slowness in starting the insurrection, the lack of resolution in seizing power, [which] encouraged the reactionaries, especially the French colonialists and pro-French Vietnamese traitors.[8]

8 Truong Chinh: *The August Revolution*, p. 35.

The momentary suspension of the international forces imping-
ing on Viet Nam at the Japanese capitulation had presented the
first real opportunity for the development of widespread political
power by Vietnamese during the twentieth century. Yet the
presence of the Japanese and the colonial commitments of the
French meant that this hiatus would be of short duration. Before
international pressures began to reappear, the Vietnamese had
not developed enough power to prevent a reimposition of colonial
rule. Time was, of course, a major limiting factor, but in the
space of a month before the reoccupation occurred in the south,
most of the features of Vietnamese society which facilitated or
circumscribed the development of revolutionary power were
demonstrated rather clearly. Thereafter, these advantages and
obstacles to the extension of Vietnamese political power remained to be employed and overcome in the drive to win independence from France.

PART SIX

The Revolutionary Opportunities in the Chinese Occupation of Northern Viet Nam, September 1945–March 1946

✖
✖
✖

CHAPTER 17 ✵ ✵ ✵

THE WARLORD OCCUPATION

OF NORTHERN VIET NAM

✵
✵
✵

With the arrival of Chinese troops in Hanoi on September 9, 1945, a new phase of the August Revolution in the north began. The unfettered latitude which the Viet Minh had enjoyed for almost a month, during which time the Japanese had neither prevented it from establishing its provisional revolutionary government nor prohibited it from proclaiming a declaration of independence, had come to an end. While the Chinese occupation was to circumscribe the political opportunities of the Viet Minh, the purpose of its leaders—in sharp contrast to the British in the south—was not to pave the way for the reestablishment of French sovereignty. Because of the history of Chinese relations with France in Indochina and the warlord involvement in Vietnamese exile politics, there was great interest in delaying the return of the French. Thwarting the growth of the Viet Minh and facilitating an orderly resumption of colonial authority would not prove to be goals of the Chinese occupation.

Although this delay was in the general interest of all Chinese associated with the occupation, it did not lead to any comprehensive or consistent exploitation of the opportunities presented. Through the divergent and often conflicting purposes of various Chinese governmental echelons, the occupation reflected many of the chaotic conditions of internal politics in China. The consequences of this situation meant that the Viet Minh, while having its purpose served by the blocking of the return of the French, now had a more complicated political environment within which to attempt to develop its revolutionary power. Their difficulty stemmed from the utilization of the Vietnamese exile groups by the Chinese occupation command to explore the possibilities of political influence in Viet Nam, and from the demands for privileges and largess made by these temporary Chinese overlords. These pressures obviously restricted the Viet Minh's freedom of maneuver, which had been at a maximum with the hiatus in established authority when the Japanese capitulated. But the Chinese did not completely eliminate this latitude; sensing the divisive character of Chinese motivations, the Viet Minh leaders successfully manipulated them to yield an extensive degree of operational autonomy. While this maneuvering placed great demands on the Viet Minh's capacity, it was out of this interaction between occupation and revolution that the underlying nature of both the August Revolution and Chinese interests in Viet Nam were demonstrated.

The Chinese occupation was a projection of the warlord politics of south China onto the revolutionary scene of northern Viet Nam. The confusing and often contradictory Chinese actions during the twelve months before the last remnants of their occupation forces left Indochina become more intelligible when analyzed in the context of China's domestic politics. The dispatch of troops into Tonkin, northern Annam, and upper Laos played an important role in efforts to curb warlordism—the existence of autonomous concentrations of regional political power beyond central control—which had plagued the republican government of China since its inception. It was this consideration which was the origin of the divergence in Chinese purposes during the occupation of Viet Nam.

One particularly annoying source of this type of political power was in the border province of Yunnan, where Lung Yun had ruled as governor since 1927. During the course of the anti-Japanese war, Lung Yun's strength had been diminished because of the proximity of the central government installed in Chungking, the location of armed divisions of the national regime in Yunnan, and the presence of American forces in the province. As World War II ended, it was clearly anticipated that Lung Yun would make strenuous efforts to reassert his autonomy and for this reason the central authorities moved to siphon off his power. Rather than employing troops of the central government exclusively for the Vietnamese occupation, Yunnanese forces under the command of Lu Han, a cousin and trusted lieutenant of Lung Yun's, were thrown upon what was considered the rich booty of northern Viet Nam.

Political competition in China caused the sending of a force which mounted to 150,000—and averaged 125,000 Chinese troops between October 1945 and April 1946—to supervise the surrender of 48,000 Japanese in northern Viet Nam, a task which the Chinese consistently neglected and never completed. At a minimum, 60,000 of these troops were always of Yunnanese origin. With his power resources thus depleted Lung Yun was brought under control by the central government on October 5, 1945, in what was known as the "Kunming incident," when he was arrested and Lu Han appointed to replace him. But Lu Han did not return permanently to Kunming to administer the affairs of Yunnan, for his base of strength was obviously with his troops in Viet Nam. Instead he would make brief air trips to south China to care for his interests.

Understandably, these circumstances did not lead Lu Han to regard his position or future with respect to the central government as secure, nor did they bring him any more closely under its control. Therefore, a curious situation developed. The French were attempting to obtain assistance for their military men and civilians still suffering from the effects of the Japanese occupation in northern Viet Nam and to minimize the political opportunities of the Viet Minh there; yet their diplomatic negotiations were with the central government of China, which did not have firm control over its representatives in Indochina. Although pre-occupied with the problems of Manchuria and the armed challenge of the Communists, the Chiang Kai-shek government expected to use its occupation of Viet Nam as an opportunity to renegotiate its treaty relations with France, with the hope of bringing an end to French extraterritorial rights in China. On the other hand, the interests of the Lu Han and other warlord factions were necessarily more short range and immediate because of their own uncertain positions. The situation became more complicated when in late December the 53rd Army of the Chinese central government arrived in Viet Nam to relieve the Yunnanese troops, who began to return to China by the beginning of February 1946. Even though this eliminated his real source of strength, Lu Han was allowed to remain in Viet Nam as the chief of the occupation forces, but now he was more firmly under the command of Nanking.

In the five months prior to the forced return of all his Yunnanese troops to China, Lu Han was able to follow an autonomously conceived path. Only partially was he restricted by visiting delegations of the central government, which periodically demanded more forthright action on the stated goals of the occupation. Lu Han was not interested in the Japanese, who, fortunately for him, managed to make themselves inconspicuous and avoided any clash with Chinese interests. More important for the Yunnan warlord were opportunities to damage French prestige, to dabble in Vietnamese politics, and to provide for his own enrichment.

Lu Han's pursuit of his goals began immediately upon the arrival of Chinese troops in Hanoi. At that moment the principal symbol of French sovereignty and authority was the handful of men in the French mission—led by Jean Sainteny—who had flown into the city shortly after the Japanese capitulation and installed themselves in the ornate and imposing palace of the governor general of Indochina. Had Lu Han been interested in abiding by Chiang Kai-shek's position on Viet Nam that ". . . China had no territorial ambitions there and that while sympathetic to the freedom of 'weak nations' the Chinese troops in northern Indochina would neither encourage the independence movement nor assist French soldiers in suppressing the rebels . . ."[1] he would have at a minimum allowed the small and ineffectual French mission to remain as it was. Instead, on the evening of September 9, only a few hours after the arrival of the mission, several Chinese officers appeared at the palace with the obvious intention of taking it over. They were put off temporarily, but on the 10th Sainteny was forced out of the palace in a maneuver that was unmistakably directed at embarrassing the French, diminishing their prestige with the Vietnamese, and asserting the predominance which the Chinese expected to exercise during their occupation.[2] Since the governor general's palace had such a symbolic importance in the August Revolution, its control was a key political barometer. Therefore, it was significant that after his brief occupancy Sainteny was unable to regain the building for more than a year, until December 23, 1946, when the clash with the Viet Minh in Hanoi ended the urban phase of the Vietnamese Revolution.[3]

Of greater potential to French authority in northern Viet Nam than possession of the governor general's palace were the approximately four thousand troops of the Colonial Army who had been interned in the citadel of Hanoi by the Japanese since March 9. In contrast to the British, who had released and rearmed the French troops in Saigon, the Chinese regarded their counterparts in the north as prisoners of war and not official representatives of the French government. As a further insult, the citadel of Hanoi was carefully searched to determine if the French troops interned there had by chance obtained any weapons.[4] The effect of these actions was slightly mitigated when the Chinese permitted the families of the colonial troops to visit the troops in detention, but only a month after the beginning of the occupation.

1 *The New York Times*, October 14, 1945, p. 12. Statement was reported to have been made on August 24, 1945.
2 Sainteny: *Histoire d'une paix manquée*, pp. 98–9.
3 Ibid., p. 226.
4 Ibid., p. 152.

The Chinese also blocked the restoration of colonial authority when they denied permission to approximately five thousand French troops, who had managed to escape capture during the Japanese *coup de force,* to return from south China until January 1946. Even then they were not permitted to enter Tonkin but were required to pass through Laos to central Viet Nam. This pattern of refusing to recognize the existence of French authority was also followed in the Chinese occupation of Laos, where French guerrillas who had held out against the Japanese were disarmed and the official French representative in Vientiane was arrested. Moreover, the Chinese 93rd Independent Division took up positions in the highlands of Laos where no Japanese forces had ever been stationed so that it might control the opium poppy harvest. The division refused to leave Indochina until September 1946, a year after its arrival, when a second crop became available.

At the formal ceremony in Hanoi accepting the surrender of the Japanese on September 28, 1945, the confrontation between the French and the Chinese on the questions of status and prestige became more antagonistic. The French representative to this affair, General Alessandri, who had just arrived from Yunnan for the ceremony, was not allowed to attend in an official capacity because of what was termed his "unclear position." By this it was meant to emphasize that he had served the Vichy administration in Indochina, which had cooperated with the Japanese. Although Alessandri had exonerated himself with the French by his service to de Gaulle after March 9, 1945, his taint provided the Chinese with their opportunity for embarrassing France. When Alessandri noted the absence of the French flag on September 28 and requested that it be raised for the ceremony, he was refused. It was explained that Lu Han feared that the disturbances which had occurred in Saigon at a surrender ceremony where the French flag had been flown might also result in Hanoi. Alessandri was outraged but his embarrassment for the day was far from ended.

Later, undoubtedly as a retort for Alessandri's angry departure from the ceremony, where he was seated 114th in order of priority, Lu Han issued a statement in which he warned " 'the enemy of Viet Nam' that if they dared to cause any troubles or to stir up any bloody tragedy then he would severely punish them . . ."[5] Little doubt was left as to the identity of the "enemy of Viet Nam." Affronts of this sort to the French representative in Hanoi continued to mount, and on October 2, in an interview with the visiting delegate of the Chinese central government in Chungking, Marshal Ho Ying-ch'ing, Alessandri was told that his official position was not recognized and that the question of French sovereignty in Indochina was a matter for further diplomatic discussion.

While this attitude from the emissary of the central government seemed to indicate a unanimity with the warlord factions in Viet Nam, such was not the case. Marshal Ho had also told Alessandri that China did not have the least desire of seizing Viet Nam but, on the contrary, hoped to aid in its gradual realization of independence according to a program to be determined by the great powers.[6] Moreover, one of the principal reasons for Marshal Ho's visit to Hanoi was to expedite the disarmament and the regrouping of the Japanese.[7] In addition, the central government of China had disavowed Lu Han over the issue of not releasing French prisoners from the Hanoi citadel. Through Marshal Ho's visit it was emphasizing to its commander on the scene that it wanted a purely military occupation, avoiding any political involvement in Vietnamese affairs while negotiations with France on outstanding diplomatic issues were being conducted. Although its lack of firm control over the Yunnanese occupation troops meant that a certain amount of embarrassment to the French was unavoidable, this could hardly undermine the strong bargaining position which the Chungking government had.

Lu Han's interests were motivated by entirely different considerations. He disagreed fundamentally with the occupation

5 Chu Ch'i: *Yueh-nan shou-hsiang jih-chi* ("Diary of Accepting [the Japanese] Surrender in Viet Nam") (Shanghai: Commercial Press Company; 1946), pp. 19–20. This is an account by a Chinese occupation official and is considered the only dependable source on these events. Cited in King Chen: "China and the Democratic Republic of Viet Nam," p. 80.

6 Devillers: *Histoire du Viet Nam*, p. 193.

7 King Chen: "China and the Democratic Republic of Viet Nam," p. 82.

policy of Chungking. The Yunnanese warlord-politician desired "a long period of occupation and to place Viet Nam under China's trusteeship while supporting and assisting the Vietnamese to obtain their independence."[8] Obviously such a situation was highly desirable from the perspective of a political leader in a south China border province, for whom opportunities for expanding influence seemed naturally to point southward. If Ho Ying-ch'ing's mission had real expectations of dissuading Lu Han from such purposes and prodding him on to the task of dealing with the Japanese, then the timing of the "Kunming incident" on October 5, while the marshal was in Hanoi, could hardly have been more inappropriate. With Lung Yun arrested the key issue for the Yunnanese chief in Viet Nam was to maintain what power he had by virtue of his occupation command position.

Since it seems certain that Chungking was determined to eliminate Lung Yun, antagonizing Lu Han would appear to have been unavoidable. But once the antagonism had emerged, the only alternative available to the central government in prosecuting its policy in Viet Nam was to replace Lu Han and take away his power. Eventually this was done, but the challenges it faced in north China meant that the central government could not do it immediately and never with the confidence that the replacement troops it sent would not develop autonomous interests of their own. In the meantime, Lu Han's objective became understandably narrowed from what was advantageous for a Yunnanese warlord faction in an adjacent territory to what was good for Lu Han stripped of his territorial base and aware that efforts to reduce his strength further would be forthcoming. Possessing a sizable and undisciplined armed force, facing few sanctions, and having few long-range prospects for political survival, Lu Han's potential to affect the August Revolution was as great as his purposelessness and opportunism. With such a combination of circumstances it was not surprising that the course he chose had only a modicum of consistency.

8 Chu Ch'i: *Yueh-nan shou-hsiang jih-chi*, p. 10. Cited in King Chen: "China and the Democratic Republic of Viet Nam," p. 79.

CHAPTER 18 ✿ ✿ ✿

VIET MINH MANEUVERS

AGAINST THE VIETNAMESE

NATIONALISTS

✿
✿
✿

Lu Han's occupation policies were not designed to bring Viet Nam under China's trusteeship; they did not serve to establish firm Chinese ties with Vietnamese politics except in an almost accidental and pragmatic manner. When the Chinese troops arrived in northern Viet Nam in early September 1945, their retinue included the Vietnamese exile political groups that they had nurtured and sustained during the Japanese war. Just as they had been maintained for intelligence-gathering during the war, now the exiles were being employed as instruments of the occupation command in the politics of Viet Nam. Unhappily for the Chinese, the exiles' capacity for effectiveness in this task was no greater than that which they had demonstrated in attempting to obtain information on the Japanese occupation in Indochina.

While Lu Han had the option of establishing a political alliance with the Viet Minh, the greater political capacity of the Communist organization also gave it greater autonomy. The exiles, on the other hand, were easier to control because they were almost totally dependent on the Chinese for their strength. They were useful in opposing the Viet Minh's designs for total political hegemony, thus allowing the Chinese to secure actions from the Communist-led group which might have been more costly to obtain otherwise. These potential costs would have included the creation of a truly effective client Vietnamese political group or a resolution of Chinese interests with those of the Viet Minh. Such alternatives were too long range for either the occupation leadership or the Viet Minh, so out of the desire of both the Chinese and the Viet Minh to fulfill immediate goals, a complex pattern of competition and cooperation arose.

One of the limiting factors of the Vietnamese nationalist exiles as effective revolutionaries was their fragmentation. This characteristic had been demonstrated in the efforts of Chang Fa-k'wei to organize them into a coherent political organization. Many of the obstacles to this goal had been of his own creation in trying to force a consensus upon them, but the fragmentation was also, and perhaps primarily, due to the fact that the exile groups were personal followings rather than broad structures of interest. Since personal prestige was easily affronted in working out organizational priorities, fragmentation was not an unexpected consequence. A final attempt to heal these fissures by the formation of a provisional Vietnamese government in March 1944 had only made the antagonism more irreconcilable. Ho Chi Minh and Vu Hong Khanh deserted this government, and the Kwangsi warlord, Chang Fa-k'wei, was ironically left with the least competent of the exiles, the aging Nguyen Hai Than, and his impotent Dong Minh Hoi.[1] It was this division among the exiles that existed when the Chinese occupation of northern Viet Nam began. Moreover, the ties of the VNQDD (the Viet Nam Nationalist Party) to the Yunnanese, and the Dong Minh Hoi to the Kwangsi troops proved to be a source of

1 Dabezies: "Forces politiques au Viet Nam," p. 152.

friction among these two Chinese factions in the occupation command.

In early September 1945, as the Yunnanese 93rd Army moved across the Sino-Vietnamese border at Lao Kay and then down the Red River Valley to Hanoi, it systematically overturned whatever governmental presence it found in the towns along the route and installed the VNQDD.[2] Similarly, the Dong Minh Hoi was established in the towns along the path of the 52nd Army from Kwangsi, as it occupied Lang Son on the border and swept along the northeast coast to Haiphong. However, these non-Yunnanese troops did not remain in Viet Nam and returned rapidly to Chang Fa-k'wei's control in South China, leaving the Kwangsi leader Hsiao Wen as political advisor to Lu Han. Although he was without any real source of power, Hsiao Wen's primary objective was to place Nguyen Hai Than of the Dong Minh Hoi in power as the legitimate head of the provisional government to which the other Vietnamese political figures had been committed in March 1944. Considering the Dong Minh Hoi's relative strength, this was clearly an ill-founded goal.

Initial assessments of the strength of the three major Vietnamese political groups indicated that the Chinese-protected nationalist exiles were in a disadvantaged position in number of adherents. Even with the addition of the members of the exile Phuc Quoc movement, who had long since lost any real hope of the restoration of Cuong De to the throne, the Dong Minh Hoi was believed to have had no more than 1,500 members. The VNQDD was much stronger, with about 8,000 followers when it returned to Viet Nam with the Yunnanese forces after fifteen years of exile. In sharp contrast, the Viet Minh were thought to have 70,000 adherents, including recruits in the mountain base area. Not only did this ranking of the strength of the Vietnamese political movements demonstrate the weakness of the two Chinese-oriented exile groups, but with Hanoi having a population of 119,700 and Tonkin containing 9,851,000, it

2 Ibid.

also indicated that none of the groups had a mass following.[3]

Though social and economic distress was widespread as a result of famine, floods, and Japanese-enforced food requisitions, most of the population remained politically inert because of the absence of organized forms for popular participation. As long as distress was localized and political organization minimal, the August Revolution continued as a process of the unstable maneuvering and bargaining of political elites rather than as a mass uprising. This did not mean that there was a disinterest in a popular base among the parties competing for influence within the constraints of the Chinese occupation of northern Viet Nam. But in the space of less than two months following the capitulation, when the first real opportunities for broad political organization had occurred in the country, none of the parties, with the exception of the Viet Minh, had the capacity or decisiveness to gain a wide following. Yet the Communists also did not have a mass organization. As was observed of its character at the time, "The Communist Party is an elite of shock troops, but even in this case they are more like a clandestine group than a normal party. The masses are still lacking. No party exercises over them an immediate and profound hold. The parties then lack an essential thing: a pact with the people. . . ."[4]

In establishing such a popular alliance the Communists were over the long range committed to the use of organizational techniques which the other parties had not mastered. As a consequence of the effectiveness of these techniques the Chinese-protected, nationalist political groups launched a propaganda campaign through their respective newspapers, Đồng Minh and Việt Nam, in which they sought to discredit the Viet Minh regime and to force the formation of a government of national union.[5] They also developed shock groups which specialized in kidnapping members of the Viet Minh and, by their success in this technique, forced a showdown on the issue of a reorganized government. The Chinese feared that a showdown might lead to

---

3 *Annuaire statistique de l'Indochine, 1943–1946*, pp. 27–8.
4 Mus: *Problèmes de l'Indochine contemporaine*, P.M. I, p. 16.
5 Dabezies: "Forces politiques au Viet Nam," p. 154.

violent conflict; therefore, they quickly arranged an accord between the Dong Minh Hoi and the Viet Minh on October 23,
but this lasted only eight days and was ended when Nguyen Hai
Than resumed his denunciations of the Viet Minh.[6]

The tactics of the Dong Minh Hoi then became less crude. They
began to attack the Viet Minh for its Communist origins in an
attempt to play upon the suspicions of the Kuomintang Chinese
as well as the privileged Vietnamese in Hanoi and the provincial
towns.[7] The Viet Minh responded to this challenge by having
the Central Committee of the Indochinese Communist Party
formally proclaim the dissolution of the party organization on
November 11. There was little meaning in this gesture, for all
the subsequent party documents demonstrate that the structure
and leadership continued to function without any fundamental
changes.[8] While it doubtless enabled the Viet Minh to strengthen
its nationalist identification, the maneuver's most important effect
was to throw the other parties back upon their limited capacities
to oppose their Communist adversaries. Not only were they de-
ficient in organization, but they were being outperformed in the
propaganda war, through which they had their best hope of winning support among the unorganized population. However, the
exile groups were not a complete failure in these verbal battles,
for their denunciation was troublesome enough for the Viet
Minh to make them take over the VNQDD newspaper, *Việt
Nam*, on November 18. Another certain clash growing out of
this incident was averted by an accord on November 19, in
which the formation of a national union government was again
pledged by the Viet Minh.[9] This too proved to be a transient
move, quickly forgotten in the rush of events.

The character of this competition among handfuls of political

6 Ibid.

7 Devillers: *Histoire du Viet Nam*, p. 195.

8 Nguyen Kien Giang: *Les grandes dates du parti de la classe ouvrière du Viet Nam*,
pp. 53–4, records that the Central Committee of the party issued an important directive
on November 25, 1945, after the party was publicly dissolved. This book does not
mention the dissolution of the party. It avoids the problem of the change of the
name of the party by identifying it as the Worker's Party, or Lao Dong Dang,
the appellation adopted February 11, 1951, for the Indochina Communist Party,
which was founded in 1930.

9 Dabezies: "Forces politiques au Viet Nam," p. 154.

activists in northern Viet Nam was the result of the small size of the groups out of power, their lack of armed units for more overt action, and their inability to translate popular uncertainty and discontent into political strength. Within these limits there were few alternatives open to the VNQDD and the Dong Minh Hoi other than trying to force the Viet Minh to share governmental power with them by propaganda attacks which questioned its legitimacy. The non-Communist groups had little capacity for broadening the political context of the August Revolution to develop an effective challenge to the Viet Minh. Unlike the parties of southern Viet Nam—the religious-political sects and the Trotskyites, which were powers to be reckoned with—the exile parties of the north were not serious competitors for power. But by their foothold of strength and their limited challenges, they were able to cast in relief some of the essentials by which the Viet Minh was holding power.

Beyond its armed units, its control over the vestiges of the colonial administrative structure, and its advantage in number of followers, there was a more fundamental source of Viet Minh strength. That the Viet Minh had institutionalized itself as a revolutionary government, been the first to succeed to authority upon the Japanese capitulation, and established a legitimacy based on an identification with national independence was the real demonstration of its strength. The Viet Minh's experience seems to support Paul Mus's observation that "The only revolution that the Sino-Vietnamese political wisdom, in its classical expression, holds as authentic is that which changes things completely. It is a major proof of the right to power that a program with new solutions for all things is offered. This conception has been, in the Far East, familiar for all times to the most modest countryman."[1] The Viet Minh had, as Mus points out, an ability to present its actions as a "renovation of the state," while its competitors had only parochial concepts and goals for power.[2]

The parochialism of its opponents became more conspicuous during the controversy which resulted over the Viet Minh's de-

[1] Mus: *Viet Nam: Sociologie d'une guerre*, p. 30.
[2] Ibid.

termination to hold general elections for a national assembly on December 23. Since this would be the first experience of the Vietnamese with universal suffrage, it would obviously be an event of great impact in establishing an identity between the population and the revolutionary government. It was primarily General Hsiao Wen rather than the exile parties themselves that tried to block the Viet Minh's maneuver. The Kwangsi political adviser still had hopes of being able to reconstitute the coalition of the Dong Minh Hoi, the VNQDD, and the Viet Minh as it had existed in March 1944.[3] This was not only unrealistic from the perspective of the relative strengths of the groups, but also beyond Hsiao Wen's political or coercive capacity to achieve. What he could and did secure on December 19 was a delay in the elections until January 6, 1946, but this did not really satisfy his objectives. His apprehension over the decline of influence for his clients was well founded. Beyond the areas where their meager armed units were located, the VNQDD and the Dong Minh Hoi did not have the provincial political organization which the Viet Minh had constructed. While the VNQDD could count on some of the contacts it had cultivated before its downfall following the Yen Bay revolt of 1930, the Dong Minh Hoi could claim little support other than the followers it brought with it from China.

Hsiao Wen continued to press what advantage he possessed, and on December 23 he obtained an accord for the exile nationalists with the Viet Minh which called for (1) the formation of a provisional government of national union while awaiting the constitution of a permanent government by the national assembly, (2) support of general elections by all parties, and (3) the allocation of seventy "special" seats in the national assembly, fifty for the VNQDD and twenty for the Dong Minh Hoi, in addition to those which might be won in the election. However, this accord was not respected by any of the parties; the Viet Minh did not cancel the elections originally called for December 23 in remote areas, which it claimed could not be reached by a counter order, and the Dong Minh Hoi and the

3 Devillers: *Histoire du Viet Nam*, p. 200.

VNQDD continued to lead a campaign against the elections, hoping ultimately to sabotage them by not putting up any candidates. This abstention had little effect, and the resulting vote reported for the Viet Minh was massive. In Hanoi, Ho Chi Minh received 169,222 votes or 98 per cent of the 172,765 cast from 187,880 registrees, a figure which strains belief, since population statistics show that there were only 119,000 persons in the city.[4] In his native province of Nghe An, Vo Nguyen Giap received 97 per cent of the votes cast.[5] The countrywide results, giving the Viet Minh 90–92 per cent of the total vote, aroused such passions from the opposition that they were not published for three months, when other issues had intervened to divert attention from their incredible disparity.[6]

What had these elections demonstrated about revolutionary politics in Viet Nam? Did they communicate some underlying feelings of the population or did they merely ratify the existing situation? Did they represent a competition for political support among autonomous groups or were they a controlled demonstration of political strength? One observer has noted:

> The choice of the voters among the various candidates appeared to have been free on the whole, but the choice was limited. There were hardly any other candidates than those agreed on by the Viet Minh Front. "Collaborators," "corrupt" and suspect elements were eliminated. But wasn't this the common lot in all liberated countries? In France itself at this time was the choice before the voters so wide, could one then conceive of the candidacy of a Maurras, a Flandin, a Georges Bonnet, or a Paul Faure? The Ho Chi Minh government created a democratic base by the same methods and the same means as those of General de Gaulle and M. Bidault, methods it must be said, which were more liberal than those that prevailed behind the iron curtain or in Algeria.[7]

But are these conclusions justified in light of the discrepancies which have been noted in the course of the election?

---

4 Devillers: *Histoire du Viet Nam*, p. 201. *Annuaire statistique de l'Indochine, 1943–1946*, p. 27.
5 Ibid.
6 Dabezies. "Forces politiques au Viet Nam," p. 155.
7 Devillers: *Histoire du Viet Nam*, p. 201.

In the provincial towns controlled by the VNQDD or the Dong Minh Hoi—such as Vinh Yen, Viet Tri, Phu Tho, Yen Bay, Lao Kay, Mon Cay, and Ha Giang—elections did not take place at all. Yet when the National Assembly convened, Viet Minh representatives were seated from these localities. Moreover, there was the question of geographic distribution of the seats in the National Assembly. Of the 374 elected members only 18 came from southern Viet Nam (Cochinchina) while the north and center had 356 representatives. However, the south had 5,500,000 inhabitants or a little less than 25 per cent of the total population of approximately 22,000,000 in Viet Nam.[8] Although the assembly was to have a truly national character, there were no elections in the French-controlled southern area and only 1 representative out of the 18 allotted to the south ever attended any of the brief sessions. This put the bulk of the constituencies in the north, where the influence of the Viet Minh was predominant. But even in locations where it was not paramount, the Viet Minh carefully managed the election of its candidates, sometimes placing them on the lists of subsidiary parties.

The underlying significance of the election seems to go beyond the Viet Minh's gerrymandering to establish a national legislature in its own image. The most important aspect of the effort to strengthen its political legitimacy was that voting was practically obligatory for every man and woman above the age of eighteen in areas under Viet Minh influence. Food ration cards had to be presented when an individual voted, and without the stamp given to the card it was no longer valid. Under the conditions of food scarcity and near-famine then existing in the north, this was undoubtedly an extremely effective means of bringing the urban population more firmly under the Viet Minh's control. It demonstrated a capacity for the exercise of authority which no other indigenous group could approximate and thus increased the compliance toward the Viet Minh regime on a purely pragmatic basis. Legitimacy was not only to be consolidated by an identification with aspirations of the moment, but also through

8 *Annuaire statistique de l'Indochine, 1943–1946*, pp. 27–8.

administrative performance to meet basic public needs. The unusual sagacity of the Viet Minh was in using its administrative capacity in order to strengthen popular identification with the revolutionary regime through the requirement of the ration card stamp in voting. This technique seemed to ensure that what was not secured through popular enthusiasm over the first opportunity to participate in choosing a government in Viet Nam would be obtained on a more certain basis.

CHAPTER 19 ✖ ✖ ✖

THE CHINESE ROLE

IN THE REVOLUTION

✖

✖

✖

The fact that elections for a national assembly occurred in December 1945 and January 1946 demonstrated again that the Viet Minh had opportunities to consolidate its revolutionary power in northern Viet Nam which were denied to it in the south by the determined reoccupation of the French. The Chinese occupation had substantially restricted but not eliminated the hiatus in international power which had permitted the August Revolution to occur. The situation reflected the very different diplomatic status that China had with France as contrasted with that of Britain. But it was also an indication of the totally different relationship that the Viet Minh had been able to develop with the Chinese occupiers, which the diplomatic position of the British made difficult if not impossible to achieve in the south. This is not to imply that the Chinese desire to improve its diplomatic relations with the French automatically brought the Viet Minh advantages in consolidating its power. The significant divergence in purpose between the occupation forces under Lu Han and the Chinese central government, with whom the French were negotiating for their own reoccupation, meant that special efforts were required of the Viet Minh.

From the very outset of the occupation these efforts were made with shrewdness and determination. Without these important qualities, Lu Han could have potentially eliminated the Viet Minh regime and established his own Vietnamese followers in power. But the Viet Minh showed, at least to Lu Han's satisfaction, that they could provide more of what the occupiers wanted than any other Vietnamese group. Necessarily, their overthrow would have required the substitution of a group with similar capacities or the use of coercive force to get the same results. In a situation reminiscent of the Allied intervention during the Russian Revolution, it is a remarkable dimension of the August Revolution that the Viet Minh was able to manage the demands of the Chinese occupation and not only maintain but extend its own power.[1]

Although the Viet Minh abolished all taxes in a sweeping propaganda gesture at the beginning of September 1945, it organized "voluntary" subscriptions from the rich to sustain its administration. It was in this context that a "Gold Week" was held September 16–23, during which the private gold hoards that were the savings of a people living in wartime insecurity were solicited.[2] When Lu Han arrived in Hanoi by plane from Yunnan September 18, he was presented a gold opium pipe by Ho Chi Minh.[3] From this auspicious beginning Ho developed a relationship by which he was able to thwart Hsiao Wen's objective of placing Nguyen Hai Than in power as a Kwangsi puppet. More vital than the "Gold Week" tactics to the solidification of this tie with the Yunnanese leader was the willingness of the Viet Minh to accept favorable exchange rates for Chinese

1 A comparison between the August Revolution and the October Revolution has been drawn by George Modelski: "The Viet Minh Complex," in Cyril E. Black and Thomas P. Thornton, eds.: *Communism and Revolution: The Strategic Uses of Political Violence* (Princeton: Princeton University Press; 1964), p. 206.

2 Volait: *La vie économique et sociale du Viet Nam*, pp. 16–17.

3 Devillers: *Histoire du Viet Nam*, p. 193.

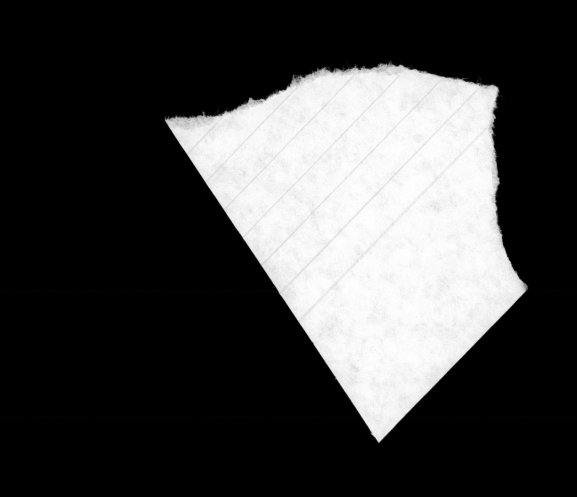

currency, which eventually enabled the occupation forces to extract enormous profits from Viet Nam.

The question of the exchange rate was one of the first tasks which the Chinese dealt with. It appears that it was an arbitrary Chinese decision to set the rate at 1.50 Bank of Indochina piasters to 20 Chinese dollars. This meant that the value of Chinese money in Hanoi was roughly three to five times higher than in Kunming, the capital of Yunnan province.[4] In Hanoi 1 piaster was worth 13.33 Chinese dollars, while in Kunming its value was between 45 and 70 dollars. Consequently, every airplane arriving from Kunming brought with it great quantities of money to be exchanged, and in one instance 60 million Chinese dollars were reported on a single flight.[5] The Chinese began to buy up hotels, shops, houses, and similar sorts of real estate in yet another form of speculation. By these and a wide variety of other financial operations, including loans received from the Bank of Indochina, the Chinese occupation was estimated to have extracted 400 million Bank of Indochina piasters as well as 14,000 tons of rice valued at 27 million piasters.[6] This booty did not include the returns from the opium harvests which the Chinese 93rd Independent Division was able to acquire in northern Laos. Nor did it reflect the contraband trade in Viet Nam which official and unofficial Chinese carried on in items ranging from armaments to foodstuffs.

While it is virtually impossible to establish a more precise measure of the financial burden of the Chinese occupation, a rough order of magnitude can be estimated. In 1939, governmental expenditures for all of Indochina were 114 million piasters at the existing valuation, which constituted about 10 per cent of the annual product of the Indochinese states, or 1.14 billion piasters.[7] In their occupation of only the northern portion of Viet Nam, it appears that the Chinese were able to secure fi-

4 Sainteny: *Histoire d'une paix manquée*, p. 149.

5 Chu Ch'i: *Yueh-nan shou-hsiang jih-chi*, pp. 25, 43, 63, as cited in King Chen: "China and the Democratic Republic of Viet Nam," p. 89.

6 Sainteny: *Histoire d'une paix manquée*, p. 148.

7 McCall: "The Effects of Independence on the Economy of Viet Nam," p. 7.

nancial and other resources equivalent to at least half of the annual prewar product of the whole of Indochina. Another measure of this burden is the estimate that all war damages totaled 2.8 billion piasters. In less than one year the Chinese were able to obtain about a fifth of what the Japanese had siphoned off in five years of occupation of the whole of Indochina.[8]

Measured against such substantial material return, any political advantages that the Chinese could have potentially secured would seem at best ephemeral. Unless the Chinese had been willing to make a more determined effort to resist French reoccupation, there would seem to have been no long-range purpose served by placing Nguyen Hai Than or any other puppet in power. The warlord occupiers undoubtedly knew the limitations of the Vietnamese nationalist exile groups. Certainly their resiliency against a reestablished French colonialism was not hard to assess. In the shorter range, the option of overturning the Viet Minh for the benefit of the exile politicians could have offered few advantages as long as the Communists were responsive to the interests of the occupiers. While Viet Minh power was minute in comparison to the Chinese occupation forces, it was, especially in its political dimension, significant enough to have caused Lu Han considerable trouble had a relatively harmonious relationship not been developed. From the outset, Ho Chi Minh showed his understanding of Lu Han's desires for largess and took no action to thwart them even though it meant the further impoverishment of his flood- and famine-ravaged country.

Whether these were the terms on which Lu Han decided to give no more than token support to the VNQDD and the Dong Minh Hoi cannot be determined from available evidence. However, the Viet Minh, which potentially could have staged a boycott of the Chinese exchange rate, did not receive a clear field from its acquiescence. It had to deal with Hsiao Wen's political ambitions for the exile groups, and although Lu Han did not offer this project any support, he did not actively discourage it. In addition to participating in Hsiao Wen's periodic accords with

8 Ibid., p. 73.

the exiles, as occurred on October 23 and November 19, 1945, the Viet Minh also had to make substantial efforts to satisfy or neutralize the VNQDD and the Dong Minh Hoi. Such was the intent of the December 23 agreement in which the two nationalist parties received seventy seats in the National Assembly. This agreement also stated that Nguyen Hai Than would become vice-premier and that two cabinet positions, ministries of economy and health, would be reserved for the Dong Minh Hoi, while two other posts were allotted to the VNQDD.[9]

Obviously, the Viet Minh expected that tactics of this sort would fulfill the demands of the opposition parties. Although they initially rejected these cabinet and legislative positions, the exile nationalists eventually agreed to participate in a Viet Minh-led government. This change did not represent an ideological transformation but, with the departure of Yunnanese troops from the ranks of the occupation forces by the beginning of February 1946, there was the realization that continued opposition to the Viet Minh offered few advantages. As long as the exile nationalists remained without a mass base and without effective political tactics, few alternatives were open to them. During the early phases of the occupation, their main alternative came from Hsiao Wen's unrelenting prodding of the Viet Minh. But the latter was adept enough to provide an outlet for its political competitors while preserving its own initiative in the August Revolution. This strategy, along with that of ensuring that Lu Han's purposes did not remain unfulfilled, obtained for the Viet Minh a vital measure of latitude within which it could continue to develop its revolutionary power.

This interaction of occupation and revolution which characterized the August Revolution in northern Viet Nam showed that in a colonial society the criterion for revolutionary success was not only holding power internally, but also manipulating international forces. These internal and international dimensions were intimately linked in Viet Nam. Although substantial advantage accrued to the Viet Minh from its wider base of popular support, it was not the utilization of popular strength which circum-

9 Dabezies: "Forces politiques au Viet Nam," p. 155.

scribed the exile nationalists and satisfied the Chinese occupiers. The political skills that accomplished these tasks were an ability to sense the presence of power and to respond to its pressure. Through the expansion of its military and political capacities, the Viet Minh displayed many of the characteristics that were to persist through seven years of revolutionary war. Getting external assistance was an important one of them.

That the Chinese occupation troops played a part in the arming of the Viet Minh has been suggested by French observers and publicly asserted by an agent of the exile nationalists.[1] From Hong Kong in 1947 there was a press dispatch which quoted the declaration of a verified Vietnamese nationalist source that "most of the arms being used by resistance groups against the French in Indochina were brought through private channels while General Lu Han's government forces occupied the northern half of the country at the end of the war."[2] The source indicated that he had purchased as much as 30,000 U.S. dollars' worth of arms from the Chinese and that anyone with the cash could get arms. His testimony underscored the fact that the selling of arms "consisted of private and not official transactions." However, it was reported that "Chinese officers and men disposed of both Japanese arms taken over from the enemy depots and some of their own lend-lease weapons."[3]

Although there is little doubt that the Viet Minh obtained armaments through the Chinese, it is difficult to determine the exact amount. In order to define more precisely the importance of the Chinese as a source of weapons, a comparison is required with the arms secured earlier from French stocks either with the complicity or acquiescence of the Japanese. According to available information, as of March 6, 1946, there were almost 32,000 weapons from the following three sources in the hands of the Viet Minh north of the 16th parallel (in addition to the approximately 4,600 arms air-dropped to them by the Allies before August 19, 1945): (1) from stocks of the Garde Indo-

1 Marchand: *Le drame indochinois*, p. 75, says that weapons were purchased through the Chinese.
2 *The New York Times*, April 1, 1947, p. 15.
3 Ibid.

chinoise allegedly acquired with the help of the Japanese; (2) from stocks of the French Colonial Army obtained with Japanese help; and (3) from Japanese army stocks, some ceded directly, others received through the Chinese. Together with the arms air-dropped to them, this gave the Viet Minh armed forces a total of 35,600 individual and 750 automatic weapons, plus 36 artillery pieces and an indeterminate number of mortars and heavy weapons.[4]

Official estimates suggest that less than 20 per cent of this armament available to the Viet Minh in the spring of 1946 was obtained through the Chinese, but this information concerned only known stocks of weapons. Many more arms than these specifically documented came into the possession of the Communist revolutionaries. The most accurate estimate of their material resources at any one time during the August Revolution is probably the one given for December 19, 1946, the day the Viet Minh initiated its general attack against the French. The estimate indicates that it had arms sufficient for approximately 150 battalions. Using the allowances of weapons thought to be available to such units, the Viet Minh had roughly the following amount of equipment in excess of known stocks in the hands of the French prior to the Japanese *coup de force*:

INCREASE IN VIET MINH WEAPONS
STOCKS DURING 1946

Aggregate Estimate for December 19, 1946	Amount Increase over March 6, 1946	Percentage Increase
75,000 individual weapons	40,000	114%
2,250 automatic weapons	1,500	300%
300–450 mortars	indeterminate	indeterminate
4,500 submachine guns	3,900	900%

In attempting to account for this increase over nine months of approximately 45,000 arms it seems probable that the 6,000 weapons estimated to have been acquired from 48,000 Japanese

4 Data is from archival sources; see also Marchand: *Le drame indochinois*, p. 75.

troops is understated. However, in the absence of more extensive information it is impossible to suggest a more accurate estimate. While these Japanese arms and those of the Chinese occupation troops were undoubtedly prime items in the contraband trade, a source of greater supply was the sea and overland shipments from China. This contraband trade was facilitated by the extremely unsettled situation in the area along the Sino-Vietnamese border and the continued predominance of warlordism adjacent to the frontier, both during the Chinese occupation of Viet Nam and afterward.

With the attention of both the major political forces in China focused on the conflict of the civil war in the north, the task of containing the power of southern warlords was less pressing. The border area, which came less and less under the control of any authority, was to remain in an anarchic state for several years until the Chinese Communists were able to impose their centralizing force on the southern region. Therefore, the Viet Minh, maintaining its mountainous base contiguous with the China border, continued to secure armaments without interruption after December 1946, when the French occupied many of the key coastal towns which were centers of the sea trade.

Before this inconvenience occurred, a lively junk trade in contraband arms was taking place between Hai Nan Island, the south China coast, and the Vietnamese coast. This traffic was originally set in motion by Japanese deserters but was later picked up by Chinese promoters. As a representative case, a junk carrying a load of 22 submachine guns, 2 automatic rifles and a stock of ammunition was known to have arrived in the northern coastal town of Quang Yen in December 1945. With cargoes of this size it would have required only twenty junks with such loads to have supplied the Viet Minh during 1945–6 with the total increase of submachine guns above known stocks. There are indications that this level of activity was completely within the capacity of the external supply operations that the Viet Minh had established. In one day, December 15, 1945, an eleven-junk convoy reportedly deposited an estimated 1,500 metric tons of arms and ammunition on the island of Hon Me, between Thanh Hoa and Vinh on the coast of central Viet Nam. On the same day another four junks arrived in the town of Thanh Hoa with American arms which were being supplied by Chinese commercial intermediaries.

There was no question of any of this supply of arms being a gift, and as the trade developed, procedures became more standardized. The Viet Minh sent a representative, Nguyen Van Cam, to make purchases in Canton and Hong Kong on the basis of exchange of opium, gold, and rice for weapons. Like the arrangements made with the Chinese occupation forces, these agreements were not so much politically inspired as they were financially motivated. Although it seems that some of the arms supplies were facilitated by Chinese Communist units in south China, their assistance was on a strictly *quid pro quo* basis. Another element in this pattern of external supply was the purchase of arms in Thailand for the Communist-led resistance in southern Viet Nam. This task was undertaken in Bangkok by Tran Van Giau, who had been removed as military commissar for the Nam Bo Committee. Through him, arms were sent by sea from a small port east of Bangkok to towns and secret locations in Viet Nam along the Gulf of Thailand, as well as overland through the central Viet Nam mountains from the northeastern Thai town of Oubon.

The ability to obtain resources sufficient to sustain such a contraband trade was another indication of the organizational capacity of the Viet Minh. One important means of raising the items of exchange for weapons was through the purchase of opium on the Laotian frontier. Salt worth 1,000 piasters was given for a kilogram of opium; the opium was resold to Chinese traffickers in Hanoi at 15,000 piasters per kilogram in hard currency.[5] But as the Viet Minh strengthened its hold on the north, it developed an even more remunerative and sophisticated means of financing governmental and military operations. This involved the Bank of Indochina, which, with its authority to issue currency, had always been a hated symbol of colonialism and during the August Revolution had been the chief obstacle

5 Volait: *La vie économique et sociale du Viet Nam*, p. 30.

to the Viet Minh's sovereignty. One of the shortcomings of the August Revolution from the Viet Minh's point of view was that it had "failed to seize the Bank of Indochina and suppress the privileges of the magnates of the money-market. . . . The colonialists availed themselves of this opportunity to attack us later on in the financial field . . ."[6]

Because of this French control over finances, the Viet Minh decided to issue its own currency and make its use obligatory while collecting the Bank of Indochina piasters in exchange. By retiring piasters backed by the French franc from use inside the country and printing a Ho Chi Minh piaster on flimsy paper of very limited durability, the Viet Minh expected to acquire hard-currency backing for its own money.[7] The first Viet Minh money was printed in February 1946, but the Chinese occupiers, seeing that its use would restrict their opportunities to get Bank of Indochina piasters, blocked the project.[8] After the Chinese departure an order was issued, on June 9, 1946, by the Viet Minh regime stating that the utilization of the Bank of Indochina piaster by Vietnamese would come to an end within two months. The French were permitted to use the Bank of Indochina piaster for purchases, but their change would be given in the Ho Chi Minh piaster.[9] Not only did this provide the funds with which to obtain additional armaments, but it also increased the psychological bond between the monetized sector of the population and the Viet Minh regime. This tactic, similar to the requirement for the stamping of ration cards during the voting of January 1946, was yet another design to strengthen the legitimacy of the Viet Minh and develop its revolutionary power.

While the availability of hard currency facilitated the contraband trade in weapons, the Viet Minh was also able to expand its military power through another important activity. Estimates indicate that, during 1946, the Communist-sponsored independence movement was able to manufacture in hastily constructed arsenals 20,000 to 30,000 weapons which were copies

6 Truong Chinh: *The August Revolution*, p. 37.
7 Volait: *La vie économique et sociale du Viet Nam*, p. 33.
8 Ibid.
9 Ibid.

of American carbines, Sten guns, and other foreign arms. The establishment of these rudimentary arsenals in northern Viet Nam was another advantage to the Viet Minh of the absence of the French or a restrictive foreign occupation there. Besides seizing what industrial raw materials were available in the north, the Viet Minh obtained control over machine shops and repair facilities, especially those of the Trans-Indochina railway at Truong Thi, in Nghe An province, and at Ha Dong, just outside Hanoi. In addition, the match factory at Thanh Hoa was transformed for the production of explosives.[1] With about 400 tons of cast iron and pyrotechnics found in the warehouses of French commercial firms, the Viet Minh set its rapidly constructed arsenals into operation. Obviously, the quality of their product was not high, since these raw materials were not intended for such purposes; but despite their inferiorities, these weapons proved effective in a guerrilla war of short-range fire.

It appears that at least one half of the increase of approximately 45,000 weapons over the arms acquired from the stocks of the French and the Japanese was produced inside Viet Nam. Although this seems like a fantastic achievement for a political movement without great organizational experience, it was not accomplished without the important assistance of deserters from the Japanese army. Of the 48,000 Japanese troops and 2,000 civilians located north of the 16th parallel at the end of the war, 30,500 had surrendered and embarked for Japan by April 20, 1946. The remainder had fled to the sanctuary of Hai Nan Island, joined with the Chinese army upon its withdrawal, or were merely at large in unorganized units. A disputed number, somewhere between 2,000 and 4,500, was estimated to have actively joined the Viet Minh.

Those who did join were part of a group known as the "Japanese Organism for Collaboration and Aid for the Independence of Viet Nam," which was headed by Lieutenant Colonel Mukaiyama, who with his principal assistant, Major Oshima, was located at Thai Nguyen, in the Viet Minh mountain-base area. Although Japanese groups were located at other strategic spots,

1 Ibid., p. 43.

the one at Thai Nguyen, comprising about 1,500 combatants and 600 technicians and workers, accounted for almost half the largest estimate of the total number of deserters. The second most important concentration of Japanese was at the central Viet Nam port town of Quang Ngai, where 300 men were grouped under the command of Major Saito, who had been the chief of the Kempeitai at Da Nang. At this location, as well as at Thai Nguyen, the Japanese were staffing training schools and arms-production facilities, while some of their men were grouped into guerrilla units which accompanied the Viet Minh into combat, especially as experts in heavy weapons.

Largely because of this Japanese technical assistance, the Viet Minh arsenals were able to achieve a substantial production. The pace was set at Thai Nguyen, where the output was 10 pistols per day and 50 rifles and 3 to 4 machine guns per month. The total production at this one arsenal from its beginning in October 1945 until the outbreak of hostilities in December 1946 would have been approximately 700 rifles, 4,200 pistols, and 56 machine guns. For an estimated 20,000 to 30,000 weapons to have been manufactured within Viet Nam in 1946, at least five arsenals of equal capacity to the one at Thai Nguyen would have been required. In fact more than five arsenals did exist during 1946, but it is virtually impossible to establish either their individual or aggregate production with any degree of accuracy.[2]

On the basis of this information it seems certain that an indigenous production of 20,000 to 30,000 weapons was well within the capacity of the Viet Minh. Yet it must be emphasized that the data for the output at the Thai Nguyen arsenal demonstrate that this domestic production consisted primarily of pistols rather than rifles or automatic weapons. Whatever the precise quantity of weapons produced inside the country, their quality was low in terms of efficiency, and they were capable of only short-range fire. The arsenals were obviously more important in filling im-

2 Arsenals were located at (1) Chi Ne, southwest of Hanoi, (2) Thai Nguyen, (3) Bai Thuong, east of Thanh Hoa, (4) Van Ly, 40 kilometers southeast of Nam Dinh, (5) Quang Ngai, (6) Di Le, near Quang Tri, (7) Co Bi, 15 kilometers north of Hue, and (8) on the island of Cong Son. In addition, three small-scale operations were located 20 kilometers west of Quang Ngai.

mediate needs for ammunition and grenades as a stockpile against imminent conflict with the French than in the more long-range task of manufacturing higher-quality armaments.[3] Weapons of outside origin must necessarily have composed the most important source of arms for the expansion of the quality of the Viet Minh military capacity, as well as accounting for approximately one half the increase in quantity prior to the outbreak of warfare in December 1946.

Through these various sources more weapons had been set loose in Viet Nam in the chaotic aftermath of the Pacific war than had ever been available, even to the established colonial authority in the era before 1940. Without these arms the revolutionary movement would obviously have lacked an effective means for expressing and pursuing its political goals. The very fact of possessing such arms in the postwar context of Viet Nam, where almost all patterns of authority had deteriorated, endowed their possessors with great power. Therefore, this review of the origins of the armament which the Viet Minh secured is not included here as an analysis of revolutionary war logistics, but as a more precise measure of the political factors that enabled a new power configuration to be developed in Viet Nam.

These factors may be measured in statistical terms. Of the approximately 83,000 weapons of widely varying quality available to the Viet Minh in December 1946, those obtained from the Japanese upon their capitulation, those of indigenous manufacture, and those acquired from contraband trade were roughly equal in quantity. About 25,000 arms originated from each source when those guns parachuted before August 1945 are subtracted from the total. While one of the key factors in the launching of the Vietnamese revolution was the destruction of colonial authority by the Japanese, their material assistance to the Viet Minh was also vital. By ceding French arms to them instead of the nationalist government of Tran Trong Kim and by helping the Viet Minh to establish arsenals, the Japanese

---

3 The Quang Ngai arsenal turned out 12,000 grenades during 1946. Because of the scarcity of raw material, the lack of ammunition for heavy weapons remained a serious problem.

seemed to be acknowledging that the Communist-led movement was, in their view, the most capable of the Vietnamese factions to thwart the return of the French.

Unlike the Chinese, the Japanese appear not to have required Viet Minh payment for weapons and their generosity seems to have been motivated primarily by political purposes. But as a vanquished armed force the Japanese had few alternatives in late 1945, and the tie with the Viet Minh served to maximize what power remained to them. If the Chinese caused much impoverishment by their demands upon the Vietnamese economy, they were on the other hand responsible for most of the high-quality weapons which the Viet Minh received. In addition, there was established in the contraband trade a commercial contact with China that would continue to exist after the Japanese influence ceased. Such means of external supply were not only to serve the Viet Minh in organizing their guerrilla war forces initially, but they were to be an important continuing souce of matériel in the build-up of an ever larger Communist armed force. After 1950, in the diplomatic atmosphere affected by the Korean War, the Thai took steps to eliminate what advantage the Viet Minh had enjoyed for four years from their territory. But the advent of the Communist regime in China merely served to increase the possibilities for securing weapons and supplies from the north, a pattern that was an outgrowth of the Chinese postwar occupation.

Even though political conditions in both Thailand and China changed radically in the course of the nine years of the Communists' struggle for independence in Viet Nam, these developments had less effect than other factors on external supply. The geographic features of the Vietnamese borders, and the changes in the military requirements of the Viet Minh as its armed force developed in scale, contributed the most in defining the patterns of this supply. Yet the importance of external sources of arms to the Viet Minh was not so much of a quantitative as a qualitative value. The perfecting of a conventional military organization from guerrilla units progressively required more-sophisticated weapons and training. Equipment of this type was obtained almost exclusively from the contraband trade with China prior to 1947; afterward there were opportunities to capture them in battle from the French. Since this frontier trade expanded into one of the most significant features of the Indochina War, raising the thorny diplomatic problem of a "privileged sanctuary," it is important to emphasize that several of its initial characteristics persisted despite political changes in China.

Not only did the quality of the matériel remain more important than quantity, but it continued to be a trade for which the Viet Minh had to pay with its scarce and meager resources. Moreover, the remoteness of the Sino-Vietnamese frontier and its political-military instability facilitated the transfer of the matériel, as did the Viet Minh control of certain key coastal areas. Inevitably, the opinion developed that the elimination of this source of arms would have resulted in the strangulation of the revolutionary movement. Yet this seems hardly tenable. The blocking of external supplies certainly could have had an important effect in checking the growth of Communist military strength. But a critical threshold in Vietnamese politics had been crossed with the August Revolution, and as a consequence it was political organization and not weapons that was the primary support of the Viet Minh's military operations. The difference between the August Revolution and the abortive prewar attempts to challenge French authority was not just in the opportunities for securing arms; more important was the difference in the extent of the organization for political participation. In the expansion of this organization, the presence of the Chinese in Viet Nam was a vital factor.

CHAPTER 20 ❁ ❁ ❁

THE EXPANSION

OF THE VIET MINH

❁
❁
❁

The presence of Chinese occupation forces in northern Viet Nam until the spring of 1946, delaying the attempted reestablishment of colonial rule, gave the Viet Minh time to expand its political organization. When it made its bid for power in Hanoi in August 1945, the Viet Minh had called for the creation of "People's Committees," *Ủy Ban Nhân Dân,* which were supposed to have "mobilized the masses and encouraged them to participate in revolutionary struggle."[1] Since the Viet Minh's organizational capacity was limited by a relatively small number of trained political organizers, this technique allowed them to extend their influence by giving a rationale and legitimacy for the formation of local groups. This process was described by Paul Mus as follows:

> At the outset it was possible to credit the Viet Minh with a name, a tradition, and a means of liaison in great part inherited from

1 Truong Chinh: *The August Revolution,* p. 25.

the Communists, but without any real control over the people. Above all the Viet Minh knew how to seize their chance. Vietnamese society had been deserted by its Confucian cadre and had not been re-encadred by those imitating European values. It seemed to the villagers that the time had come for a new reign. Taking Hanoi had given the Viet Minh an initial success, but the movement could not get to the countryside. The contact with the people, the primary element in the revolutionary adventure could not be made. It was urgent that the Viet Minh stir the people.[2]

Stirring appeals to the people of northern Viet Nam had to take into account the famine which had ravaged the provinces of the Red River Delta in the spring of 1945. Unusually heavy rains during the summer of that year raised the river level to a perilous point. Dikes had been neglected and French technicians responsible for water control had been imprisoned by the Japanese. Attempting to remedy the situation, Vietnamese subordinates opened the flood gates on the Day River dam south of Hanoi but at too rapid a speed, with the result that a deluge was loosed upon the Delta. Eight out of the fourteen provinces in the Red River Delta were inundated by July 1945, and there was no possibility of drying out the fields for immediate use. A frightened people fled southward from the Delta, fearing the plague.[3] Although the Communists have claimed that between 2 and 3 million persons perished, it appears that 500,000 to 600,000 is a more accurate measure of the tragedy.[4] Whatever the true toll, such devastation undoubtedly had an important impact on the attitude of the populace, since even at the lowest estimates the calamity eliminated almost 6 per cent of the population of northern Viet Nam (Tonkin).[5]

While the reaction to such a tragedy created the potential for a popular uprising, it could also have resulted in a passive population. People might be expected to concern themselves with

2 Mus: *Problèmes de l'Indochine contemporaine*, P.M. V, pp. 18–19.
3 Volait: *La vie économique et sociale du Viet Nam*, p. 9.
4 Ibid., p. 7. Devillers: *Histoire du Viet Nam*, p. 131, says that "nearly a million people died."
5 *Annuaire statistique de l'Indochine, 1943–1946*, p. 28. The population of northern Viet Nam was 9,851,200.

immediate personal problems rather than with political protest against either the authority presumed responsible for the flood and famine or the broader issues of colonial reoccupation. Neither extreme—mass uprising nor widespread apathy—resulted. The calamity was not localized but was felt outside the Red River Delta and throughout northern Viet Nam by soaring prices of rice. In October 1945, rice was selling for 250 piasters a quintal (approximately ½ kilo) in the rice-producing province of Bac Giang, but was almost three times higher in Hanoi.[6] Obviously conditions of food scarcity, flood, and famine caused life to be uncertain and contributed to the support of charismatic appeals. Therefore, during the August Revolution,

> a task of the greatest importance for the Communist and Viet Minh cadres was to lead the armed masses to seize Japanese rice stores and French concessions full of stocks of agricultural produce. It was precisely thanks to these attacks on granaries and colonialist plantations that the national salvation movement could be developed intensely, the people rapidly armed, the self-defense brigades quickly founded where the movement had never been organized. . . .[7]

Natural calamities were not the only, or even the primary, factor creating unstable conditions and giving opportunities for the organization of a revolutionary political structure. Of more fundamental importance was Paul Mus's observation that Vietnamese society had been deserted by its Confucian cadre and not been re-encadred. The disintegration was not merely the consequence of the Japanese occupation and the rise of the Viet Minh. It was only the final blow, which in extensive areas of Viet Nam exposed the decay that had occurred in the administrative system of the country.

Prior to the French intervention in the nineteenth century, the "recruitment of the mandarinal [administrative] corps within the village meant that the highest ambitions were permitted to the young villagers according to their abilities."[8] These talents were

6 Volait: *La vie économique et sociale du Viet Nam*, p. 18.

7 Truong Chinh: *The August Revolution*, pp. 24–5.

8 Mus: *Problèmes de l'Indochine contemporaine*, P.M. I, p. 3.

determined on the basis of examinations in the Confucian classics, which were held on a quarterly basis. The incentive for the candidates at these examinations was not just the opportunity for administrative position and prestige; there was also an exemption from military service and *corvée* duty for those successful in the first echelon in the hierarchy of tests for selection.[9] As a result of this process, there was, in addition to the recruitment of a well-educated bureaucratic cadre, a commitment established to the method of selection. This occurred because there were rewards even for those not chosen for administrative careers and because the examinations gave an easily understood purpose to the whole educational system.

This aspect of social control was of vital importance to the peaceful functioning of the country. Other than this political structure there was no comprehensive economic, social, or religious organization to provide a framework of unity for the autonomous villages of largely self-sufficient peasant farmers that composed Vietnamese society. The Vietnamese revere the spirits of their ancestors and other venerable souls through rituals conducted by the elders of the village, with neither an ordained nor specially educated priestly class nor a hierarchical ecclesiastical body.[1] Since there has traditionally been little diversity in agricultural produce or occupation, economic organization has been localized. Kinship has always been the most important social grouping. And although kin ties often extended beyond the village clan, relations rarely went beyond nine generations and usually were organized into subordinate groups with a more recent common ancestor.[2] Because of the forms of ancestor veneration these ties, too, were localized. These otherwise self-contained villages, where more than 80 per cent of the population of Viet Nam lived before 1945, formed a part of a larger community almost solely on a political basis. The lines of authority and compliance knitting these villages together were

9 E. Luro: *Le pays d'Annam* (Paris: Ernest Leroux; 1878), p. 145.

1 This religious tradition is discussed in Kenneth P. Landon: "Annamese Folkways Under Chinese Influence," in Landon: *Southeast Asia: Crossroads of Religion* (Chicago: University of Chicago Press; 1949), p. 57 *passim*. The rituals involved are described in Hickey: *Village in Vietnam*, pp. 55–81.

2 Huard and Durand: *Connaissance du Viet Nam*, p. 91.

founded on the local recruitment of a bureaucratic cadre and an accepted tradition of Confucian politics.

The imposition of the French colonial state brought the ruin of ". . . the Confucian balance between the ritualistic state and the autarchic village . . . without anything to replace it."[3] While it had been primarily a bureaucratic structure, the traditional political system of Viet Nam had not been unresponsive to popular pressures. Indeed, one of its chief functions was communicating such pressures and gathering information so that the Confucian state could be kept in "equilibrium." Moreover, it could absorb certain shifts in social influence by providing a legitimate avenue for political mobility to the ambitious and the capable. For those who challenged its legitimacy, sanctions were imposed to reinforce social control, but even though "equilibrium" and "harmony" were the goals of the system, these were rare in Vietnamese history. Yet the many centuries of internecine warfare and the struggle for power had the Confucian model for its political ideal. With its destruction by colonial rule, there was only the most narrowly circumscribed legitimacy for political action. All else was illegal and therefore revolutionary.

The deterioration which colonialism brought to traditional politics in Viet Nam went beyond its effects on the bureaucratic structure. It also had a damaging impact on the Vietnamese village. By requiring that village officials be chosen by elections based theoretically on the equality of the individual voter, the French were imposing a system of politics which did not reflect the distribution of social influence within the Vietnamese village. This did not mean that traditionalism in the village was dead, but that the notables of the customary councils remained in the background, resisting French reforms and at each opportunity reestablishing themselves in their former positions.[4] Had it simply been a question of election procedures enforced from the outside, traditionalist politics might have been expected to reemerge when the void in the central authority occurred with the Japanese capitulation, and in many cases such a reemergence

---

3 Mus: "Viet Nam: A Nation Off Balance," p. 531.
4 Mus: *Viet Nam: Sociologie d'une guerre*, p. 26.

did result. But something more than the election regulation had taken place to prevent the leaders from resuming a place of authority in the village. The basis for the social hierarchy no longer had its customary vitality; literary accomplishments could not be demonstrated by the prestige which came with success in the mandarinal examinations, and consequently, classical learning had become moribund and ties with the Confucian cultural tradition weakened. Not only did the villages become isolated from an integrating structure of society and politics, they also lost one of the important bonds that had united the village community.

While respect for learning diminished, the regard for age and the accumulation of wealth continued. Yet with the village patriarchical system curtailed, age alone could not enjoy the prestige with which it had once been endowed. The imposition of money tax and the money economy increased the importance of wealth as a measure of social influence. Unfortunately, the concerns with money and wealth did not strengthen the cohesion of the village; taxes became more an individual affair rather than continuing to be a collective responsibility of the village. Wealth tended to draw social distinctions more sharply and produced envy as much as respect. Because of the scarcity of economic opportunity, wealth, unlike literary achievement, could not even theoretically be available to all; its social function did more to fragment than to unify. Wealth operated as one of the chief forces in the colonial impact on the vitality of the Vietnamese village. Because of these pressures, "The traditional village could not survive. It continued to look the same, at least in Tonkin and Annam, but it became an empty shell, void of any social substance it had once had and which had kept life constantly renewed. With the heart gone out of it, even the appearance of the village was in a precarious position . . ."[5]

These details point up how the imposition of alien regulations on village affairs and the ending of political recruitment through literary examinations brought on the disintegration of the traditional system of politics in Viet Nam. Except for two restraining

5 Mus: "Viet Nam: A Nation Off Balance," pp. 530–1.

factors, this atrophy in patterns of authority and political mobility might have resulted in sustained violent protest prior to 1945. One control was the presence of the colonial administrative and police apparatus; the other was the ineffectiveness of a Vietnamese elite to exploit the potential for revolution. Because of the inconsequential challenges to French rule, administrative control was achieved with a relatively small cadre of colonial officials. Until March 9, 1945, there were 5,100 French administrators and 28,000 indigenous officials in addition to the French army to maintain order in the whole of Indochina, which at that time had a population of 27 million.[6] Moreover the civil administrative cadre had only varied between 4,500 and 5,100 among the French, and 20,800 and 28,000 for the indigenous officials over two decades.[7]

Obviously, this ratio of administrators to population depended on a considerable degree of political inactivity, either from compliance or apathy. In the absence of institutionalized political life the only major outbursts of rebelliousness prior to the Japanese intervention had been within the capacity of the colonial administration to quell. But its success in putting down the Nghe An revolt and the VNQDD uprising in Tonkin was also due to the shortcomings of the Vietnamese revolutionaries. Their leadership did not have a broadly structured base of operations because of a limited capacity for revolutionary organization. A simple lack of organizers was one of the limits, but "One of the distinctive features of the 1930–31 'unrest' was . . . a cleavage between the programs put forward by the more (and prematurely) active political leaders of the new generation and the dissatisfaction and sporadic uprisings in the rural areas; in other words between the modernized ideas and approaches of the former and the traditional tempo of the latter."[8]

Overcoming this cleavage between the modern elites created by the colonial education and economy and the more than 80 per cent of the population living in the remains of the traditional Vietnamese village was the primary task of revolutionary politics

6 *Annuaire statistique de l'Indochine, 1943–1946*, pp. 303, 28.
7 Ibid., p. 303.
8 Paul Mus: "Foreword," in Hickey: *Village in Vietnam*, p. xix.

in Viet Nam. This required the social and political reintegration of a society that had become—underneath the façade of the colonial administration—almost amorphous. Because the social cohesion of Vietnamese in the countryside had been sapped and their ties with an organizing cultural force greatly attenuated, the leadership in this task necessarily had to come from the new but alien elites. They had to impose a structure that would unite the village population into a framework of compliance and control if the French were to be prevented from restoring their rule and a central revolutionary authority were to be established. In northern Viet Nam, where the Chinese occupation helped to facilitate the course of the August Revolution, the villages appeared "isolated and trying to live on a closed economy. Their council of notables had disappeared, there are no more *Ly Truongs* [i.e., a traditional village official who was a sort of executive secretary of the Council of Notables], each village lives with rules adopted by the strongest opinion or the influence of the remaining notables."[9]

Whether this situation was more the result of wartime occupation and subsequent famine than of a continuation of the deterioration initiated by the effects of colonial rule, the consequences would appear to be the same. The villages had lost whatever internal resilience they once possessed and were extremely vulnerable to the imposition of a new structure of external political control. A new hierarchy could find its roots by filling the gap created by the breakdown in colonial administration. Seeking to avoid its ephemeral experience in the Nghe-Tinh soviet in 1930–1, the Viet Minh hoped to implant its framework of control by regrouping Vietnamese village society according to a new concept. Due to the lack of a wide social differentiation and the decay of the customary hierarchy of village society, the Viet Minh promoted the organization of the village on the basis of natural groupings. Thus, there were committees formed among women, youth, elderly persons, merchants, militia veterans, and especially the farmers.[1]

9 Volait: *La vie économique et sociale du Viet Nam*, p. 15.
1 Mus: *Viet Nam: Sociologie d'une guerre*, p. 26.

Unlike the Nghe-Tinh soviet but building on the experience of the Viet-Bac guerrilla zone, these groups were coordinated in such a way that they went beyond being units for village action to become organizations for participation in politics outside the village. This development reinforced their role of restructuring village society by giving them a meaning in the larger context of the tumultuous events of the August Revolution. Each of the village groups was connected through an elaborate hierarchy with the Vietnamese League for National Salvation, known as the Cuu Quoc, which was theoretically represented in the Central Committee of the Viet Minh. At the base of the hierarchy were cells of three to five members with an elected chief; a village would comprise several cells of the same functional group, just as would a neighborhood in the urban organization of the Viet Minh. Then the revolutionary strategy of the Cuu Quoc called for the cells to elect members for the next highest echelon in the organizational hierarchy, a village committee, which in turn would elect representatives for superior committees. The process of democratic centrism would be continued until the national level of the organization was reached.

It was largely because Vietnamese society in 1945 had become relatively amorphous that a superstructure of this type enabled the Viet Minh to win recruits without having to bring them into the Communist Party. It provided an opportunity for participation and protest to those who had been dispossessed of their social status or their intangible cultural ties. At the same time that it was offering means for a structured expression of discontent, it also served to bridge the cleavage between the modern urban classes and the distressed countryside. Rather than abstract programs, it was an intricate organization that served as this integrative tie.

The revolutionary structure took form gradually. Soon after the August Revolution began, the Viet Minh formally recognized the Ủy Ban Nhân Dân (People's Committees), which it had urged to be organized during the days following the seizure of power. A decree of September 2, 1945, gave some form to these committees by prescribing their composition and method for selecting their members. As the challenge of holding power increased, with the influx of the Chinese occupation troops and their sponsorship of Vietnamese exile nationalists, the Viet Minh issued a new decree on November 22. This created the *Ủy Ban Hành Chánh* (Administrative Committees), whose membership at the level of the province and above in the hierarchy had to be approved by the ministry of the interior. While in theory the Viet Minh had not previously controlled the administrative committees below the provincial level, this became an unacceptable condition for them. By order #54 of November 23, a corps of Special Inquiry Functionaries was established who were authorized to examine and regulate the operations of the lower-echelon administrative committees.

This trend toward greater central control over local units of political action was reinforced by a decree of December 30. It appointed inspectors of political affairs and from this momentum there was issued decree #96 of June 5, 1946, which established Committees of Harmonization charged with consolidating and unifying the structure of administration and political control that joined the elite with the population of the country. Before the end of 1946 there was a hierarchical organization of control in which regional committees supervised the provinces, whose committees in turn managed subordinate districts that were directly responsible for village activities. Committees at each of these echelons were composed of seven members, including the president, vice-president, and secretary—who together formed the Permanent Commission for decision-making—and members assigned for political, military, social, and economic affairs.

The People's Committees and their successors were the symbol, as well as the substance, of governmental power in the rural areas of Viet Nam. Great stress was laid upon their executive power in carrying out the decrees of the revolutionary government, raising taxes, creating local self-defense units, and making provisions for social progress in mass education and welfare. It was the demonstration of the capacity to act as a government which concerned the Viet Minh. Confirmation of the legitimacy it sought required the Viet Minh to fill the void resulting from the dissolution of the colonial administration. Yet more than an administrative structure was sought by the Viet Minh. It hoped to accommodate political interests so as to develop a structure of compliance and mobility as well as execution. Based on this objective the decree of September 1945 called for the village committees to be elected by all persons above the age of eighteen.[2] However, it appears that their members were elected from within the ranks of the Viet Minh or else appointed, although the evidence is limited. In one village in the Mekong Delta south of Saigon,

> . . . the Viet Minh party members elected six members to their *Uy Ban Hanh Chanh* (Administrative Committee). The committee chairman and his assistant were brothers from a relatively well-to-do family; the other four members were tenant farmers. When the French re-occupied Indochina in January 1946 and re-established the colonial administration the Viet Minh committee disbanded and the traditional Village Council was reinstated.[3]

Although this makes it appear that the village was open to control by the strongest external force, there was a lively contention for advantage internally. The village "was split in its sympathies, and accusations of being pro-French or pro-Viet Minh were common. Those identified as pro-French—usually big land owners and members of the Village Council—were likely victims of periodic punitive Viet Minh raids on the village at night."[4] These observations indicate that there were economically privileged persons on both sides of the political conflict in this village. The significance of this divisiveness would seem to be that respect for traditional position and institutions had given way to a scramble for advantage that bore little relation to larger issues. While

> . . . the village councillors were particularly susceptible to accusations of being pro-French or pro-Viet Minh and from time

2 Devillers: *Histoire du Viet Nam*, p. 179.
3 Hickey: *Village in Vietnam*, pp. 8–9.
4 Ibid.

to time some of them were forced to flee the village. . . , several villagers contend that the confusing war years provided an opportunity for unscrupulous members of the council to exploit their authority and it was widely known that one village official was guilty of having extorted money from villages by threatening to denounce them to the Viet Minh.[5]

By contrast, another village in the Mekong Delta located in Ha Tien province, bordering on the Gulf of Thailand had a slightly different experience. In this case the village committee was appointed by a Viet Minh political inspector, Nguyen Van Tay, on September 14, 1945, before the French reoccupation of the south took place. The committee's membership consisted of three representatives from the Advanced Guard Youth, three from the Indochinese Communist Party, and three from the "workers." Unlike the previous example it was continuity rather than conflict which was the goal of the Viet Minh in this Ha Tien village. It allied with the communal council by choosing some of the council's members—three former notables well versed in village affairs—to advise the Ủy Ban Hành Chánh. Moreover, the emphasis on continuity with tradition was indicated by the Viet Minh's assigning to the police chief on the village committee the duties involved in the village religious cult that had been performed by the Hương Hào in former times.

For all their striking dissimilarities, these two examples demonstrate that village committees were creations of the Viet Minh rather than popularly elected bodies. But their location in the southernmost areas of Viet Nam where the Communist organization was suffering its most severe blows showed another important characteristic. The Viet Minh could extend its influence over wide areas of the Vietnamese countryside. Yet in the absence of spontaneous local organizations the structure of revolution in Viet Nam would have to be imposed from the top down by an active and politically conscious elite. However, the limitations imposed by the quantity and quality of the cadres would substantially restrict the momentum of the revolution.

5 Ibid., p. 181.

The Viet Minh was thoroughly aware that "one of the short-comings of our present movement lies in the lack of cadres." Among the revolutionaries, ". . . first of all it is the cadres, who are the vanguard elements devoting themselves actively to the work of propaganda and organization, who devote them-selves to leading the masses to carry out the policies of the Government and the Party, and to serving as good examples for the people."[6]

Obviously, a high priority was placed on developing additional cadres. But in fulfilling this objective the Viet Minh was faced with a complication arising from the colonial background of Vietnamese society. There was a contradiction in that

> The great majority of cadres, schooled by the revolutionary strug-gle, are loyal, eager, and skillful elements with a good political background, and a fair degree of organization, but most of them have a poor educational level. . . . On the other hand, the tech-nicians and intellectuals who formerly graduated from the French Universities have a certain cultural level but know little about politics.[7]

As has been seen from the days of the VNQDD in 1930–1, there were those among the educated who did know something about politics. Although the educated frequently did not side with the Communists, it was in the competition for their loyalties that the Viet Minh excelled in the August Revolution.

Beyond this success in winning the loyalties of the educated, the task of developing revolutionary power was twofold. The size of the trained elite the Viet Minh had won was small; yet, upon the political capacities of this elite depended the consolida-tion of routine administration and the expansion of the revolu-tionary structure. To Truong Chinh a more pressing limitation was the low level of political awareness not only among the educated, but throughout Vietnamese society. In a rhetorical query he asked, ". . . have the imperialists ever thought of edu-cating the Vietnamese people to study or go into politics? Their

6 Truong Chinh: *The August Revolution,* p. 71.
7 Ibid., p. 73.

sole concern was the formation of a class of young Vietnamese intellectuals who would serve them merely as tools . . ."[8] Without political sensitivity, the disruption in the countryside would be turned to narrow advantage, as was shown in the two contrasting cases of villages in the Mekong Delta, instead of to the consolidation of control. In the absence of political consciousness, the political activists which the Viet Minh had in large part recruited from the colonial regime would view its role in bureaucratic terms. Therefore, one of the crucial dimensions of revolutionary success for the Viet Minh was its capacity for political mobilization of the mass of the Vietnamese population. In turn, this depended on the energies of a politically shrewd cadre in establishing a structure of participation and control to overcome the cleavage which had separated the modern classes of Viet Nam from its village society.

Significantly, it was the demands created by military preparation and operations which eventually offered the greatest stimulus to political mobilization. Through the physical mobilization of villagers into the nascent Viet Minh armed force, the coordination of local guerrilla efforts of village self-defense units, and the organization of propaganda units, the capacity of this structure was tested. Without the military threat posed by the French reoccupation, the Viet Minh would have had to devise other forms of participation and psychological motivation for the political mobilization of the village population. Moreover, as the military requirements of the Viet Minh increased, efforts were made to expand its local organizational capacity. This resulted in the creation of Resistance Committees, or *Ủy Ban Kháng Chiến,* during the second half of 1946. The purpose of these committees was to provide local liaison for the armed forces as a source of supplies and support for mobile combat units: reporting on the political and military situation in its locality and furnishing combatants for the regular forces, in addition to organizing local self-defense units and maintaining village security.

Although the *Ủy Ban Kháng Chiến* were supposedly sub-

8 Ibid.

ordinate to the Administrative Committees, a rivalry developed during the initial phases of the resistance war between the military and civilian leaders, which meant that this organizational relationship did not work out in practice. Therefore, by a decree of October 1, 1947, these organisms were unified into a single entity which was known as *Ủy Ban Kháng Chiến Hành Chánh* (UBKCHC) and organized from the village to the national level in a hierarchy of control and execution. At the village and district levels, the military members of the committee were representative of the popular militia, and at the province and above, members of the regular army held this position.

Such was the political-military structure with which the Viet Minh entered into the conflict with the French. Its great attribute was that it allowed for decentralization in initiative compatible with centralization in control. Through the structure a bridge was laid from the urban areas, which were the focus of the struggle in the August Revolution, to the countryside, where the resistance war would be fought. Without such careful preparation the Viet Minh could not have immediately launched and sustained guerrilla warfare. And without the opportunity created north of the 16th parallel by the absence of the French until March 6, 1946, and the avoidance of warfare there for almost nine months after the French returned, the Viet Minh could not have developed so strong a revolutionary organization. The freedom to maneuver, which contributed so decisively to the Viet Minh's political success, would obviously have been an impossibility without the extended Chinese occupation. Whether in view of the Chinese financial demands the price was too great cannot be easily determined. It seems clear that, given its revolutionary goals, the Viet Minh had no choice. Undoubtedly it was glad to get a political foothold no matter what the price.

PART SEVEN

*The French Response to
the Vietnamese Revolution:
Political Community Versus
Military Reoccupation,
March - December 1946*

✖
✖
✖

CHAPTER 21 ✿ ✿ ✿

CONFLICTING FRENCH VIEWS

ON COLONIAL REOCCUPATION

✿
✿
✿

The political power that the Vietnamese revolutionaries had been able to develop north of the 16th parallel during the Chinese occupation presented the French with a challenge they had not faced in the south. When the Chinese agreed in the Sino-French Treaty of February 28, 1946, to withdraw their troops, the problem of Viet Minh power confronted France for the first time. But long before the signing of the treaty, two sharply opposing views developed within official French circles over the procedure to be followed in this reoccupation of northern Viet Nam. One view was that negotiations with the Viet Minh leading to a formal accord were a vital prerequisite. Otherwise, it was argued, strong resistance would be encountered: the Viet Minh would take to the maquis and fight tenaciously against the reinstallation of French sovereignty.

Such was the clairvoyant reasoning of General Philippe Leclerc, a hero of the liberation of France, who had been appointed Supreme Commander of French Troops in the Far East.[1] However, his views were regarded as a "capitulation" by his immediate superior, the de Gaulle-appointed High Commissioner for Indochina, Admiral Georges Thierry d'Argenlieu.[2] As the admiral interpreted his mission, reoccupation came first, with negotiations of an unspecified nature to follow at a later date. Before their views could reach a showdown, the situation was radically altered by the resignation of General de Gaulle on January 20, 1946, and the return of party government to French politics.

Until this time d'Argenlieu had operated on the basis of a declaration issued by the French government on March 24, 1945. This statement, while acknowledging that Indochina "was to enjoy freedom in keeping with its stage of evolution and capacities," obviously held those capacities in low regard. It provided a framework for only the most limited self-government, and even that was to be dominated by a French-appointed governor general. The crux of the declaration was that "The Indochinese Federation shall form with France and the other parts of the community a 'French Union,' the interests of which abroad shall be represented by France. Indochina shall enjoy within that union liberty of its own."[3]

But when these words were written, there was neither a French Union nor an Indochinese Federation. There was also little reason for Vietnamese political activists to believe that they would have a part in shaping either of these institutions. This could be concluded from the guarded phrase that "The statute of Indochina . . . will be put into final form after consultation with the qualified agencies of liberated Indochina."[4] Moreover, the declaration was based on principles formulated at a conference on postwar colonial problems held in Brazzaville in early 1944. The final communiqué of this meeting had stated in part

1 Sainteny: *Histoire d'une paix manquée*, p. 172.
2 Devillers: *Histoire du Viet Nam*, p. 212.
3 Cole: *Conflict in Indochina*, p. 5.
4 Ibid., p. 6.

that "the aims of the work of civilization which France is accomplishing in her possessions exclude any idea of autonomy and any possibility of development outside the French Empire bloc. The attainment of 'self government' in the colonies, even in the most distant future, must be excluded."[5]

The irrelevance of the March 24 declaration to the developing political realities in Viet Nam was not primarily due to these abstractions formulated in the wartime isolation of Brazzaville. Moreover, the statement on the future status of Indochina had not been issued because of a desire to prepare a program to deal with indigenous political movements in France's principal East Asian possession. Rather, it had been made in anticipation of the hostile ideas of international trusteeship that General de Gaulle felt were likely to be submitted the following month to the San Francisco Conference for the organization of the United Nations.[6]

The French leader's fears were not idle ones, for in a press conference aboard the USS *Quincy* on February 23, on his return from Yalta, President Roosevelt had told a reporter of his concern for the future of Indochina:

> The first thing I asked Chiang was, "Do you want Indo-China?" . . . He said, "It's no help to us. We don't want it. They are not Chinese. They would not assimilate into the Chinese people." . . . With the Indochinese, there is a feeling they ought to be independent but are not ready for it. I suggested at the time, to Chiang, that Indo-China be set up under a trusteeship—have a Frenchman, one or two Indochinese, and a Chinese and a Russian because they are on the coast, and maybe a Filipino and an American—to educate them for self-government. It took fifty years for us to do it in the Philippines.[7]

5 *La conférence africaine française, Brazzaville, 30 janvier 1944–8 février 1944* (Algiers: Commissariat aux Colonies; 1944), p. 35, as cited by Lancaster: *The Emancipation of Indochina*, pp. 122–3.

6 This idea was expressed in a dispatch from Paris in *The New York Times*, March 24, 1945, p. 9.

7 Samuel I. Rosenman: *The Public Papers and Addresses of Franklin D. Roosevelt: Victory and the Threshold of Peace* (New York: Harper & Brothers; 1950), pp. 562–3, as quoted in Cole: *Conflict in Indochina*, p. 48.

The fears of trusteeship stemming from these remarks and the urgency it engendered in French political plans for the future of Indochina were dissipated by two events. One was the death of President Roosevelt in April 1945. The other was the resolution of the "non-self governing territories" problem in the United Nations Charter, which ended the threat of United States pressure to take Indochina away from France. But with the pressure removed, the refinement of a political program in response to the situation in Viet Nam was not forthcoming. However, direct contact was established with Vietnamese exiles in south China through the French military mission headed by Jean Sainteny. Among his tasks was the preparation for the French return to Indochina. Yet this was plainly conceived as an administrative and operational problem rather than a political one. Ironically, this approach was to be complicated by the Viet Minh leaders with whom Sainteny was in contact. Their proclamation of an independent government and the development of revolutionary power in Viet Nam probably could not have been anticipated in the spring of 1945.

By contrast, the fragmented and uncertain French approach to the future was easily perceived. Their lack of preparation was apparent in that a high commissioner for Indochina, Admiral d'Argenlieu, was not appointed until the Japanese were capitulating. Moreover, d'Argenlieu was judged a shockingly poor choice since he had no experience in Asia and was not a career naval officer but had been a Carmelite monk before the war.[8] In addition to the haphazardness in choosing the leadership there seemed little or no coordination among the various French agencies concerned with the reoccupation. For example, when Sainteny returned to Paris from Kunming in July 1945, he found the ministry of colonies indifferent to his mission. The ministry's attention was focused on Calcutta, where its own mission was waiting to return to Indochina.[9] Of greater consequence to the French for regaining their position was the absence of French armed forces in East Asia, a condition which resulted in the

8 Bernard Fall has called d'Argenlieu's selection France's "major postwar blunder in Southeast Asia." *The Two Viet-Nams*, p. 72.

9 Sainteny: *Histoire d'une paix manquée*, pp. 47–8.

Chinese and British occupation of the two halves of Viet Nam. This obstacle to French reoccupation yielded political advantages to the Viet Minh, allowing it to expose the gap between France's postwar political goals for Indochina and its capacity to achieve them.

The Communists in Viet Nam saw the French declaration of March 24 as a cynical act. In their view, "It was only after the French surrender in Indochina [March 9, 1945] that the de Gaulle government agreed to issue the Proclamation recognizing the autonomy of Indochina. This hypocritical proclamation was, for the Indochinese peoples, as stupid as it was ridiculous because it was published just at the time when the French had no more authority in Indochina."[1] Although its public pronouncements attacked the French and asserted the independence of Viet Nam, the Viet Minh quietly sought an accommodation with France. This trend had dated from July 1945, when a Viet Minh *aide-mémoire* was passed through an American OSS intermediary. The document demanded that its proposals for independence be "announced and observed by the French in their future policies in *French Indochina*."[2] Key to their demands was that "Independence . . . be given to this country in a minimum of five years and a maximum of ten." Moreover, the Viet Minh said that it was willing to accept a French governor until independence was granted.

In retrospect, these demands are so modest as to appear fantastic and to question the authenticity of the *aide-mémoire*. Could the Viet Minh at one time have really been willing to settle for gradual independence? But these demands were formulated well before the airdrops of weapons to the Viet Minh, the sudden capitulation of the Japanese, and the seizing of Hanoi during the August Revolution. What they demonstrate is that France was not able to take advantage of the position of the Viet Minh before its demands lost their modesty. The absence of a policy closely related to the political reality in Viet Nam was a striking liability.

1 Truong Chinh: *The August Revolution*, p. 30.
2 Sainteny: *Histoire d'une paix manquée*, p. 57, for text. Italics added.

Jean Sainteny did not have such luxury of hindsight in his negotiations with the Viet Minh for the French reoccupation of northern Viet Nam. He did not even have the benefit of the support of his superior, the high commissioner of Indochina, in these negotiations. But in carrying the burden of the discussions with the Viet Minh from the summer of 1945 through the signing of the accords for the reoccupation until the outbreak of hostilities in December 1946, Sainteny did have the important asset of continuity. He had been in touch with Ho Chi Minh as early as July 1945, through the intermediary of Laurie Gordon, a Canadian businessman who had been trapped in wartime Indochina.[3] Although Sainteny did not meet Ho until after the August Revolution in Hanoi, he did send a French mission to the headquarters of the Viet Minh. During the autumn of 1945, Sainteny had periodic meetings with the Viet Minh leader, but due to the Viet Minh's preoccupation with the Chinese and the exile nationalists, these meetings accomplished little. Not until January 1946, after Viet Minh elections and the beginning of serious bargaining on the Sino-French Treaty, did Sainteny's talks with Ho reach a meaningful stage.

One of the surprising aspects of these negotiations was Sainteny's discovery that Ho felt he needed the support of the French to maintain his power and to neutralize his opposition. These adversaries included not only the exile nationalists, but also a vehement group of five men who formed the Tổng Bộ (Direction Committee) of the Viet Minh. In Sainteny's view the Tổng Bộ closely controlled the actions of Ho Chi Minh. Their overriding concern was symbolized for the French representative by the propaganda slogans they had plastered throughout Hanoi, which read, "Independence or Death," while Ho's approach is pictured as being one of realistic moderation. Although he was no less deeply committed to independence, the Viet Minh leader did not in private demand it immediately or unconditionally.[4]

Explanations of the outbreak of hostilities in December 1946 emphasize Ho's inability to secure sufficient concessions from

3 Ibid.
4 Ibid., pp. 167–9.

the French to placate the *Tổng Bộ* extremists.[5] Whether Ho found it convenient to strike a moderate pose and thus use the extremism of his colleagues as a lever has not become clear. What is apparent is that the middle-ground position grew less and less tenable during the course of 1946, and the French position turned progressively more intransigent. Without any meaningful response to its expectations of independence, the Viet Minh became increasingly aggressive; inevitably, this polarization of positions led to a confrontation which threatened the very existence of the Viet Minh.

But in the first months of 1946 there was nothing inevitable about these negotiations. Ho Chi Minh showed himself well aware of the Viet Minh's limitations in strength and was eager to avoid a violent test of wills. Although the discussions concerning the French reoccupation were protracted, they were not conducted in an atmosphere of crisis. It was not until the signing of the Sino-French Treaty that an accord with the Viet Minh became a matter of priority. On February 16 the basis for an accord had already been established through Ho Chi Minh's defining what Sainteny felt were not unacceptable conditions.[6] The task remained to convince Paris of their utility.

General Leclerc, whose job it was to achieve the military reoccupation of northern Viet Nam, considered an accord with the Viet Minh as indispensable. His first responsibility was for the safety of approximately 30,000 French citizens north of the 16th parallel since, without adequate protection, they were in effect the hostages of the Viet Minh. A more fundamental consideration was the potential for protracted resistance by the Viet Minh armed forces. If such a conflict had broken out, the only partially disarmed Japanese troops and the Chinese occupation soldiers could not have been expected to have remained on the sidelines. Given his pacification mission in southern Viet Nam, Leclerc could spare only 20,000 men for the reoccupation of the north. The French general fully appreciated that if the almost 200,000 armed men of three nationalities in the north were to

5 Ibid., p. 223.
6 Ibid., p. 175.

oppose him, the 10 to 1 ratio against his troops could lead to their destruction.[7] In his post-mortem report, Leclerc observed that "if we had found . . . a land risen up against us or simply in disorder, we could obviously have landed at Haiphong, but —I affirm categorically—the reconquest of Tonkin, even in part, would have been impossible." Moreover, the bloody en-counter with the Chinese garrison at Haiphong which the French experienced upon arrival March 6, 1946, strengthened Leclerc's view that "despite the accords of Chungking we are certain that in case there had been serious combat with the Vietnamese, the Chinese would have immediately exploited these difficulties in order to prevent us from reoccupying Tonkin."[8]

The possibilities of a negotiated accord with the Viet Minh concerning reoccupation were vastly increased with the resigna-tion of the de Gaulle government at the end of January. With the return of party government the Socialist, Marius Moutet, replaced Jacques Soustelle as Minister of Overseas France. This removed the principal source of strength in Admiral d'Argenlieu's pro-gram to reoccupy the north without conditions. General Leclerc did not neglect this sudden opportunity; he dispatched General Valluy on a mission to Paris to emphasize the necessity of nego-tiations and to underscore their urgency. After the first week in March the tides would make a landing at Haiphong harbor —filled with silt due to wartime neglect—by deep-draft French troopships an impossibility. The need for a timely conclusion to the diplomatic bargaining with the Chinese and a resolution of the issues with the Viet Minh was grasped thoroughly in Paris. But Leclerc's success in persuading the authorities in France to his views merely provoked Admiral d'Argenlieu to increased efforts. On February 13 the admiral departed for Paris to argue his own case, leaving General Leclerc as acting High Com-missioner of Indochina.[9]

The day following d'Argenlieu's departure, General Leclerc telegraphed Paris informing them of his belief that it was neces-

7 Ibid., p. 181.
8 Ibid., p. 245.
9 Devillers: *Histoire du Viet Nam*, p. 212.

sary to go to the extent of "pronouncing immediately the word 'independence,' " in an accord with the Viet Minh.[1] This important word was such an emotional and political obstacle that it proved to be almost insurmountable in French efforts to define a stable relationship with political movements in Viet Nam. Both in the problems of reoccupation and the negotiations in the years which followed, the word "independence" came to imply a complete and decisive break with previous political patterns. The French refused to use it until the Russian and Chinese recognition of the Viet Minh in 1950 made it mandatory.

The possibility of using the word "independence" while devising subtle techniques for preserving the substance of French influence seems not to have been considered seriously. This would have required a more specific political program than the French had been able to formulate, and in the absence of such a program they found it necessary to construct *ad hoc* solutions with the Viet Minh under the pressures of competing French political cliques. These pressures did not allow for a careful definition of French interests in response to the conditions and their capacities in Viet Nam. Lacking such a definition, France moved toward an armed conflict that was definitely not in its interest.

Surprisingly, it appears that Ho Chi Minh was more concerned with the word "independence" than its substance. As he told the French journalist Jean-Michel Hertrich in 1945, "France and Viet Nam concluded a marriage a long time ago. The marriage has not always been happy, but we are not interested in breaking it. . . ."[2] Ho put it more specifically to Jean Sainteny: "Even though we want to administer ourselves and though I ask you to withdraw your administrators, I still need your professors, your engineers, and your capital in order to build a strong and independent Viet Nam."[3]

By February 18 the French had spelled out the formula which was the best solution that Leclerc could secure in his bargaining with Ho Chi Minh; it called for France to recognize the Republic

1 Sainteny: *Histoire d'une paix manquée*, p. 175.
2 Quoted in Jean Lacouture: *Cinq hommes et la France* (Paris: Éditions du Seuil; 1961), p. 57.
3 Sainteny: *Histoire d'une paix manquée*, p. 168.

of Viet Nam as "A Free State in the Indochinese Federation and in the French Union."[4] This arrangement was much more qualified than Ho had expected, and he would not agree to it. Although Ho wanted to keep talking in hopes of a better formula, he did take some of the actions which Sainteny considered prerequisites to an accord. A coalition government was formed by the National Assembly, meeting in its first session since the elections of January 1946. At this point, Sainteny let it be known that the French had gone as far toward an accord as they would go. It was imperative that the French ships enter Haiphong harbor between March 5 and 7, and if by this time there had been no agreement, the French relief troops would have to disembark with full knowledge of the consequences that this would have for the French hostages in Hanoi and the political future of the Viet Minh. A little before sunrise on the morning of March 6, as the French flotilla was making its preparations for a landing, Hoang Minh Giam, a close confidant of the Viet Minh leader, came to Sainteny's residence to notify him that President Ho was ready to accept his conditions.

Out of this test of wills came an accord which Ho Chi Minh felt was a victory for France. As he said to Sainteny, ". . . it is you who have won; you know very well that I wanted much more than that—well, I understand also that one cannot have everything in a day."[5] If Sainteny had won, his victory was only relative; it did not mean that Ho Chi Minh had lost. If the March 6 accords did not recognize the independence which Ho Chi Minh had declared Viet Nam to have on September 2, 1945, they did bring the recognition of the legitimacy of his government. It sanctioned the existence of the parliament, treasury, and most important of all, the Viet Minh army. Besides this recognition there were three other key points bearing on the future of the Viet Minh in the accord. First, concerning the unification of Viet Nam, "the French government binds itself to carry out the decisions taken by the population through a referendum." In addition to this opening for the potentially

4 Ibid., p. 176.
5 Ibid., p. 167.

peaceful extension of its power throughout Viet Nam, the Viet Minh also received a French commitment to future negotiations. These discussions were to bear "on the diplomatic relations of Viet Nam with foreign states; the future status of Indo-china; and French economic and cultural interests in Vietnam."[6]

Perhaps the most substantial and immediate advantage to the Viet Minh in the accords was an annex dealing with the military aspects of the French reoccupation and the disarmament of the Japanese. This document defined the relief forces for Viet Nam north of the 16th parallel as consisting of 10,000 Viet Minh and 15,000 French troops, including those who had been imprisoned by the Japanese or had escaped and returned from China. These forces were to be placed under French command with Vietnamese representation, but the French elements were to be divided into three categories: (1) units guarding Japanese prisoners, who would be repatriated within ten months or before, if all prisoners had been evacuated, (2) units charged with the maintenance of public order, a fifth of whom were to be relieved by the Vietnamese army every year until at the end of five years their mission would be terminated, and (3) units charged with the defense of air and naval bases, the length of whose mission was to be determined by conference.[7]

Unlike their counterparts in the south, who never had a chance to negotiate with the French and who were forced into guerrilla warfare when public buildings were taken over in Saigon, the Viet Minh in the north at least had a sanction against a build-up of French troops and a tenuous commitment to their withdrawal within five years. While this agreement facilitated the military reinstallation of France in northern Viet Nam, it did not give her unquestioned predominance of strength in the area. The Viet Minh had at least 25,000 men under arms at the time, although it was committing less than half of them to French operational control.[8] The maintenance of this favor-

6 The text of the agreement is found in Cole: *Conflict in Indochina*, pp. 40–2.
7 Ibid.
8 Marchand: *Le drame indochinois*, p. 74, says that the Viet Minh had 30,000 men at this time and that contrary to the March 6 accords its 10,000-man contingent never effectively came under the French operational control.

able balance of forces was theoretically guaranteed by the French agreement to limit their forces to 15,000 men. As a practical factor the French troop strength was also limited by the lack of fresh replacements for their prewar contingents still in the north. The Viet Minh was under no such restraint not to augment its forces by recruitment and training. And as it became more and more apparent that the French were not going to move beyond the March 6 agreement to define areas of Vietnamese political autonomy, the Viet Minh did in fact double its armed force from its early-1946 strength.

The political turmoil which ensued during 1946 tended to obscure the meaningful character of the March 6 accords. Given the elements of strength of both parties, these agreements were an extremely good beginning since they resolved the thorny problem of the French reoccupation without resort to violence and, in turn, led to a conclusion of the Chinese occupation and the repatriation of the bulk of the Japanese soldiers. If these measures eliminated important resources for the expansion of the Viet Minh armed forces, the precise limitation on French military strength tended to balance the advantages. But the recognition of the Viet Minh government as "A Free State . . . in the French Union" hardly acknowledged the commanding revolutionary power it had been able to develop. At the same time, the accords provided an avenue for the expansion of the Viet Minh's power through bargaining rather than forcing it into protracted political conflict. Taken as a whole, these provisions were an effective political response to a revolutionary movement still in its formative stage. They institutionalized what power had already developed, and they offered the creation of new political institutions in which that power could be increased. Above all they established a precedent and a framework for dealing with a revolutionary elite which was aware of the limitations to its strength and of the problems of developing greater power.

Of larger significance were the questions that the agreements did not resolve. France's desire to preserve its position in Indochina remained greater than its military capacity to achieve this goal by force. But this desire was also greater than France's political ingenuity to create institutions which could channel the strength of the Viet Minh without provoking it to general warfare. This was a corollary of the imprecise character of French interests in Indochina and the indecision as to how to secure them through political relations with the Vietnamese. Largely because Indochina was the most pressing colonial problem that France faced, it felt compelled to transform its empire into an institution with more legitimacy in the postwar world; thus Indochina begat the French Union. Because Viet Nam was the most pressing problem within Indochina, the French felt obliged to remold Vietnamese ambitions by an institution which would allow them to maintain their influence among contiguous dependencies with quite different levels of political development; thus Viet Nam begat the Indochinese Federation.

Whether the Viet Minh could have been prevented by political action alone from eventually launching a war against France is an open question. More to the point is the fact that in 1946 the Viet Minh had a level of political and military power that was more easily dealt with than at any other moment. It seems that the Viet Minh was under no spell of enthusiasm to undertake a war against the French unless its alternatives were blocked. Ho Chi Minh's willingness to spend four months in futile bargaining in France at the crucial point in the Viet Minh's revolutionary development—from June through September 1946—seems clearly to have demonstrated such a desire for a political solution.

CHAPTER 22

THE ABSENCE OF FRENCH IDEAS

FOR POLITICAL COMMUNITY

✹

✹

✹

The reactions to the March 6 accords clearly defined the positions of the parties to the Viet Nam conflict. For General Leclerc, the French military reconquest of the north had not been a realistic option. "We never intended to launch an armed conquest of north Indochina. The Cochin Chinese experience demonstrated that to accomplish that, we would need forces much stronger than those which we now have," was Leclerc's analysis of the results. Moreover, "At the present time," he said, "there is no question of imposing ourselves by force on masses who desire evolution and innovation."[1] The accords clearly bore the stamp of Leclerc's perspective; they had been reached under the coercive force of military power for the purpose of avoiding an armed clash and defining means for future agreements. While the Leclerc position was based straightfor-

[1] Adrien Dansette: *Leclerc* (Paris: Flammarion; 1952), pp. 209–10, 199, as cited in Hammer: *The Struggle for Indochina*, pp. 152, 155–6.

wardly on a precise assessment of the conditions which the French faced, the Vietnamese point of view was more complex.

The March 6 accords were a "Vietnamese Brest-Litovsk," Vo Nguyen Giap explained in an emotional speech to a Hanoi crowd of 100,000. He told them that the accords had the same purpose as the truce Lenin had arranged with the Germans during World War I to stop the invasion of Russia so that the Soviets could consolidate their political power. "We have especially negotiated in order to protect and reinforce our political, military, and economic position," said the Viet Minh military leader. Moreover, Giap asserted, the alternative to negotiation was a long-term resistance for which the Viet Minh was not then prepared. Furthermore,

> . . . at certain points where the revolutionary movement is not very deep many people have not taken it very seriously, and if we had prolonged the resistance, there would have been a collapse in certain sectors or a loss of fighting spirit. In continuing the military struggle, we would have lost our forces and gradually our soil. We would have only been able to hold several regions . . .

Then taking on potential critics who might point out that the accords did not contain the important word "independence," Giap argued, "They do not see that the independence of a country results from objective conditions and that in our struggle to obtain it, *there are moments when it is necessary to be firm and others when it is necessary to be pliant.*"[2]

It was Ho Chi Minh who created the greatest sensation at the public meeting, called especially to explain the Franco-Vietnamese accords. He pointed out that Viet Nam had been independent since August 1945, but that no country had recognized it diplomatically. The March 6 accords, he reasoned, opened the way for international recognition while they limited the French military strength in northern Viet Nam to 15,000 for only five years' duration. However, it was on the basis of his personal prestige that the Vietnamese leader sought to clinch all arguments: "I, Ho Chi Minh, I have always led you along

2 Text is from *Quyết Chiến* (a daily newspaper) of Hue, March 8, 1946, as quoted in Devillers: *Histoire du Viet Nam*, p. 229.

the path of liberty, I have fought all my life for the independence of the Fatherland. You know that I would prefer death to selling out the country. I swear to you that I have not sold you out."[3]

If the March 6 accords were to the Viet Minh a Brest-Litovsk, they were regarded as a Munich by Admiral d'Argenlieu and those of a Gaullist orientation in the French circles in Indochina. Although in public the French high commissioner approved and praised the accords, his attitude in private was vehemently different. On March 8, less than a week after his return from consultations in Paris, d'Argenlieu told General Valluy, who had been sent by Leclerc to inform him of the details of the French landing at Haiphong, "I am amazed, yes General, that's the word, I am amazed that France has in Indochina such a fine expeditionary force, and that its chiefs prefer to negotiate rather than to fight . . ."[4] D'Argenlieu matched these fighting words with negotiations of a quite different character. The purpose of his bargaining was emphatically not to reach an accommodation with the Viet Minh; the admiral's initiatives were designed to circumscribe the Viet Minh and to check its ability to attain its goals.

The first indication of this opposing trend was the statement by the French commissioner for Cochinchina, Jean Cédile, that the March 6 accords did not apply south of the 16th parallel. Although this assertion was quickly disavowed by General Leclerc, Vo Nguyen Giap ordered the troops in Nam Bo to continue their guerrilla warfare against the French. Secondly, there was the election of Dr. Nguyen Van Thinh as President of the provisional government of the Republic of Cochinchina on March 26, 1946, by the reconstituted version of the Colonial Council which had ruled the south before the Japanese occupation. While this provisional government did not have any legality until recognized by France, it was the beginning of a southern separatist movement that would be d'Argenlieu's counterweight to the Viet Minh.[5]

3 Ibid., p. 231.
4 Ibid., p. 242.
5 Ibid., pp. 248–51.

However, the negotiations called for in the March 6 accords were set in motion by a communiqué signed by Admiral d'Argenlieu and Ho Chi Minh on board the high commissioner's flagship anchored off the coast northwest of Hanoi on March 24, 1946. They announced that a preparatory conference would be held at Dalat, a mountain resort in southern Viet Nam, during the beginning of April, which would conclude its discussions in time for a Vietnamese delegation to be dispatched to Paris before the end of May for "official definitive discussions."[6] This Dalat conference gave the Viet Minh the occasion to demonstrate the broad nationalist base it had been able to establish by its championing of Vietnamese independence. Its delegation was led by Nguyen Tuong Tam, minister of foreign affairs and a leader of the VNQDD, and although it included two high-ranking Communist Party leaders, Vo Nguyen Giap and Duong Bach Mai, the bulk of the delegates were nonpolitical specialists in financial and technical problems. The composition of the Viet Minh delegation also probably reflected its belief that little of consequence could be decided before the departure of a different delegation for Paris.

The key issue for the Vietnamese delegation at Dalat was the question of the unity of Viet Nam. In order to undercut the emerging French maneuver to proclaim the independence of Cochinchina, the Viet Minh got an unauthorized delegation into Dalat from the south to support the position of unity of Viet Nam. This group included Pham Ngoc Thach, who had come to political prominence with the Advanced Guard Youth, and Nguyen Van Sam, a non-Communist journalist who ironically was later assassinated by the Viet Minh. Although the Nam Bo representatives did not help the cause of unity, the Viet Minh delegation continued to be adamant in attacking this fundamental question. Meanwhile the French delegation of technical experts was concerned with laying the groundwork for future discussions on such problems as customs regulations, economic development, and the role of the French language in Vietnamese education. Moreover, France was not to be budged

6 Sainteny: *Histoire d'une paix manquée,* p. 197, for text.

easily on the question of Cochinchina. It was here that she had her major chance to preserve what she had built up in Indochina.

The French delegation at Dalat undertook to argue that there were objective reasons for the separate autonomy of the south of Viet Nam. In their view no natural unity existed between the south and the northern Tonkin Delta, which was considered to be geographically a part of the high plateau of Yunnan and Kwangsi. The French also pointed out that prior to the seventeenth century the Vietnamese had not come into Cochinchina; they also asserted that it was the French who had seen the great possibilities for the future development of the area and had invested capital there. As far as the d'Argenlieu administration was concerned, France would not tolerate a solution to the problems of Viet Nam that was contrary to the interests of the "Cochinchinese." Yet virtually the only people feeling a "Cochinchinese" identity were those who had profited from the French presence to become wealthy landholders, get a French education, and receive French citizenship.

The Indochinese Federation, which had come closer to reality by the March 6 accords, would also provide a convenient means of recognizing the autonomy of Cochinchina. From d'Argenlieu's perspective this federation would be useful in checking the spread of the Viet Minh's political strength. He identified the source of its power as nationalism, a pervasive force which he feared would not only overrun Cochinchina but also the neighboring states of Cambodia and Laos. This Viet Minh political drive was equated with the centuries of Vietnamese expansion southward from the Tonkin Delta and with their military forays westward to the countries on their border.

The tide of Vietnamese expansion was at its height when the French had intervened in the middle of the nineteenth century, and France's relatively unopposed occupation of Laos and Cambodia can be attributed in large measure to the protection they guaranteed against Vietnamese "expansionism." Moreover, their fragmentation of Viet Nam into three "countries"—with one of them, Cochinchina, being made a French colony—was designed to restrict the unity which the Vietnamese had painfully achieved. This colonial policy had the effect of encouraging regional and local forces which were latent in Vietnamese society. The revolutionary fervor which the Viet Minh had generated now threatened to overcome these parochial tendencies, and in response the French were arguing, at least through d'Argenlieu's propaganda, that nationalism in general, and Vietnamese nationalism in particular, was an outmoded nineteenth-century doctrine which the French were justified in opposing.[7] France's purpose, according to d'Argenlieu, was to provide the benefits of the modern world to the people of Indochina without the complications of politics.

Rather than channeling the energies of the Viet Minh so that they might have been dissipated by the enormity of the task of developing revolutionary power, the admiral's program was to meet them head on. In retrospect, the adamancy of the opposition to the Viet Minh appears to have won them more adherents than they might otherwise have expected. Since nationalism in Viet Nam was essentially an anti-French reaction rather than a defined positive force, a policy of intransigence gave it increased substance and purpose. The paradoxical nature of the general and parochial trends in Vietnamese politics in 1946 were summarized by General Leclerc's political adviser, Paul Mus. In a conversation with the high commissioner he offered the view that if the admiral tried to divide Viet Nam, there would be a strong trend toward unity. If, on the other hand, he tried to unite Viet Nam, he could expect a vigorous regionalism and parochialism.

The views of the high commissioner in Indochina reflected the feelings of local colonial interests and the French-oriented Vietnamese elite in the south, rather than those of the ministry of overseas France (the former ministry of colonies) or the French parliament. In fact, it was the unsettled political situation within France following the resignation of de Gaulle and the defeat of the proposed constitution on May 5, 1946, that permitted Admiral d'Argenlieu so much latitude. It was this condition that

7 See Pierre Gourou: "For a French Indo-Chinese Federation," *Pacific Affairs*, Vol. XXI (March 1947), pp. 18–29.

allowed factions to develop within the French administration in
Indochina over a policy of concessions versus one of force.
Sensing that these circumstances might also lead to his being
checked again, as on March 6, the high commissioner wanted to
be able to recognize the autonomy of Cochinchina before the
Viet Minh delegation left for Paris at the end of May. But this
required the ratification of the parliament and the backing of
the ministry of overseas France, and at that moment France had
no parliament and it was caught up in an election fever. Marius
Moutet, the minister of overseas France, was campaigning in
his home district and in no position to respond to d'Argenlieu's
proposals even if he had wanted to do so.[8]

Frustrated in his designs to restrict the Viet Minh through
established procedures, Admiral d'Argenlieu took it on his own
initiative to recognize the Republic of Cochinchina as a "free
state having its own government, parliament, army and finances,
being a part of the Indochinese Federation and the French
Union."[9] When this government was formally proclaimed in
Saigon on June 1, 1946, two thirds of the audience at the ceremony were, according to an observer, French military and civilians.[1] French overattendance emphasized that the Cochinchinese
republic was a political force founded on some 8,000 large
landholders, approximately 1,500 Vietnamese with French citizenship, and about 15,000 resident Frenchmen, all living in
southern Viet Nam.[2] D'Argenlieu had now checkmated Leclerc's
move of March 6; they had both recognized autonomous governments at either end of Viet Nam. Each of these governments
was to have a surprising capacity for endurance—surprising,
because it was widely expected that the Viet Minh would be
crushed militarily, and because the Associated State of Viet Nam,
which grew out of the Cochinchinese republic, was thought sure
to fall from lack of popular support.

In their endurance these two governments demonstrated some

8 Devillers: *Histoire du Viet Nam*, p. 269.
9 Ibid., p. 270.
1 Ibid.
2 *Annuaire statistique de l'Indochine, 1936–1937*, p. 23. *Annuaire statistique de l'Indochine, 1943–1946*, p. 29.

fundamental characteristics of the revolution in Viet Nam. The fact that unrepresentative leadership elites could remain in authority in southern Viet Nam was another indication that there was not a broad popular uprising throughout Viet Nam. But the inability of military force to eliminate the politically sophisticated and purposeful Communist movement proved there was much more to the revolution than the protest of a discontented *bourgeoisie* and intellectuals. At the outset neither group was able to predominate and the majority of the population remained unaffected. Yet, beyond the complexity of the situation it seems clear that the French could still have created institutions to reconcile the conflicting revolutionary political forces being asserted in 1946.

In the absence of these institutions, the contending parties launched a violent competition to achieve a predominance of political power. In this conflict the population could not remain unaffected; they were the object of the competition in which the goal was a new structure of political power. Inevitably there was a strong French opinion which did not believe that a thwarted elite could make a full-scale revolution, for this would require a political mobilization of the Vietnamese population on a scale never before approached. Moreover, France had in Viet Nam, especially in the south, an elite through which it seemed possible to maintain colonial influence. A measured response to the convulsion in Viet Nam could have been devised by the French; they could have created institutions granting power to indigenous citizens and permitting them opportunities for political mobilization on French terms, but this appeared to be unnecessary and the institutions seemed difficult beyond comprehension to construct. For this miscalculation France was to pay a dear price. Yet, as her officials faced the pressures in Viet Nam, they seemed not to be interested in dealing with them in ways that could be useful to France by institutionalizing the revolutionary process that had already been set in motion.

The prime opportunity for the French to respond to the Vietnamese revolution by devising new political institutions came in the summer of 1946. The "official definitive negotiations" called for by the Ho–d'Argenlieu communiqué of March 24 did not commence for more than a month after the Viet Minh delegation arrived in France. This delay was caused by the political instability out of which the Fourth French Republic was being created. The conference did not begin until July 6 at the Palace at Fontainebleau, and from the outset, the tone and character of the discussion was significantly different from that of the Dalat meeting. The Vietnamese delegation was almost exclusively composed of high-ranking Viet Minh leaders, headed by Ho Chi Minh. In the opening remarks, Pham Van Dong, Ho's chief lieutenant, vehemently attacked the policies of Admiral d'Argenlieu, directing his protest against the formation of the Cochinchinese republic and the military occupation of the central Viet Nam plateau which had taken place during June.[3]

Before the discussion had gone very far, d'Argenlieu posed another embarrassing problem. He called a second Dalat conference to which he invited Cambodia, Laos, and Cochinchina, as well as observers from south-central Viet Nam (below the 16th parallel) and from the mountain ethnic minorities; their purpose was to examine the problems involved in the formation of the Indochinese Federation. The conference was announced on July 25, to be convened on August 1, and it immediately had its effect on the deliberations at Fontainebleau. Pham Van Dong emphasized that the proposed meeting at Dalat called in question the purpose of the Fontainebleau conference. He wondered if it would not be better to suspend the discussions in France until the ambiguity between the two conferences had been resolved.[4] This tense atmosphere of the conference was heightened further by a Viet Minh ambush of French troops in the northern Viet Nam town of Bac Ninh on August 4, in which twelve French soldiers were killed and forty-one wounded.[5]

Despite these tensions, the negotiations dragged on through August and into the first weeks of September with the status of southern Viet Nam being the intractable point of the discussions.

3 Devillers: *Histoire du Viet Nam*, p. 295.
4 Ibid., p. 300.
5 *The New York Times*, August 6, 1946, p. 12.

Finally, on the night of September 9, 1946, a *modus vivendi* was drafted which was a last effort at conciliation, but rather than resolving major issues, it discussed secondary problems without any agreement on fundamentals. For example, French nationals were to be given preference in the employment of technicians and advisers by the Viet Minh government; schools in Viet Nam would follow French programs; Viet Nam was to form a customs union with the Indochinese Federation; and a commission was to be established to study postal, telegraph, and telephone communications between Viet Nam and the rest of the states of Indochina. But all of these clauses were conditional ones; they depended on what Viet Nam was to become politically, and on this point there was an agreement to disagree, but at a later date.[6]

The story of the Fontainebleau negotiations tells much more about French colonial policies and domestic politics than it does about revolution in Viet Nam. More than two months of intense wrangling yielded inconclusive results, which are best summarized in the last article of the *modus vivendi*. In it France and the Viet Minh "agree to seek together the conclusion of special agreements on all questions which may arise, in order to strengthen their friendly relations and prepare the way for a general final treaty. The negotiations will be resumed to this end as soon as possible and at the latest in January 1947." In retrospect it seems almost laughable that the French and the Viet Minh were discussing problems of telephone communications just three months before their armed confrontation in the streets of Hanoi. But the irreality of this *modus vivendi* was forceful evidence that two months of hard bargaining had not given the French any clearer conception of how they might come to terms with the revolution in Viet Nam. Lacking a consensus within their own circles, the French sought to defer the question.

When the final draft of the *modus vivendi* was considered on the morning of September 10, Pham Van Dong demanded that the agreement include the date and the modalities for a referendum on the status of Cochinchina, as was called for in the

6 Text of *modus vivendi* in Cole: *Conflict in Indochina*, pp. 43-5.

March 6 accord. He asserted that the Vietnamese delegation would not sign the document if it did not contain these details.[7] This reluctance was based on the fear of repercussions in Hanoi from signing a *modus vivendi* without receiving the least assurances of Viet Nam's independence and unity. If such was the overriding concern of Pham Van Dong, there were other considerations which Ho Chi Minh thought primary. He did not want to return to Viet Nam empty-handed because he felt that without some sort of tangible shred of hope indicating that the French would fulfill the March 6 accords, there would be no means of stopping those within the Viet Minh who wanted to launch an all-out fight for independence.

Ho Chi Minh allowed the Viet Minh delegation, with Pham Van Dong at its head, to leave Paris for Hanoi. But within a day after its departure he had signed a *modus vivendi* lacking the conditions that Pham Van Dong had demanded. This was not done without substantial misgivings by the Viet Minh leader, who commented on his decision by saying, "I have just signed my death warrant."[8] Moreover, he pleaded that the insufficiency of the statement would make it difficult, if not impossible, to assuage the emotions of the Viet Minh leadership. To Jean Sainteny, who had come to France to facilitate the work of the Fontainebleau conference, he pleaded, "Don't let me leave this way; arm me against those who seek to surpass me. You will not regret it."[9] Prophetically, he covered his disappointment over the meager results of his negotiation with the assertion that "If it is necessary for us to fight we shall fight. You will kill ten of our men, but we will kill one of yours and it is you who will finish by wearing yourself out."[1]

7 Devillers: *Histoire du Viet Nam*, p. 305.
8 Sainteny: *Histoire d'une paix manquée*, p. 209.
9 Ibid.
1 Ibid., p. 210.

CHAPTER 23

THE COMING SHOWDOWN

WITH FRANCE

🟌

🟌

🟌

From the first indication that the d'Argenlieu clique of officials was not going to give a very broad interpretation to the March 6 accords, the Viet Minh had been preparing for the military showdown its negotiators sought to avoid. One of its immediate concerns was that southern Viet Nam not be gotten under firm control and separated by the French from the rest of the country through lack of political and guerrilla activity to oppose them. Thus the smoldering remains of the August Revolution in the south were fanned to a new intensity. By comparison, there was no significant military provocation north of the 16th parallel —with the exception of the Bac Ninh ambush in early August— since such confrontations, it was felt, would have prejudiced the outcome of the conferences at Dalat and Fontainebleau. However, upon the departure of Ho Chi Minh for France at the end of May 1946, Vo Nguyen Giap, who then became the most potent leader remaining in the country, began to build up the

Viet Minh armed forces in the north. His goal was to be prepared for whatever contingencies the breakdown in negotiations might bring.

Meanwhile, the guerrilla action south of the 16th parallel was being directed toward eliminating the village-level social and administrative leadership in the localities where there were Viet Minh forces to carry out this terror. Where the opportunity presented itself, French convoys and installations were ambushed. In these operations the southern guerrilla forces were limited by two key factors: There was a divisiveness in the Nam Bo command, which stemmed from the Viet Minh's continuing reliance on the Cao Dai, Hoa Hao, and Binh Xuyen forces, and there was a relative paucity of the Viet Minh's men and equipment as compared with its resources in the north and the strength of the French in the south. By the end of 1946 the Viet Minh had only an estimated 25,000 men under arms south of the 16th parallel; a substantial portion of them, estimated at 5,000 men, was located in central Viet Nam between Da Nang and Nha Trang, a territory which remained unoccupied by the French. As these figures indicate, during the summer of 1946 the approximately 35,000 French troops concentrated in the Cochinchina region in the south were opposed by a guerrilla force of almost half their number.

Despite severe losses in weapons and casualties inflicted on them by the French, the Viet Minh Nam Bo forces were able to create widespread political instability. In the rural areas of the south this was achieved through the assassination and kidnapping of at least 368 village leaders during 1946. The Viet Minh was able to direct its attacks at various levels, shifting operations to take advantage of changing opportunities. From late August until the cease-fire provisions of the *modus vivendi* went into effect on October 30, it concentrated its attacks on French posts and convoys. For example, there were 212 attacks on posts in the south during October but only 17 in November. There were 84 ambushes in the month preceding the cease-fire and only 13 following it. After the cease-fire the Viet Minh then shifted its operations by concentrating on assassination. In the first two weeks of November, 17 village notables were killed in the south, with 32 reported missing, and before the outbreak of general hostilities an additional 48 notables were killed.

Under the terms of the *modus vivendi* cease-fire the French could not respond militarily to these attacks on village leaders without violating the agreement. At least this was what the Viet Minh maintained. Freed of the threat of reprisal and with the structure of rural society weakened by its loss of leadership, the Viet Minh was able to expand its own political framework behind the screen of the cease-fire. Although the French intransigence over a more far-reaching *modus vivendi* had predictably strengthened the determination of the Viet Minh, it had, ironically, not benefited the Cochinchinese republic. Because of its effective tactics of infiltration and subversion, the Viet Minh could continue to extend its political influence in the south even when the French did try to check it militarily. The French predicament became increasingly unpleasant.

In their policy of postponing negotiations the French were caught between the self-imposed sanctions against a military response to the Viet Minh and the expansion of the independence movement's influence by means of political violence. The delay in negotiating seemed certain to give the Viet Minh time to increase its strength, which would in turn make its demands for concessions more extensive and forceful. Since the French position already allowed for very little flexibility, the successful campaign of guerrilla terrorism in the south pressed the followers of Admiral d'Argenlieu to seek a showdown. In the period of diplomatic inactivity following the signing of the *modus vivendi,* d'Argenlieu chafed at the restrictions these agreements imposed. As the admiral began to prepare for a confrontation with the Viet Minh, the wisdom of Vo Nguyen Giap's military development program became apparent.

When the Viet Minh delegation departed for the Fontainebleau conference at the end of May 1946, the armed forces at the Viet Minh's disposal north of the 16th parallel numbered approximately 31,000 men.[1] Although estimates are conflicting, it ap-

1 Devillers: *Histoire du Viet Nam,* p. 283.

pears that at this time there were approximately 20,000 loosely organized guerrilla forces in Cochinchina and that their number, generally balancing losses with new recruitment, was relatively stable during 1946. Six months later, as a consequence of a rapid program of expansion, the Viet Minh had throughout Viet Nam about 100,000 men under its control.[2] Doubling its armed force in that short a period of time was obviously a spectacular organizational achievement. Yet it did not mean that the Viet Minh had created a uniformly disciplined and trained fighting force; there were strong regional variations in size and quality.

While force levels in the far south remained unchanged, the greatest increase in military strength occurred in northern Viet Nam, where most of the twofold increase in quantity was concentrated. Central Viet Nam, in the area of Quang Ngai and Qui Nhon, was another location of energetic organizational activity. In this central area it was estimated that the Viet Minh had about 25,000 out of 65,000 men who could be termed regulars when the armed confrontation came in December 1946. The greatest concentration of regulars, approximately 40,000, was in Tonkin. Supplementing the regulars there were about 15,000 troops of secondary quality in northern and central Viet Nam and about 20,000 poorly armed guerrillas in Cochinchina.

The creation of such a force was all the more remarkable for the fact that few of its members had received military training before joining the Viet Minh. There were four sources from which members of the Viet Minh forces with previous military experience were recruited. First, there were the most loyal and seasoned of them all, the veteran Viet Minh guerrillas, numbering at a maximum 5,000 persons, who had been organized by Vo Nguyen Giap and Chu Van Tan in the mountain areas of northern Viet Nam before August 1945.[3] Another element in the small nucleus was a group of about 4,000 men who had been recruited by the Japanese for a volunteer armed force after March 9, 1945. There was also a group of approximately 3,000

2 This did not include approximately 35,000 paramilitary forces.

3 Democratic Republic of Viet Nam: *Ten Years of Fighting and Building of the Vietnamese People's Army,* p. 15.

men who had served with the French army in Europe and other parts of the empire and had returned home to join the Viet Minh. Of potential, but uncertain, utility to the Viet Minh were the 24,000 members of the French-led militia force, the Garde Indochinoise, who were inducted into the Viet Minh only with great care because of suspected psychological commitment to their old units. A similar attitude was adopted toward the approximately 55,000 men who had served with the French Colonial Army in Indochina during the Japanese occupation.

There is no accurate indication of how many experienced military men joined the Viet Minh from the Garde Indochinoise or from service as regulars with the French army, but it would have required their complete defection, a total of 79,000 men, in order to have accounted for the expansion of the Viet Minh armed forces without popular mobilization. On the basis of fragmentary information it seems that the Garde Indochinoise veterans were more likely volunteers in the Viet Minh than were the regulars among the Vietnamese in the French army, because army units were concentrated at certain key locations and were more distinctly military than their militia counterparts. At least 3,100 of the 55,000 showed themselves disciplined enough to follow their French officers into Chinese exile when the Japanese *coup de force* occurred. The Garde Indochinoise, however, was scattered throughout the country in small units, with few French command personnel, and with a local paramilitary rather than military role. The militiamen made almost no attempt to retreat into China or to oppose the Japanese.

Beyond these organizational factors there are other reasons why it appears that there was no wholesale transfer of loyalties by those Vietnamese with French military backgrounds. Not only was suspicion of the Viet Minh a barrier, but also there was no universal reaction against the French regime in Viet Nam. For example, in the midst of the revolutionary fervor in the summer of 1946, Vietnamese accounted for approximately 6,300 men out of the 35,000 French forces in Viet Nam south of the 16th parallel. Although it is impossible to determine whether these 6,300 were part of the 55,000 who had previously served with the French during the occupation, it seems likely that they were. This impression is based on the strong trend of indigenous co-operation with the colonial regime in the military sphere. During November and December 1946 the French were able to recruit an additional 18,000 Vietnamese, bringing them into their ranks as trained troops by June 1947.[4] Moreover, nearly 12,000 partisans were recruited for counterguerrilla duty and a militia of 8,700 was organized. Before the end of 1947, Vietnamese troops composed two thirds of the French forces south of the 16th parallel.

While this competition with the Viet Minh for the loyalties of Vietnamese military recruits yielded the French the best results in the south, their success was not confined there. As a consequence of their continued role in the Indochina War, there were, by the spring of 1954, nearly 300,000 Vietnamese fighting against the Viet Minh under French leadership. This French capacity to mobilize substantial Vietnamese manpower for military purposes at the beginning as well as at the conclusion of the war suggests an important commentary on the revolution in Viet Nam. Since the military recruitment of the Viet Minh was a close corollary of its program of political mobilization, it was severely restricted by the continuing ability of the French to secure the support of widespread segments of Vietnamese society. Although there was broad opposition to France in Viet Nam and great deterioration in the structures of traditional social commitment, there were still means of organizing political structures around the old colonial regime. Though this did not minimize the revolutionary character of Vietnamese society, it did mean that the decay of the old regime was not thorough and that the form of a new order was far from complete. This characteristic of revolutionary politics in Viet Nam became clearer as the two opponents worked to establish increasingly larger military forces.

In addition to the political restrictions the Viet Minh faced, there were factors of internal military organization which also tested its capacity as a revolutionary movement. Even if there

4 Marchand: *Le drame indochinois,* p. 77.

had been a mass defection of the 79,000 French-trained Vietnamese military men, they would not have brought with them an officer or noncommissioned officer corps sufficient to provide the encadrement for a fighting force of 100,000 men. Moreover, it was undoubtedly the officers, the more privileged Vietnamese among the French troops, who were the most psychologically committed to their French units. Even the existing Vietnamese officer corps was too small for Viet Minh requirements; among the 55,000 Vietnamese in the French Colonial Army in Indochina, less than 1 per cent were officers, 27 being recognized as regulars and 23 as reserves, while 2,342—about 5 per cent of the total—were noncommissioned officers.

In order to meet its leadership requirements, the Viet Minh established training schools in two towns: Tong, northwest of Hanoi in the upper Red River Valley, on the site of a former French base, and Quang Ngai, in central Viet Nam. At both of these locations, Japanese instructors and their program of instruction played an extremely important role. The instructors at Tong were part of Lieutenant Colonel Mukaiyama's "Japanese Organism for Collaboration and Aid for the Independence of Viet Nam." The 300-man group at Quang Ngai was the same one that had set up arsenals under the direction of Major Saito. By the end of 1946 these two schools apparently had been able to train 1,500 noncommissioned officers. Although the number of officers graduated, if any, is not available, it would appear that it was clearly insufficient to meet the Viet Minh's requirements. In order to provide leadership for its 80,000-man main force, it seems reasonable to expect that the Viet Minh would have needed at least 10 per cent officers, or 8,000, and about 18,000 noncommissioned officers, or 25 per cent of its total strength. There is little evidence to suggest that it had this level of experienced personnel.

The shortage of officers placed an especially heavy burden on those Viet Minh military leaders who had received their training through the channels of revolutionary politics. Of the prominent military chiefs of the Viet Minh, at least five had had experience in China, either at the Whampoa Military Academy or with

Chinese Communist guerrilla units. Two of these Whampoa graduates were given special responsibilities in developing the Viet Minh armed force. One of them, Nguyen Son, was placed in charge of the central Viet Nam operational and training command at Quang Ngai, where, with his Japanese colleagues, he trained noncommissioned officers and organized two units of undetermined strength which were called "divisions." During the gestation period of 1946, Nguyen Son had as his command deputy a Chinese-trained Viet Minh officer, Le Thiet Hung, while in an analogous position to Nguyen Son was Vong Thua Vu, another Whampoa graduate, who was in charge of military training at the upper Red River base at Tong.

Perhaps the best indication of the various predominant elements in the Viet Minh military tradition is demonstrated in the backgrounds of the six men who were chosen to command the infantry divisions which slowly began to emerge from guerrilla units in 1949: Two were men with Chinese military training; two were of Tho origin and had risen through the guerrilla movement started by Giap in the Tonkin mountains during the Japanese occupation; one was a former noncommissioned officer in the French army; and the remaining division commander had progressed through the revolutionary movement inside Viet Nam after 1946 without having had any outside military training.

The character of this latter-day military structure reflected some of the particular features of the Viet Minh's revolutionary politics. The emergence of the Tho generals betrayed a continuing reliance on this key mountain minority for manpower as well as bases. The Chinese background of officers given vital training and operational responsibilities in conjunction with Japanese deserters recalls the role of external aid in the expansion of the Viet Minh force. Whether or not the approximately 80,000 weapons obtained through the aid of the Chinese and Japanese were a limit to the Viet Minh's manpower recruitment, they do indicate that the men were relatively well provided for in armament. Also, this profile of its division commanders indicates from another perspective that the development of the Viet Minh military strength depended on the leadership of men without extensive prior experience. Moreover, the mobilization of a 100,000-man armed force in a little over a year was not only a spectacular achievement, it was a vital prerequisite if the revolutionary movement were to be sustained. Against the pressures of the French, the Viet Minh's ability to field such a fighting force stood out as a striking claim to legitimacy.

Measured against the approximately 350,000 men that the Viet Minh had brought into its combat units by 1954, this initial achievement gives evidence of the capacities that the Viet Minh was to demonstrate on numerous occasions in stalemating the French militarily. By the autumn of 1946 the Viet Minh had established a unique military position: It had increased its armed forces to a larger size than the French then had in Viet Nam, and of more importance to its strategy, it had expanded its strength to approximately 75,000 men north of the 16th parallel, where the French were restricted by the March 6 accord to 15,000 men. With the continued effectiveness of the guerrillas in Cochinchina, the French were caught in a double-pronged strategy. Giap had done his work well; through his efforts the Viet Minh was prepared to wait out the hiatus in diplomatic bargaining or to resist the initiatives of d'Argenlieu.

CHAPTER 24 ✿ ✿ ✿

THE COUP DE FORCE

IN HANOI: BEGINNING OF

REVOLUTIONARY WAR

✿

✿

✿

The trend toward a French confrontation with the Viet Minh was not averted by the Fontainebleau conference and the signing of the *modus vivendi*. Indeed, the trend was purposefully sustained by the French high commissioner in Indochina; Admiral d'Argenlieu's second Dalat conference in August had created much hostility among the Viet Minh because there was no masking the event as a transparent attempt to shore up the prestige of the Cochinchinese republic. Dalat was followed by another provocative action which the admiral initiated even as the *modus vivendi* was being signed; on September 10, 1946, he ordered the French commissioner for Tonkin to establish control over customs collection in northern Viet Nam.[1] In particular, d'Argenlieu wanted to bring to an end the freedom with

1 Sainteny: *Histoire d'une paix manquée*, p. 214.

which the Viet Minh had been able to use the port of Haiphong.

Concerning this issue the *modus vivendi* had stated, "Viet Nam forms a customs union with the other countries of the Indochinese Federation. Consequently, there will be no internal customs barriers and the same tariffs will be applied everywhere on entry and departure from Indochinese territory."[2] However, the Viet Minh did not regard this statement as superseding the March 6 accords, which recognized its government as having the right to maintain a treasury. In addition, the *modus vivendi* called for the formation of a coordinating commission on customs. D'Argenlieu's action would seem to have prejudiced the work of such a commission before it could be established. Not unexpectedly, his initiative caused a violent reaction by the Viet Minh, and on November 14 the Vietnamese National Assembly passed a resolution demanding that France "respect the customs sovereignty" of Viet Nam.[3] Before its demands could be pressed further, events brought the issue to a head.

The incident that was to set off a chain reaction leading to the general conflagration between France and the Viet Minh occurred on November 20. A boat belonging to a Chinese trader bringing motor oil into the port of Haiphong was confiscated by French authorities. As they were towing the craft away from its mooring, a vehicle with Vietnamese militiamen, or *Tự Vệ*, as they were called, approached the scene and opened fire on the French. Although no one was injured in the exchange of fire, the noise attracted additional Vietnamese forces who arrested a French officer and two enlisted men trying to locate the storehouse of goods taken from the boat, which they considered contraband. In the ensuing attempts to liberate the French personnel, fighting broke out with great intensity and, before it subsided during the night, twenty French soldiers were killed and twenty wounded.

During the course of the following day, November 21, a cease-fire agreement was reached in Hanoi between French and Vietnamese representatives. It was identified by the name of its

2 Cole: *Conflict in Indochina,* p. 44.
3 Sainteny: *Histoire d'une paix manquée,* p. 215.

signers as the Lami-Nam agreement. At the same time Admiral d'Argenlieu, then in Paris for consultations, is reported to have instructed his deputy, General Valluy, in Saigon to use force to settle the Haiphong incident. Before his orders could be implemented, the fighting had stopped.[4] But the situation was soon inflamed again. Whether by coincidence or in retaliation, another incident occurred at the border town of Lang Son later in the day on November 21. A French team attempting to locate the graves of their comrades killed by the Japanese on March 9, 1945, was fired on by the Viet Minh, and in an hour and a half of fierce combat, eighteen Frenchmen were killed or wounded.[5]

Despite the response from the French military representatives in the north that measures were being taken to resolve the crisis, the high command in Saigon overruled these officials. General Valluy feared these incidents might multiply while negotiations were being conducted so he gave the following order to Colonel Dèbes, the French commander in Haiphong:

> It appears clearly that we are up against premeditated aggressions, carefully staged by the Vietnamese Regular Army which no longer seems to obey its government's orders. Under these circumstances, your commendable attempts at conciliation . . . are out of season. The moment has come of giving a severe lesson to those who have treacherously attacked you. Make use of all the means at your disposal to master Haiphong and so bring the leaders of the Vietnamese to a better understanding of the situation.[6]

On November 22, Colonel Dèbes informed his Vietnamese counterpart in Haiphong that in view of the violations of the Lami-Nam agreement, he was demanding that the Viet Minh forces evacuate the Chinese quarter of the city before nine o'clock on he morning of the 23rd. In responding to Dèbes' letter, the Vietnamese commander denied all of the French officer's charges and called his attention to the continuing negotia-

---

4 Hammer: *The Struggle for Indochina*, p. 183.
5 Marchand: *Le drame indochinois*, pp. 78–9.
6 Institut Franco-Suisse d'Études Coloniales: *France and Viet Nam: The Franco-Vietnamese Conflict According to Official Documents* (Geneva: Éditions du Milieu du Monde; 1947), p. 45.

tions in Hanoi, which had, early on the morning of the 23rd, reached an agreement for the reestablishment of a mixed guard at the railroad station in Haiphong. This exchange of letters was followed by another set in which Dèbes repeated his accusations and demands and the Vietnamese commander denied them. The verbal battle was ended by the French commander, who gave the order to open fire at five minutes past ten o'clock on the morning of the 23rd, unleashing not only a bombardment by ships of the French fleet in Haiphong harbor, but also barrages by marine artillery and strikes by fighter aircraft. Before the day was over the Viet Minh forces had been neutralized and about 6,000 persons, including civilians fleeing the town, had been killed.[7]

After this carnage of an innocent population the atmosphere in northern Viet Nam was supercharged with suspicion and hostility on both sides. One important reaction in France to mitigate the tension was the naming of Jean Sainteny as a special envoy with full civil and military powers in northern Viet Nam. Because of his close relations with Ho Chi Minh, it was felt in Paris that Sainteny could do much to alleviate the anger and hatred caused by the Haiphong incident. But when he returned to Hanoi on December 2, he found the situation filled with an air of desperation. However, it seemed widely accepted that the reciprocal confidence between Ho and Sainteny could still have served to reestablish calm and prevented the clash that otherwise appeared inevitable.[8] Yet, if this were to occur, decisions would have had to be made in Paris on the content of negotiations to prevent further incidents and on the future of the broader agreements called for in the *modus vivendi*. But France still faced the problems of domestic politics, which had shunted the Indochina controversy to the sidelines of decision-making.

---

7 Paul Mus: *Témoignage Chrétien* (No. 292, 10 février 1950), as cited in Devillers: *Histoire du Viet Nam*, p. 337. The same figure is also used in Sainteny: *Histoire d'une paix manquée*, p. 216. The most detailed account of the Haiphong incident, including a special emphasis on the relationship between d'Argenlieu in Paris, Gen. Valluy in Saigon, and Gen. Morlière, who tried hard for a reconciliation in Hanoi, is contained in Chapter 19, "Haiphong," in Devillers: *Histoire du Viet Nam*, pp. 331–43.

8 Sainteny: *Histoire d'une paix manquée*, pp. 217–19.

While Paris seemed to want to avoid a showdown, it also appeared unable to control the largely independent actions of Admiral d'Argenlieu. Although Sainteny's belated mission was indicative of a desire for conciliation, he was not specifically authorized to take any new initiatives. In a letter of December 8 to his father-in-law, the former governor general of Indochina and former president of France Albert Sarraut, Sainteny expressed his own predicament and at the same time perceptively summarized the French problem in Indochina:

> . . . all the ground gained before and by the 6 March [accords] is lost. Everything has to be done again . . . we are here to execute orders, but we must receive these orders. France ought to know if it wants to conserve its Empire and how it expects to do it. It is necessary to abandon for a few moments the preoccupations of narrow minded politicians and give the orders to those who are attempting to save it. There is not a moment to lose. . . .[9]

Even as Sainteny wrote these lines, Hanoi seemed, at least to one observer, to be ". . . a city preparing for disaster."[1] Shady streets were being barricaded with felled trees, roadblocks had isolated the city from the surrounding countryside, and wide segments of the civilian Vietnamese population had fled the northern capital. "No one in his right mind wants fighting in Indochina" was certainly a widely held view, but in a dispatch filed three days before the clash it appeared that "the prospect of it is increasingly sinister unless irresponsible violence and bickering over technicalities can be curbed."[2]

One of the key "technicalities" was the landing by the French of a Foreign Legion battalion on December 5, 1946, at Da Nang, a central Viet Nam port north of the 16th parallel, without consulting the Viet Minh.[3] Although under the tense circumstances, consultation might have been considered unexpected, the action was a violation of the March 6 accords as well as the spirit of

9 Ibid.
1 Robert Trumbull, in *The New York Times*, December 18, 1946, p. 20.
2 Ibid.
3 *The New York Times*, December 15, 1946, p. 5.

the *modus vivendi*. Obviously, these reinforcements accelerated the trend toward a military confrontation. Even though Paris had reaffirmed its recognition of the September 14 *modus vivendi* as the legal basis of its relations with the Viet Minh, there was, for an obvious reason, little confidence in this pronouncement in Hanoi. The reaffirmation was coupled with an announcement that France was going to increase its total armed strength in Indochina because of the situation created by the Haiphong incident.[4]

The increase in French military strength north of the 16th parallel and the indication of a continued expansion of French armed forces in Indochina was an unmistakable development. It must have suggested to the Viet Minh leadership that they had little to gain by deferring whatever action they planned to retaliate against France for the Haiphong tragedy. Their advantage of holding the French forces to 15,000 men, as prescribed in the March 6 agreements, would certainly be lost in this French build-up. By July 1946 there were 67,000 Frenchmen and Legionnaires under arms in all of Indochina. The 18,000 additional Vietnamese recruits inducted in November and December 1946 would bring the French military strength up to about 95,000 men by the early spring of 1947.

The training of these recruits and the announced dispatch of additional forces from France meant a short-time lag in the build-up. In the estimated six months before this expansion could be completed, the Viet Minh still had an important advantage from the March 6 accords. This came from the scattered pattern in the stationing of the 15,000-man French contingent in northern Viet Nam. Although one third of France's strength, 5,000 men, was concentrated around Hanoi, the remainder were dispersed throughout the territory in detachments of 1,000 men or less.[5] This pattern increased the vulnerability of the reoccupation forces, which were under restrictions to remain in garrisons at fixed points. Even though the approximately 75,000

---

4 *The New York Times*, November 30, 1946, p. 6.

5 Marchand: *Le drame indochinois*, p. 63, enumerates the garrison locations of the French reoccupation troops.

Viet Minh under arms were clearly inferior in both training and equipment to the French, they would never again have so favorable a balance of forces. Between the mounting pressure of French military expansion and inflexibility in negotiations, the Viet Minh had few durable advantages. Since there seemed no foreseeable improvement in its relations with the French, time was against the Viet Minh.

Of more immediate concern than the gradual expansion of France's military force was the fear that the French would launch a *coup d'état* in Hanoi similar to the one that had broken the hold of the revolutionary movement in Saigon. Whether or not the Viet Minh was aware of them, it appears certain that there were several French contingency plans for the seizure of Hanoi. What the Viet Minh did discover, at Haiphong in December 1946, was a directive issued by General Valluy more than seven months before, on April 10, 1946, which required the French garrisons in northern Viet Nam to gather information in order to be prepared to neutralize local Viet Minh forces by surprise.[6] Obviously, this aroused the suspicions of the Viet Minh to a new height. In particular, Vo Nguyen Giap became adamant in his advocacy of the view that "The best means of not being surprised is to strike first . . ."[7] Thus on December 7, in response to the landing of the French Foreign Legion battalion at Da Nang, Giap issued a directive ordering his forces to be prepared for a "preventive coup" by December 12.

In the midst of the gathering storm a brief ray of hope was seen in mid-December by the Viet Minh as a result of the election of Léon Blum to head a new French government. These expectations stemmed from an article that Blum had written before his election in a Socialist newspaper, *Le Populaire,* on December 10, 1946. In it he had said, ". . . there is one way and only one way of preserving in Indochina the prestige of our civilization, our political and spiritual influence, and also of our material interests which are legitimate: it is sincere agreement

6 Devillers: *Histoire du Viet Nam,* p. 345, contains the text of the directive which was confirmed as authentic in the version published by the Viet Minh.
7 Ibid., p. 346.

[with Viet Nam] on the basis of independence. . . ."[8] Immediately upon hearing of these views Ho Chi Minh dispatched a message, on December 15, to this new Socialist premier of France which called for (1) the return of French and Viet Minh troops to the positions they had held prior to November 20 in Lang Son and Haiphong, (2) the withdrawal of the troops landed at Da Nang by the French on December 5, and (3) the cessation of French mopping-up operations in Cochinchina. Even in retrospect it is difficult to determine if this message would have made any difference in Paris. Its substance was virtually the same as a telegram (to which there was no response) sent by Jean Sainteny shortly after his return to Hanoi. Whether a direct appeal to the new French premier might have averted the clash will never be known. Ho's message was held up in Saigon by French authorities and did not reach Paris until December 26, seven days after the fighting had begun in Hanoi.[9]

Meanwhile, beginning on December 17, a series of incidents between the *Tự Vệ* and French units in Hanoi resulted in several deaths on both sides. On the morning of December 19, 10,000 Viet Minh troops were grouped in three sections on the outskirts of Hanoi, and an approximately equal number of militiamen was alerted that an attack would be launched that evening. At the same time the French commander for northern Viet Nam, General Morlière, demanded that the *Tự Vệ* be disarmed as an indication of the peaceful intentions of the Viet Minh. This demand was the reason later given by Ho Chi Minh as the instigation of the outbreak of the fighting, for it was considered an ultimatum.[1] Before noon on the 19th, Ho sent a letter to Sainteny in which he asked the French commissioner to search for a way to ameliorate the ominous climate developing in Hanoi.[2] General Morlière responded sympathetically to this spirit of relaxing tensions by acceding to Vo Nguyen Giap's request that a part of the French troops be given leave from their posts.

---

8 As quoted in Hammer: *The Struggle for Indochina*, p. 186.
9 Devillers: *Histoire du Viet Nam*, pp. 348–52. Text of Ho's message on p. 351.
1 This was contained in Ho's Christmas Day broadcast on Viet Minh radio, as reported in *The New York Times*, December 28, 1946, p. 1.
2 Text of letter is found in Devillers: *Histoire du Viet Nam*, p. 354.

For the first time in about fifteen days over 1,200 French soldiers were allowed to visit the cafes and cinemas of Hanoi.[3]

As the tense day of December 19 was moving toward dusk, a Eurasian agent of the French who had infiltrated the Viet Minh armed forces informed his superiors that the Vietnamese were preparing a *coup de force* for eight o'clock that evening. Shortly after this news was received, a letter arrived from the Viet Minh indicating that it was prepared to hold a meeting on the following morning to consider the demand of General Morlière to disarm the militia. Whether this was just a guise to keep them off-balance, the French could not be sure. Yet it was a great relief to their military command to hear the clocks of Hanoi sound the hour of eight without incident. Four minutes later the city was plunged into darkness as the central power station was taken over by the Viet Minh, and fierce fighting erupted in the shadowy streets.[4]

Although the exact moment for the outbreak of hostilities may not have been chosen until very soon before the attack, there was little question that there had been substantial preparation for the affair. The Vietnamese and Chinese quarters of Hanoi had been well stocked with food and ammunition. Holes had been cut between adjoining houses to facilitate passage. Tunnels to points outside the city had also been carefully prepared. These provisions made it possible for elements of the Tự Vệ to hold out for almost two months before the French were able to make themselves complete masters of the city, on February 19, 1947.[5] After three weeks of fighting against the estimated 10,000 Tự Vệ, the 5,000-man French garrison was able to lift the state of siege that had been proclaimed when the fighting broke out. At the same time the Hanoi-Haiphong Highway, the veritable lifeline for food and supplies of the 5,500 French civilians in Hanoi, was reopened.[6]

The garrisons in the other northern Viet Nam locations were

3 Ibid.

4 Sainteny: *Histoire d'une paix manquée*, p. 224. An hour-by-hour account of the street fighting in Hanoi is found in Contre-Amical. Robert Kilian: *Les fusiliers marins en Indochine* (Paris: Éditions Berger-Levrault; 1951), pp. 149–62.

5 *The New York Times*, February 20, 1947, p. 19.

6 *The New York Times*, January 10, 1947, p. 4.

not quite so fortunate. Hue was under constant attack until reinforcements arrived to drive off the Viet Minh on February 5.[7] Less fortunate still was the French detachment at Vinh, a central Viet Nam town 155 miles south of Hanoi, which capitulated to the Viet Minh on December 21. The reinforced garrison at Da Nang was the object of a fierce Viet Minh attack, but it was able to hold both the town and the airfield there. Viet Minh attempts were also made to take the Red River Delta towns of Bac Ninh, Phu Lang Thuong, and Nam Dinh, with the latter being under the most severe pressure until March 12, 1947, when a ground column finally arrived from Hanoi.[8]

These attacks served to demonstrate that the Viet Minh had the capability to coordinate its military operations over all Viet Nam. Moreover, these operations against the French garrisons in the north were matched by an intensification of the guerrilla war in the south. Before two months had passed, the French in northern Viet Nam were subjected to almost 10 per cent casualties, with 1,855 men reported killed or wounded from December 19, 1946 to February 7, 1947.[9] Although this was far from devastation, it was probably also far from being an accurate figure of French losses.

General Leclerc's worst fears of having the Viet Minh withdraw to the countryside for a guerrilla war had now been confirmed. Nonetheless, it seems that there was no real change in French thinking caused by the December 19 events in Hanoi. In their aftermath, Marius Moutet, the minister for overseas France, was quoted as saying that "Before there can be any negotiation it will be necessary to get a military decision."[1] In a special sense this statement could not have been more correct. However, the military decision did not come for another seven years. And when it did occur, it was the Vietnamese who did the deciding, and the ensuing negotiations at Geneva were on their terms and not those of the French.

---

7 *The New York Times*, February 7, 1947, p. 10.
8 *The New York Times*, December 22, 1946, p. 1, and March 13, 1947, p. 14.
9 *The New York Times*, February 8, 1947, p. 6.
1 *The New York Times*, January 5, 1947, p. 1.

PART EIGHT

Conclusion:
The Origins of Revolution

✖
✖
✖

CHAPTER 25 ✿ ✿ ✿

FRANCE AND

THE ORIGINS OF REVOLUTION

IN VIET NAM

France failed to realize that at the end of World War II, Viet Nam was in the midst of a revolution that its colonial policies had helped to create. Moreover, the French remained unaware that this revolution had brought a configuration of power which made colonial rule an anachronism. Instead, the French appear to have calculated that the Viet Minh and other groups were so weak militarily that France could easily bring them under control by force of arms without heeding their political demands. Although General Leclerc had tried to warn his countrymen of the costs of a military occupation of Viet Nam, his assessment was given little credence. Had Frenchmen known that their military action would claim vast resources badly needed for France's postwar development, as well as the lives of more than 75,000 of their soldiers over nine years of war, they might have sought alternatives.[1] Since their calculations were so myopic that they could not foresee the tragedy that lay ahead, they chose to try to crush the revolution rather than to seek ways of sharing political power with the Vietnamese.

As if to show how little interested they were in a political settlement with the Viet Minh, the French made a final cynical gesture in the spring of 1947 before the First Indochina War began in earnest. In a move dictated largely by domestic political considerations the newly appointed French high commissioner, Émile Bollaert, tried to display apparent flexibility by sending an emissary to Ho Chi Minh. The purpose of the mission was ostensibly to satisfy the Socialist members of the French coalition government that contact with the Viet Minh leader was being maintained. But the effect of the undertaking was to demand the virtual unconditional surrender of the Viet Minh. Chosen for the mission was Paul Mus, who several months earlier had agreed to become Bollaert's political advisor in the hope that he might contribute to averting a full-scale conflict between the French and the Vietnamese. Paradoxically, Mus, a scholar and teacher who enjoyed wide respect among the Vietnamese for his service to education in Viet Nam before World War II, was to be yet another agent of French intransigence. He was also the last Frenchman to talk with Ho Chi Minh until after the Viet Minh victory in 1954.

When Mus set off by foot from Hanoi in May 1947, to walk through the Viet Minh lines in search of Ho Chi Minh, he was given no new terms with which he might initiate a more fruitful round of discussions. Instead he was instructed to inform Ho that the conditions for further discussion with the French would be for the Viet Minh to disarm its soldiers, permit free circulation of French troops throughout Vietnamese territory, concentrate its disarmed soldiers in predetermined perimeters, return hostages, and deliver into French hands non-Vietnamese within Viet Minh ranks. After he reached the mountain redoubt in the

---

[1] For statistics on casualties in the First Indochina War see Bernard B. Fall: *Street Without Joy: Indochina at War, 1946-54* (Harrisburg, Pa.: The Stackpole Company; 1961), Appendix II, p. 313.

hills of northern Viet Nam where the Viet Minh had its head-quarters, Mus conveyed these terms directly to Ho in a private discussion. Without immediately responding to the conditions, Ho turned the conversation in a leisurely manner to his impressions of the future of the French Union. He felt that if France's idea of a worldwide commonwealth were to become a reality, it had to be based on the mutual respect of the parties involved. Then abruptly, without having consulted any of his colleagues in the Viet Minh hierarchy, Ho terminated the discussion by saying, "In the French Union there is no place for cowards; if I accept these conditions I would be one."[2]

While a willingness to renew negotiations with the Viet Minh could have averted a war, it would not have led to any immediate resolution of the political problems of Viet Nam. Indeed, it was because these dilemmas of sharing political power were so difficult to resolve that the less ambiguous and more seductive road to war seemed so attractive. Perhaps more than anyone else involved, Ho Chi Minh sought to avoid this road because he probably realized more clearly than others that the Vietnamese people were not only unprepared militarily for war, but more importantly, they were not unified politically. In the sixteen years since its founding, the Indochinese Communist Party under Ho's leadership had been unable to establish a countrywide political organization free from parochial pressures or strong enough to mobilize unchallenged political power. Undoubtedly Ho had the discouraging experience of the precipitous revolt of the Communist Party in southern Viet Nam in 1940, as well as its hasty action in 1945, to remind him of the limitations in launching a countrywide resistance against France. Still, through the Viet Minh Front, the Indochinese Communist Party had done more to bring the Vietnamese people into a unified political movement than had any other group. If Ho Chi Minh could not get France to recognize the legitimacy of this power—meager though it was in relation to the armed strength of France—then he had no choice but to fight.

2 Mus: *Viet Nam: Sociologie d'une guerre*, pp. 314–16. See also Robert Shaplen: *The Lost Revolution* (New York: Harper and Row; 1965), pp. 49–54.

The fact that the Viet Minh was strong enough to challenge the French but not powerful enough to throw them out of Viet Nam was an indication of the relative strength of the revolutionaries as well as the diversity of the origins of revolution. Because the Viet Minh had been unable to surmount the parochial, especially regional, divisions in Vietnamese society, the revolutionary pressures they could bring to bear against the French were limited. Although these parochial divisions had traditionally been barriers to Vietnamese political unity, colonially sponsored social changes had tended to reinforce them, making them even more significant obstacles. Besides buttressing existing social cleavages, these changes, through which France had brought limited modernization to Viet Nam, also produced many pockets of potential political power. But because of its localized character this potential power was extremely difficult to mobilize. Spasmodic uprisings confined to local areas were indicative of the existence of revolutionary potential in the decades before Japanese intervention. Yet the swiftness and effectiveness of the colonial regime in crushing these revolts meant that there was little revolutionary space within which this potential might have been transformed into more extensive revolutionary organization.

Without a determined and effective leadership, no incipient revolutionary movement—in Viet Nam or elsewhere—has been successful in moving beyond sporadic and isolated terror to make a sustained bid for governmental power. Consequently, incumbents who place all their emphasis on crushing pockets of revolt but who fail to prevent the formation of a disciplined revolutionary leadership are overlooking the long-range source of their difficulties. With few exceptions, those who become revolutionaries are politically skilled individuals whose talents are potentially available to the incumbent government. This was especially true in Viet Nam, where the revolutionaries were almost exclusively the product of the colonial education system which the French had established to provide a trained body of functionaries for their commerce and administration.

If the opportunities in commerce and governmental administration had been extensive enough to have given the rising generations of French-educated Vietnamese a stake in the continuation of colonial rule, it is conceivable that they might never have sought the path of revolution. But prior to the Japanese occupation, colonial institutions offered little upward mobility or expanding opportunity. Indeed, institutions which were sources of employment for educated Vietnamese remained relatively static in size and number primarily because of budgetary limitations. But the paucity of colonial revenues merely reflected restrictions on colonial economic growth. Industry in France feared the loss of export markets if Viet Nam became highly industrialized and consumer goods were manufactured locally.[3] Because such policies gave colonial society a static quality, sharp antipathies developed between the French directors of colonial institutions and their Vietnamese subordinates. No matter what their educational background, individual Vietnamese had little prospect of rising to positions where institutional policy was made. For most of those who became revolutionaries, it was clear that their own opportunities for advancement were inseparably bound up with eliminating French rule in Viet Nam.

Not all Vietnamese, of course, were excluded from positions of privilege and influence in Viet Nam's colonial society. For those who had become large landholders, prosperous merchants, or high-ranking bureaucrats and had capped their achievements by becoming French citizens, the rewards of colonial rule were gratifying indeed. Their sentiments were hardly revolutionary, and when revolution did occur, the object of their loyalty was clear. These Vietnamese sought the continuation of French rule because their personal fortunes depended on it. But their support was anything but decisive for France, since they numbered probably less than one half of one per cent of the Vietnamese population.[4] And for a larger number of Vietnamese to have

---

3 The problems of employment, mobility, and economic growth are discussed by McCall: "The Effects of Independence on the Economy of Viet Nam," pp. 31–2, 50.
4 There were 5,926 Vietnamese with French citizenship in 1948 out of an estimated population of 22.7 million. This represented more than a twofold increase from 1937, when there were 2,555 "naturalized" French citizens in Viet Nam. See *Annuaire statistique de l'Indochine, 1947–48,* pp. 19, 23.

been identified with French rule, a broader sharing of the fruits of colonial society would have been necessary.

But economic growth in Viet Nam was so limited by the mercantilist policies of the colonial regime that its advantages could not be widely distributed without being dissipated altogether. Moreover, those Vietnamese who received the greatest economic rewards from the colonial economy had sealed their loyalty to France by acquiring political status through French citizenship. While it is unlikely that France would ever have made citizenship available outside of the indigenous oligarchy through which it ruled Viet Nam, it is also unlikely that French citizenship would have been very satisfying to rising generations of Vietnamese. Without providing a legitimate means for Vietnamese to have political status other than as colonial subjects or to share in governmental authority in Viet Nam, France alienated those whose power they were eventually unable to control through force.

CHAPTER 26 ✠ ✠ ✠

VIET NAM AND REVOLUTION

Men cannot make revolutions unless they have an acute sensitivity toward the social bases of their country's political difficulties and a capacity to create new forms of popular participation in politics which link people together in a common effort to change the society in which they live. Revolutionaries in Viet Nam have had this sensitivity and capacity. The way they have formed a new system of politics by overcoming some —though by no means all—of the traditional antipathies in Vietnamese society and by laying the foundation of a new political community based on mass participation in politics is the most important contribution of this Vietnamese experience to an understanding of revolution.

Conditions in a society may be ripe for revolution—just as they were in Viet Nam when Japan's occupation of the country collapsed at the end of World War II—but without the creation of a viable political alternative there seems little likelihood that a revolution will actually occur. What are the specific qualities that a revolutionary leadership must possess in order to launch a revolution even when conditions are ripe? Why—and how—

does a revolutionary leadership take form from among those politically talented people in a society who are thwarted in finding opportunities within a prevailing regime? And what does the emergence of such a leadership indicate about the incumbent political system and the society it is trying to govern?

A major conclusion of this study is that the circumstances which led to the emergence of a revolutionary leadership in Viet Nam are strikingly similar to other instances of revolution. For example, an investigation into the nature of the Bolshevik elite in Russia and the Nazi elite in Germany concluded that, despite the radically different ideological images these two groups had of themselves, they had both arisen from "frustrated segments of the middle classes who had been denied access to what they considered their proper place and organized violent action to gain what they had been denied."[1] These Russian and German revolutionary leaders were people who "had experienced some upward mobility, gained some economic rewards and wanted political power." But they "had been denied access to politics."[2]

While there are obviously profound dissimilarities between political upheaval in Russia and Germany and revolution in Viet Nam, this description is, in the details that really matter, also an accurate portrayal of the reasons why a revolutionary leadership arose in Viet Nam. The existence of this similarity does not mean, of course, that whenever new rising elite groups are thwarted in their aspirations, a revolution will automatically result. But it does suggest that such groups are probably the most capable of providing revolutionary leadership and that their alienation from the existing system has been a conspicuous event leading to revolution. Primarily because of their educational achievements these rising middle groups have been the "symbol specialists" in the revolutionary leadership. Without them "to speak the words that caught the ears, touched the hearts, activated the behavior of the radicalized cohorts, the specialists in violence might have murdered and pillaged but they could not

1 Daniel Lerner: "The Coercive Ideologists in Perspective," in Harold Lasswell and Daniel Lerner, eds.: *World Revolutionary Elites: Studies in Coercive Ideological Movements* (Cambridge: The MIT Press; 1965), pp. 463–4.
2 Ibid., p. 459.

have built a revolutionary movement capable of seizing state power."[3]

However, these symbol specialists have not been mere street-corner orators who have exhorted the mob. Instead their chief role has been to "shape the images and teach the rites of the new ideology they dispensed."[4] Through their revolutionary ideology they have established contact with a wider and wider range of the population and brought them into a revolutionary movement poised for mobilizing power against an incumbent regime. As studies of China, Russia, and Germany show, the "intellectuals of higher social status founded the [revolutionary] movements through which people of lesser status subsequently made their way to the top."[5] So it was in Viet Nam that the ideological and organizational efforts of Truong Chinh, a technical school student, and Vo Nguyen Giap, the holder of a doctor of laws degree, were responsible, for example, for the rise of Chu Van Tan, an uneducated mountaineer, to Minister of Defense in the revolutionary government. Indeed, the success of the revolution launched by the thwarted Vietnamese intelligentsia depended vitally on mobilizing the less privileged portion of the population of Viet Nam.

Without the effects of modernization it seems unlikely that a revolutionary intelligentsia would have taken form and led revolutions such as those in Russia and China.[6] Certainly in Viet Nam the modernizing effects of the colonial education system were instrumental in the emergence of effective revolutionary leaders. Through education they got the opportunity for some upward mobility and some economic rewards, but their mobility into a potentially modern world was limited by the narrow contours of colonial society. Most of all, they got the chance to develop skills that made them significant competitors for political influence. But in colonial Viet Nam there were no legitimate means by which emergent groups of Vietnamese could use their political

3 Ibid., pp. 460–1.
4 Ibid., p. 461.
5 Ibid., p. 466.
6 Ibid., George K. Schueller: "The Politburo," pp. 97–178, and Robert C. North with Ithiel de Sola Pool: "Kuomintang and Chinese Communist Elites," pp. 319–455.

skills to compete for influence over governmental decisions. Only by organizing themselves into a revolutionary movement could they share in the governing of the country—a role which they felt their political strength entitled them to and which French intransigence prevented.

Older generations of Vietnamese revolutionaries had also felt themselves entitled to share in the governing of the country, but they lacked the cohesion and strength to challenge the French successfully. They could not bring about changes in the politics of Viet Nam that would displace France and create a unified political order. By contrast, rising generations of French-educated Vietnamese distinguished themselves from these earlier, ineffective revolutionaries through their capacity to forge a revolutionary strategy and with it establish an organization which was the nucleus of an alternative government. In initiating their revolution, this later generation of revolutionaries was not merely attempting to overthrow French rule; they were trying to achieve fundamental changes in Vietnamese politics by creating new ways of mobilizing and sharing power.

But there were other reasons besides the level of political skills that made emergent revolutionaries more effective than their traditionalist predecessors. During the first four decades of the twentieth century the political environment in Viet Nam underwent radical changes. The transformation of Vietnamese society brought on by the partial modernization of the country by France made it easier to mobilize power against the colonial regime than was the case during earlier phases of French rule. First of all, the disaffected French-educated class—though still small in relation to the whole of Vietnamese society—was much larger than any preceding revolutionary elite. But more importantly, the population of the country, which these revolutionaries would have to arouse against France, had become more highly mobile as a result of the modernizing influences of colonial policies.

Since both the upper class as well as nearly all the modern segments of the population were limited in their chances for further opportunity in the relatively static prewar society, they shared a common frustration against France which gave them a cohesiveness they manifested in their nationalist aspirations. In the minds of these Vietnamese, nationalism meant driving France from Viet Nam so that those who had developed political talent and social skills would have a greater control over their own destiny. Appeals to nationalism, therefore, were ultimately successful—as they had not been earlier—in launching revolution because this ideology could galvanize into action the large numbers of people who had acquired social mobility and political cohesiveness from the colonial impact on Vietnamese society.

Instead of winning the allegiance of those whom it was bringing into the modern world, the French had to face mounting opposition from them. Increasingly, the Vietnamese were frustrated by the incapacity of colonial institutions to adapt to the challenge of changes which they were responsible for initiating. Such inflexibility and intransigence in colonial social and political institutions resulted in the denial of access of rising middle groups to what they considered their proper place. It is the pressure of this inflexibility that George Pettee calls "cramp," by which he means that institutions have not grown to meet the needs of society, and therefore a tension is produced that only a revolution may relieve. A revolution, says Pettee, "takes place when the great majority of the society feel cramped beyond tolerance." But, he cautions, a revolution "never can happen until a great proportion of the culture has already developed under purposes which cannot be satisfied under existing institutions, and the existing contradictions have integrated the will of the revolutionists and disintegrated that of the conservatives."[7]

In a similar vein, Chalmers Johnson has asserted that all revolutions are caused by multiple dysfunctions in society. When such dysfunctions are left unresolved by an intransigent ruling class, revolutionaries seek to correct the situation by far-reaching change. Dysfunction occurs, says Johnson, when one of the component parts of society "does not function in the way it must in order to maintain equilibrium," and "if no remedial action occurs, the entire [social] system will move out of equilibrium."

7 George Pettee: *The Process of Revolution* (New York: Harper and Bros.; 1938), p. 33.

Revolution, he believes, "is the preferred method of change when (a) the level of dysfunctions exceeds the capacities of traditional or accepted methods of problem solving; and when (b) the system's elite, in effect, opposes change."[8]

In the concepts of "cramp" and unresolved "multiple dysfunctions" there is once again emphasis on the disparity between social instability and the lack of institutional response to it that is mentioned so frequently by scholars as a major source of revolutionary potential. Whether or not Pettee's and Johnson's particular analytical concepts are valid for all revolutions, the disparity that concerns them was conspicuously present in the origins of revolution in Viet Nam. Here, the most significant source of "cramp" or "multiple dysfunction" arose from the tensions of the partial modernization of the country. Because of the restrictions of colonial policy a French-educated Vietnamese elite, though trained for modernity, did not have the opportunity to make Viet Nam a more thoroughly modernized society. In the countryside the demands of modernity were imposed—especially in monetary taxation—without providing institutions for the eventual modernization of village Viet Nam.

Since colonial programs were so pervasive but yet not far-reaching enough to modernize the whole country, they produced tensions which resulted in a potential for revolution. Men who had acquired new skills and talents but had no sanctioned means for employing the potential power afforded by these attributes of modernity sought outlets in political change and violence. When Viet Nam became a "nation off balance," it also became a society with a substantial potential for revolution:[9] The demands upon the colonial government were greater than its performance to meet them.

The concepts of "cramp" and "multiple dysfunction" might seem to point to the conclusion that revolution results when certain conditions of social imbalance are ignored by governments. But neither Pettee nor Johnson believes that revolution

<hr/>

8 Chalmers Johnson: *Revolution and the Social System* (Stanford: The Hoover Institution; 1964), pp. 5, 10.
9 Mus: "Viet Nam: A Nation Off Balance."

inevitably occurs when a certain set of social conditions appear. Both of them would agree with Harry Eckstein that "one should not seek explanations . . . in specific social conditions, but rather in ways in which social conditions may be perceived. . . ."[1] As James C. Davies has put it, political stability is "ultimately dependent on a state of mind, a mood in a society. . . . It is the dissatisfied state of mind rather than the tangible provision of 'adequate' or 'inadequate' supplies of food, equality, or liberty which produces the revolution."[2]

Yet Davies thinks that there is one particular condition which always produces the state of mind for revolution. He asserts that "Revolutions are most likely to occur when a prolonged period of objective economic and social development is followed by a short period of sharp reversal." A period of rising economic performance results in "an expectation of continued ability to satisfy needs—which continue to rise—" but in the period of reversal there develops "a mental state of anxiety and frustration when manifest reality breaks away from anticipated reality."[3]

Davies' assertion, though a valid generalization about the causes of revolution, leaves so many factors unaccounted for that its significance is restricted to a narrow spectrum of events; it is an explanation of one way that revolutionary potential can develop rather than how revolutions actually occur. Although Davies stresses that it is a state of mind that leads to revolution, he does not account for such a development in societies, like colonial Viet Nam, which have not experienced prolonged periods of economic advance. Moreover, he offers no discussion about how an organization for revolution emerges once a revolutionary state of mind has evolved. In addition, there is no allowance in Davies's view for the possibility that an incumbent government might have the means of force or the political legitimacy to maintain itself despite the popular reaction to an economic setback. Finally, Davies does not make an effort to

1 Harry Eckstein: "On the Etiology of Internal War," *History and Theory*, Vol. IV, No. 2 (1965), p. 149.
2 James C. Davies: "Toward a Theory of Revolution," *American Sociological Review*, Vol. XXVII, No. 1 (February 1962), p. 6.
3 Ibid. See also James C. Davies: "The Circumstances and Causes of Revolution," *The Journal of Conflict Resolution*, Vol. XI, No. 2 (June 1967), pp. 247–57.

distinguish between revolutions and rebellion. Consequently, his generalization is really more appropriate as an explanation for the likelihood of the occurrence of civil violence than it is for far-reaching changes in the way that politics are conducted in a society.

In striking contrast to Davies's limited attempt to develop a theory of revolution is the effort by Ted Gurr to set forth a theoretical model on the conditions of civil violence. Instead of postulating a single condition which is assumed to produce a state of mind conducive to violence as Davies does, Gurr has grounded his theory on the interaction of several general factors. His basic premise is that "the necessary preconditions for violent civil conflict is *relative deprivation*," which is people's "perceptions of discrepancy between their *value expectations* and their environment's *value capabilities*." Value expectations are "the goods and conditions of life to which people believe they are justifiably entitled," while value capabilities are "the conditions that determine people's chances for getting or keeping the values they legitimately expect to attain."[4]

Gurr's theory accounts for a wide range of cross-pressures in the world of political conflict by emphasizing the interaction of factors which can facilitate as well as prevent the occurrence of civil violence. If people are willing to accept deprivation as being legitimate, says Gurr, then their value expectations will be reduced. By such an assertion, Gurr is acknowledging that people may not become frustrated in the face of adversity if they feel they have been dealt with justly. On the other hand, people whose frustrations have reached the level of persistent anger will only be able to commit violence to the extent that the facilities for violent action are greater than those of social control.

In Gurr's theory, social control means the amount of physical or social retribution people anticipate, their fear of retribution, and their options for expressing their frustration nonviolently through social institutions. The social facilitation of civil violence

4 Ted Gurr with Charles Ruttenberg: *The Conditions of Civil Violence: First Tests of a Causal Model* (Princeton, N.J.: Center of International Studies, Research Monograph No. 28; April 1967), pp. 3–4.

consists of common experiences and beliefs that sanction violent responses to anger as well as the amount of group support for violence.[5] Thus in contrast to Davies's statement that a particular condition is a cause of violence, Gurr's theory points to a probability statement: The likelihood and scale of civil violence will vary, he is saying, with the degree of severity of relative deprivation and the extent to which social facilitation is greater than social control.

Although Gurr has not specifically concerned himself with revolution, his theory is extremely valuable in understanding the revolutionary process. The sense of relative deprivation which he feels is a crucial explanation for violent behavior also seems, at least on the basis of the Vietnamese experience, to be at the heart of the origins of revolution. Because Gurr is more interested in the preconditions of civil violence, his measures of relative deprivation have been focused on the kinds of frustration he thinks are most likely to result in violent responses. But revolution does not necessarily involve violence, and therefore a different set of measures seems required if relative deprivation is to contribute to a greater understanding of the origins of revolution. From both the general literature as well as an inquiry into revolution in Viet Nam, it seems clear that a denial of the exercise of political power is the most conspicuous source of a sense of relative deprivation leading to revolution. Since the very essence of the process of revolution is change in the way power is shaped and shared, the denial of the exercise of power seems especially appropriate as a measurement of the kind of sense of deprivation that results in revolution.

Obviously, a sense of deprivation may never arise if people have little or no expectation of enjoying political power. The key question, then, in understanding revolution in Viet Nam or elsewhere is: Why do people come to expect and demand political power which is denied to them? Although it is impossible to account for all the reasons why people become dissatisfied with their political status, the experience of Viet Nam and much of the literature on revolution offer some significant insights for

5 Ibid., pp. 6–14.

understanding why political expectations rise. If people find new opportunties for individual achievement through education, commerce, industry, communications, religion, etc., they acquire talents and skills which make them more nearly equal in ability to those exercising governmental authority. Political expectations will tend to rise as these individuals achieve social attributes which are similar to or greater than those who have the greatest enjoyment of political power in the society.

Of course, the enjoyment of political power does not mean merely holding governmental office or exerting widespread political influence. From the perspective of the individual it also means the enjoyment of personal liberties, a dependable way of seeking redress of grievances, and the absence of formal barriers to positions of decision-making authority. When those with rising achievement and political expectations are systematically excluded from such power, their frustration usually leads them to question the basis on which governmental authority is founded.

As observers have frequently noted, revolutions are not made by impoverished and downtrodden men. They are launched by men who are rising in individual achievement but whose expectations for political status have been frustrated. Theirs is a state of mind out of which revolutions develop. As Aristotle put it, the "principal and general cause of an attitude of mind which disposes men toward . . ." revolution is ". . . a passion for equality, which arises from their thinking that they have the worst of the bargain in spite of being the equals of those who have the advantage."[6]

In Viet Nam this state of mind was undoubtedly present from the very beginning of French rule, but initially it was not widespread or intense enough to result in anything more than abortive revolts. These uprisings were led by mandarins who were trying to regain the political status they had enjoyed prior to French control. But France's power proved to be overwhelming against the meager strength the mandarins were able to mobilize. Strictly speaking their leadership was not revolutionary since they were

6 *The Politics of Aristotle*, ed. and trans. by Ernest Barker (London: Oxford University Press, 1952), p. 207.

not asserting a new system of politics in which the Vietnamese people might share power more widely than they had before colonial rule. The mandarinal revolts were merely attempts to reestablish an old form of politics to its previous position of predominance, and few Vietnamese were willing to risk their lives for such a restoration.

But political expectations became more widespread and intense as colonial programs transformed Vietnamese society. For the approximately 10 per cent of the population who found opportunities for social mobility and personal achievement through colonial institutions, there was a new awareness of the importance of political status. They were reminded of their inferior position when their occupational mobility was thwarted by more-privileged but often less-qualified Frenchmen, when their educational opportunities proved to be greater than their employment opportunities in relatively static French institutions, and when decisions affecting their interests were made by French councils.

Inevitably, personal frustrations over thwarted mobility led to political expectations that the ending of French rule would end the barriers to individual opportunity. And for those who had avoided obstacles to occupational advancement, their achievements made them more nearly equal to their French rulers and raised their expectations as to the political status they should enjoy. Significantly, a small portion of them were successful in having their social and political status recognized when they acquired French citizenship. But the great majority of Vietnamese had developed political expectations that were not easily satisfied by citizenship or any other token response of the French regime.

Because of the colonial government's limited responsiveness, these rising political expectations became the major source of revolutionary potential in Viet Nam. Such a discrepancy between political expectations and capabilities does not appear, on the basis of the literature on revolution, to be unique in Viet Nam. Rather it seems to be the most significant way of expressing the various factors that contribute toward or against the development of revolutionary potential. But despite the apparent utility of this analytical expression—revolutionary potential—it is still hard to be precise about the details of the process that is taking place.

While political capabilities or performance can be measured by criteria such as the extent to which power is shared through the decentralization of decision-making, the extent of participation in politics through access to positions of authority and expressions of the popular will, and the extent of legitimacy as evidenced in popular compliance, political expectations are more elusive. They are difficult to measure because political expectations are the way men perceive social conditions rather than the objective state of conditions themselves. In this respect the Vietnamese experience seems to offer some useful examples of ways to account for the rise of political expectations, since French intervention stimulated expectations that were not present when they arrived.

With the rise of individual achievement and mobility among the Vietnamese, individual expectations rose too. These new aspirations were expressed through demands for higher education, appeals for broader opportunities in the civil service, and the formation of political parties. For example, there was the creation of the Constitutionalist Party in the 1920's in southern Viet Nam by a handful of wealthy Vietnamese who wanted only limited self-government for their country. Other kinds of expectations were demonstrated in the abortive Yen Bay uprising of 1930. The most conspicuous participants in this revolt were lower- and middle-rank civil servants who, like the wealthy southern Vietnamese, would not have had any comparable opportunity for social mobility prior to French intervention. And of course there was the leadership of the Indochina Communist Party, which arose in part from those with backgrounds of traditional status but who coalesced with modern men during its rise through the colonial education system.

If there were a direct relationship between this rising mobility and rising expectations, if the adage "The more people get, the more they want" is correct, then a measure of the social mobility of a population would be a good measure of their rising expectations. Whether or not mobility is the most precise measure of expectations, it seems to be the best available one. Such a measure can allow one to determine the point where personal expectations are most likely to take on a political character. From the Vietnamese experience it appears that political expectations are most likely to develop (1) when people's achievements increase their status relative to the status of those enjoying the greatest amount of political power and (2) when people can identify their personal frustrations in thwarted mobility or opportunity with the action or inaction of those in political authority.

When political expectations are rising and political performance is not, the discrepancy between the power people expect and what they get will produce the potential for revolution. If their expectations are continually frustrated and they see no hope of fulfillment under existing conditions, people will question the basis on which political authority is founded. The extent of this potential for revolution may, of course, be quite limited either because expectations are not widespread or because the performance of the incumbents has responded to all but a portion of the people's expectations. But as unfulfilled expectations become more extensive, the potential for revolution will increase.

This potential results because people's expectations usually reflect achievements which have brought them considerable potential power in terms of skills, wealth, or influence over others. Thus the greater the political expectations, the greater the potential power to affect political life. Understandably, institutions of authority cannot long maintain their legitimacy when substantial amounts of potential power are denied formal expression and a share in political privileges. If the denial persists, then popular compliance with governmental decisions can be expected to decline, with the result that political crises may arise over "illegal" actions, budgetary difficulties from a popular refusal to pay taxes, or similar conflicts. The larger the number of people who feel deprived politically, the greater the revolutionary state of mind and the greater the potential for revolution.

However, the existence of revolutionary potential, even when it is relatively widespread, does not mean that a revolution will inevitably occur. Unless the capabilities of the revolutionaries in mobilizing potential political power are greater than those of the incumbents either to crush this mobilization by force or blunt it by token concessions, a revolution is unlikely to take place. Without the creation of an opposition political structure— a revolutionary political structure—the frustrated expectations of the revolutionaries may simply result in sullen apathy or feeble protest. But with a burgeoning political organization, revolutionaries can became the credible competitors of an ineffective and intransigent incumbent.

Among the various competive capabilities that revolutionaries require for success, three appear to be critical. First, and most important, the revolutionary political structure must become a distinctively new way of sharing power. Only by a new approach to sharing power can the revolutionaries hope to mobilize in support of the revolutionary cause those whose expectations have been thwarted by the incumbents. Secondly, a revolutionary ideology must establish the legitimacy of the revolutionary structure by rationalizing the way the revolutionaries are trying to fulfill popular expectations which the "illegitimate" incumbents have failed to heed. Finally, a revolutionary military organization must be created in order to prevent the incumbents from crushing the mobilization of revolutionary power and—by undermining the incumbents' instruments of force—to aid in the expansion of the revolutionary political structure.

In achieving these competitive capabilities the Vietnamese revolutionaries were effecting changes in the politics of their country that challenge many commonly held assumptions about the nature of revolution in a modernizing society. Too often the protractedness and destructiveness of revolutionary violence— in Viet Nam and elsewhere—have obscured the political significance which lies behind them and have led to the assumption that social deterioration and chaos are the inevitable results of such conflict. But, on the contrary, the level of violence that revolutionaries can sustain is a clear indication of the capacities of their political structure as compared with the strength or weakness of existing political institutions. Although revolution can occur without violence, it is unusual unless an incumbent government either lacks instruments of force (police and armed forces), has lost control over them, or decides to carry out a revolution itself rather than face a challenge from an opposing political structure. Consequently, the amount of popular strength required to displace an incumbent is a prime determinant of the extent to which changes in the structure of politics are likely to occur during a revolution.

Because the French had, at least up until 1945, control over Viet Nam, it seemed unlikely that any revolutionary group, no matter what its capacity for bringing change to Vietnamese politics, could develop the strength to displace colonial rule. While there was great disaffection with the French among the modernized segment of Vietnamese society who lived in the cities, there was little opportunity to exploit such feelings since demands for a change could be ignored or else conveniently crushed by force. Rural areas, on the other hand, were under much less firm control, and protests there were harder for the French to put down; but the peasant-village population was also more difficult for revolutionaries to mobilize due to their sedentary existence and unfamiliarity with large-scale organization.

So long as the French kept popular discontent under control, the challenge to the political skills of the Vietnamese revolutionaries remained profound: They could mount random uprisings, but could they achieve the fundamental changes in Viet Nam's politics required to mobilize the power to replace French rule? The twofold challenge these Vietnamese revolutionaries faced was that, in an only partially modernized society, it is relatively easy for incumbents to keep the small, modern—usually urban —sector under political control; while it is exceedingly difficult for a modernized though alienated upper class to form resilient political links with the more traditionalist-oriented population in the countryside—even when they are in open revolt.

Obviously, the formation of a revolutionary political party was an indispensable first step toward exploiting the potential for revolution in Viet Nam. Before the twentieth century, however, political parties of any description had not existed in the country; yet they became recognized as a necessity because pre-existing institutions had been conspicuously ineffective in mobilizing the power to thwart the imposition of French rule. Gradually, clandestine parties began to take the edge over more parochial groups such as families, mandarinal cliques, etc., in rallying the Vietnamese for participation in politics, and thus they set an important trend. But early Vietnamese parties did not achieve much success. In trying to avoid detection by French security forces, these clandestine parties found it necessary to work through traditionalist groups such as secret societies and provincial associations rather than making direct appeals to the more modernized though unaffiliated portions of the population. As a result, they only rarely surmounted the factionalism and parochialism that had rendered preceding political institutions ineffective.

Ideological shallowness was a basic cause of the shortcomings of these early parties. Their incapacity to conceive and communicate a strategy for revolution inhibited their organizational effectiveness because they could not be specific about their goals for new ways of shaping and sharing power. By comparison, the revolutionary ideology of the Indochinese Communist Party was instrumental in the coalescence of those rising middle groups in Vietnamese society who were frustrated at being denied access to formal positions of political influence. Of course, this coalescence did not happen all at once; it occurred gradually and in response to the slow evolution of Communist ideology. From 1930, when the Communist Party was founded in exile, to the August Revolution of 1945, this ideological evolution was focused on specifying ways in which the nationalist aspirations of frustrated middle groups could be achieved. As the Communists developed increasingly precise techniques for mobilizing and sharing power—as they became more specific about who was to get what, when, and how—they steadily achieved a commanding position of revolutionary leadership in Viet Nam.

Even though they eventually outstripped their revolutionary competitors, the Communists still remained essentially an elite political party. Their ideological successes prior to the August Revolution did not result in a mass following but rather in a well-disciplined party of the type required by the circumstances of revolution in Viet Nam. Nor could it have been otherwise. One of the important lessons of this study of Viet Nam is that the emergence of a revolutionary leadership is a vital factor in the unfolding of revolution. And without the framing of an effective revolutionary ideology, it seems most unlikely that a successful leadership could have been formed. Yet it is still surprising to note how small the Communist Party really was. As Ho Chi Minh has recalled:

> When the August Revolution took place, there were about 5,000 Party members, including those in jail. Less than 5,000 Party members have thus organized and led the uprisings of twenty-four million fellow-countrymen . . . to victory.[7]

Less surprising is the fact that the Communist Party's initial attempts at exploiting the potential for revolution in Viet Nam were failures. Naturally, these early attempts were made in areas where the French were especially weak rather than in places where the opposition to colonial rule was necessarily the most intense. They came in the Nghe-Tinh uprising in central Viet Nam in 1930–1, the Mekong Delta revolt of 1940, and the Bac Son uprising in northern Viet Nam during 1940–1. In all of these cases there was a similar pattern in which revolutionary leaders from the modernized sector of Vietnamese society were trying to mobilize into larger-scale resistance those rural people whose discontent with colonial rule had broken out into open revolt. But in the intensity of these uprisings the revolutionaries could not implant the organizational structure to transform these pocket revolts into the nucleus of a broader revolutionary movement. Despite their gradual success in winning the allegiance of a revolutionary elite, the Communist Party still faced the challenge of using these leaders to forge political links with the mass of Viet Nam's population in the countryside.

7 Ho Chi Minh. "Our Party Has Struggled Very Heroically and Won Glorious Victories," p. 12.

Only during the last of these pocket uprisings—at Bac Son—were the revolutionaries successful in establishing a durable enough political structure to gain control over a portion of Vietnamese territory and create a revolutionary "base area." However, this limited success was due as much to fortuitous circumstances as it was to the skills of the leaders of the Indochinese Communist Party. Unlike the earlier uprisings in the rice-growing lowlands of Nghe-Tinh and the Mekong Delta, the Bac Son revolt occurred in a remote mountain region which, even in the best of times, the French probably could not have controlled in the face of such a virulent protest. But with the indirect Japanese assistance to the revolutionaries and the restrictions imposed by their occupation on the French, the colonial government's grip on the countryside was gradually ebbing away.

Despite the fortuitousness of this situation it was the way in which the revolutionaries exploited it that not only was seminal for events in Viet Nam, but also illustrative of an important lesson in understanding revolution. The mere fact that the Communists had gained control over Vietnamese territory—even though the territory was small and remote, and even though this control was often disputed—gave the party an image of legitimacy which none of its revolutionary competitors could match. Yet the party realized how tenuous its hold over the Bac Son base area really was; in this first firm political linkage to the population outside the party, the Communists were almost exclusively dependent on guerrilla bands organized among the mountain minority people, the Tho. And while the party was aware that a larger, more conventional armed force was a necessity if it were to exploit other, broader revolutionary opportunities, it also recognized that the building of a revolutionary army is essentially a political task and that even a burgeoning armed force could not achieve all of the party's revolutionary goals. In moving beyond the Bac Son base area the party's need to create a more diverse and more penetrating set of political links with the Vietnamese people was clear.

But how could a political party of no more than 5,000 members form organizational ties with enough of Viet Nam's population to create a governmental alternative to the colonial regime? Since the Communist Party could not hope to recruit into its membership such a popular following and, at the same time, maintain its necessarily tight discipline, the party had to establish new institutions for rallying the Vietnamese to participate in the revolutionary politics of their country. In addition to an expanded revolutionary army, the most important new organization was an alliance of mass-membership groups known as the Viet Minh, which, for the first time in Viet Nam, provided a stimulus and a rationale for popular participation in politics. Under the overarching control of the Viet Minh a widely diverse set of political parties and popular associations allowed people of often conflicting affiliations to identify with the party's revolutionary cause.

In forming the Viet Minh the Communist Party was taking advantage of the effects of the Japanese occupation which had made the Vietnamese conscious of the vulnerabilities in French rule even before the elimination of the colonial government in March 1945. Sensing that the wind was blowing in a new direction, the Vietnamese felt that they must anticipate what the wind would bring with it. By joining the Viet Minh they could identify with the cause of national independence without necessarily incurring all the commitments of membership in a clandestine revolutionary party. Of course, new recruits soon learned that their share in the expected fruits of independence would depend on their role in preparations to exploit the growing weaknesses in colonial rule. So, gradually, many of those attracted to the Viet Minh found their way into the Communist Party and the revolutionary army being formed in the Bac Son base area.

But the principal purpose of the Viet Minh was not just to act as a conduit for party recruitment; its primary function was to enhance the legitimacy of the party's slowly emerging revolutionary structure so that it would be recognized as the sole reliable force seeking independence for Viet Nam. In pursuing this goal the Viet Minh's success was extensive enough for it to be virtually the only visible revolutionary group when the Japanese collapse occurred and the cry for independence went up. Yet despite their preparations, the Japanese capitulation caught the Viet Minh leaders by surprise: They had not had the time to develop a governmental structure which could completely fill the political void left by the Japanese. Even though they reacted quickly by taking control over Hanoi, Saigon, and other major cities, there was no preexisting political structure—with the exception of the now impotent administrative institutions of the colonial regime—which these Communist leaders might seize and through it rule the country.

With the collapse of Japan's occupation of Viet Nam, the potential for revolution had reached its most extensive point; there was, for the moment, no incumbent which could prevent the revolutionaries from making their bid for governmental power and legitimacy. But, as the Viet Minh leaders learned first-hand, the brute force of the incumbent is not necessarily the most formidable obstacle which revolutionaries must confront. Their greatest challenge is to exploit the potential for revolution by creating an alternative political structure which can win the allegiance of a people and thereby achieve governmental legitimacy. Without such an effort, revolutionary potential may continue to exist even though a revolutionary government has displaced an incumbent and taken control of a country. So long as the potential for revolution persists, the stability of a new revolutionary incumbent remains in doubt.

In proclaiming the Democratic Republic of Viet Nam, holding elections for a national assembly, and forming a coalition government with opposition parties, the Viet Minh was responding to this challenge of revolution. While these actions did serve to galvanize popular feelings into support for the Viet Minh, this support was not widespread or deep enough to ensure that the revolutionary government would control all of Vietnamese territory. Such absence of support did not mean that intense opposition had developed, except in certain areas of southern Viet Nam. It simply meant that most Vietnamese had no commitment to any political movement beyond their village and that until they did, the full potential for revolution would continue unexploited. Moreover, as the British and then the French began to reoccupy Viet Nam, the possibilities of exploiting revolutionary potential were progressively reduced as more and more of the country was brought under colonial military control.

Here were the sources of protracted revolution in Viet Nam: The Communist Party through its Viet Minh front had launched a revolutionary government which—though it could not gain control over the whole country—had gained enough popular strength to prevent itself from being wiped out. In response, the French, who were both unwilling and incapable of creating a competitive political alternative to the Viet Minh—at least not until after 1950—attempted to stop the expansion of its revolutionary structure by force. The inevitable result was a tenacious revolutionary war in which the steady development of the Viet Minh's political structure during seven years of conflict enabled it to tie down the French army to fixed-position defense and, ultimately, to defeat it at Dien Bien Phu in 1954.

In trying to stop the Viet Minh, the French faced a dilemma that was impossible to resolve. If they abandoned territory, even temporarily, in order to achieve military flexibility and mobility, it also meant their abandoning the tenuous political commitment of the people living in the area. Since they could not mobilize the troops—either at home or in Viet Nam—to occupy the entire country and, at the same time, match the flexible strength of the Viet Minh's regular forces, the French had, progressively, to sacrifice control over territory. Had they, instead, been able to sponsor a government capable of establishing new institutions for sharing and mobilizing political power and forging political links with the countryside, then there might have been some rationale for the use of French military power.

France's military capacity to control territory was steadily worn down by the Viet Minh's strategy of revolutionary war in which force was made subordinate to the task of developing an alternative political system. By expanding their political structure from base areas to which they had retreated after French forces drove them from the cities in late 1946 and early 1947, the revolutionaries won increasing commitment among the Vietnamese population. The greater their popular commitment, the more difficult it was for the French to control territory and the easier it was for the Viet Minh to mobilize the population for service in politics and warfare. An even greater advantage accrued to the Viet Minh because it was not forced to defend territory in order to win the political commitment of the population. Its military forces were able to maneuver the French into unfavorable territorial positions where they were forced to fight if they were to maintain even their dwindling political credibility among the Vietnamese. Thus, the acceptance of the Viet Minh as the legitimate government in broader and broader areas of the country marked political milestones on the road to Dien Bien Phu.

In expanding its political structure, the Viet Minh relied upon techniques which in a more rudimentary form had been instrumental in its launching the August Revolution. By refining these techniques the revolutionaries took advantage of the added stimulus for popular participation in politics that resulted from the intensification of warfare in Viet Nam. As the dangers and destructiveness of war mounted, the rural population felt an increasing need for mutual assistance and self-protection—in other words, the need for a sense of order in the midst of the disorder of war. Responding to these heightened expectations, the revolutionaries appealed for a rallying behind the Viet Minh's popular participation associations as the only means of eliminating French rule, ending the war, and restoring order to the countryside.

Despite their propagandistic tone these were not hollow appeals. At the same time, the Viet Minh was calling upon local groups to form administrative committees which would be prepared to receive and carry out directives from the leaders of the revolutionary movement. Then the Viet Minh brought these committees together into an administrative hierarchy which was supported by, and parallel to, a hierarchical organization among the popular associations. Although the Communist Party maintained a tight hold over these "parallel hierarchies," its real source of political control over the countryside came from its ability to base an administrative hierarchy on popular participation. Through this technique the Viet Minh bypassed those traditional elements of village society which were either unable or unwilling to engage in politics except on a basis of status rather than a basis of performance.

By instituting a totally new approach toward political mobility and status, based almost exclusively on performance in revolutionary war, the Viet Minh was not dispensing with ideology. On the contrary, it was trying to replace the vestigial Confucian concepts of society and politics, as well as certain local traditions, with a new ideology—a new rationale for a new system of politics. Instead of the Confucian tradition of politics in which there had been mobility and status for only the very few with an extensive classical education, the Vietnamese revolutionaries wanted to institute a political system of mass mobilization. Because its principal goal had been to achieve social harmony and institutionalized authority in a relatively static society, the Confucian state system in Viet Nam never developed a great degree of power. Only a new system—one capable of generating the power to defeat France and lay the foundation of national unity—could fulfill the goals of the revolutionaries. Thus a new basis for political mobility was required. Thus a new means of sharing—of distributing—political power was required.

Here in Viet Nam was the beginning of revolution—a revolution that remains incomplete, and is the underlying cause of the war now raging there. Here was the start of fundamental changes in the way who gets what, when, and how in Vietnamese society. Men who had obtained some mobility and some economic rewards from the colonial system of politics had been denied the formal political power they thought due them and were creating a new system of politics to link them with their society so that they might overcome the weaknesses and armed opposition of the old regime.

Epilogue

※ ※ ※

THE FUTURE OF

REVOLUTION IN VIET NAM

※
※
※

Although it stopped the First Indochina War, the partitioning of Viet Nam by the Geneva Conference of 1954 did not bring an end to revolution. While it separated adversaries who had been locked in combat for seven years, this division of the country was intended to be only temporary, until elections could be conducted in 1956. But there were no binding international guarantees that these elections would in fact be carried out; nor was there any promise that the Vietnamese followers of the non-Communist State of Viet Nam, who had withdrawn south of the 17th parallel, would participate in such elections or respect their results.[1]

1 The unexcelled study of the Geneva Conference by an impressive French team of scholar and journalist is Lacouture and Devillers: *La fin d'une guerre*, pp. 111–288. Also see "The Geneva Conference," in Coral Bell: *Survey of International Affairs, 1954* (London: Oxford University Press; 1957), pp. 42–72. For a useful but polemical study see Victor Bator: *Viet Nam: A Diplomatic Tragedy* (Dobbs Ferry, N.Y.: Oceana Publications; 1965).

This lack of guarantees was in part a reflection of the in-ability of the conference participants to determine the exact purpose the proposed elections were expected to serve. Article Seven of the Final Declaration of the Geneva Conference says that general elections "shall be held in July 1956," but it does not specify what issues were to be voted upon.[2] Though this article calls for consultations to define the issues to be decided in elections, such meetings never occurred. These proposed sessions were boycotted because the representatives of the State of Viet Nam had, in effect, been excluded from the cease-fire negotiations at Geneva and their newly appointed Prime Minister, Ngo Dinh Diem, had denounced the cease-fire agreements by proclaiming the date of their signing as a national day of shame.[3]

Despite the controversy over Diem's refusal to participate in general elections, it should have been clear that elections alone could not resolve revolutionary conflict in Viet Nam—particu-larly after the partitioning of the country. Since the future political order of Viet Nam was what the seven years of war had been all about, it seemed most unlikely that the Vietnamese could simply stop fighting and settle their differences without the benefit of new institutions for sharing power and resolving conflict. But the creation of new institutions in which Communist and non-Communist Vietnamese might share political power and unite their country was regarded as an impossible task, especially during the emotional intensity of the Geneva Conference.

Because the conference participants did not wish to confront the complex dilemma of how a unified political order might be established in Viet Nam, they decided to separate the antagonists rather than try to resolve the bases of their revolutionary con-flict. In the absence of an agreement at Geneva on the funda-mental issues in Viet Nam, the great powers found a convenient substitute in proposing elections among the Vietnamese on is-sues which were left unspecified. Although masked by a decla-

---

2 See the text of the Final Declaration in B. S. N. Murti: *Vietnam Divided: The Unfinished Struggle* (New York: Asia Publishing House; 1964), pp. 220-2.
3 Ibid., pp. 16-17.

ration of apparent consensus, the Geneva Conference participants only agreed on the points on which they disagreed, and thus they set the stage for a new phase of revolutionary war.

With the division of Viet Nam at the 17th parallel, the areas under the political control of the revolutionary opponents took on a clearly defined territorial configuration for the first time in the Indochina War: The Communist-led Viet Minh were in the north, and the non-Communists were in the south. The partition had the effect of strengthening the control of the State of Viet Nam over the southern areas of the country where it enjoyed its greatest political support. No longer would its strength be diluted by efforts to maintain military control over rural areas in the north, where its political support, except for Catholic bishoprics, was nil. But this relative improvement in the non-Communist government's position of political strength did not mean that the State of Viet Nam had achieved unqualified independence from France. On the contrary, France, in getting itself out of an embarrassing and militarily untenable situation via the Geneva Conference, exposed more conspicuously than before the impotence of the State of Viet Nam.

Although the State of Viet Nam army fought as distinct national units alongside the French, none of its representatives signed the cease-fire agreement with the Viet Minh military command.[4] While Prime Minister Ngo Dinh Diem and the State of Viet Nam diplomatic delegation at Geneva opposed the cease-fire, this was not the reason their military representatives failed to sign the agreement. France was making all the decisions for the non-Communist side in the war in Viet Nam, and though it had created the State of Viet Nam as a political alternative to the Viet Minh, France, at Geneva in 1954, still had not accorded it the substance of sovereignty. Not only had the State of Viet Nam failed to develop the strength to become a serious political competitor to the Viet Minh, it had not even been able to overcome its dependency on France for survival. But with United States support, Ngo Dinh Diem in 1954 signaled his determina-

4 For text of cease-fire agreement see ibid., pp. 205–19.

tion to create in southern Viet Nam a government that was sovereign—at least to the extent that it was free of French control.

In declaring Viet Nam to be an independent republic and forcing the French to leave the country by the spring of 1956, Diem claimed he had carried out a revolution.[5] In a limited sense he had. But the political changes that Diem brought to southern Viet Nam were deceptive. Though he had succeeded in crushing the power of the political-religious sects which had been dependent on France for their autonomy, he had not created any political organization capable of integrating these groups into resilient governmental institutions. Nevertheless, it appeared that Diem had achieved a strong central administration free from the internecine squabbling that had marked the life of the State of Viet Nam. And while many problems remained, it was thought that he had established a viable political order.[6] In fact Diem had merely made his own narrowly based group—composed primarily of Catholics and northern refugees—having a parochial outlook uniquely its own, supreme over all the other non-Communist political groups in southern Viet Nam.

To accomplish this, Diem had needed control over the French-led national army of Viet Nam. In the non-Communist political system in southern Viet Nam, where power was so narrowly defined that it was the same thing as force, mastery over the army also meant having a predominance of political power. Although Diem's political shrewdness played a large role in his success, it was the support of the United States that was decisive in his wrestling control of the army away from its French-appointed commander—a Vietnamese of French citizenship. The United States simply redirected its military aid and financing of the national army through Diem's government, an act which left the French without their accustomed resources to maintain lever-

5 The most outstanding study of the Diem era is Robert Scigliano: *South Vietnam: Nation Under Stress* (Boston: Houghton Mifflin; 1963); see especially "The Limited Revolution," pp. 62–8. An impressive journalistic account is Denis Warner: *The Last Confucian* (New York: The Macmillan Company; 1963).

6 See William Henderson: "South Viet Nam Finds Itself," *Foreign Affairs*, Vol. XXXV (October 1956), pp. 283–94, and Wesley R. Fishel: "Free Vietnam Since Geneva," *Yale Review*, Vol. XLIX (September 1959), pp. 68–79.

age over the army or to sustain the private armies of the political-religious sects.[7] Lacking these American resources the French could not continue to manipulate the parochial groups toward their interests unless they were willing to use French army units —which on occasion they did. But once the national army was under Diem's authority, there was little to stop him from becoming master of the territory south of the 17th parallel. The political-religious sects—the Hoa Hao, the Cao Dai and the Binh Xuyen, etc.—were crushed or driven into hiding.[8] For the time being no other groups risked challenging Diem's supremacy.

Diem's "revolution," which brought the appearance of viable order and stability to politics in southern Viet Nam, was accomplished by military force and not by political mobilization. Through the success of the national army, Diem did not have to share power with any group, and as long as his military force was strong enough to thwart those capable of mobilizing power against him, he was secure. But Diem's sense of security was not well founded. While the political-religious sects had organized substantial numbers of villagers for political and military action, their strength was sharply limited by a rudimentary ideology and poor organization. Diem seemed to assume that all political groups in southern Viet Nam suffered from these same limitations and that therefore they could be conveniently managed by force. Moreover, he must have believed that the northward withdrawal of Viet Minh regulars had rendered their political base ineffective. Yet Diem's only safeguard against the revival of the Communists' expansion of their revolutionary structure was to oppose it by force. He had no thought of a political alternative which might develop a deep commitment among the rural populace because it offered them a means of participating in the politics and affecting the decisions of the Republic of Viet Nam.

The revolution that Ngo Dinh Diem brought about had its effect in the superstructure of politics in southern Viet Nam; it did not reach the village foundation of Vietnamese society.

7 Lancaster: *The Emancipation of French Indochina*, pp. 348–54.
8 Roy Jumper: "Sects and Communism in South Vietnam," *Orbis*, Vol. III (spring 1959), pp. 85–96.

The essence of this revolution was to eliminate the fratricidal competition between Vietnamese political cliques by the emergence of the faction around Diem and the exclusion of the French from the politics of the country. In effect, Diem had scored a successful *coup d'état*, yet the political establishment he acquired through this stroke was weak indeed. It consisted primarily of the national army and the shell of a countrywide administrative hierarchy, but there were no mass political parties, viable local institutions, or other similar organizations through which it could exercise power without force.

One of the main reasons the French had relied on the political-religious sects and comparable parochial groups was as a compensation for the lack of such political institutions. In suppressing these groups, Diem was merely confronting himself with a more troublesome dilemma: How was he to gain political power in the rural areas—the political substructure—of the country? If his revolution was to have had significance beyond the cities and provincial towns, then Diem would have had to create a legitimate means of access to the political superstructure, a way of sharing power between local and central institutions, and an ideology that reached the interests of the villagers.[9] Since Diem was uninterested and incapable of these changes, his revolution remained unfulfilled. Instead of political mobilization he saw his major task as political control of such effectiveness that it prevented anyone else from mobilizing power.

Diem's efforts in this direction were futile. Greater and greater amounts of military force were required in a vain attempt to maintain control over the countryside, but force alone could not prevent large portions of the rural areas from slipping away from Saigon's authority.[1] As the pace of military operations heightened, the strains on the national army mounted. Since the army was Diem's principal source of power, he was especially

9 For a discussion of Diem's attempts at ideology see John C. Donnell: "National Renovation Campaigns in Viet Nam," *Pacific Affairs,* Vol. XXXII, No. 1 (April 1959), pp. 73–88.
1 Bernard Fall has perceptively analyzed the renewal of conflict in Viet Nam in his "The Birth of Insurgency," in *Viet-Nam Witness* (New York: Frederick A. Praeger; 1966), pp. 169–89. Also see his "The Second Indochina War," *International Affairs,* Vol. XLI, No. 1 (January 1965), pp. 59–73.

concerned lest these strains of combat result in his losing control over the military establishment. As a precaution against cliques forming within the army, Diem rotated troop commanders at such ridiculously short intervals that they had little opportunity or incentive to make their units effective in combat.[2] This only made matters worse; it produced incentives among key military leaders to cease Diem's destructive manipulation of the army. If Diem had been assured of the loyalty of those officers to whom he delegated authority, such sharp antipathies might never have arisen. But the problem of loyalty within the army was a microcosm of the larger political dilemma in the country: There was no predictable pattern of upward mobility; there was only Diem's personal choice of those he felt to be most reliable.[3] From these demands of loyalty to a person rather than to institutions, a sense of arbitrariness arose which sapped the morale of the armed forces.

Because of the relative ineffectiveness of his troops and the rising tide of armed opposition, Diem, on American advice, found it necessary on several occasions to increase the size of the armed forces. Obviously a larger army only compounded the problem of keeping it under his political control. Abortive *coups d'état* launched against Diem in 1960 and 1962 by dissident officers should have been warnings, but the self-confident Diem was on a seemingly irreversible course.[4] He did not appear to doubt his ability to continue manipulating the army commands or the advisability of using manipulation as a prime means of political control. Yet his greatest source of security was probably his belief that the United States would not abandon him because of its anxiety about the consequences for the war against the Communists in the countryside. But Diem had left no margin for

2 When the author was adviser to the River Force of the Vietnamese navy in the Mekong Delta, 1959-61, while on active duty in the U.S. Navy, the unit had four different commanding officers, none of whom held command for more than nine months. Rotation in other units was often much faster.

3 For an inside view of Diem's political attitudes see Nguyen Thai: *Is South Vietnam Viable?* (Manila: Carmelo and Bauermann, Inc.; 1962). Mr. Thai was a close associate of Diem's before breaking with him in 1962. A major scholarly source is Jumper: "Vietnam," pp. 406-59.

4 The story of the 1960 abortive *coup d'état* is found in Stanley Karnow: "Diem Defeats His Own Best Troops," *The Reporter,* Vol. XXIV, January 19, 1961, pp. 24-9.

error. When an urban-based revolt led by an emergent yet parochial religious group—the Buddhists—erupted in the summer of
1963, Diem's predictable but ineffective attempt to suppress
it by force shocked the world. Severely embarrassed by his blunt
repressions, the United States dissociated itself from Diem and
his family—a move which Vietnamese military leaders interpreted as opening the way for them to remove Diem from the
politics of the country.[5] Since he had created no other sources
of power, there was no counterweight to the army. Thus, Ngo
Dinh Diem left power in Viet Nam just as he had come to it:
through a *coup d'état*.[6]

In their victory over Ngo Dinh Diem in November 1963, the
Vietnamese military confronted the same kind of problems that
Diem had when he came to power in 1954–5. But in 1963 the
problems had become compounded and solutions were more
urgently required if the Republic of Viet Nam was to become
something more than an institution for holding power by force.
Like Diem, the military leaders proclaimed their *coup d'état* to
be a revolution. But unlike Diem, they seemed to be more gen-
uinely concerned with the institutionalization of political power
and more aware of the limits of holding power through force.
Yet this awareness and concern did not result in a specific program of action designed to change the way in which power was
mobilized and shared.

In effect these military leaders were confronting the age-old
dilemma of establishing a viable political order—a dilemma
which the Vietnamese had dealt with unsuccessfully since they
had thrown off Chinese domination in 939. During the millennium which followed, numerous dynasties came to power through
military force, just as the military leaders did in 1963, but none
of them resolved the dilemmas of institutionalizing political
power. In contrast to the situation in earlier centuries these mili-

5 The best account of the attitude of the Kennedy administration toward Diem's
handling of the Buddhist crisis is contained in Roger Hilsman: *To Move a Nation:
The Politics of Foreign Policy in the Administration of John F. Kennedy* (Garden
City, N.Y.: Doubleday; 1967), pp. 413–537.

6 See Shaplen: "The Untold Story of the 1963 Coup," *The Lost Revolution*, pp.
188–212, and David Halberstam: *The Making of a Quagmire* (New York: Random
House; 1964), pp. 244–99.

tary leaders in 1963 were opposed by a regime, in northern Viet Nam and in wide areas of the countryside of the south, which had gone further than any previous regime in mastering this perennial challenge of power. If those who overthrew Diem were to become credible competitors for legitimate political authority, then they clearly would have to become a revolutionary government in fact as well as in name.[7]

The evidence from events since 1963 strongly suggests that the Republic of Viet Nam has made only a half-hearted attempt to effect a political revolution. The motivation for this attempted revolution has quite clearly arisen from the conspicuous ineffectiveness of instruments of force to sustain the government's power, especially against non-Communist groups in urban areas. For instance, the civil disobedience of the Buddhists which reached a crescendo in the provinces just south of the 17th parallel during the spring of 1966, resulted in concessions leading to the election of a Constituent Assembly, which drafted a new constitution for the republic.[8] While this constitution is an indication of an intent to share authority more widely in the hopes of enhancing the power of the government, there is no certainty that the military will permit the new institutions to function as they were intended. The military might once again fall back upon a reliance on force.

At best, even if the military does not block the process, the new constitutional framework proposed in March 1967 can only effect the superstructure of politics in southern Viet Nam. But this would be no mean achievement; it would, if successful, mark the unification of a multiplicity of parochial groups in what would become pluralistic institutions. By contrast with the totalitarian nature of the Communist regime in the north, this would be a historic accomplishment indeed. Yet it would not have very substantial impact in the village substructure, where institutions offering mobility into the superstructure would still not be pro-

[7] See George Carver: "The Real Revolution in South Viet Nam," *Foreign Affairs*, Vol. XLIII, No. 3 (April 1965), pp. 387–408, and Edward G. Lansdale: "Viet Nam: Do We Understand Revolution?," *Foreign Affairs*, Vol. XLIII, No. 1 (October 1964), pp. 75–86.

[8] Beverly Deepe: "U.S. Role in Vietnam Pivots on Elections," *Christian Science Monitor*, July 31, 1967.

vided. Instead, the new constitutional superstructure would be imposed on the countryside in the hope that it would somehow develop order and security there. In lieu of political mobilization a program of "pacification" or "revolutionary development" is being carried out in an effort to gain control over rural areas cleared of the regular units of the enemy. Obviously, such political control, even if it is attained, will not afford the villagers a stake in the power of the Republic of Viet Nam.[9]

Through these random efforts the Republic of Viet Nam has been groping toward revolution. Even if these efforts have been genuine, no political movement can simply grope toward revolution and expect to achieve a fundamental change in the way power is shaped and shared. The inadequacy and ineffectiveness of such actions have been made dramatically clear by the decision to increase United States armed forces in Viet Nam to almost twice the size of the contingent that was needed in Korea.[1] These larger United States forces have been required because the Republic of Viet Nam has been unable either to mobilize political support to resist the enemy or to raise the manpower to sustain its own armed forces. Certainly the willingness, or lack of it, of people to participate in military service is a good measure of the legitimacy of a government, especially when that government is fighting for its life.

The people of Viet Nam appear to regard the military as an arbitrary institution that is trying to get control over the countryside without sharing power with the peasant villagers. Yet, unless it can maintain adequate numbers of troops, the Republic of Viet Nam will, in the short run, have very little power to share. The inability to resolve such dilemmas of power has been a strong indication that the leaders of the Republic of Viet Nam,

9 In 1949 a ranking French army officer advocated abandonment of the concepts of "pacification" because political consciousness of peasant villagers had made this tactic a relic of the colonial era. See Col. J. Marchand: "Pacification en Indochine," *Tropiques: Revue des Troupes Coloniales,* janvier 1949, pp. 3–12.

1 On August 3, 1967, President Johnson announced that there would be 525,000 United States troops in Viet Nam by June 30, 1968. See *The New York Times,* August 4, 1967, p. 1. The maximum strength of United States troops in Korea reached 328,000. See Fall: *Viet-Nam Witness,* p. 309.

both military and civilian, have had little conception of the requirements for political revolution. Nor have they been aided very significantly in this regard by their American advisers.

With few exceptions those who have understood the meaning of revolution in Viet Nam have been members of the Vietnamese Communist movement. Thus far their understanding has been expressed in action and not in any comprehensive, published source where one can turn for information. Yet the need to understand this revolution has become an urgent task. Not only is the revolutionary conflict in Viet Nam consuming lives and wealth on a tragic scale, but it also portends the type of experience that many other peoples may share in their advance toward modernity. This book was undertaken out of a desire to comprehend revolution in Viet Nam and written in the hope that an examination of the Vietnamese experience could contribute to a more perceptive understanding of revolution in general.

In making such an analysis, this book has set forth a concept of what revolution is and how it occurs. That concept says that revolution is a process in which the structure of political power is permanently changed so that new ways of mobilizing and sharing political strength become established. Revolution occurs when an existing political structure has to be changed in response to a new configuration of power within a society. This does not mean that revolution is inevitable; it simply means that if a new configuration of power arises, an incumbent must either change his governmental structure to accommodate it or face the possibility that someone will mobilize new forms of power against him. More often than not, revolution occurs by the violent overthrow of an existing political establishment and its replacement by a new structure, but it need not happen this way. Incumbents can achieve revolution within their own governmental framework—although the experience of the republic in southern Viet Nam indicates that revolutionary change is difficult to achieve even when it is recognized as a necessity.

From this study of Viet Nam several aspects of the process of change in the structure of political power stand forth conspicuously as contributions to an understanding of revolution. The lack of a strong tradition of political unity in Viet Nam has meant that revolution has had to contend with unresolved problems of politics persisting into the present. Thus the revolutionary conflict which has resulted as a response to colonialism and moderniza- tion has divided the Vietnamese people against each other as they once were a little more than a century and a half ago. Per- haps this experience indicates that where modernization is only partial and not expanding, old antipathies may be reinforced instead of there being a new sense of community which develops to bind people closer together. If this is a general phenomenon valid beyond Viet Nam, then it may foreshadow a bitter future for unintegrated societies in other parts of the world which are struggling with the effects of modernity. In such circumstances those individuals who feel thwarted in their aspirations within the modernized sector of the society and ascribe political causes to their frustration may play on traditional antipathies as a means of acquiring political strength. But unless they can create a de- pendable political structure for mobilizing potential political power, they are unlikely to achieve a revolution.

Such a revolutionary political structure, capable of organizing vast portions of the rural population for military and political action has been the distinguishing feature of revolution in Viet Nam. While this mobilization has been the achievement of the Vietnamese Communist movement, it has not resulted simply because of its identification with Communist ideology. Its success is attributable to its own efforts in developing a form of political organization uniquely adapted to Viet Nam but which could be applicable to other modernizing countries. By providing peasant villagers with new forms of political participation, political status, and equality, this organization has bridged the gaps between the relatively nonmodernized areas of Vietnamese society. In this effort the Communists have not only brought many of the oppor- tunities of modernity to the countryside: literacy, organizational ability, and familiarity with machines, but they have also created a new sense of community.

At the heart of this sense of community has been a new structure of power which has won widespread popular commitment because it has rewarded popular participation. Through such a dependable sharing of power the Communists have been able to mobilize substantial popular strength with which to expand their revolutionary structure. Yet the power of the Communists is still insufficient to bring the whole country under control; revolution in Viet Nam continues. But the juxtaposition of such radically different political communities—at first the French and the Viet Minh and now the two republics of Viet Nam—serves to emphasize the problems of change in the structure of power, which is the essence of revolution.

Despite the many unique factors in the Vietnamese experience, it is this competition between political communities which links revolution in Viet Nam with revolution in other countries at different periods of history. Instead of there being a contest between incumbent and insurgents, there is a conflict between two separate political communities, each of which is claiming to be sovereign over the whole of Viet Nam. Revolution is not simply an overturning of an incumbent by violence, but a confrontation between contrasting forms of political organization which are trying to respond to similar needs of political community. And as R. R. Palmer has noted in his study *The Age of the Democratic Revolution,* it is the substitution of one political community for another that is the central focus of revolution. As he has seen it, a revolutionary situation is

> one in which the confidence in the justice or reasonableness of existing authority is undermined; where old loyalties fade, obligations are felt as impositions, law seems arbitrary, and respect for superiors is felt as a form of humiliation; where existing sources of prestige seem undeserved, hitherto accepted forms of wealth and income seem ill-gained, and government is sensed as distant, apart from the governed and not really "representing" them. In such a situation *the sense of community is lost,* and the bond between social classes tends to jealousy and frustration. People of a kind formerly integrated begin to feel as outsiders, or those who

have never been integrated begin to feel left out. As a group of
Sheffield workingmen demanded in 1794: "What is the constitution to us if we are nothing to it?"[2]

In Viet Nam a century and a half later this question is just
as germane to an understanding of the origins of revolution as it
was in the eighteenth century.

2 R. R. Palmer: *The Age of the Democratic Revolution: A Political History of
Europe and America, 1760–1800*, Vol. I, *The Challenge* (Princeton, N.J.: Princeton
University Press; 1959), p. 21. Italics added.

BIBLIOGRAPHY ✿ ✿ ✿

This book is based primarily on documents consulted in the archives of the French army on the Indochina War which are located in the Service Historique de l'Armée at the Château de Vincennes, on the eastern edge of Paris. From the more than fifteen thousand cartons of documents covering the entire war up to early 1955, items relating to the period 1940 to early 1947 were assembled and, after close scrutiny, information drawn from forty key documents was ultimately utilized in writing the book. For the most part, these forty documents were lengthy staff studies which summarized the available intelligence on the Viet Minh at the time of their preparation. The studies were prepared by the operations and intelligence staffs of the French army in Indochina and were used in making operational decisions during the course of the conflict. While the documents do confirm and clarify many points (for example, the supply of weapons parachuted by the Allies to the Viet Minh at its guerrilla bases in northern Viet Nam before the Japanese surrender in 1945), they also emphasize the confusion of the period, especially France's lack of information on the depth and extensiveness of revolution in Viet Nam.

Obviously, the information in these forty reports and staff studies does not exhaust the official French documentary evidence on the period covered in this book. Many items could not be located in the mass of documents at the army archives, and on several sensitive issues there was not even any record of documentation. Since a continuing effort is being made to reclassify and recatalogue these documents with greater precision, it may well be that the French army archives will yield additional information in the future. However, a more certain source of documentation will be the archives of the Ministère de la France d'Outre-Mer (ministry of overseas France), the post World War II successor to the ministry of colonies, when they are opened to scholars. Not only are these archives now completely inaccessible, but also most of the relevant documents that reached Paris from Viet Nam still remain in their packing cases while scarce archival manpower and resources are devoted to other projects. Whenever the archives at the ministry of overseas France become accessible, they will surely provide scholars with a great fund of information against which our present understanding of the origins of revolution in Viet Nam will have to be tested. Until then, the documentary evidence from the Service Historique de l'Armée, on which this book has been based, will be the major source of information on the way revolution began in Viet Nam.

If, however, the Democratic Republic of Viet Nam were to release documentation about the August Revolution, say in 1970 on the twenty-fifth anniversary of the event, then our dependence on French sources would be balanced by a more detailed view from the other side of the conflict. Already, Hanoi has published several sources on the period which are extremely informative and which this book has drawn upon heavily. The most important of these documents are:

Nguyen Kien Giang: *Les grandes dates du parti de la classe ouvrière du Viet Nam.* Hanoi: Éditions en Langues Étrangères; 1960.

Tran Huy Lieu: *Les soviets du Nghe-Tinh (de 1930–1931) au Viet Nam.* Hanoi: Éditions en Langues Étrangères; 1960.

Truong Chinh: *The August Revolution.* Hanoi: Foreign Languages Publishing House; 1958.

Viet Nam, Democratic Republic of, Central Committee of Propaganda of the Viet Nam Lao Dong Party and the Committee for the Study of the Party's History: *Thirty Years of Struggle of the Party,* Book One. Hanoi: Foreign Languages Publishing House; 1960.

Ten Years of Fighting and Building of the Vietnamese Peo-

ple's Army. Hanoi: Foreign Languages Publishing House; 1955.

Breaking Our Chains: Documents of the Vietnamese Revolution of August 1945. Hanoi: Foreign Languages Publishing House; 1960.

A Heroic People: Memoirs from the Revolution. Hanoi: Foreign Languages Publishing House; 1960.

Documents. Hanoi, n.d.

Vo Nguyen Giap: *People's War and People's Army*. Hanoi: Foreign Languages Publishing House; 1961.

There are also important documentary sources published by the French colonial government in Viet Nam which contain valuable information on the pre-1940 social and political situation. Among these publications there is the only thorough study of land tenure available for Viet Nam as well as detailed police reports on the origins of revolutionary political parties. The most significant of these documents are:

Gouvernement Général de l'Indochine, Direction des Affaires Politiques et de la Sûreté Générale: *Contribution à l'histoire des mouvements politiques de l'Indochine française*. Hanoi, 1933:
  Vol. I. *Le Tân Việt Cách Mệnh Đảng*
    (Parti Révolutionnaire du Nouvel Annam).
  Vol. II. *Le Việt Nam Quốc Dân Đảng*
    (Parti National Annamite du Tonkin).
  Vol. III. *Le Việt Nam Quôc Dân Đảng*
    (Les Émigrés du VNQDD).
  Vol. IV. *Le Đong Dương Công Sản Đảng*
    (Parti Communiste Indochinois).
  Vol. V. *La Terreur Rouge en Annam*.
  Vol. VI. *Le Cao Dai*.
———— Direction des Services Économiques: *Annuaire statistique de l'Indochine, 1913–1922, 1936–1937, 1943–1946, 1947–1948*.
———— Inspection Générale de l'Agriculture et de l'Élevage et des Forêts: *Économie agricole de l'Indochine*. Par Yves Henri, Inspecteur Général de l'agriculture des Colonies. Hanoi, 1932.
———— Office Indochinois de la Propagande: *Les administrations et les services publics indochinois*. Par J. de Galembert, Administrateur de 1ère Classe des Services Civils de l'Indochine. Deuxième Édition revue et augmentée par É. Érard. Hanoi, 1931.

The most useful bibliography on Viet Nam is Roy Jumper: *Bibliography on the Political and Administrative History of Vietnam* (Saigon: Michigan State University Vietnam Advisory Group; 1962). The selected bibliography in Joseph Buttinger: *Vietnam: A Dragon Embattled* (New York: Frederick A. Praeger; 1967), pp. 1258–82, is especially useful for recent publications. A more comprehensive bibliography covering the period focused on in this book is Cecil Hobbs: *Indochina: A Bibliography of the Land and People* (Washington, D.C.: Library of Congress; 1950). Another useful bibliographic source is John F. Embree and Lillian O. Dotson: *Bibliography of the Peoples and Cultures of Mainland Southeast Asia* (New Haven: Yale University, Southeast Asia Studies Program; 1950). Most of the books listed in the following selected bibliography contain helpful information on sources; see especially the works of Bernard B. Fall, Donald Lancaster, Ellen J. Hammer, and Virginia Thompson.

SELECTED BIBLIOGRAPHY

Anh Van and Jacqueline Roussel. *Mouvements nationaux et lutte de classes au Viet Nam.* Paris: Publications de la IVe Internationale; 1947.

Apple, R. W., Jr.: "Vietnam: The Signs of Stalemate." *The New York Times,* August 7, 1967.

Aurousseau, L.: "La première conquête chinoise des pays annamites." *Bulletin de l'École Française d'Extrême-Orient,* Vol. XXIII (1923), pp. 137–264.

Bauchar, R.: "Fleuve Rouge-Rivière Noire," *Tropiques: Revue des Troupes Coloniales* (juin 1947, numéro 289), pp. 17–31.

Benda, Harry J.: "Political Elites in Colonial Southeast Asia: An Historical Analysis." *Comparative Studies in Society and History,* Vol. VII, No. 3 (April 1965), pp. 233–51.

Bernard, Paul: *Le problème économique indochinois.* Paris: Nouvelles Éditions Latines; 1934.

Black, Cyril E., and Thomas P. Thornton, eds.: *Communism and Revolution: The Strategic Uses of Political Violence.* Princeton, N.J.: Princeton University Press; 1964.

Bốn Mắt [pseud., in Vietnamese means "Four Eyes"]: *La nuit rouge de Yen Bay.* Hanoi: Imprimerie Le Van Tau; n.d.

Brinton, Crane: *The Anatomy of Revolution.* New York: Vintage Books; 1957.

Buttinger, Joseph: *The Smaller Dragon: A Political History of Vietnam*. New York: Frederick A. Praeger; 195.

———: *Vietnam: A Dragon Embattled*. 2 vols. New York: Frederick A. Praeger; 1967.

Cadière, L.: "Le mur de Dong Hoi: étude sur l'établissement des Nguyen en Cochinchine." *Bulletin de l'École Française d'Extrême-Orient*, Vol. VI (1906), pp. 87–254.

Cady, John F.: *The Roots of French Imperialism in Eastern Asia*. Ithaca, N.Y.: Cornell University Press; 1954.

———: *Southeast Asia: Its Historical Development*. New York: McGraw-Hill; 1964.

Canada, Department of Mines and Technical Surveys, Geographical Branch: *Indo-China: A Geographical Appreciation*. Ottawa, 1953.

Catroux, Gen.: *Deux actes du drame indochinois*. Paris: Plon; 1959.

Chesneaux, Jean: *Contribution à l'histoire de la nation viêtnamienne*. Paris: Éditions Sociales; 1955.

Cho Huan-Lai: *Les origines du conflit franco-chinois à propos du Tonkin jusqu'en 1883*. Paris: Jouve; 1935.

Coedès, G.: *The Making of South-East Asia*. Translated by H. M. Wright. Berkeley and Los Angeles, Calif.: University of California Press; 1966.

Cole, Allan B.: *Conflict in Indo-China and International Repercussions: A Documentary History, 1945–1955*. Ithaca, N.Y.: Cornell University Press; 1956.

Condominas, Georges: "Aspects of a Minority Problem in Indochina." *Pacific Affairs*, Vol. XXIV (March 1951), pp. 77–82.

———: "L'Indochine" in André Leroi-Gourhan and Jean Poirier: *Ethnologie de l'Union Française (territoires extérieurs)*. Tome second: *Asie, Océanie, Amérique*. Paris: Presses Universitaires de France; 1953. Pp. 514–680.

Coulet, Georges: *Les sociétés secrètes en terre d'Annam*. Saigon: Imprimerie Commerciale, C. Ardin; 1926.

Coyle, Joanne Marie: "Indochinese Administration and Education: French Policy and Practice, 1917–1945." Unpublished Ph.D. dissertation, Fletcher School of Law and Diplomacy, Tufts University; 1963.

Dabezies, Pierre: "Forces politiques au Viet Nam." Thèse pour le doctorat, Université de Bordeaux, 1955.

Dansette, Adrien: *Leclerc*. Paris: Flammarion; 1952.

Davies, James C.: "Toward a Theory of Revolution." *American*

Sociological Review, Vol. XXVII, No. 1 (February 1962), pp. 5–19.

———: "The Circumstances and Causes of Revolution." *The Journal of Conflict Resolution,* Vol. XI, No. 2 (June 1967), pp. 247–57.

Decoux, Adm. Jean. *À la barre de l'Indochine.* Paris: Plon; 1949.

Deutsch, Karl W.: *Nationalism and Social Communication.* Cambridge, Mass.: M.I.T. Press; 1953.

———: "The Growth of Nations." *World Politics,* Vol. V, No. 2 (January 1953), pp. 168–95.

———: "Social Mobilization and Political Development." *The American Political Science Review,* Vol. LV, No. 3 (September 1961), pp. 493–514.

Devillers, Philippe: *Histoire du Viet Nam, 1940 à 1952.* Paris: Éditions du Seuil; 1952.

Dorsenne, Jean: *Faudra-t-il évacuer l'Indochine?* Paris: La Nouvelle Société d'Édition; 1932.

Ducoroy, Maurice: *Ma trahison en Indochine.* Paris: Les Editions Internationales; 1949.

Dumarest, André: *La formation des classes sociales en pays annamite.* Thèse, Université de Lyon, Faculté de Droit. Lyon: Imprimerie P. Ferrol; 1935.

Eckstein, Harry: "On the Etiology of Internal War." *History and Theory,* Vol. IV, No. 2 (1965), pp. 133–63.

"L'église catholique en Indochine." *Tropiques: Revue des Troupes Coloniales* (février 1947, numéro 285), pp. 39–46.

Elsbree, Willard H.: *Japan's Role in Southeast Asian Nationalist Movements, 1940 to 1945.* Cambridge, Mass.: Harvard University Press; 1953.

Emerson, Rupert: *From Empire to Nation.* Boston: Beacon Press; 1960.

Ennis, Thomas E.: *French Policy and Developments in Indochina.* Chicago: University of Chicago Press; 1936.

Fall, Bernard B.: "The Political Development of Viet Nam: V-J Day to the Geneva Cease-Fire." Unpublished Ph.D. dissertation, Syracuse University, October 1954.

———: *Le Viet Minh: La République Démocratique au Viet Nam, 1945–1960.* Paris: Librairie Armand Colin; 1960.

———: *Street Without Joy: Indochina at War, 1946–54.* Harrisburg, Pa.: The Stackpole Co.; 1961.

———: *The Two Viet Nams: A Political and Military Analysis.* New York and London: Frederick A. Praeger; 1963.

————: *Viet-Nam Witness, 1953–66.* New York and London: Frederick A. Praeger; 1966.

Furnivall, J. S.: *Colonial Policy and Practice.* New York: New York University Press; 1956.

Gaudel, André: *L'Indochine en face du Japon.* Paris: J. Susse; 1947.

Gittinger, J. Price: *Studies on Land Tenure in Viet Nam.* Saigon: U.S. Operations Mission to Viet Nam; December 1959.

Gobron, Gabriel: *Histoire et philosophie du caodaïsme.* Paris: Derby; 1949.

Gottman, Jean: "Bugeaud, Galliéni, Lyautey." In E. M. Earle: *Makers of Modern Strategy.* Princeton, N.J.: Princeton University Press; 1943. Pp. 236–49.

Gourou, Pierre: *The Peasants of the Tonkin Delta: A Study of Human Geography.* New Haven, Conn.: Human Relations File; 1955.

Great Britain, Admiralty, Naval Intelligence Division: Geographical Handbook Series, B.R. 510, *Indo-China.* Cambridge, England: Cambridge University Press; 1943.

Gurr, Ted, with Charles Ruttenberg: *The Conditions of Civil Violence: First Tests of a Causal Model.* Princeton: Center of International Studies; 1967.

Halberstam, David: *The Making of a Quagmire.* New York: Random House; 1964.

Hall, D. G. E.: *A History of South-East Asia.* New York: St. Martin's Press; 1955.

Hammer, Ellen: *The Struggle for Indochina.* Stanford, Calif.: Stanford University Press; 1954.

Hertrich, Jean-Michel: *Doc-Lap: L'indépendence ou la mort.* Paris: Jean Vigneau; 1946.

Hickey, Gerald C.: "Social Systems of Northern Viet Nam." Unpublished Ph.D. dissertation, Department of Anthropology, University of Chicago, 1958.

————: *Village in Vietnam.* New Haven, Conn.: Yale University Press; 1964.

Hoang Van Chi: *From Colonialism to Communism: A Case History of North Vietnam.* New York and London: Frederick A. Praeger; 1964.

Ho Chi Minh: "Our Party Has Struggled Very Heroically and Won Glorious Victories." In *A Heroic People: Memoirs from the Revolution.* Hanoi: Foreign Languages Publishing House; 1960. Pp. 11–18.

—————— (Nguyen Ai Quoc): *Le procès de la colonisation française.* Paris: Librairie du Travail; 1925.

Honey, P. J.: "The Position of the DRV Leadership and the Succession to Ho Chi Minh." *The China Quarterly,* No. 9 (January–March 1962), pp. 24–36.

Huard, Pierre, and Maurice Durand: *Connaissance du Viet Nam.* Hanoi: École Française d'Extrême-Orient; 1954.

Hull, Cordell: *The Memoirs of Cordell Hull.* New York: The Macmillan Company; 1948.

Isoart, Paul: *Le phénomène national viêtnamien: De l'indépendence unitaire à l'indépendence fractionnée.* Paris: Librairie Générale de Droit et de Jurisprudence; 1961.

Johnson, Chalmers: *Peasant Nationalism and Communist Power.* Stanford, Calif.: Stanford University Press; 1962.

—————: *Revolution and the Social System.* Stanford University: The Hoover Institution; 1964.

—————: *Revolutionary Change.* Boston: Little, Brown & Co.; 1966.

Jones, Robert B. Jr., and Huynh Sanh Thong: *Introduction to Spoken Vietnamese.* Washington, D.C.: American Council of Learned Societies; 1957.

Jumper, Roy: "Vietnam: The Historical Background." In George McTurnan Kahin, ed.: *Governments and Politics of Southeast Asia.* 2nd edn. Ithaca, N.Y.: Cornell University Press; 1964.

—————, and Nguyen Thi Hue: *Notes on the Political and Administrative History of Viet Nam, 1802–1962.* Saigon: Michigan State University, Viet Nam Advisory Group; 1962.

Kaufman, H. K.: *Bangkhuad: A Community Study in Thailand.* Locust Valley, N.Y.: Association for Asian Studies; 1960.

Kilian, Rear-Adm. Robert: *Les fusiliers marins en Indochine.* Paris: Éditions Berger-Levrault; 1948.

King Chen: "China and the Democratic Republic of Viet Nam, 1945–1954." Unpublished Ph.D. dissertation, Pennsylvania State University, September 1962.

Kohn, Hans: *The Idea of Nationalism.* New York: The Macmillan Co.; 1961.

Kunstadter, Peter, ed.: *Southeast Asian Tribes, Minorities and Nations.* Princeton, N.J.: Princeton University Press; 1967.

Lacheroy, Col. Charles: *Une arme du Viet Minh: Les hiérarchies parallèles.* Paris, 1953.

Lacouture, Jean: *Cinq hommes et la France.* Paris: Éditions du Seuil; 1961.

————, and Philippe Devillers: *La fin d'une guerre*. Paris: Éditions du Seuil; 1960.

Lancaster, Donald: *The Emancipation of French Indochina*. London: Oxford University Press; 1961.

Landon, Kenneth P.: "Annamese Folkways Under Chinese Influence." In Kenneth P. Landon: *Southeast Asia: Crossroads of Religion*. Chicago: University of Chicago Press; 1947.

Lanessan, Jean M. A. de: *La colonisation française en Indochine*. Paris: Félix Alcan; 1895.

Lasswell, Harold D.: *Politics: Who Gets What, When, How*. Cleveland and New York: The World Publishing Co.; 1958.

————, and Daniel Lerner: *World Revolutionary Elites*. Cambridge Mass.: The M.I.T. Press; 1965.

League of Nations, International Labour Office: *Labour Conditions in Indo-China*. Geneva, 1938.

Le Thanh Khoi: *Le Viet-Nam: Histoire et civilisation, le milieu et l'histoire*. Paris: Les Éditions de Minuit; 1955.

Levy, Roger: "Indo-China in 1931–1932." *Pacific Affairs*, Vol. V, No. 3 (March 1932), pp. 205–17.

Lhermite, Lt. Col.: "Les opérations 'Bénédictine' et 'Geneviève.' " *Tropiques: Revue des Troupes Coloniales* (juin 1948, numéro 300), pp. 27–31.

Luro, É.: *Le pays d'Annam*. Paris: Ernest Leroux; 1878.

Lyautey, Lt. Col.: "Du rôle colonial de l'Armée." *Revue des Deux Mondes*, Vol. CLVIII, février 15, 1900, pp. 308–28.

Lyautey, L. H. G.: *Lettres du Tonkin et du Madagascar, 1893–1899*. Paris: Librairie Armand Colin; 1920.

Mao Tse-tung: *On New Democracy*. Peking: Foreign Languages Press; 1954.

Marchand, Gen. Jean: *Le drame indochinois*. Paris: J. Peyronnet; 1953.

————: "Pacification en Indochine." *Tropiques: Revue des Troupes Coloniales*, janvier 1949, pp. 3–12.

Maspéro, Georges: *Le royaume de Champa*. Paris: Van Oest; 1928.

Maspéro, Henri: "La dynastie des Li antérieurs." *Bulletin de l'École Française d'Extrême-Orient*, Vol. XVI, No. 1 (1916), pp. 1–26.

————: "L'expédition de Ma Yuan." *Bulletin de l'École Française d'Extrême-Orient*, Vol. XVIII, No. 3 (1918), pp. 11–28.

————: "Le protectorat général d'Annam Sous les T'ang." *Bulletin de l'École Française d'Extrême-Orient*, Vol. X (1910), pp. 590–610.

Masson, André: *Histoire du Vietnam.* Paris: Presses Universitaires de France; 1960.

Maybon, Charles: *Histoire moderne du pays d'Annam, 1592–1820.* Paris: Plon; 1920.

McAlister, John T., Jr.: "Mountain Minorities and the Viet Minh: A Key to the Indochina War." In Peter Kunstadter, ed.: *Southeast Asian Tribes, Minorities and Nations.* Princeton, N.J.: Princeton University Press; 1967. Pp. 771–844.

————: "The Possibilities for Diplomacy in Southeast Asia." *World Politics,* Vol. XIX, No. 2 (January 1967), pp. 258–305.

McCall, Davy Henderson: "The Effects of Independence on the Economy of Viet Nam." Unpublished Ph.D. dissertation, Department of Economics, Harvard University, 1961.

Mérimée, J.: *De l'accession des indochinois à la qualité de citoyen français.* Thèse, Université de Toulouse, Faculté de Droit. Toulouse: Imprimerie Andrau et LaPorte; 1931.

Miyakawa, Hisayuki: "The Confucianization of South China." In Arthur F. Wright, ed.: *The Confucian Persuasion.* Stanford, Calif.: Stanford University Press; 1960.

Modelski, George: "The Viet Minh Complex." In Cyril E. Black and Thomas P. Thornton, eds.: *Communism and Revolution: The Strategic Uses of Political Violence.* Princeton, N.J.: Princeton University Press; 1964, pp. 185–214.

Murti, B. S. N.: *Vietnam Divided: The Unfinished Struggle.* New York: Asia Publishing House; 1964.

Mus, Paul: *Problèmes de l'Indochine contemporaine: La formation des partis annamites.* Paris: Collège Libre des Sciences Sociales et Économiques; n.d.

————: *Le Viet Nam chez lui.* Paris: Centre d'Études Politiques Étrangères; 1946.

————: "The Role of the Village in Vietnamese Politics." *Pacific Affairs,* Vol. XXIII (September 1949), pp. 265–72.

————: "Viet Nam: A Nation Off Balance." *Yale Review,* Vol. XLI (Summer 1952), pp. 524–38.

————: *Viet Nam: Sociologie d'une guerre.* Paris: Éditions du Seuil; 1952.

Nash, Manning: "Southeast Asian Society: Dual or Multiple." *The Journal of Asian Studies,* Vol. XXIII, No. 3 (May 1964), pp. 417–24.

Navarre, Henri: *Agonie de l'Indochine (1953–1954).* Rev. edn. Paris: Plon; 1956.

Nguyen Xuan Dao: *Village Government in Viet Nam: A Survey*

of Historical Development. Saigon: Michigan State University, Viet Nam Advisory Group; September 1958.

Ory, Paul: *La commune annamite au Tonkin.* Paris: Augustin Challamel; 1894.

Paret, Peter: *Internal War and Pacification: The Vendée, 1789–1796.* Princeton, N.J.: Center of International Studies; 1961.

Pasquier, Pierre: *L'Annam d'autrefois.* Paris: Société d'Éditions Géographiques, Maritimes et Coloniales; 1929.

Pettee, George: *The Process of Revolution.* New York: Harper & Brothers; 1938.

Pye, Lucian: *Guerrilla Communism in Malaya.* Princeton, N.J.: Princeton University Press; 1956.

Redfield, Robert: *The Little Community and Peasant Society and Culture.* Chicago: University of Chicago Press, Phoenix Books; 1953.

Reischauer, Edwin O., and John K. Fairbank: *East Asia: The Great Tradition.* Boston: Houghton Mifflin Company; 1960.

Robequain, Charles: *The Economic Development of French Indo-China.* London and New York: Oxford University Press; 1941.

Rosenman, Samuel I.: *The Public Papers and Addresses of Franklin D. Roosevelt: Victory and the Threshold of Peace.* New York: Harper & Brothers; 1950.

Royal Institute of International Affairs. *Survey of International Affairs, 1939–1946: The Far East, 1942–1946.* London: Oxford University Press; 1955.

Sabattier, Gen. G.: *Le destin de l'Indochine.* Paris: Plon; 1952.

Sacks, I. Milton: "Marxism in Viet Nam." In Frank N. Trager, ed.: *Marxism in Southeast Asia.* Stanford, Calif.: Stanford University Press; 1960. Pp. 102–70.

Sainteny, Jean: *Histoire d'une paix manquée: Indochine 1945–1947.* Paris: Amiot-Dumont; 1953.

Sarraut, Albert: *La mise en valeur des colonies françaises.* Paris: Payot; 1932.

Scigliano, Robert: *South Vietnam: Nation Under Stress.* Boston: Houghton Mifflin Company; 1964.

Shaplen, Robert: "The Enigma of Ho Chi Minh." *The Reporter,* Vol. XII, January 27, 1955, pp. 11–19.

———: "Letter From South Vietnam." *The New Yorker,* June 17, 1967, pp. 37–91.

———: *The Lost Revolution.* New York: Harper & Row; 1965.

Taboulet, Georges: *La geste française en Indochine: Histoire par les textes de la France en Indochine des origines à 1914.* 2 vols. Paris: Adrien Maisonneuve; 1955–6.

Tanham, George K.: *Communist Revolutionary Warfare.* New York: Frederick A. Praeger; 1961.

Thompson, Laurence C.: *A Vietnamese Grammar.* Seattle, Wash.: University of Washington Press; 1965.

Thompson, Virginia: *French Indochina.* London: George Allen and Unwin; 1937.

Tilly, Charles: *The Vendée.* Cambridge, Mass.: Harvard University Press; 1964.

To Nguyen Dinh: *Tàn Phá Cổ Am* ["Destruction of Co Am"]. Saigon: Tấn Phát Xuất Bản; 1958.

Trang Liet: *Cuộc Đời Cách Mạng: Cường Để* ["Life of a Revolutionary"]. Saigon: Tôn Thất Lễ; 1957.

Tran Trong Kim: *Việt Nam Sử Lược* ["History of Viet Nam"] 6th edn. Saigon: Tân Việt; 1958.

Tran Van Giap: "La vie d'un mandarin annamite du XVIe siècle." *Cahiers de l'École Française d'Extrême-Orient,* Vol. XXVI (1941).

Truong Buu Lam: "Sino-Vietnamese Relations at the End of the Eighteenth Century: A Study of the Tribute System." Paper No. 3 prepared for the Conference on the Chinese World Order, September 1965. Cambridge, Mass.: East Asian Research Center, Harvard University.

U.S. Department of State: *A Threat to Peace: North Viet-Nam's Effort To Conquer South Viet-Nam.* Publication 7308, Far Eastern Series 110. Washington, D.C.: Government Printing Office; 1961.

———: *Aggression from the North: The Record of North Viet-Nam's Campaign to Conquer South Viet-Nam.* Publication 7839, Far Eastern Series 130. Washington, D.C.: Government Printing Office; 1965.

U.S. Department of State, Office of Intelligence Research: *Political Alignments of Vietnamese Nationalists,* by Milton Sacks. OIR Report #3708. Washington, D.C., 1949.

U.S. Department of State, Office of Intelligence Research, Research and Analysis Branch: *Programs of Japan in Indochina.* OIR Report #3369. August 10, 1945.

Volait, André: *La vie économique et sociale du Viet Nam du 9 mars 1945 au 19 décembre 1946.* Paris: École Nationale de la France d'Outre-Mer, Section Afrique-Noire; 1948.

Vu Quoc Thong: *La décentralisation administrative au Viet Nam.* Hanoi: Presses Universitaires du Viet Nam; 1952.

Warner, Denis: *The Last Confucian.* New York: The Macmillan Company; 1963.

Weinstein, Franklin B.: *Vietnam's Unheld Election.* Ithaca, N.Y.: Southeast Asia Program, Cornell University, Data Paper No. 60; July 1966.

Wiens, Harold J.: *China's March Toward the Tropics.* Hamden, Conn.: Shoe String Press; 1954.

Woodside, A. B.: "Early Ming Expansionism (1406–1427): China's Abortive Conquest of Vietnam." *Papers on China,* Vol. XVII. Cambridge, Mass.: East Asian Research Center, Harvard University; December 1963.

————: "Some Features of the Vietnamese Bureaucracy Under the Early Nguyên Dynasty." *Papers on China,* Vol. XIX. Cambridge, Mass.: East Asian Research Center, Harvard University; December 1965.

BIBLIOGRAPHY

A NOTE ABOUT THE AUTHOR

John T. McAlister, Jr., is a lecturer at the Woodrow Wilson School of Public and International Affairs and a research associate at the Center of International Studies at Princeton University. He was born in Spartanburg, South Carolina, in 1936 and has received three degrees from Yale—B.A. in 1958, M.A. in 1964, and Ph.D. in 1966. For three years he served as a reserve officer in the U.S. Navy, and from 1959 to 1961 he was adviser to the River Force of the Vietnamese navy in the Mekong Delta.

In March 1968 Mr. McAlister testified before the Senate Foreign Relations Committee on the nature of revolution in Viet Nam. His articles and reviews have appeared in *The American Political Science Review*, *The Journal of Asian Studies*, *World Politics*, and *The New York Times Book Review*.

A NOTE ON THE TYPE

The text of this book was set on the Linotype in a face called
TIMES ROMAN, designed by Stanley Morison for *The Times*
(London), and first introduced by that newspaper in 1932.

Among typographers and designers of the twentieth century,
Stanley Morison has been a strong forming influence, as typo-
graphical adviser to the English Monotype Corporation, as a
director of two distinguished English publishing houses, and as
a welter of sensibility, erudition, and keen practical sense.

Composed, printed and bound by
The Haddon Craftsmen, Inc., Scranton, Pennsylvania

Maps by Jean Paul Tremblay

Typography and binding design by Golda Fishbein